Legal Issues of Services of General Interest

Series Editors
Johan Willem van de Gronden
Markus Krajewski
Ulla Neergaard
Erika Szyszczak

For further volumes:
http://www.springer.com/series/8900

Erika Szyszczak · Jim Davies
Mads Andenæs · Tarjei Bekkedal
Editors

Developments in Services of General Interest

T·M·C·Asser Press

Springer

Editors
Prof. Erika Szyszczak
School of Law
University of Leicester
University Road, Leicester
LE1 7RH
UK
ems11@leicester.ac.uk

Dr. Jim Davies
Department of Law Park Campus
University of Northampton
School of Social Sciences
Boughton Green Road
NN2 7AL Northampton
UK
jim.davies@northampton.ac.uk

Prof. Mads Andenæs
Department of Private Law
University of Oslo
Domus Media
Karl Johans Gate 47
0162 Oslo
Norwaymads.andenas@nchr.uio.no

Dr. Tarjei Bekkedal
Department of Private Law
University of Oslo
Domus Exilii
St. Olavs Gate 23
0166 Oslo
Norway
tarjei.bekkedal@jus.uio.no

ISBN 978-90-6704-831-6 ISBN 978-90-6704-734-0

DOI 10.1007/978-90-6704-734-0

Softcover reprint of the hardcover 1st edition 2011

Published by T.M.C. ASSER PRESS, The Hague, The Netherlands www.asserpress.nl

Produced and distributed for T.M.C. ASSER PRESS by Springer-Verlag Berlin Heidelberg

Cover design: eStudio Calamar, Berlin/Figueres

Printed on acid-free paper

Springer is part of Springer Science+Business Media (www.springer.com)

Series Information

The aim of the series *Legal Issues of Services of General Interest* is to sketch the framework for services of general interest in the EU and to explore the issues raised by developments related to these services. The Series encompasses, inter alia, analyses of EU internal market, competition law, legislation (such as the Services Directive), international economic law and national (economic) law from a comparative perspective. Sector-specific approaches will also be covered (health and social services). In essence, the present Series addresses the emergence of a European Social Model and will therefore raise issues of fundamental and theoretical interest in Europe and the global economy.

Series Editors

Johan Willem van de Gronden
Faculty of Law
Radboud University
Comeniuslaan 4
6525 HP Nijmegen
The Netherlands
e-mail: J.vandeGronden@jur.ru.nl

Markus Krajewski
Fachbereich Rechtswissenschaft
Universität Erlangen-Nürnberg
Schillerstraße 1
91054 Erlangen
Germany
e-mail: markus.krajewski@jura.uni-erlangen.de

Ulla Neergaard
Faculty of Law
University of Copenhagen
Studiestræde 6
1455 Copenhagen K
Denmark
e-mail: ulla.neergaard@jur.ku.dk

Erika Szyszczak
School of Law
University of Leicester
University Road, Leicester
LE1 7RH
UK
e-mail: ems11@leicester.ac.uk

Acknowledgments

This is another book in the series Legal Issues of Services of General Interest. This volume is based upon papers presented at a Seminar and Workshop in London in June 2009, introducing some new researchers in the field of Services of General Economic Interest and also some new dimensions.

The Seminar and Workshop was hosted by the Institute of Advanced Legal Studies and we thank Belinda Crothers for the administrative help in making the event successful. We also acknowledge the financial support from the Centre for Research on Markets, Innovation and Technology (CeRMIT), the University of Oslo, the Centre for European Law and Integration (CELI), University of Leicester and the Society of Advanced Legal Studies (SALS). Finally, we are grateful to all of the participants of the Seminar and Workshop for their stimulating contributions.

Contents

List of Contributors

Pierre Bauby is a researcher and Professor of Political Science [Paris 8 University, French National School of Public Administration (ENA), Centre National de la Fonction Publique Territoriale]. He holds a Ph.D. degree in Political Science from the Institut d'Etudes Politiques of Paris. He is Special Advisor on Services of General Interest of the General Secretariat of CEEP (European Centre of Employers and Enterprises providing Public Services) and expert of the Rapporteur on Services of General Interest of the European Economic and Social Committee (EESC). He is Chairman of the French Association *Reconstruire l'Action Publique* and member of the International Scientific Commission 'public services–public enterprises' of CIRIEC (International Centre of Research and Information on the Public, Social and Cooperative Economy). His main publications focus on the reform of the State and on Services of General Interest. Recent publications include: *Europe: une nouvelle chance pour le service public!*, Fondation Jean Jaurès, 2010; *Les services publics en Europe, Pour une régulation démocratique*, Publisud, 2007; *Reconstruire l'action publique*, Syros, 1998; *Le service public*, Flammarion, 1997; *L'Etat-stratège*, Editions ouvrières, 1991.

Tarjei Bekkedal is a post-doctoral Research Fellow at the Department of Private Law, University of Oslo. He holds a Ph.D. degree in European Law from the University of Oslo and specialises in the law relating to the European Internal Market. He has been a lecturer in law for 12 years and teaches Constitutional Law, Administrative Law, Contract Law, Family Law and Inheritance Law. He has previously worked as legal advisor for the Norwegian Ministry of Culture, where he was responsible for the regulation of broadcasting and electronic communications.

Jim Davies is a Research Fellow at the University of Northampton and has a Ph.D. from the University of Leicester where he was awarded a *Modern Law Review Scholarship* for doctoral research. His Ph.D. degree research was entitled

The European Consumer Citizen: A Coherent, Tangible and Relevant Notion of Citizenship and is now being developed into a monograph. In 2009, he published 'Entrenchment of New Governance in Consumer Policy Formulation: A Platform for European Consumer Citizenship PracticeL', in the *Journal of Consumer Policy* and has a chapter titled *Consumer Protection in a Normative Context: The Building Blocks of a Consumer Citizenship Practice*, in Mel Kenney and James Devenney (eds), *European Consumer Protection: Theory and Practice* (Cambridge University Press, forthcoming). He was the author of the European Law article in all three volumes of the *Student Law Review* during 2008 and has written a *Glossary of EU Law*, with Professor Erika Szyszczak. Before reading law as a mature student Jim spent many years as a senior manager in the telecommunications industry and has expertise in organisational change and strategic process development.

Johan van de Gronden is a Professor of European Law at the Faculty of Law of the Radboud University Nijmegen in the Netherlands having previously worked at the Europa Institute of the University Utrecht (the Netherlands). His research focuses on EU internal market law, competition law and the relationship between these law areas and (national) policies regarding issues of general interest (like health care). Since October 2003 he has also served as a deputy judge at the District Court of Rotterdam (additional function) mainly sitting on competition law cases. He is a founding editor of the TMC Asser series *Legal Issues of Services of General Interest* and a founding member of the *Transformation of the Market and the State* Project (ToMaS).

Martin Hennig is a Research Fellow at the University of Tromsø, Norway. He is currently in the process of researching for his Ph.D. degree in law on the subject 'Public Service Obligations in the EU Inland Transport Sector'.

Markus Krajewski holds the Chair in Public and International law at the University of Erlangen-Nuremburg, Germany. Recently, he was a guest professor at the Collaborative Research Centre Transformations of the State (TranState) of the University of Bremen, on leave from a position as Assistant Professor at the University of Potsdam, where he taught European, International and German public law. Prior to this he was Lecturer in German Law at King's College London. His research interests include WTO law, European external relations and the treatment of public services under European and international law. Since 2007 he has been a member of the International Department of the World Trade Institute in Bern. Markus advises international organisations and NGOs on issues of European and international law. In the academic year 2009/2010 he headed up a project for the development of WTO law teaching and research capacities of law schools in Ethiopia at the Addis Ababa University. He is a founding editor of the

TMC Asser series *Legal Issues of Services of General Interest* and a founding member of the *Transformation of the Market and the State* Project (ToMaS).

Ulla Neergaard is a Professor of EU Law at the University of Copenhagen. She holds a Ph.D. degree from the European University Institute, Florence, Italy. Her doctoral thesis is in the area of competition law, and is published under the title *Competition & Competences. The Tensions between European Competition Law and Anti-Competitive Measures by the Member States*. From 1998–2009 she was an academic in the Law Department at the Copenhagen Business School, Denmark, and was a Professor of Competition Law. Since 2009 Ulla Neergaard has been Professor of EU Market Law at the Law Faculty at the University of Copenhagen, moving over to a Professorship of EU law in 2010. Since 1999 Ulla Neergaard has been an expert member of the Danish Council of Competition and since 2005 also of the Danish Energy Regulatory Authority. She has published widely in EU competition law as well as in the more fundamental aspects of EU law. Among others, she is a co-author of a text book on EU Law and another on EU Competition Law. She has been involved in various research projects, for example, 'Blurring Boundaries: EU Law and the Danish Welfare State', which has led to several books. In the coming years, among others she will be involved in a research project concerning 'European Legal Method: Synthesis or Fragmentation?'. She is a founding editor of the TMC Asser series *Legal Issues of Services of General Interest* and a founding member of the *Transformation of the Market and the State* Project (ToMaS).

Priscilla Schwartz is a lecturer in law at the University of Leicester. She is a graduate of the University of London—Queen Mary (Ph.D. in Law), King's College (LL.M.) and Fourah Bay College University of Sierra Leone [LL.B. (Hons) and BA]. Her areas of expertise are: international economic law, law and development, public international law and environmental law and policy. Priscilla convenes LL.M. courses in International Law and Development, Law and Organisation of the World Trading System and Contemporary Legal Problems of World Trade and supervises Ph.D. research. She is also a teaching associate at Queen Mary, London and is visiting scholar at the Institute of Public Administration and Management, Sierra Leone. Priscilla is also co-convenor of the African IEL Network (Society for International Economic law), consultant adviser, Directorate of Research, Innovation and Publication, Tertiary Education Commission, Sierra Leone, co-ordinator of research in Law and Development at the Centre for European Law and Integration Leicester, and the Book Review Editor *Manchester Journal of International Economic Law*. Priscilla maintains research interests in international public policy and law relating to economic development, especially their implication for developing countries. Particular areas include international (global) trade, foreign investment, development financing, natural resource exploitation and sustainable development; and she has a good record of publication in these areas. Priscilla is also a Barrister and Solicitor (BL). Prior to her academic career, Priscilla was Sierra Leone Government (GOSL) legal counsel and was also special assistant to the Attorney General and Minister of Justice. She conducted several domestic and international negotiations on behalf of the GOSL including, with the World Bank and the United Nations. She was instrumental in the setting up of the UN Special Court for Sierra Leone, and participated in the drafting of its Statute and Agreements. She also initiated and coordinated implementation of projects for the development of the rule of law.

Grith Skovgaard Ølykke is an Assistant Professor at the Law Department at Copenhagen Business School, Denmark, where she studied for her Ph.D. in EU public procurement law. Her research interests include EU rules on public procurement, competition, State aid and the interaction of these law areas. Grith teaches EU Law, Public Procurement Law, Competition Law and a course involving Article 106 TFEU and State Aid Law.

Erika Szyszczak is a Jean Monnet Professor of European Law *ad personam* and Director of the Centre for European Law and Integration (CELI) at the University of Leicester. She is a practising Barrister at Littleton Chambers, Temple, London and an ADR Accredited Mediator. She has written extensively in the area of SGEIs and published *The Regulation of the State in Competitive Markets in the EU* (Hart, 2007) which is being revised in 2011. She is one of the founding editors of the TMC Asser series and the *Transformation of the Market and the State* (ToMaS) research project. She sits on the Editorial Boards of the *Modern Law Review, Journal of European Social Law and the European Law Review.*

List of Abbreviations

A

AG	Advocate General
AJDA	L'actualité juridique Droit administratif
AMC	Advanced Market Commitment
AU	African Union

B

BUPA	British United Provident Association

C

CARIFORUM	Caribbean Forum of ACP States
CEEP	Centre européen des entreprises à participation publique et des entreprises d'intérêt économique général (European Centre of Employers and Enterprises providing Public Services)
CEER	Council of European Energy Regulators
CELSIG	European Liaison Committee on Services of General Interest
CFI	Court of First Instance
CMLRev	Common Market Law Review
CRM	Cause Related Marketing
CSR	Corporate Social Responsibility

D

DFID	Department for International Development (UK)

E

EAGCP	Economic Advisory Group for Competition Policy
ECHR	European Convention for the Protection of Human Rights and Fundamental Freedoms
ECJ	European Court of Justice
ECLRev	European Competition Law Review
ECSC	Treaty establishing the European Coal and Steel Community
EDC	European Defence Community
EEA	European Economic Area
EESC	European Economic and Social Committee
EFTA	European Free Trade Association
EIA	Economic Integration Agreements
EIPR	European Intellectual Property Review
ELPA	Automobile and Touring Club of Greece (Ελληνική Λέσχη Περιηγήσεων & Αυτοκινήτου, Elliniki Leschi Periigiseon kai Aftokinitou
ELRev	European Law Review
EPA	Economic Partnership Agreement
EPSU	European Federation of Public Service Union
ERGEG	European Regulators Group for Electricity and Gas
ETUC	European Trade Union Confederation
EU	European Union

F

FAQ	Frequently Asked Question
FTA	Free Trade Agreement

G

GATS	General Agreement on Trade in Services
GATT	General Agreement on Tariffs and Trade
GC	General Court (of the EU)
GDA	Global Framework Alliance
GDA	Global Development Alliance
GDP	Gross Domestic Product
GFA	Global Framework Agreements
GSM	Global System for Mobile Communications

H

HFA	Housing Finance Agency (Ireland)

I

IDRC	International Research Development Centre
IHPs	International and Global Partnership on Health
IPR	Intellectual Property Rights

J

JCMS	Journal of Common Market Studies
JIEL	Journal of International Economic Law

L

LDC	Least Developed Countries

M

MDG	(United Nations) Millennium Development Goal

N

NEPAD	New Partnership for African Development
NESGI	Non-Economic Services of General Interest
NGO	Non-Governmental Organisation
NRA	National Regulatory Authority
Nyr	Not yet reported

O

ODA	Overseas Development Administration
OECD	Organisation for Economic Cooperation and Development
ONP	Open Network Provision

P

PPP	Public–Private Partnership
PSE	Parti socialiste européen (Group of the Progressive Alliance of Socialists and Democrats in the European Parliament)
PSPP	Public–Social–Private Partnerships
PSO	Public Service Obligation

S

SGEI	Service of General Economic Interest
SGI	Service of General Interest

SNCF	Société Nationale des Chemins de Fer (France)
SSGI	Social Services of General Interest

T

TEC	Treaty establishing the European Community
TEU	Treaty on European Union
TFEU	Treaty on the Functioning of the European Union
TNC	Transnational Corporation
TRIPS	Agreement on Trade Related Intellectual Rights

U

UNDP	United Nations Development Programme
UNFPA	United Nations Population Fund
UNICEF	United Nations (International) Children's (Emergency) Fund
USO	Universal Service Obligation

W

WB	World Bank
WHO	World Health Organisation
WTO	World Trade Organisation

Chapter 1
Introduction: Why Do Public Services Challenge the European Union?

Erika Szyszczak

Contents

1.1 Introduction

Writing in May 2010 Mario Monti, a former Commissioner for Competition stated:

> Since the 1990s, the place of public services within the single market has been a persistent irritant in the European public debate.[1]

[1] Monti 2010, p. 73.

Jean Monnet Professor of European Law ad personam, University of Leicester, Barrister, Littleton Chambers, London

In writing this Introduction I have benefitted enormously from the discussions of seminar and conference papers presented at Oxford University, EUI (Florence), ERA (Trier) as well as the conferences which have been the basis of the books published in the *Legal Issues of Services of General Interest* series.

E. Szyszczak (✉)
School of Law, University of Leicester, Leicester, UK
e-mail: ems11@le.ac.uk

E. Szyszczak et al. (eds.), *Developments in Services of General Interest*,
Legal Issues of Services of General Interest, DOI: 10.1007/978-90-6704-734-0_1,

What has been a persistent irritant for the Single Market project has created a rich source for investigation by academic researchers, an increasing amount of legal work for practioners and discussion between policy-makers. This in turn has led to an explosion of ideas in what Ross has described as 'this short history of chaos'[2] on what is the modern role for public services. However, there are few concrete solutions to this 'irritant' of the Single Market. This Introduction follows the pattern of the book and analyses why public services are viewed in this way by the European integration project. Section 1.2 charts the evolution of public services as an 'irritant' in EU law and the legal and political responses. Section 1.3 examines three areas where public services are responding to the challenges of modernisation in their function, definition and funding: the new EU concept of 'Social Services of General Interest', the development of 'Universal Service Obligations' and the role of 'Public Service Obligations' in retaining the values of the Member States and their citizens in a new 'European Social Model'. Finally Sect. 1.4 takes the reader outside of the inward EU perspective to examine if public services are also irritants in modernising public services in least developed countries (LDCs) and in the globalised economy regulated by WTO rules. The globalisation of services and the fact that the EU has a developed external relations policy has led to the inclusion of universal service provisions in international trade agreements of the EU. Thus the final section of this chapter examines how far international agreements enhance an understanding of modern public services.

1.2 The Evolution of a European Public Service Concept

Increasingly the public services of the Member States of the EU have been subjected to a Europeanisation process.[3] The initial interference with Member States' control over their public services came early, in 1957, in the new nomenclature given to them in the original Article 90 EEC. Article 90(2) EEC created an 'exemption' for 'services of general economic interest' from the full application of the EEC Treaty rules. This 'exemption' has subsequently created confusion. Is it an exemption or a justification or a switch rule?[4] Are public services economic activities when they pursue social objectives? *Johan van de Gronden* explores whether a public service is an 'economic' activity caught by the Treaty rules, how experimentation with new mixes of public and private provision of social services

[2] Ross 2007, p. 1058.

[3] I use the concept of Europeanisation as defined by Radaelli 2009: a set of processes of construction, diffusion, and institutionalisation of formal and informal rules, procedures, policy paradigms, styles, 'ways of doing things' and shared beliefs and norms which are first defined and consolidated in the EU policy process and then incorporated in the logic of domestic (national and sub-national) discourse, political structures, and public policies.

[4] See Buendia Sierra 2000; Baquero Cruz 2005.

may be seen as economic activities carried out by undertakings and, also, as is discussed by *Tarjei Bekkedal* and *Grith Skovgaard Ølykke*, whether the exemption applies to all the 'market law' rules of the Treaty or merely the application of the competition rules.

Pierre Bauby begins his chapter with a discussion of the historical, political, and cultural specificity of the generic concept of 'public services' in Europe. The enlargement of the EU in 2004 and 2007 added even greater complexity to the diversity of concepts of public services already found in the EU. It is interesting to see that in 1957, what is now Article 93 TFEU in the chapter on Transport, used the term 'public service' but as 'certain obligations inherent in the concept of a public service',[5] whereas, Article 106(2) TFEU [ex Article 90(2) EEC, Article 86(2) EC] created a new concept of 'services of general economic interest'. This was an entirely new concept which was not recognised in any language of the original Member States or in scientific literature. However, as a concept, it has withstood the test of time and continues to remain in the TFEU and to be the source for the emergence of new European concepts. 'Services of general economic interest' have also held their own and withstood challenges to their existence from the European integration project.

For a long time services of general economic interest were derogations from the European rules of competition and internal market. New concepts have gradually been introduced into the framework of EU law and official documents, firstly through the liberalisation processes starting in the 1980s and discussed in the chapter by *Jim Davies and Erika Szyszczak* and secondly, through a Commission soft law programme, discussed in the chapter by *Ulla Neergaard.*

Bauby also indentifies other aspects of Treaty amendment which have had an impact on the growing importance of services of general interest, for example, in the Treaty of Maastricht 1992, the inclusion of a concept of 'Citizenship of the Union', 'consumer protection' and 'trans-European networks', alongside aims to provide an efficient infrastructure to provide the conditions necessary for the competitiveness of the Union's industry, economic and social cohesion, extended competence in the environmental field and the Protocol on social policy. Gradually what were seen as services to protect the national interest were seen as vital parts of the European integration project. Overall the objectives of the Union required 'balanced and sustainable economic and social progress' which could be delivered by strong services of general interest. *Bauby* also notes the Court's responsiveness to the sensitivity of Member States' public services by limiting the full application of the competition laws to such services.[6] The Court has held that restrictions on competition from other economic operators must be allowed in so far as they are necessary in order to enable the undertaking entrusted with the service of general economic interest to provide the service in question. It is necessary to take into

---

[5] See Chap. 8 by Hennig.

[6] ECJ, Case C-320/91 *Corbeau* [1993] *ECR* I-2533 and ECJ, Case C-393/92 *Commune Almelo* [1994] *ECR* I-1477.

consideration the economic conditions in which the undertaking operates and the constraints placed on it, in particular the costs which it has to bear.[7] The ECJ has held that the exclusion may apply where the restriction on competition is necessary for an undertaking to perform the service of general economic interest under economically acceptable conditions.[8]

During the 1990s, a number of opportunist litigants took advantage of the moves towards liberalisation of markets to challenge State monopolies which had originally been tolerated when the original EEC Treaty was drafted. In particular the combination of what are now Article 106 and 102 TFEU allowed litigants to challenge State monopolies which had become inefficient, out of date, complacent and expensive. However, the move towards greater liberalisation and the inclusion of Article 4 EC[9] also raised fears of the disintegration of national social models and the lack of consensus upon whether a 'European Social Model' could be constructed and what it should look like.

The increased attacks on public services using the competition and free movement rules of the Treaty led the Member States to give services of general economic interest a greater prominence in the Treaty by the insertion of a new Article 16 EC by the Treaty of Amsterdam 1997. This Article was a melting pot of different preferences from the Member States. Its purpose is to define a shared competence between EU and Member States and the need to integrate, or harness, the important roles such services play in European integration, ensuring social and territorial cohesion as well as ensuring that national patriotism does not offend the principles of a competitive and integrated market. This Article recognised the place occupied by services of general economic interest in the *shared values* of the Union, as well as their role in promoting social and territorial cohesion. It also emphasised the application of some the competition rules to services of general economic interest. However, the Article is also concerned to show that there are shared competences between the Member States and the Union in relation to services of general economic interest. The importance of Article 16 EC is signified by Ross who argues that public services are no longer a derogation, an 'irritant' in Monti's language, but a positive part of the European integration process.[10]

---

[7] ECJ, Case C-393/92 *Municipality of Almelo and Others* v. *NV Energiebedrijf IJsselmij* [1994] *ECR* I-1477. See Fiedziuk 2010, 271; Gyselen 2010.

[8] ECJ, Case C-157/94 *Commission* v. *the Netherlands*, Case C-158/94 *Commission v. Italy* [1997] and Case C-159/94 *Commission* v. *France* [1997] *ECR* I-5815, *ECR* 1-5699, 5789, 5815.

[9] Article 4 EC stated: 'For the purposes set out in Article 2, the activities of the Member States and the Community shall include, as provided in this Treaty and in accordance with the timetable set out therein, the adoption of an economic policy which is based on the close co-ordination of Member States' economic policies, on the internal market and on the definition of common objectives, and conducted in accordance with the principle of an open market economy with free competition.'

[10] Ross 2000, p. 22.

Three years later, in 2000, Article 36 of the Charter of Fundamental Rights of the European Union declared that the Union 'recognises and respects' *access* to services of general economic interest as provided for in *national laws and practices* and in accordance with the (then) EC Treaty, in order to promote the social and territorial cohesion of the Union. As *Bauby* notes, as with Article 16 EC, the text has many contradictory interpretations and may well give rise to litigation before the European Courts. The Charter also refers to a number of rights and principles which may be encapsulated under the traditional national ideas of public services.[11] Since 1 December 2009 the Charter has the same legal value as the Treaties.[12]

Finally *Bauby* assesses the impact of the Treaty of Lisbon 2009. Here Article 14 TFEU creates an explicit legal base for secondary law in the form of regulations establishing "principles and conditions, particularly economic and financial conditions, which enable them [SGEIs] to fulfil their missions" involving the Council and the Parliament in the Co-decision process. Thus the Commission no longer retains the exclusive legislative control over the management of public monopolies and undertakings granted exclusive rights, as it does under Article 106(3) TFEU. The use of Regulations as the legal device to regulate such principles and conditions for SGEIs at the EU level is a significant move. Bauby sees Regulations as a positive instrument which can penetrate directly into the Member States' legal and constitutional systems. However, even before the Treaty of Lisbon 2009 was ratified, the Commission announced that it would not use the legislative powers unless it added value. The Commission sees the new Protocol on Services of General Interest annexed to the Treaty of Lisbon 2009 as a coherent framework for EU action and a sufficient benchmark for developing and protecting SGEIs in the future.[13] It may be that the new competence is too far-reaching and that the Commission continues to think that a softer approach should continue in this area. This is a theme taken up in the chapter by *Ulla Neergaard* where she argues that an 'in between layer' of EU governance is perhaps required in this area, maybe in the form of Directives rather than the deeply penetrating Regulation.

Article 14 TFEU also provides for the mainstreaming of services of general economic interest through all EU policies. The provision also recognises the competence of the Member States and their communities, in compliance with the Treaties. Significantly also, there is Protocol No. 26 which is annexed to the TEU and the TFEU reinforces the role of SGEIs at the national and the European integration level. The Protocol also mentions, for the first time in primary EU law the, concept of 'non-economic' services of general interest and that these shall be

[11] For example, Article 29 (right of access to placement services); Article 34 (social security and social assistance); Article 35 (healthcare); Article 37 (environmental protection); Article 38 (consumer protection). See Kenner and Hervey 2003.

[12] Article 6 TEU.

[13] Communication from the Commission to the European Parliament, the Council, the European Economic and Social Committee and the Committee of the Regions accompanying the communication on 'A single market for twenty first century Europe' Services of general interest, including social services of general interest: a new European commitment, COM(2007) 724 final, 9.

within the competence of the Member States to provide, organise, and commission. *Bauby* concludes by addressing the many problems which remain in accommodating SGIs into the European integration process and by showing that solutions are available within the existing framework of regulation.

Ulla Neergaard pays close attention to the Commission's soft law documents, an area neglected by academic scrutiny in the past. Initially the Commission engaged sparingly with SGEIs in its annual Competition Reports, the use of Article 106(3) TFEU, or in intervening in Article 267 TFEU (ex Article 234 EC) references to the ECJ. The turning point is in 1996 with the publication of the Commission Communication, *Services of General Interest in Europe.*[14] This is a notable development raising an issue, seen in other chapters in this volume, of the EU's use of new concepts to create ownership over an idea which is firmly rooted in *national* cultural, conceptual, constitutional, and political backgrounds. The 1996 document is an attempt to clarify some of the definitions used at the EU level, as well as to clarify the emerging ECJ case law which was not entirely consistent or coherent in its approach to defining when a Member State's public service was an economic activity and caught by the Treaty rules or how the justifications and derogations for public interests could be raised under the free movement and competition rules.

Neergaard charts the subsequent development of soft law against the political developments of the EU. At issue at the start of the twenty-first century was whether the EU had the capacity and the competence to develop framework laws to regulate SGEIs. The European Parliament has taken a keen interest in these debates and has called for a Framework law on a number of occasions. Much of the Commission's work at this time was in Working Papers and documents, treading gingerly to test the capacity of the EU to take such a bold approach, especially in the light of the weak legal competence to legislate in the area.[15] There followed a Green Paper[16] and a White Paper[17] but both documents acknowledged that the role of SGEIs was an ongoing debate in Europe.

Action is seen in 2007 when the Commission adopted a package of initiatives to transform its Citizens' Agenda[18] into a more concrete form and consistent set of actions. *Neergaard* assesses the significance of the use and role of soft law. It can be criticised as evading democratic decision-making processes and it is often vague and non-justiciable. On the other hand, it has flexibility. It can be used to test the water with ideas and can be used to pull-together the Courts' case law with political thinking. *Neergaard* notes that a common factor in the Commission's approach is to set out definitions of central concepts in the regulation of SGEIs at the EU level. Finally, it should be noted that, rather ironically, once EU legislative competence was

---

[14] 96/C 281/03.

[15] Rodrigues 2009, p. 255 and Szyszczak 2009.

[16] European Commission, *Green Paper on Services of General Interest* COM(2003) 270 final.

[17] European Commission, *White Paper on Services of General Interest*, COM(2004) 374.

[18] European Commission, *Communication on Services of General Interest, Including Social Services of General Interest: A New European Commitment* COM(2007) 725; Szyszczak 2009.

granted in Article 14 TFEU the Commission decided *not* to introduce hard legislation, especially in the much anticipated form of a Framework Regulation but instead continued with its use of soft law techniques. *Neergaard* concludes that the continued use of soft law in this area may eventually prove to be problematic. The overall impression from the chapters by Bauby and Neergaard is that the policy approach towards SGIs is rather like a set of tectonic plates which are constantly shifting against each other in the creation of a new public, economic and social space of Europe.

The creation of a legal base for legislation on SGEIs has eclipsed the already limited role performed by Article 106 TFEU (ex Article 86 EC).[19] Although Article 106(1) TFEU played an influential role in the early case law challenging the behaviour of State monopolies, more recently its role has been confined to providing a justification for alleged state aid. *Tarjei Bekkedal* raises the question of what then is the purpose of Article 106 TFEU (ex Article 86 EC)? In particular he analyses Article 106(2) TFEU which is traditionally seen as a derogation to the Treaty provisions.[20] The inclusion of Article 106 TFEU in the original EEC Treaty provisions reveals an awkward role for this provision. It is found in the Treaty chapter on competition. As *Bekkedal* notes the conventional reading of the provision is that it is an autonomous exception to all of the Treaty provisions and is not confined to specific types of infringement of the TFEU. As an exception or derogation to the basic Treaty provisions it should be interpreted narrowly and according to the principle of proportionality. The conventional view also takes the position that Article 106(2) TFEU can be invoked by the Member States *and* undertakings. *Bekkedal,* in contrast, takes a more radical view. He argues that the recent ruling in *MOTOE*[21] where the ECJ established that the exception of Article 106(2) TFEU can only be invoked by *undertakings* denies the application of Article 106(2) TFEU to justify barriers to freedom of movement used by the Member States. He argues that it is questionable as to what is the value-added of a competition approach to Internal Market law? He makes the point that Article 106(2) TFEU should not be turned into a general clause in EU law because it should be an exception primarily targeted at economic objectives. In relation to the fundamental free movement provisions economic objectives are not, in principle, accepted as legitimate justifications to the free movement rules. *Bekkedal* also notes that the European Courts take a softer approach to the application of the principle of proportionality when applying Article 106(2) TFEU, whereas, a classical application of the principle should be strict: 'a least restrictive alternative' assessment of the challenged restriction on competition and cross-border trade. If Article 106(2) TFEU is applied as a general clause with these softer standards for review it could compromise the Internal Market project.

---

19 See Davies 2009a, p. 51 and Davies 2009b, p. 549.

20 Cf. Baquero Cruz 2005, who describes the provision as a 'switch-rule'.

21 ECJ, Case C-49/07 *MOTOE* [2008] *ECR* I-4863, para 46. But compare: ECJ, Case C-157/94 *Commission* v. *Netherlands* [1999] *ECR* I-5751.

Bekkedal finds a new role for Article 106 TFEU in that it could be considered as a value statement fulfilling the concept of a 'European Social Model'. By recognising the concept, and role, of services of general economic interest, Article 106 TFEU confirms a role for SGEIs and this is enhanced with the teleological values of Article 14 TFEU and Protocol No. 26 annexed to the TEU and TFEU and the role of Article 36 Charter of Fundamental Rights of the Union. Read together these legal and constitutional provisions express a constitutional approval of the social importance of SGEIs.

Another potential use of Article 14 TFEU is for creating a transparent framework for the selection of undertakings entrusted with a SGEI. This would further diminish the role played by Article 106(2) TFEU. *Grith Skovgaard Ølykke* takes up a new dimension: the fact that the public procurement Directives apply to contracts for the provision of SGEIs and this ensures transparency in the entrustment of SGEIs. This then raises the question of whether the privileged rules of Article 106 TFEU apply alongside the specific public procurement rules, which are set out in secondary EU legislation. Looking at Article 106 TFEU through public procurement spectacles, *Skovgaard Ølykke* identifies the determination of 'what is a contract' as a central issue for the application of the public procurement Directives. Where SGEIs are provided through in-house arrangements there will not be a 'contract'[22] and where an SGEI is entrusted through a legislative act this will also not satisfy the requirements of a 'contract'.

This question of 'what is a contract' for the purposes of the procurement law of the EU has been addressed by the ECJ in two strands of case law. The first strand of cases has developed a doctrinal approach in the creation of the *Teckal*[23]criteria, whereas, the second strand concerns the imposition of obligations to provide an SGEI by a legislative act. *Skovgaard Ølykke* points out that even though detailed rules exist in the public procurement Directives, these are subject to the primary law rules of Article 106 TFEU, as well as other relevant Treaty rules, for example, the rules on discrimination. The entrustment of a SGEI has been further refined by the ECJ in *Altmark.*[24] In a series of cases the ECJ has been asked to analyse whether a 'contract' existed when the entrustment of a SGEI was regulated by a legislative act and different interpretations have been given.

A second set of problems arise where the entrustment of a SGEI take place by a service concession. The procurement Directives subject service concessions to a special regime and service concessions are exempted from the Directives but under tight conditions. This raises the question as to whether Article 106(2) TFEU could be applied. Although this question has been debated in the academic literature it has not been explicitly applied in litigation before the ECJ. However, *Skovgaard Ølykke* argues that in recent cases Article 106(2) TFEU could be the explicit basis

---

[22] See Frenz and Schleissing 2009, p. 171.

[23] ECJ, Case C-107/98 *Teckal* [1999] *ECR* I-8121, paras 49–50. .

[24] ECJ, Case C-280/00 *Altmark* [2003] *ECR* I-7747, paras 89–93. Cf. General Court, Case T-289/03 *BUPA* v. *Commission* [2008] *ECR* II-81, para 182.

for the rulings, creating a new approach to contracts where SGEI are provided even where the *Teckal* criteria are not fulfilled.[25] If this is the outcome of the case law, it gives a renewed role for Article 106(2) TFEU at a time when many commentators are questioning its continued existence in the TFEU.

1.3 New Dimensions: Social Services of General Interest, Universal Service Obligations and Public Service Obligations

In the early 1990s the Commission began to take an interest in the modernisation of social security issues. The Member States were facing common problems of long-term unemployment, demographic changes with an aging population, and increased reliance upon migrant labour and pressures to cut public spending on welfare. Some social welfare agencies were also facing rising costs, for example, in long-term care and health care services. This in turn led the Member States to experiment with different kinds of public and private provision of social services. The use of non-State undertakings to provide social services and the Member States' involvement in subsidising some of these ventures inevitably led to conflicts with the free movement and competition rules.[26] This in turn has led to conflicts within the EU as to the level of EU competence to regulate *social* services of general interest (SSGI). *Johan van de Gronden* explores these themes in his chapter. His starting point is that SSGI are not a legally distinct category in EU law. It will be recalled that Protocol No. 26 annexed to the TFEU and TEU refers to 'non-economic services of general interest'.

Van de Gronden traces the case law whereby issues of SSGI are analysed by the ECJ, first in relation to the free movement rules and then in relation to competition law. The cases are few and raise a range of diverse issues. One of the early cases, *Freskott,*[27] concerned the application of the free movement rules to a social security scheme. This case has been neglected by legal scholars and yet, as *Van de Gronden* shows, the Court gave a broad reading to the application of the free movement rules. Although the Court held that the services provided did not fall within the ambit of Article 56 TFEU, it did find that when a Member State introduces a social scheme that covers insurable risks it is obliged to design that scheme to conform with the requirements of the Treaty provisions on free movement. However, a Member State may justify any restrictions of services'

---

[25] ECJ, Case C-84/03 *Commission* v. *Spain* [2005] *ECR* I-139, para 9; ECJ, Case C-480/06 *Commission* v. *Germany* [2009] I-*ECR* 4747.

[26] The Europeanisation of health care has emerged as a discrete area as the free movement and competition rules have been tested against national schemes. This is the subject of the second volume in this series: Van de Gronden et al. 2011.

[27] ECJ, Case C-355/00 *Freskot* AE v. *Elliniko Dimosio* [2003] *ECR* I-5263.

trade by using Article 52 TFEU as developed as an 'overriding requirement of general interest' or 'Rule of Reason'. More recently issues of Citizenship of the Union have started to appear in the free movement cases. This is a development whereby the liberalisation of the economic space of European integration is matched by the liberalisation of the public space of national social and welfare schemes in opening up access to non-nationals.[28]

In addition to social insurance services, that are supplied directly to the person, have also featured in litigation before the ECJ. In *Sodemare*[29] the Court found that social care services for the elderly fell within the free movement rules but that a Member State could attach conditions to the way in which such services were provided without infringing the freedom of establishment rules.[30]

More recently issues of social housing have created problems in the United Kingdom, Ireland, and The Netherlands (and under the EEA Agreement for Iceland and Norway). Of central concern is the question of whether social housing schemes are economic activities, whether they fulfil the requirements of being a service of general economic interest and whether the subsidisation of such housing is a state aid which is compatible with the Internal Market. These are central questions which need guidance because Member States would be under a duty to notify any state aid to the Commission unless it complies with the *Altmark*[31] criteria or satisfies the *de minimis* rules of the Commission's Framework and Decision.[32] Complaints have been brought by competitors who would like to access the market for low cost housing. This is an area where the Commission may have the power to challenge a Member State's definition of a SGEI if the housing scheme does not have a sufficiently 'social objective'. *Van de Gronden* analyses the rather disappointing ruling of the ECJ in *Sint Servatius*[33] where the Court analysed the Dutch social housing scheme only in the context of the free movement of capital. Not surprisingly the Court found that a prior authorisation scheme for cross-border investment projects constituted a restriction on the free movement of capital but it could be justified by an overriding reason of general interest ('the Rule of Reason'). The Court missed the opportunity to examine whether Article 106(2) TFEU could be applied and the latitude of discretion left to a Member State in determining the scale of a SGEI in such a sector. Procurement activities are viewed as part of the free movement rules under EU law and as States have

---

[28] See Szyszczak 2009.

[29] ECJ, Case C-70/95 *Sodemare* [1997] *ECR* I-3395.

[30] For a discussion of the case law see: Hancher and Sauter 2010, 117.

[31] ECJ, Case C-280/00 *Altmark Trans and Regierungsprasidium Magdeburg* [2003] *ECR* I-7747.

[32] 2005/C 297/04; *OJ* C 297/4 2005 and C(2005) 2673, *OJ* L 312/67 2005. At the time of writing, the Commission has published Reports on how the Member States have applied the Framework and Decision (available at: http://ec.europa.eu/competition/consultations/2010_sgei/reports.html) and begun a review of the application of the Framework and the Decision see: Public Consultation on State Aid Rules, available at: http://ec.europa.eu/competition/consultations/2010_sgei/index_en.html.

[33] ECJ, Case C-567/07 *Sint Servatius* [2009] *ECR* I-9021.

increasingly cut back on direct provision of social services, there is the likelihood that their procurement activities may be caught by EU law. However, as *Van de Gronden* shows the procurement rules appear to have carved out a number of safe havens for the procurement of social services. These resonate with the exceptions found in the Services Directive[34] and the Framework and Decision[35] adopted by the Commission in the wake of the *Altmark* ruling.[36]

Van de Gronden also examines the application of the competition rules to SSGIs. Several of these cases are well-known, for example, the *Poucet and Pistre, Albany, Brentjens* and *Drijvende Bokken* judgments.[37] Whereas, social security schemes which are universal and are based upon the principle of solidarity are not seen as economic activities, complementary schemes will usually be caught by the competition rules, but may be exempted from the full force of these rules if they are a SGEI.

The application of the Treaty rules to SSGIs creates questions on competence. Member States continue to retain competence in the creation of SSGIs but the Commission is able to question whether there has been a manifest error in these definitions. The Commission has also made it clear that the modernisation of SSGIs and the introduction of competition makes SSGIs susceptible to scrutiny under the competition law rules of the Treaty. In 2006, the Commission issued its first Communication dedicated to SSGIs and this was quickly followed by a second Communication in 2007 and two sets of 'Frequently Asked Questions'.[38] By 2008 the Commission was publishing biennial reports on SSGIs. Thus in a short space of time, SSGIs have become a focal point of concern for the Commission. The potential application of the Treaty rules to SSGIs instigated the Protocol No. 26 annexed to the TEU and TFEU reaffirming Member State competence in the area of SSGIs and also creating clearer concepts on the functions of SGEIs in general.

Universal service obligations (usos) were the price extracted by the Member States in agreeing to liberalise the core networked industries in the EU. Their role is to ensure social and regional cohesion within the Member States as well as maintaining and improving the quality of core services. The latter is achieved by guarantees of quality, affordability, continuity. For some commentators usos have a role to play in protecting the vulnerable consumer, contributing to the evolution of a *social* European private law.[39] However, usos have a much wider remit. The Monti Report 2010 recognised the importance of usos in providing citizens with access to the benefits of European integration:

---

[34] Directive 2006/123/EC, *OJ* L 376/36.2006.

[35] *Supra* n. 32.

[36] *Supra* n. 31.

[37] ECJ, Joined Cases C-159/91 and C-160/91 *Poucet and Pistre* [1993] *ECR* I-637; ECJ, C-67/96 *Albany* [1990] *ECR* I-5751; Joined Cases C-115/97, C-116/97 and C-117/97 *Brentjens* [1999] *ECR* I-6025 and Case C-219/97 *Drijvende bokken* [1999] *ECR* I-6121.

[38] *Communication from the Commission of 20 November 2007, Services of General Interest Including Social Services of General Interest: a New European Commitment,* COM(2007) 275.

[39] Micklitz 2009.

> In order to be able to effectively participate in the single market citizens need access to a number of basic services of general economic interest, in particular in the area of network industries, such as postal services, transport services or telecommunications services. In network industries, market opening at EU level has, therefore, always been accompanied by measures ensuring that a universal service continued to be provided.[40]

The chapter by *Jim Davies and Erika Szyszczak* charts the development of usos in the EU liberalisation programme. Noting that services of general economic interest and usos are EU nomenclature for traditional public services previously delivered by the nation state, and often by a public monopoly, the authors see an expanding role for the concept of usos in the future development of the EU, from a social perspective as well as a commercial perspective.

The authors note that, whereas, a Member State has a wide competence to define a SGEI, this is no longer the case when a uso is found in liberalising legislation. The authors question whether the use of usos is a temporary device and whether they will survive if, and when, there is full market liberalisation of a sector. Their chapter charts the various stages of the evolution of an EU concept of a usos and their analysis of usos concludes that far from the gradual demise of the usos in the liberalisation process, they see the concept changing and evolving, and expanding in its role of protecting the consumer-citizen interest in the Internal Market.

A second focus of this chapter is to place the consumer–citizen at the heart of the usos. Academics have argued that usos have a role to play in protecting the *vulnerable* consumer contributing to the evolution of a *social* European private law.[41] However, usos have a much wider remit in contributing not only to the inclusiveness of EU society but also the *effectiveness* of the benefits brought by an Internal Market.

The chapter argues that the simple triangle of relationships traditionally used to describe the new 'State–provider–user (consumer) relationship' of liberalised markets is too simple and that 'a geometry of triangles' should be used to chart the complexity of the various triangular relationships which are emerging in liberalised markets. Even so, the visualisation and description of these relationships in this way does not capture the dynamics of the regulation and role of usos in liberalised markets. To this end a more fluid description appears necessary, placing the consumer-citizen of EU law at the heart of a complex web of networked relationships. By viewing the consumer–citizen through a lens of networked relationships, issues emerge of governance of the processes and outcomes through which consumer, competition and integration issues are mediated.

The theme of public service obligations (psos) is taken up by *Martin Hennig* who argues that the concept of psos has not received as much attention from the academic or practising community in contrast to the attention given to 'usos', 'services in the general interest' and 'services of general economic interest'. In order to rectify this anomaly *Hennig* focuses upon Article 93 TFEU which

---

[40] Monti 2010.

[41] See Micklitz 2009.

explicitly mentions public service obligations and state aid in EU transport law. However, the inter-changeability of concepts in EU law causes semantic confusion and *Hennig* begins with an examination of the concept of psos in France and the United Kingdom in order to unravel how closely the national concepts can be translated into EU law. In fact the investigation shows very differing concepts between the United Kingdom and France. In France public services enjoy a constitutional status, whereas, in the UK public service values are protected through political rather than legal mechanisms. The chapter then argues that Article 93 TFEU contains a functional concept of 'public service' allowing the Member States to protect public service values through financing mechanisms to facilitate the coordination of transport or where state authorities compensate operators for the costs of providing services which undertakings are required to perform by law, or under acts of public authority. However, *Hennig* finds that public service obligations have the same functions as the new EU terminology of services of general economic interest, but the use of the latter terminology undermines the mission of protecting common shared values in the EU. *Hennig* is, therefore, curious *why* the term public service obligations has been retained in Article 93 TFEU, despite the various revisions of the original Treaty and why the concept is not used more widely in EU law.

1.4 Global Issues

Section 1.3 of the book looks at a different dimension to SGIs. As many services are liberalised they open up new global markets. Concerns to protect functional public services do not stop at the EU external borders: they are now global concerns. These themes are taken up by *Priscilla Schwartze* in discussing the regulatory paradoxes that emerge as public private partnerships (PPP), used to supply traditional government services in least developed countries (LDCs). PPP were first developed in industrialised States (most notably in the United Kingdom[42]) to improve the quality and economic efficiency of public services in industrialised countries using market-based solutions. They have become more important as governments have attempted to keep public spending under control and a general reluctance of electorates to pay higher taxes for public services. In LDCs, the issue is different: governments frequently do not have the funds to develop and maintain

[42] See HM Treasury, *Public Private Partnerships: The Government's Approach*, London, HMSO 2000; HM Treasury, *PFI: Meeting the Investment Challenge*, London, HMSO, 2003. The EU has endorsed the use of PPP as part of the Initiative for Growth for the development of trans-European transport networks and the delivery of SGEIs: European Commission, Green Paper on Public–Private Partnerships and Community Law on Public Contracts and Concessions, COM(2004) 327 final; *European Commission, Green Paper on Services of General Interest* COM(2003) 270 final.

public services. The United Nations has endorsed the use of PPP as a means of realising the Millennium Development Goals that benefit the public and deliver economic development and an improvement in the quality of life. PPP is seen as:

> innovative methods used by the public sector to contract with the private sector, who bring their capital and their ability to deliver projects on time and to budget, while the public sector retains the responsibility to provide these services to the public in a way that benefits the public and delivers economic development and an improvement in the quality of life.[43]

Gradually a revolution has taken place with use of private capital harnessed to deliver public services and infrastructure projects.[44] As *Schwartze* points out there appears at first sight an inherent conflict between the *commercial* interest underpinning PPP for social services, especially health care, and the goals of a public policy. Both goals seem irreconcilable. Yet these solutions have been transplanted to LDCs to ensure that basic social services are provided. *Schwartze* takes as a case study the use of PPP in delivering health care services in Sierra Leone. As she shows, this is a complex lens through which to examine the role of PPPs since health objectives do not easily translate into private economic objectives and the cooperation models of inter-state, multi-lateral, and regional settings must work within the WTO rules, especially the WTO TRIPS Agreement and intellectual property rights. Health care, as the United States and the EU has discovered,[45] is not an easy sector to classify in terms of economic and social activities and this dichotomy is enhanced when analysing the appropriateness of marketing health care as a 'public–private for profit partnership' as a development tool in poor countries. Thus the chapter offers an analytical model to identify the concept of PPP in a developmental context of government health services in LDCs. *Schwartze* is able to offer a model which allows for the possibility of using PPPs for facilitating increased aid flows for funding a technical solution to problems encountered in health care systems in LDCs. As she shows, the model is complex which leaves many questions to be addressed. These encompass the legal arrangements, rights, obligations, and responsibilities of the various parties, the indicators and standards used to measure gains, should the PPP apply to the whole country or are the gains to be made for selective investment? *Schwartze* concludes by stating that whatever model is adopted, LDC should retain the autonomy to choose the right regulatory mechanisms and provide the institutional capacity to meet the health challenges they face.

The EU is aware that international trade agreements such as the WTO and the GATS may affect the internal EU response to trade in public services and the Commission has publicly stated that international trade agreements should not impede the EU capability to pursue its policies on public services.[46] *Markus*

---

[43] UN Economic Commission for Europe 2008.

[44] Grimsey and Lewis 2007.

[45] See Van de Gronden et al. 2011.

[46] European Commission, *White Paper on Services of General Interest*, COM(2004) 374 final at 20.

Krajewski adopts a different approach and asks the question: to what extent can the international agreements signed by the EC/EU reflect, or even advance, a *positive* understanding of public services? This is an important perspective now that the Treaty of Lisbon 2009 places external relations policy in a larger value, and principle, driven framework. *Krajewski* also examines the role of the WTO and in particular the GATS but in this chapter the telecoms sector is the focus of attention. As was shown in the chapter by *Davies and Szyszczak*, telecoms provides an important model for liberalisation and the development of usos which are mirrored in other sectors opened up to competition. Two case studies follow, first the EC-Chile bilateral association agreement and second, the EU-CARIFORUM Economic Partnership Agreement which is of particular interest in that it contains positive usos. *Krajewski* also examines a number of agreements which are currently under discussion to determine if there is an emerging trend to include and define public service and usos in the external agreements of the EU. Underlying this approach is a quest to determine whether in its external role the EU is continuing internal trends of seeing public services not only as exemptions and derogations from EU law—the irritant of the Single Market—but also as a positive requirement: a move 'from derogation to obligation?'[47]

This Introduction began with the theme that public services were viewed as an irritant in the European integration project and that the case law and policy responses towards public services have created an explosion of ideas. These ideas are responses to questions of: what is the *role* of public services in the liberalisation and privatisation of markets; what should modern public services look like; are there bright lines distinguishing social services of general interest; are the legal tools out-dated (for example, is the *economic/non-economic* distinction functional today); is *solidarity* a useful concept; what is *legitimate* financing of public services; are public services provided for consumers or citizens; what is the *role* of the *State;* is it possible, or useful, to have a Framework Regulation on SGIs; what is the effect of the Treaty of Lisbon 2009 on the future of SGIs, the role of competition as a value in the future of EU integration, values in the 'European Social Model' and the integration of national social welfare schemes into EU law? More recently the effects of the current recession have made an impact upon the funding of public services at a time when more people look to public services as the traditional safety net against poverty and social exclusion. Thus the future role and 'reform' of public services in a climate of austerity is firmly on the EU political agenda. Not all of the answers to these questions can be explored immediately but many ideas are to be found in the chapters of this book.

---

[47] Ross 2000.

References

Baquero Cruz J (2005) Beyond competition: services of general interest and European Community law. In: de Búrca G (ed) EU Law and The Welfare State. OUP, Oxford

Buendia Sierra J (2000) Exclusive rights and state monopolies under EC law. OUP, Oxford

Davies G (2009a) What does article 86 actually do? In: Krajewski M, Neergaard U, Van de Gronden J (eds) The changing legal framework for services of general interest in Europe. TMC Asser, The Hague

Davies G (2009b) Article 86 EC, the EC's economic approach to competition law, and the general interest. 5.2 Compet Law J 549

Fiedziuk N. (2010) Towards a more refined economic approach to services of general economic interest. 16.2 Eur Public Law 271

Frenz W, Schleissing P (2009) The never ending story of 'in-house' procurement. In: Krajewski M, Neergaard U, Van de Gronden J (eds) The changing legal framework for services of general interest in Europe. TMC Asser Press, The Hague, p 171

Grimsey D, Lewis M (2007) Public private partnerships: the worldwide revolution in infrastructure provision and project finance. Edward Elgar, Cheltenham

Gyselen L (2010) Services of general economic interest and competition under European law: a delicate balance. J Eur Compet Law Pract

Hancher L, Sauter W (2010) One step beyond? From sodemare to docMorris: The EU's freedom of establishment case law concerning healthcare. 47.1. CMLRev 117

Kenner J, Hervey T (eds) (2003) Economic and social rights under the EU charter of fundamental rights: a legal perspective. OUP, Oxford

Micklitz H-W (2009) Universal services: nucleus for a *Social* European private law, EUI working papers law 12, Department of Law

Monti M (2010) A new strategy for the single market. At the service of Europe's economy and society. Report to the President of the European Commission José Manuel Barroso, 9 May 2010

Radaelli C (2009) Europeanisation: solution or problem? 8.16. European integration online papers. http://eiop.or.at/eiop/texte/2004-016.htm

Rodrigues S (2009) Towards a general EC framework instrument related to SGEI? Political considerations and legal constraints. In: Krajewski M, Neergaard U, Van de Gronden J (eds) The changing legal framework for services of general interest in Europe. TMC Asser Press, The Hague, p 255

Ross M (2000) Article 16 E.C. and services of general interest: from derogation to obligation? 25 ELRev 22

Ross M (2007) Promoting solidarity: from public services to a European model of competition? 44 CMLRev 1057

Szyszczak E (2009) Legal tools in the liberalisation of welfare markets. In: Neergaard U, Roseberry L, Nielsen R (eds) Integrating welfare functions into EU law: from Rome to Lisbon. DJØF Publishing, Copenhagen

UN Economic Commission for Europe (2008) Guidebook on promoting good governance in public private partnerships, ECE/CECI/4, United Nations

Van de Gronden J et al (eds) (2011) Health care and EU law. TMC Asser Press, The Hague

Part I
Background Issues

Chapter 2
From Rome to Lisbon: SGIs in Primary Law

Pierre Bauby

Abstract This chapter is a discussion of the historical, political and, cultural specificity of the generic concept of 'public services' in Europe. The enlargement of the EU in 2004 and 2007 has added even greater complexity to the diversity of concepts of public services already found in the EU. Bauby notes that it is interesting to see that in 1957 (what is now) Article 93 TFEU (in the Chapter on Transport) used the term 'public service', whereas, Article 106(2) TFEU (ex Article 90(2) EEC, Article 86(2) EC) created a new concept of 'services of general economic interest' but this was a derogation from the fundamental economic freedom and competition law of the EU. This was an entirely new concept which was not recognised in any language of the original Member States or in scientific literature. However, attempts to put SGEIs on a positive footing in EU legislation have met with resistance and it is questionable how far the new Treaty of Lisbon 2009 will provide an adequate legal basis for EU legislation.

Contents

P. Bauby (✉)
Paris 8 University, 66 rue de Rome, Paris, 75008, France
e-mail: bauby.pierre@orange.fr

E. Szyszczak et al. (eds.), *Developments in Services of General Interest*,
Legal Issues of Services of General Interest, DOI: 10.1007/978-90-6704-734-0_2,

Each society, within its long history, built and defined its 'Public Services', according to its own way of development, its traditions, institutions, culture, social movements, and the relations of force that structured it. So, it is nothing surprising that we find in Europe a series of diversity in the field of 'Public services'.[1]

2.1 Diversity and Unity in Europe

The first element to take into account is the terms and concepts used to define the 'Public Services'. They reflect historical developments, national cultures, and politico-ideological conceptions, and they are not necessarily equivalent in the actual 23 official languages of the EU.

The British use the expression either as singular concept—'Public service' equivalent to the concept of 'Civil Service', which means essentially, the administration and the civil servants, or as a plural concept 'Public Services', which refers to the various services provided to citizens by local authorities, central government, health care, education, policing, etc. The British also use the expression 'Public Utilities', which corresponds to the major network services (gas, electricity, water and wastewater, post and, telecommunications), but does not have a genuine explanatory value.[2]

We cannot establish a univocal glossary setting up the exact equivalent of 'Public Services' in all 23 official languages of the EU and each Member State. The successive enlargements, especially those of 2004 and 2007,[3] came to complicate the situation. In this field, each language refers to national histories, cultures, traditions, identities, etc., on the basis of which a national vocabulary, sometimes a specific doctrine has been developed: 'public services', 'public service', 'public utilities', 'service public', 'öffentliche Dienstleistungen', 'öffentlicher Dienst',[4] 'Daseinsvorsorge', etc., terms that cover various concepts in the European Member States.[5]

In attempting to develop a better comprehension between different languages and cultures, European construction had to create a common language, here by creating new terms—'services of general interest SGIs', 'services of general economic interest—SGEIs', we will return to that.

---

[1] According to, in particular, *Cahiers français*, no 339, Les services publics, juillet-août 2007, La Documentation Française; Valin 2007.

[2] Marcou and Moderne 2005; Bell and Kennedy 2001.

[3] Andreff 2007; Atilla 2003.

[4] Forsthoff 1969; See also the translation of the term 'service of general interest'—*Dienste von allgemeinem Interesse*, or of the concept 'public service' used in the Community law—*öffentlicher Dienst*.

[5] Mangenot 2005.

More deeply, behind the same expression 'Public Services', there is often an amalgamation or confusion between missions, objectives, finalities, and organisation.

Thus, it coexists in two particular conceptions:

- a functional conception, which emphasises objectives and finalities of 'Public Services';
- an organic conception, which assimilates 'Public Services' to the entity that provides the service.

We also often understand 'Public Services' as public enterprises. The attribute 'public' within the expression 'Public Service' is sometimes considered as a reference to an enterprise having a public statute, or even activities of the state or communities, while 'Public Service' missions can also be entrusted to private enterprises (delegation, concession, etc.).

Another diversity is reflected in the fact that the competent territorial levels are not the same in the sectors and the structure of each state: between local, regional and national levels, the activities in question can have a market or non-market nature; organisation methods may be subject to different types of actors—public, mix, private or associative; doctrines and concepts, in particular the legal ones, are more or less formalised.

Thus, France built a strong concept of 'Public service' (*service public*), a sound legal doctrine (the principles drawn by the Council of State for more than one century of equality, continuity, and mutability-adaptability), a series of economic reasons (linked to 'market failures') and finally a political content, assimilating it to social link, the Republic, and the national identity. Other countries, as for example, the countries of Northern Europe (Sweden, Finland, Denmark) and The Netherlands, have not adopted a legal definition of 'Public Services', but based on the legislative intervention; there is no equivalent concept of 'Public Services' in Sweden and Finland, even if these countries are considered as typical examples of a welfare state thanks to a very active social policy and the relative autonomy of public law as developed in both countries.[6]

But, within this diversity, there is in Europe a profound unity[7]: in all European countries, public authorities—local, regional and/or national, were led to consider that some activities could not only be subject to the common law of competition and market rules, but to specific rules of definition, organisation and, regulation, with three objectives:

- to guarantee the right of each inhabitant to access basic goods and services (right to education, health, security, transport, communications, etc.);
- to build solidarities, guarantee economic, social and territorial cohesion, develop social link and promote the general interest of concerned community;

[6] Modeen 2001.

[7] According to, in particular, Bauby 1997; Lyon-Caen and Champeil-Desplats 2001; Bauby 2008, 2007.

- to take into account the long-term and the interests of future generations, to create conditions for a sustainable development, both economic, social, and environmental.

These aims and objectives of general interest are at the centre of the system of values that characterises all European countries and form a set of common value for Europe. 'Public Services' (or their equivalent) represent a key element of the European social model characterised by interactions and the integration of economic and social progress, which shape a 'social market economy'.

Thus, 'Public Services' are both characterised by their important national specificity, revealing a real diversity, and by a unity of tasks, resulting from history.

How should the European integration process approach 'Public Services'? Will they continue to lie outside the process, thus continuing to be defined and organised within the national framework, or will they be the subject of Europeanisation process? This question was not clarified by the Treaty of Rome of 1957, whose object was to progressively eliminate different obstacles to exchanges of goods.

2.2 The Treaty of Rome of 1957

The process of European integration began after the Second World War with the ECSC Treaty of 1951, and then with the Treaty of the European Defence Community (EDC) of 1953, it rests on an approach of progressive political integration starting with six Member States. But the failure of the EDC led to a clear inflexion, because the way for a direct political integration seemed impossible in the short term: instead, governments decided to follow the way of a progressive economic integration, starting with the construction of a 'Common market'.

This is what the Treaty of Rome of 1957 embraced. European construction was defined by three characteristics: a progressive supranational set, with common policies and some delegated powers to new institutions; its intimate legal nature (treaties, regulations and directives with a priority legal position over the national law); economic liberalism and the principles of free exchange and free competition, then free movement (workers, goods, services and capital), thus making the market the main regulator of European integration. Nevertheless, for the founders of Europe, the economy was only a way of integration that served a political objective with a federal nature.

The Treaty of Rome objective was to progressively eliminate different obstacles to goods exchanges, both by creating four common policies (commercial, competition, agriculture, and transport) but not to harmonise 'Public Services'. It evokes them only twice: Article 93 TFEU of the Chapter on Transport[8] refers to

[8] We use the numbering of articles in the current treaties (the so-called Lisbon), in force since 1 December 2009.

'obligations inherent in the concept of a public service',[9] whilst Article 106(2) TFEU recognises possible derogations from competition rules for 'services of general economic interest'.

Article 106 TFEU (ex Article 90 Rome, Article 86 EC)

1. In the case of public undertakings and undertakings to which Member States grant special or exclusive rights, Member States shall neither enact nor maintain in force any measure contrary to the rules contained in the Treaties, particularly those rules provided for in Article 18 and Articles 101–109.
2. Undertakings entrusted with the operation of services of general economic interest or having the character of a revenue-producing monopoly shall be subject to the rules contained in the Treaties, in particular to the rules on competition, in so far as the application of such rules does not obstruct the performance, in law or in fact, of the particular tasks assigned to them. The development of trade must not be affected to such an extent as would be contrary to the interests of the Union.
3. The Commission shall ensure the application of the provisions of this Article and shall, where necessary, address appropriate directives or decisions to Member States.

We should note here the innovative approach of the authors of the Treaty of Rome: in order that representatives of different countries with different histories, cultures, and languages understand themselves, they create the expression 'services of general economic interest', which pre-existed in no national language or tradition. And to avoid any misunderstanding, in particular between French and German, they did not use the word 'public', that could lead to confusion (Is it about services' beneficiary or of the status of entities providing them?), but they clearly accentuate the objectives and finalities, the general interest, suggesting a functional meaning. Besides, they insist on 'the particular tasks assigned to them'. Certainly, the expression 'services of general economic interest' is particularly improper, because the authors' main aim was the 'economic' nature of the services rather than any particular 'economic' category of general interest. But even if invented in 1957, this expression has not been changed and Article 106 TFEU remains unaffected by the multiple revisions of the treaty.

In the White Paper on SGIs, the European Commission proposes a clarification of the terminology and definitions of the Community terms which are subject to a certain consensus among all stakeholders[10]: 'services of general interest covers both market and non-market services which the public authorities class as being of general interest and subject to specific public service obligations' and that 'services of general economic interest refers to services of an economic nature.' Thus, it appears clear that this expression reflects the only common conception for European countries, the functional sense, which focuses on objectives, missions and finalities, general interest, and not the organic sense and the ownership type of operators.

---

[9] 'Aids shall be compatible with the Treaties if they meet the needs of coordination of transport or if they represent reimbursement for the discharge of certain obligations inherent in the concept of a public service.'

[10] COM(2004) 374.

Even if before, the Single Act of 1986, Article 90 EC (Article 106 TFEU) did not produce effects, it led to very different representations and interpretations by the Community institutions, including in the last period, and most often presented as allowing 'derogations' of Community rules in the field of SGIs. In particular, derogations from competition or of freedom of movement rules,[11] on the condition that they are justified and proportionate and often identified as an 'exception' to these same rules. The White Paper of the European Commission of 2004[12] said that 'the effective performance of a general interest task prevails, in case of tension, over the application of Treaty rules.'

The expression of 1957 'services of general economic interest' (SGEIs), was not changed by the adoption of new treaties,[13] and is now expressed in the primary law of the European Union, by the Treaty of Lisbon, as 'services of general interest' (SGIs) and 'non-economic services of general interest' (NESGIs). Furthermore, from the Community debates and the communications of the Commission has emerged the concept of 'social services of general interest' (SSGIs).

A careful study of, on the one hand, the secondary law and, on the other hand, the judgments of the Court of Justice and of the General Court reveals a frequent use of the term 'public service', but never in a general or global sense, as is the case in France or in certain countries of Roman law. It is always used as a qualifying term, a concept or a particular service: 'public service mission', 'public service obligation', 'obligation inherent in the concept of public service', 'public service requirement', 'delegation of public service', 'public service concession', 'public service contract', 'concessionaire or manager of a public service', 'public transport service', 'public service delivery of drinking water or gas distribution', or, furthermore, in respect of a particular service, 'guaranteeing that the public service will be executed', 'object of the public service', etc. It is through an improper extension that the use by the Court of the expression 'postal public services' was sometimes interpreted as a general or nominal definition of 'the public service' or of 'the public services'.[14]

But between 1957 and 1986, there is a consensus: each Member State continues to be responsible for defining, organising, implementing, financing its public services of general interest, according to its history, traditions, institutions, and culture. For almost 30 years there is no European integration of 'Public services'.

2.3 The Single Act of 1986: Nothing Changes, All Changes!

The Single Act of 1986, which amended and completed the Treaty of Rome, entrusted European institutions with the mission to implement the four freedoms of movement (people, goods, services, capital) and the single market. The articles

[11] Directive 2006/123/CE on services in the internal market.

[12] COM(2004) 374, point 3.2.

[13] It is significant that Article 90 of the Treaty of Rome has not been changed since 1957.

[14] For example, Guglielmi and Koubi 2009.

that made reference to public services and services of general economic interest were not changed, but the objective of free movement of services gave a mandate to the European institutions to eliminate obstacles to exchanges and to realise the internal market of … 'services of general economic interest', but without defining the specific provisions that would ensure their goals and develop European solidarity.[15] Even though not defined, the consensus of that time limited 'services of general interest' to the sectors of communications, transport and energy, key infrastructure networks necessary to the realisation of internal market and the four freedoms of movement.

A process of Europeanisation of services of general economic interest started then, sector by sector with three possible directions for the Europeanisation of public services[16]:

- Reject Europeanisation on behalf of specificities of SGIs or of each national state (on behalf of the principle of subsidiarity). This led to defensive strategies, which delayed the process and deadlines, but did not hinder the process, because they did not fall within European integration.
- Building European SGIs, as each member state did in its history, but no actor has proposed at this time, as this would put into question the practices, traditions, and usual organisational methods.
- To use the arms of the Treaty, developed since 1957 (competition, free trade), to break frontiers and improve the efficiency of often inefficient services. It is this strategy that will prevail. Why?

The implementation of the four freedoms of movement resonated with the essential changes of the 1980s and 1990s: rapid technological changes; internationalisation of economies and societies; diversification and territorialisation of needs; questioning burdens and inefficiencies of many public services; the strategies of major industrial and financial services groups; the development of the influence of the neo-liberal theories and the virtues of competition, etc.

The combination of these factors has led to a growing gap between national modes of definition and organisation of public services (communication, transport and energy) and the EU objectives of free movement. Europeanisation aimed both at breaking down national barriers, implementing European integration and introducing greater efficiency in areas that were often 'protected' by monopolies or exclusive local, regional and/or national rights.[17]

The European Union gradually called into question the national forms of organisation and regulation of public services that had been defined by the history of each EU Member State as it developed strategies for the creation of internal markets in network sectors, based on 'liberalisation', the introduction of competition and market logic.

---

[15] See in particular CEEP 1995; Mangenot 2005.

[16] Bauby 2007–2008.

[17] Bauby 1998; Savary 2005.

However, these network sectors cannot be totally liberalised in order to make them subject only to the Community law of competition. The liberalisation logic leads to a series of polarisations in the network sectors calling into question some SGI objectives. There can be an oligopolistic competition among a few large groups, leading to new concentrations, to the detriment of users. Liberalisation overvalues the short-term, for which the market provides valuable information, to the detriment of the long-term for which the market is myopic. It focuses on large consumers who have 'market power' over small ones. It calls into question the equal treatment and the opportunities for equalisation (*péréquation*) of tariffs. Liberalisation takes into account neither territorial effects nor environmental consequences. It leads to forms of social dumping.

Under these conditions, apart from some pressure groups proposing a complete deregulation of SGIs by removing them from the common law of competition, the European rules, resulting from debates, initiatives of actors, and social movements, implement a controlled, organised and regulated liberalisation. The European Union has had to complete sectoral projects of liberalisation by creating new concepts and norms. We saw the concept of 'universal service' appear in telecommunications and postal services, then for electricity, guaranteeing some basic services to all residents and citizens; the public service was defined in energy and transport. The European Commission held public debates and proposed a set of principles that could form the basis of a Community doctrine.

2.4 Premises for a Community Doctrine

Progressively, a series of elements came to testify the research of a European conception of Public Services or Services of General Interest.

The Treaty of the European Union (Maastricht) of 1992 had already opened the potential for taking better account of and legitimising public service missions, even if most of these provisions continued to be often no more than potentials and subject to the priority of competition rules. The potentialities of the Treaty of Maastricht included:

1. The Article 8, establishing 'citizenship of the Union', whose content was largely to develop, for example, in terms of guaranteeing access to certain essential goods and services.
2. The Title XI (Article 129 A) 'Consumer protection': the satisfaction of consumer needs is their *raison d'être*, their purpose, the foundation of their legitimacy.
3. The Title XII (Articles 129B, C and D) 'Trans-European networks' provides for their development, interconnection, interoperability, and reveals a collective European interest.
4. The Title XIII aims to provide 'conditions necessary for the competitiveness of the Community's industry', whose foundations are based largely on the existence of efficient infrastructure.

5. Title XIV 'Economic and social cohesion' set the goal of 'reducing disparities between the levels of development of the various regions', which directly affects the services of general interest (social, territorial and generational solidarities)
6. Title XVI extended EU responsibilities in the area of protection of environment and concerned services of general interest, whose feature is to generate significant externalities.
7. The Protocol on the social policy, annexed to the treaty, established as objectives 'the promotion of employment, improved living and working conditions, proper social protection, dialogue between management and labour, the development of human resources with a view to lasting high employment and the combating of exclusion.' Services of general interest can contribute to realise these objectives.
8. More generally, the Articles A and B set objectives for a balanced and sustainable economic and social progress, 'to promote economic and social progress which is balanced and sustainable, in particular through the creation of an area without internal frontiers, through the strengthening of economic and social cohesion.'

In parallel, the case law of the Court of Justice has recognised since the *Corbeau*[18] and *Commune Almelo*[19] judgements that Article 106(2) TFEU can justify a limitation of competition for some services of general economic interest, which has been confirmed since then in many judgements. Thus, the Court of Justice defined progressively a jurisprudence recognising that services of general interest may fall within other objectives, missions, and forms of organisation than the general laws of competition.

Other evolutions occurred, resulting from debates, initiatives of different actors and of European networks such as the European Centre of Employers and Enterprises providing Public Services (CEEP), the European Trade Union Confederation (ETUC), the European Liaison Committee on Services of General Interest (CELSIG), and social movements, in particular of November–December 1995 that called into question the issue of total liberalisation and proposing a re-balancing of competition rules and general interest: both being considered not as finalities but as two ways for advancing EU objectives.

However, we had to wait 11 years after the Single Act, for the Treaty of Amsterdam to refer, in Article 16 EC, to SGEIs (without clear definition of the conditions of their particular tasks) as part of the common values of the European Union, with regard to their role in social and territorial cohesion and for which it establishes a shared competence between the EU and the Member States to enable them to fulfil their missions. However, this Article provided merely for a general, rather than legally specific, Treaty objective for SGEIs.

---

[18] ECJ, Case C-320/91 *Procureur du Roi v Paul Corbeau* [1993] *ECR* I-2533.

[19] ECJ, Case C-393/92, *Municipality of Almelo v NV Energiebedrijf IJsselmij* [1994] *ECR* I-1477.

Article 16 EC
Without prejudice to Articles 83, 106, and 107, and given the place occupied by services of general economic interest in the shared values of the Union as well as their role in promoting social and territorial cohesion, the Community and the Member States, each within their respective powers and within the scope of application of this Treaty, shall take care that such services operate on the basis of principles and conditions which enable them to fulfil their missions.

In 2000, the Charter of Fundamental Rights of the European Union was proclaimed. Article 36 'recognises and respects access to services of general economic interest.' Even though the Charter was not binding for 9 years it was for the first time that a declaration of rights at supranational level embraced an article on public services. Since 1 December 2009, the Charter 'has the same legal value as the Treaties' (Article 6 TEU).

Article 36 of the Charter of Fundamental Rights of the European Union
The Union recognises and respects access to services of general economic interest as provided for in national laws and practices, in accordance with the Treaty establishing the European Community, in order to promote the social and territorial cohesion of the Union.

It seems that this article may have two contradictory interpretations. On the one hand, we could read it as giving no competence or obligation to Community institutions, because the respect for access to SGEIs makes reference to 'national legislations'. But on the other hand, this text may be interpreted as imposing on the Community institutions the obligation to respect 'the access to services of general economic interest as provided for in national laws.' It will rely on future litigation before the Court of Justice of the European Union to bring clarity to the meaning of this article.

These two advances were linked with a series of other debates and positions, which gradually came to open a Community discussion on the future of public services. Thus, the European Commission has committed itself, since 1996, to a reflective and cross-cutting series of publications: two Communications (1996 and 2000), a report (2001), a Green Paper (2003) and a White Paper (2004), all entitled *Services of general interest in Europe*.[20]

In the White Paper of 12 May 2004, the Commission stressed that the debates had revealed important differences of views and perspectives, but that they seemed to have reached a consensus on the necessity to ensure a harmonious combination of market mechanisms and public service missions. The White Paper stresses the responsibility of public authorities: whereby, if the supply of services of general interest is organised in cooperation with the private sector or entrusted to private or public enterprises, the definition of public service obligations and missions remains the responsibility of public authorities at the appropriate level. The public

[20] European Commission, *Green Paper on Services of General Interest*, 2003, COM(2003) 270 final; European Commission, *White Paper on Services of General Interest*, 2004, COM(2004) 374 final; European Commission, *Communication on 'Services of general interest, including social services of general interest: a new European commitment'*, 2007, COM(2007) 725 final.

authorities are also responsible for market regulation and the monitoring of the operators that perform the public service missions entrusted to them.

The White Paper also identifies nine principles that have emerged from European debates as the basis of a developing common doctrine. A doctrine now reinforced with Article 14 TFEU and Protocol 26 on Services of General Interest of the TFEU and the TEU, introduced in the Treaty of Lisbon in 2009, which takes up most of these principles. The nine guiding principles of the White Paper can be set out as:

1. *Enabling public authorities to operate close to the citizens*: Services of general interest should be organised and regulated as closely as possible to the citizens and the principle of subsidiarity must be strictly respected.
2. *Achieving public service objectives within competitive open markets*: the Commission remains of the view that the objectives of an open and competitive internal market and of developing high quality, accessible and affordable services of general interest are compatible: under the TFEU Treaty and subject to the conditions set out in Article 106(2), the effective performance of a general interest task prevails, in case of tension, over the application of Treaty rules.
3. *Ensuring cohesion and universal access*: the access of all citizens and enterprises to affordable high-quality services of general interest throughout the territory of the Member States is essential for the promotion of social and territorial cohesion in the European Union. In this context, universal service is a key concept the Community has developed in order to ensure effective accessibility of essential services.
4. *Maintaining a high level of quality, security, and safety*: Furthermore, the security of service provision, and in particular the security of supply, constitutes an essential requirement which needs to be reflected when defining service missions. The conditions under which services are supplied also have to provide operators with sufficient incentives to maintain adequate levels of long-term investment.
5. *Ensuring consumer and user rights*: These include in particular the access to services, including to cross-border services, throughout the territory of the Union and for all groups of the population, affordability of services, including special schemes for persons with low income, physical safety, security and reliability, continuity, high quality, choice, transparency, and access to information from providers and regulators. The implementation of these principles generally requires the existence of independent regulators with clearly defined powers and duties. These include powers of sanction (means to monitor the transposition and enforcement of universal service provisions) and should include provisions for the representation and active participation of consumers and users in the definition and the evaluation of services, the availability of appropriate redress and compensation mechanisms, and the existence of an evolutionary clause allowing requirements to be adapted in accordance with changing user and consumer needs and concerns, and with changes in the economic and technological environment.

6. *Monitoring and evaluating the performance*: in line with the prevailing view expressed in the public consultation, the Commission considers that any evaluation should be multi-dimensional and cover all relevant legal, economic, social, and environmental aspects.
7. *Respecting diversity of services and situations*: any Community policy in the area of services of general interest must take due account of the diversity that characterises different services of general interest and the situations in which they are provided. However, this does not mean that it is not necessary to ensure the consistency of the Community's approach across different sectors or that the development of common concepts that can be applied in several sectors cannot be useful.
8. *Increasing transparency*: the principle should apply to all aspects of the delivery process and cover the definition of public service missions, the organisation, financing and regulation of services, as well as their production and evaluation, including complaint-handling mechanisms.
9. *Providing legal certainty*: the Commission is aware that the application of Community law to services of general interest might give rise complex issues. It will, therefore, make a continuous effort to improve legal certainty regarding the application of Community law to the provision of services of general interest, without prejudice to the case law of the European Court of Justice and the Court of First Instance.

2.5 From the Constitutional Treaty to the Treaty of Lisbon

In these circumstances, the Convention on the Future of Europe, charged with the preparation of a draft of European Constitution, and after conducting a deep review of the framework of its Working Group XI 'Social Europe', proposed to complete and consolidate the Article 16. On the one hand, by making it a 'general provision' at the beginning of the third part of the Treaty, therefore, applicable to all policies and the functioning of the European Union (including competition and internal market), and on the other hand, by making it the basis of a secondary legislation (a European Act), allowing to guarantee the existence, operation and financing of public services, and finally by making express reference to the freedoms of national and local authorities.

> *Article III-122*
> Without prejudice to Articles I-5, III-166, III-167, and III-238, and given the place occupied by services of general economic interest as services to which all in the Union attribute value as well as their role in promoting its social and territorial cohesion, the Union and the Member States, each within their respective competences and within the scope of application of the Constitution, shall take care that such services operate on the basis of principles and conditions, in particular economic and financial conditions, which enable them to fulfil their missions. European laws shall establish these principles and set these conditions without prejudice to the competence of Member States, in compliance with the Constitution, to provide, to commission and to fund such services.

The Treaty of Lisbon, signed on 13 December 2007 by the heads of state and government of the 27 Member States of the European Union, following the 2004 rejection of the 'Constitutional Treaty' in the referendums of France and The Netherlands, came into force on 1 December 2009 after ratification by each State. It amended the Treaty of the European Union (TEU) and the Treaty establishing the European Community, which became the Treaty on the functioning of the European Union (TFEU).

The Treaty adopts, in many areas, the proposals from the Convention for the Future of Europe and the Treaty establishing a Constitution for Europe of 2004, although in some areas it is withdrawn and shows a re-focus on the role and prerogatives of the Member States and a resistance to any further Europeanisation. As regards services of general interest, it contains major innovations with Article 14 of TFEU, the legal force of the Charter of Fundamental Rights and Protocol 26 annexed to the treaties: provisions that complete themselves and set out in the primary law the framework for a European conception of services of general interest, guaranteeing their objectives and the diversity of their forms of organisation.

The Article 14 of the Treaty on the Functioning of the European Union continues the progress of Article III-122 of the draft Constitutional Treaty of 2004: it is an explicit legal basis for secondary law; the corresponding secondary law is subject to the co-decision of the Council and the Parliament and not only of the Commission (as was the case with Article 106 EC); it explicitly refers twice to the prerogatives and duties of Member States and their communities (reference to Article 4); it must be applied in all EU policies, including internal market and competition ('Provisions having general application'); and it also indicates that the legal tool for legislation should be regulations, which are immediately and directly applicable in national law.

> *Article 14 TFEU*
> Without prejudice to Article 4 of the Treaty on European Union or to Articles 93, 106 and 107 of this Treaty, and given the place occupied by services of general economic interest in the shared values of the Union as well as their role in promoting social and territorial cohesion, the Community and the Member States, each within their respective powers and within the scope of application of this Treaty, shall take care that such services operate on the basis of principles and conditions, particularly economic and financial conditions, which enable them to fulfil their missions. The European Parliament and the Council, acting by means of regulations in accordance with the ordinary legislative procedure, shall establish these principles and set these conditions without prejudice to the competence of Member States, in compliance with the Treaties, to provide, to commission and to fund such services.

With regard to the legal status of the Charter of fundamental rights, the new Article 6(1) of the EU Treaty provides that 'The Union recognises the rights, freedoms and principles set out in the Charter of Fundamental Rights of the European Union of 7 December 2000, as adapted at Strasbourg,[21] on 12 December

[21] JOEU C 303 of 14.12.2007.

2007, which shall have the same legal value as the Treaties.'[22] With regard to access to services of general economic interest, the Charter provides:

> *Article 36 Charter of Fundamental Rights*
> The Union recognises and respects access to services of general economic interest as provided for in national laws and practices, in accordance with the Treaties, in order to promote the social and territorial cohesion of the Union.

Protocol 26 TEU and TFEU on Services of general interest has, as an integral part of the Treaties, the same legal value as the remainder of the Treaties.[23] The Protocol is the result of a demand from the Prime Minister of The Netherlands at the European Council of June 2007 which adopted the contents of the reforming treaty in response to a demand from European Commission that involved the organisation of social housing in The Netherlands. In 2005, the European Commission had considered that the qualification of the housing system of The Netherlands as a SGEI was subject of an obvious error in that it went beyond the social character that a 'public service' should have: 'letting homes to households that are not socially deprived cannot be regarded as a public service.' The structural overcapacity on the housing market was not appropriate for the execution of public service; it represented a barrier to competition that should be addressed through the sale of the houses.

In doing this, the European Commission developed a restrictive conception of missions of general interest and public service obligations and called into question the competence of decision of a Member State. Primacy was given to the application of competition rules in relation to missions of general interest. To avoid such drifts, which might affect in future many other sectors or activities, the government of The Netherlands introduced the Protocol as a condition of acceptance of the reforming Lisbon Treaty and its ratification in The Netherlands:

> *Protocol (No 26) on Services of General Interest*
> The High Contracting Parties, wishing to emphasise the importance of services of general interest,
> Have agreed upon the following interpretative provisions, which shall be annexed to the Treaty on European Union and to the Treaty on the Functioning of the European Union:
>
> *Article 1*
> The shared values of the Union in respect of services of general economic interest within the meaning of Article 14 of the Treaty on the Functioning of the European Union include in particular:
>
> - the essential role and the wide discretion of national, regional, and local authorities in providing, commissioning and organising services of general economic interest as closely as possible to the needs of the users;
> - the diversity between various services of general economic interest and the differences in the needs and preferences of users that may result from different geographical, social or cultural situations;

[22] Except for the limited application in Poland and the UK.

[23] Article 51 TEU.

- a high level of quality, safety and affordability, equal treatment and the promotion of universal access and of user rights.

Article 2

The provisions of the Treaties do not affect in any way the competence of Member States to provide, commission and organise non-economic services of general interest.

Unlike the previous treaties, it concerns not only services of general economic interest but all SGIs, regardless of whether they are classified as economic or non economic. If a service is qualified as 'non economic', the Article 2 of the Protocol clearly identifies that the Treaties 'do not affect in any way the competence of Member States to provide, commission and organise…' this service. If a service is qualified as 'economic', which is the case in a growing number of areas, Article 1 of the Protocol requires the EU institutions to respect both 'the essential role and the wide discretion of national, regional and local authorities in providing, commissioning and organising' this service; to respect 'the diversity between various services of general economic interest and the differences (…) that may result from different geographical, social or cultural situations'; and also the principles 'of quality, safety and affordability, equal treatment and the promotion of universal access and of user rights.'

2.6 What Potentialities from the Lisbon Treaty?

The Treaty of Lisbon is quite a step forward compared to the earlier Treaties in that it creates new possibilities for clarifying the EU rules governing the definition, organisation, and operation of services of general interest, to guarantee and secure them. But it will require a strong political pressure for these potentials to lead to action. The Article 14 of the Treaty on the functioning of the EU provides in particular that 'the European Parliament and the Council, acting by means of regulations in accordance with the ordinary legislative procedure, shall establish these principles and set these conditions', …'particularly economic and financial conditions, which enable them to fulfil their mission.' So, the question to ask is whether the current secondary legislation of the EU is sufficient or not for this purpose. A pragmatic approach should seek not to legislate for the sake of legislation but should consider how any new EU legislative initiative could add value compared to the current situation and objectives of the treaty. In other terms, it is about examining whether the European positive law in force is sufficient or not.

Clearly, social services of general interest are, on the whole, subject to a series of legal incertitude's and insecurities detrimental to their proper operation. Of what EU standards and norms are they subject and under what conditions? Most of them are now part of a vast 'grey area'. It is a paradox, given their 'social' function, that they are less guaranteed than economic SGIs such as transport or energy whose sectoral secondary legislation contain definitions of public service obligation, universal service, or consumer protection, etc. Therefore, in the area of SSGIs, it is necessary to clarify in legislative instruments the rules necessary for them to accomplish their missions, as is the case for other sectors of SGEIs.

The Treaty of Lisbon introduced the notion of 'non-economic services of general interest' (NESGI) which is neither a matter of the internal market or the law of competition. But the lack of definition of these non-economic services in primary or secondary law generates legal uncertainties and insecurities which affect the performance of their duties. It is not the Commission nor the Court of Justice but the ordinary legislative procedure that must clarify these categories and establish the norms governing each non-economic sector.

Even if all stakeholders acknowledge the principle of subsidiarity in the context of a shared competence between the Union and the Member States in the field of SGEIs,[24] there remain a number of uncertainties and insecurities in terms of the implementation of this principle. Under what conditions can Member States or local authorities define SGEIs: their missions; their forms of organisations (for example, in the area of special or exclusive rights); the modes of management (for example, the management 'in house' is now defined and clarified only in the field of transport); cooperation and mutualisation between public authorities? What rights and duties in the areas of non-economic services of general interest? Here again, the legislative procedure should clarify the rights and duties of public authorities to define, organise, and manage the SGI(E)s.

Article 14 TFEU emphasises the economic and financial conditions relevant to the missions of SGEIs. From this point of view, the 'Monti-Kroes package'[25] came with clarifications and guarantees in the area of the compensation for a public service obligation. It exemplifies the added value of a cross-cutting European positive law and, although it needed to be re-evaluated in 2009–2010 and eventually modified, according to Article 14 TFEU by the ordinary legislative procedure, it remains that the path outlined by the ECJ in the *Altmark* judgement distinguishes such compensations from the provision of the Treaty on state aids.

In terms of economic and financial conditions, the uncertainties and insecurities of the current period have led economic operators, in some sectors, to slow or postpone some infrastructure investments which are necessary for the safe operation of SGEIs, and therefore, for the continuity of services in long-term. Here

---

[24] Hoorens 2008.

[25] Three texts concerning state aid in the form of public service compensation (two texts of 28 November 2005: a decision on the application of Article 86(2) of the EC Treaty to State aid in the form of public service compensation granted to certain undertakings entrusted with the operation of services of general economic interest and a Community framework for State aid in the form of public service compensation) and a Directive on the transparency of financial relations between Member States and public undertakings as well as on financial transparency within certain undertakings (obligation of keeping separate accounts), replaced on 16 November 2006 by the Directive 2006/111/EC. These texts are currently under review by the Commission: http://europa.eu/rapid/pressReleasesAction.do?reference=IP/10/715&format=HTML&aged=0&language=EN&guiLanguage=en

again, a clear and stable legal framework will give investors the focus they need for long-term financing.

In some sectors (transport, energy, communications), the European secondary law has provided explicit detail of the guarantees that are to be provided to consumers and end-users, thereby allowing the realisation of the content of Article 36 of the Charter of Fundamental Rights. However, a broader European base for developing consumer and end-user rights should be defined and added to the principles contained in Protocol 26 on the services of general interest that is now annexed to the Treaties.

The sectoral secondary law in force places the main responsibilities of regulation on Member States and on national sectoral agencies.[26] While the rules are defined at European level harmful distortions are created, especially as a process of oligopolisation of operators develops in each sector and at multi-service plan with few dominant players. European secondary law should, therefore, define a general regulatory framework focusing on the necessary involvement of all stakeholders in regulation development in order to help ensure that SGEIs can accomplish their missions.

Also, it is necessary to define a framework providing for the efficient monitoring and evaluation of the effectiveness and performance of services of general interest and necessary for European governance in complex fields and sectors.[27] This framework should clarify the objectives of evaluation; the methodology necessary to take into account all the objectives of the SGI by crossing indicators; the relations between the European and national level; the necessarily pluralistic and independent management arrangements and the organisation of public debates.

The secondary European law should further clarify the conditions of implementation of Article 106(2) TFEU and define under what conditions the directions proposed by the European Commission's White Paper of 2004, according to which 'the effective performance of a general interest task prevails, in case of tension, over the application of Treaty rules' can be realised.

Finally, there should be clearly established a coherence between the internal norms of the European Union on SGIs and the guidelines it defends in negotiations with WTO, the GATS and more generally in any international trade negotiation.

These 10 challenges are now the subject of actual shortcomings and insufficiencies in the European secondary law that are detrimental to the accomplishment of the tasks of services of general interest. They should, therefore, be subject to a European legislative process to ensure greater legal certainty for all actors and stakeholders. However, there is a question, should we conduct a comprehensive approach that will yield a comprehensive and coherent European legal framework or should we proceed pragmatically on a case by case basis? Certainly it is the approach that may be the most effective that should be favoured.

---

[26] Rodrigues 2005; Bell 2001.

[27] CEEP-CIRIEC 2000.

It is by responding point by point, in concrete terms, to uncertainties and insecurities of the European law for all actors concerned—public authorities (at all levels), SGI, SGEI, SSGI operators, regulatory agencies, users, staff, and trade unions—that we can both guarantee the existence of services of general interest of quality and build a European conception that will make one of the pillars of the future European Union.

References

Andreff W (2007) Economie de la transition. La transformation des économies planifiées en économies de marché, Bréal

Atilla A (2003) Public Administration in Central and Eastern Europe. In: Peters G, Pierre J (eds) Handbook of public administration. Sage

Bauby P (1997) Le service public. Paris, Flammarion

Bauby P (1998) Reconstruire l'action publique. Services publics, au service de qui? Syros

Bauby P (2007) Quels modèles de service public dans les pays de l'OCDE?, Cahiers français, Les services publics, juillet-août, La Documentation française

Bauby P (2007–2008) L'européanisation des services publics, Télescope, Vol. 14, no. 1, Le service public et la mondialisation, hiver. Ecole nationale d'administration publique, Québec

Bauby P (2008) La libéralisation des services publics, Cahiers français, no. 347, novembre-décembre, La Documentation française

Bell J (2001) L'expérience britannique en matière d'autorités administratives indépendantes, in Conseil d'Etat, Rapport public 2001. Jurisprudence et avis de 2000. Les autorités administratives indépendantes, Etudes et Documents, no. 52

Bell J, Kennedy TP (2001) La notion de service public au Royaume-Uni et en Irlande. In: Marcou G, Moderne F (eds) L'idée de service public dans le droit des Etats de l'Union européenne. L'Harmattan, Paris

CEEP-CIRIEC (2000) Services of general economic interest in Europe.

CEEP-European Centre of Employers and Enterprises providing Public Services (1995), Europe, concurrence et service public. Masson-Armand Colin

Forsthoff E (1969) Traité de droit administratif allemand (translated in French by Fromont M, Bruylant, Bruxelles)

Guglielmi G-J, Koubi G (2009) La notion de service public en droit européen. AJDA, 5 octobre

Hoorens D (2008) Les collectivités territoriales dans l'Union européenne. Organisation, compétences et finances, Dexia

Lyon-Caen A, Champeil-Desplats V (eds) (2001) Services publics et droits fondamentaux dans la construction européenne. Dalloz, Paris

Mangenot M (ed) (2005) Public administrations and services of general interest: What kind of Europeanisation? EIPA, Maastricht

Marcou G, Moderne F (eds) (2005) Droit de la régulation, service public et intégration régionale, Tome 1, Comparaisons et commentaires. L'Harmattan, Paris

Modeen T (2001) Le service public en droit finlandais et suédois. In: Marcou G, Moderne F (eds) L'idée de service public dans le droit des Etats de l'Union européenne. L'Harmattan, Paris

Rodrigues S (2005) Apports(s) du droit communautaire au droit de la régulation des services publics. In: Marcou G, Moderne F (eds) Droit de la régulation, service public et intégration régionale, Tome 1, Comparaisons et commentaires. L'Harmattan, Paris

Savary G (2005) L'Europe va-t-elle démanteler les services publics?, L'Aube

Valin S (2007) Services publics: un défi pour l'Europe, approches nationales et enjeux communautaires. Editions Charles Léopold Mayer, Paris

Chapter 3
The Commission's Soft Law in the Area of Services of General Economic Interest

Ulla Neergaard

Abstract This chapter charts the EC Commission's attempts to pull together the various interests of the Member States and the EU Institutions into integrating SGIs into the framework of EU law and policy. Starting with the EC Commission's first Communication in 1996, Neergaard examines the historical evolution and policy ramifications of the Commission's various Papers and soft law instruments to show how the political agenda has changed over time and the various attitudes towards turning soft law into hard law in the EU. This chapter examines when soft law is useful and can have a positive influence on disagreements between the various EU Institutions and the Member States, and when it becomes a convenient forum to avoid hard law initiatives.

Contents

This chapter is based on paper presented at the seminar: 'Government and Services of General Interest in a Global World', 15 June 2009 (Institute of Advanced Legal Studies, University of London). Certain parts may be seen as a development of previous related works such as Neergaard 2009a, Neergaard 2008.

U. Neergaard (✉)
Det Juridiske Fakultet, Københavns Universitet,
Studiestræde 6, 1455 København K, Denmark
e-mail: Ulla.Neergaard@jur.ku.dk

E. Szyszczak et al. (eds.), *Developments in Services of General Interest*,
Legal Issues of Services of General Interest, DOI: 10.1007/978-90-6704-734-0_3,

3.1 Introduction

> *More effective and transparent consultation at the heart of EU policy-shaping...* The Commission already consults interested parties through different instruments, such as Green and White Papers, Communications, advisory committees, business test panels, and ad hoc consultations. Furthermore, the Commission is developing on-line consultation through the inter-active policy-making initiative. Such consultation helps the Commission and the other institutions to arbitrate between competing claims and priorities, and assist in developing a longer term policy perspective. Participation is not about institutionalising protest. It is about more effective policy shaping based on early consultation and past experience.[1]

This quotation is from the White Paper on European Governance of the Commission. The use of consultation is considered as having several positive effects and may create policy as soft law. This chapter analyses the soft law of the Commission regarding one particular field of policy, namely Services of General Economic Interest. In this particular area of Commission policy soft law has been used extensively. Yet this particular area of SGEIs has only attracted scant, and rather scattered, attention in academic legal writing to date. Thus, a need for a critical examination of the soft law policy exists, as the body of knowledge on the phenomenon of soft law in the area of SGEIs is still fairly poor.

The concept of 'soft law' may be understood as:

> Rules of conduct that are laid down in instruments which have not been attributed legally binding force as such, but nevertheless may have certain (indirect) legal effects, that are aimed at and may produce practical effects.[2]

In this chapter, the soft law in focus is limited to Commission communications on SGEIs and related concepts.[3] In what follows, there is firstly an overview of the

[1] Commission of the European Communities, *European Governance. A White Paper*, COM(2001) 428,15. Footnotes have been omitted from the quotation.

[2] Senden 2004, 112, who also points out that: 'The designation as soft law of instruments such as recommendations, notices, resolutions, conclusions, guidelines, declarations, programmes, codes of practice etc. is induced by the fact that they can all be typified as Community legal instruments that have not been attributed legally binding force ...'(23). See also, for example, Mörth 2005; Senden 2005a, Soft law and its implications for institutional balance in the EC, 79–99; and Senden 2005b, Soft Law, Self-Regulation and Co-Regulation in European Law.

[3] As SGEIs stand at the centre of the analysis, sector-specific regulation and related soft law is not included here, neither is soft law relating to state aid and procurement. Only the soft law of a horizontal character is put under scrutiny in this chapter. On sector specific regulation see Chap. 7 by Davies and Szyszczak.

relevant soft law (Sect. 3.2). Then follows an analysis of certain important aspects (Sect. 3.3), and finally, certain general conclusions are stated (Sect. 3.4).

3.2 Overview of the Commission's Initiatives

The purpose of this section is to provide an overview of the Commission's initiatives towards SGEIs over the years, but does not discuss the Treaty amendments (these are discussed in Chap. 2 by Bauby). The weight of attention is given to the soft law, briefly mentioning the yearly reports from the DG Comp IV and the role taken by the Commission pursuant to the case law.

At the general level, the Commission's approach in this field of law was for a long time fairly unengaged which may be documented by reference to the annual competition reports. These demonstrate that only in more recent years, the focus on public regulation is given priority.[4] For instance, in the report concerning the year of 2004, the Director General for Competition stated:

> Regulation at both Community and national level, may unnecessarily and unintentionally hold back competition and curb the potential of the internal market. In certain sectors, such as the liberalized network industries, and in particular in the energy sector, there is a need to promote a regulatory framework creating the conditions for market entry and promoting competition. Competition advocacy and policy screening should therefore be used to influence national and EU legislation in order to ensure that safeguarding competitive markets is given due consideration.[5]

It should be noted that in reports for this period, for example in the annual report for 2004 there are relevant headlines such as: 'Application of Articles 81, 82 and 86', 'State measures (public undertakings/undertakings with exclusive and special rights)', 'Liberalised sectors', and 'Public services/services of general (economic) interest'. Similar headlines may be found in reports from other years.

---

[4] In the first years of their existence, the reports were divided into at least two parts. The first part concerned competition policy towards undertakings and the second part concerned competition policy towards state intervention. However, the actual content of the second part focused only on state aid and Articles 31 EC-undertakings (now Article 37 TFEU), and not other kinds of state intervention. In the fifth report (for the year 1975), a chapter on public undertakings was included because of the economic crisis at that time. However, the content of this chapter is related to state aid. In the following years a chapter (or section) with such a heading was retained, but consisted of only a few pages. Interestingly, the Commission in the sixth report (for the year 1976) actually tried to reflect upon the content of Article 86 EC (then Article 90 EEC, now Article 106 TFEU). In the 23rd report (for the year 1993) the subject 'Public Enterprises and State Monopolies' now gets an individual part with two chapters. In the same report, the Commission's approach to liberalisation in certain sectors is dealt with in the more general part of the report (30–34). Generally, the subject then suddenly starts to grow in respect of the pages devoted to it.

[5] See Commission, *Report on Competition Policy 2004*, SEC(2005) 805, 8.

From the case law of the European Court of Justice, it may be also be observed that the Commission did not engage in litigation. Only a few cases have been taken up on the initiative of the Commission and this has really only been a significant number in more recent years. In Article 234 EC (now Article 267 TFEU) cases, it has only seldom seriously tried to influence the development, although this to a certain degree has started to change. Regarding Article 86(3) (now Article 106(3) TFEU) the Commission has acted reluctantly.[6]

A more active approach may be said to have been taken through soft law, here understood as consisting of the various communications launched by the Commission. This development was initiated in 1996, where the Commission for the first time in a coherent manner, sets out its position on the subject.[7] This occurs in the communication entitled *Services of general interest in Europe*. The Commission states that it had felt that, '... it was time to reaffirm the principles of its policies and set out its objectives for the future'.[8] The instrument is not given any designation as such, but may probably be classified as a communication.[9] It contains the following headlines (sub-sections excluded): Introduction; Definition of terms; I. Services of general interest: a key element in the European model of society; II. The Community contribution: Dynamism, Flexibility, and Solidarity; and III. Objectives for the future.

A few years later, in 2000, the Commission again adopted a communication in this field.[10] The document in question was this time titled, *Communication from the Commission. Services of general interest in Europe*. It is stated that the communication has the purpose of updating the communication from 1996.[11]

---

[6] See for example, Szyszczak 2007.

[7] See COM(1996) 443; *OJ*/C 281/03.

[8] Ibid., Introduction.

[9] The Commission refers to it as a 'communication', for example, at: http://europa.eu/legislation_summaries/other/l26087_en.htm; Senden 2004, 132, states the following about the 'communications' of interest here: '...[C]ommunications are far from homogenous and they do not play an unequivocal role in the Community law system.' The author distinguishes between three types of communications, namely: 1. inter-institutional communications; 2. purely informative communications; and 3. individual communications (at p. 133).

[10] See COM(2000) 580.

[11] In the later *Green Paper on Services of General Interest*, COM(2003) 270, 4, see below, the Commission states that the update of the 2000 communication was made with the '... view to increasing the legal certainty for operators as regards the application of competition and internal market rules to their activities'. In the 2000 communication, it is stated in Section 6 that the aims are: '...—to provide further clarification on the respective roles of different levels of public authorities and of the competition and internal market provisions applied to services of general interest in order to respond to the request for greater legal certainty on the part of operators. Of special concern is the field of application of the rules on State aid,—to further develop the European framework relating to the good functioning of services of general interest, in which local, regional and national authorities as well as the Community have their role to play, in line with Article 16 of the EC Treaty'.

It contains the following general sections (sub-sections and annexes excluded): 1. Introduction; 2. The mission of services of general interest; 3. Services of general interest and the single market; 4. Experience with the liberalisation of certain services of general interest; and 5. A European perspective.

The Nice European Council meeting, in 2000, took note of this latter communication, but requested the Commission to report further on the implementation of these services for the Laeken European Council in 2001. Consequently, the Commission adopted a report on 27 October 2001.[12] As a response to a request from the Barcelona European Council, the Commission prepared a short communication containing a *status* of the work on the examination of a proposal for a framework directive on SGIs.[13]

In addition, in 2003, the Commission launched a debate on the role of the EU in promoting the provision of high quality SGIs on the basis of a Green Paper.[14] This document was given the title, *Green paper on services of general interest.*[15] It contains the following general sections (sub-sections, summary table and annex excluded): Introduction; 1. Background; 2. The scope of Community action; 3. Towards a Community concept of services of general interest?; Good governance: organisation, financing, and evaluation; 5. Services of general interest and the challenge of globalisation; and 6. Operational conclusion. Altogether, 30 questions were submitted for discussion.

Then in 2004, a much anticipated White Paper, *Communication from the Commission to the Council, the European Economic and Social Committee, and*

---

12 See COM(2001) 598.

13 Commission, *Communication from the Commission to the Council, the European Parliament, the Economic and Social Committee and the Committee of the regions on the Status of Work on the Examination of a Proposal for a Framework Directive on Services of General Interest*, COM(2002) 689.

14 See COM(2003) 270.

15 According to Senden 2004, 124, the following may be said about Green Papers in general: 'Green Papers are instruments used solely by the Commission, and their use dates back to the early 1980s. Since then, but in particular since 1993, the use of Green Papers has steadily increased … The Green Papers usually start with an overview of the present situation and regulatory framework in a particular area and then identify the problems and challenges in this respect. On the basis thereof, the need for future action is analysed and options or suggestions for action are presented. However, as yet these are not specific and do not contain concrete proposals. According to the Commission, Green Papers are 'reflection documents for discussion, [footnote omitted] drafted with a view to public debate and consultation… Over the last decade, it has become more of a habit to formulate specific questions in the Green Papers, to which the addressees are called upon to respond, but other comments remain equally welcome of course… Their adoption must therefore be seen against the background of the preparation and further development of Community law and policy. As such, the Green Paper can be typified as a preparatory instrument and said to fulfil a *pre-law* function in the Community law context'.

the Committee of the Regions White Paper on services of general interest[16] was published. The Commission states that the aim of the White Paper is:

> In line with the request made by that the European Parliament in its Resolution on the Green Paper of 14 January 2004 [footnote omitted], the Commission draws its conclusions from the debate in the present White Paper.[17]

Stating further that:

> By submitting this White Paper, the Commission does not intend to conclude the debate that has developed at European level. Its aim is to make a contribution to the ongoing discussion and to take it further by defining the Union's role and a framework that allows these services to function properly. The White Paper sets out the Commission's approach in developing a positive role for the European Union in fostering the development of high-quality services of general interest and presents the main elements of a strategy aimed at ensuring that all citizens and enterprises in the Union have access to high-quality and affordable services. The document focuses on just some of the key issues of the debate as it would be impossible to address all the issues raised during the public consultation. More specific issues will be addressed in the context of the relevant policies.[18]

The White Paper contains the following general sections (sub-sections and annex excluded): 1. Introduction; 2. A shared responsibility of Public Authority in the Union; 3. Guiding principles of the Commission's approach; 4. New Orientations for a Coherent policy.

Finally, in 2007, the Commission adopted a package of initiatives to turn its Citizens' Agenda into a consistent set of actions, which among others included a Communication on *Services of general interest, including social services of*

---

[16] See COM(2004) 374. According to Senden 2004, 125, the following may be said about White Papers in general: 'Subsequent to the consultation process, the Commission often draws up a communication on the follow-up to be given to the Green Paper. [Footnote omitted] Sometimes, this follow-up consists of the presentation of a White Paper. [Footnote omitted] Both of these documents give information on the outcome of the debate on the Green Paper.' At pp. 126–127, it is added: 'White Papers are also an instrument only of the Commission. They are less frequently adopted than Green Papers ... This makes clear that White Papers serve a twofold objective. On the one hand, they constitute documents for discussion and consultation; on the other, they also aim at laying down the main lines or strategy of action for the future. To this end, they usually contain concrete proposals for action. Depending on which of the two aspects is emphasized, White Papers may actually differ quite considerably; some White Papers are more directed towards debate, whereas others may already contain (detailed) work programmes or timetables for action. [Footnote omitted] For the same reasons as given above in respect of Green Papers, White Papers can be typified as preparatory instruments, or, instruments that fulfill a *pre-law* function. But, generally speaking, White Papers often go a step further than Green Papers, in that they contain (concrete) proposals'.

[17] Ibid., p. 3. Here, it is explained, *inter alia*, that the Commission staff has prepared a Report on the public consultation which analyses the contributions submitted and provides background material to the present White Paper.

[18] Ibid., p. 4.

general interest: a new European Commitment.[19] The aim of this communication is stated to be:

> The agreement by Heads of State and Government of a Protocol on services of general interest to be annexed to the Treaty of Lisbon is a decisive step towards establishing a transparent and reliable EU framework. The new Treaty on the Functioning of the European Union will also include a new Article 14 stressing the joint responsibility of the Union and the Member States and establishing a legal basis for the EU to take action. These new provisions build on a decade of debate about the responsibilities of the EU and about whether or not the EU should adopt an overarching framework for services of general interest. This debate has helped to generate converging views on the role and approach of the EU with regard to services of general interest, in particular following the 2004 Commission's White Paper [Footnote omitted] and the 2006 opinion of the Parliament [footnote omitted]. A broad agreement has emerged on the need to ensure legal certainty and consistency across EU policies, while respecting the diversity of sectors and situations. There is also broad recognition of the need to improve general awareness and understanding of EU rules. By spelling out the role of the Union, the Protocol brings the necessary clarity and certainty to EU rules. This Communication presents the Commission's views on this debate, in particular in the light of the Parliament's resolution and the Treaty of Lisbon. It also draws on public consultation on social services of general interest initiated in 2006.

The general structure of the communication is the following (sub-sections excluded): 1. Introduction; 2. The role of the EU: ensuring common rules while respecting diversity; 3. The Protocol: a coherent framework for EU action; 4. Moving forward; and 5. Conclusion.

Some of these different documents, that is, the communications under different characterisations from 1996, 2000, 2003, 2004, and 2007, are the ones to which particular weight will be given, based upon their relative importance, in the analysis to follow.

3.3 Soft Points in the Soft Law?

In what now follows, different aspects of the five sources of soft law, generally designated as communications, will be carefully analysed under four different headings:

1. The approach concerning a legislative framework;
2. The approach itself of application of soft law;
3. The approach concerning the definition of central concepts;

---

[19] See Commission, *Communication from the Commission to the European Parliament, the Council, the European Economic and Social Committee and the Committee of the Regions. Accompanying the Communication on 'A single market for 21st century Europe'. Services of general interest, including social services of general interest: a new European commitment*, COM(2007) 725. One other document included in the package may be mentioned, namely: Commission, *Commission Staff Working Document. Progress since the 2004 White Paper on services of general interest*, SEC(2007) 1515.

4. The approach concerning the distribution of competences; and
5. The approach concerning the identification of clear policies and objectives, within an overall vision.

The aim is to see, if any 'soft points' may be said to exist, but also more simply to obtain a better understanding of the content of these communications.

3.3.1 The Approach to a Legislative Framework

Certain forces have for quite some time been working on establishing a legislative framework, for instance a Directive, regarding SGEIs.[20] In this section the main developments in this process will be analysed.[21]

From the outset, it should be understood that the new legal base in Article 14 TFEU (former Article 16 EC) will be of central importance in this regard, perhaps in combination with other Treaty provisions (see Chap. 2 by Bauby). It should also be stressed that if a framework Directive is adopted using Article 14 TFEU as the legal basis—perhaps in combination with other Treaty provisions—this would only concern SGEIs and not the wider concept of SGIs in principle including both SGEIs and the even more 'sensitive' 'non-economic services of general interest'.[22]

The idea of a framework Directive, or the like, may—at least according to the official documents—be traced back to a request put forward by the European Parliament in 1998, where it called '... on the Commission to draw up a charter of principles for services of general economic interest, containing their justification

---

[20] If a legal framework is adopted, it is likely that at least the following subjects would be considered to be parts thereof: 1. objectives; 2. scope of application; 3. links with existing sector-specific legislation as well as with the Services Directive; 4. distribution of competences between the Member States and the Community, including the role of the Member States, also regarding the regional and local levels, and the Community; 5. definitions of central concepts; 6. rules on the granting of special or exclusive rights, including a clear and transparent framework for the selection of undertakings entrusted with a 'service of general economic interest'; 7. general principles regarding the provision of 'services of general economic interest' (universality and equality of access, continuity, security and adaptability; quality, efficiency and affordability, transparency, protection of less well-off social groups, protection of users, consumers and the environment, and citizen participation, non-discrimination, etc.); 8. clarification regarding the compensation of public service obligations; 9. the organisation and regulation of these services; 10. the role of regulators; 11. clarification as to the application of competition and internal market rules to these services including a point of view as to the balance between market and public service principles; 12. control issues; 13. benchmarking and quality measurement mechanisms at national and European level; 14. exchange of experience and the promotion of best practices; and 15. entry into force.

[21] Documents from other Institutions, and the like, other than the European Parliament, the Commission, and the Council, have not been examined.

[22] See, for example, Commission, *Commission Staff Working Paper. Report on the Public Consultation on the Green Paper on Services of General Interest*, SEC(2004) 326, Section 4.3.1.1., where commentators in favour of a framework instrument suggest that such should cover all 'services of general interest'.

and principles (both traditional and new), the type of missions and rights to be given to operators and a list of sectors where the notion should apply ....'[23]

The next important step was taken by the European Council of Nice of 7, 8 and 9 December 2000 as it noted, '... the Commission's intention to consider, in close cooperation with the Member States, ways of ensuring greater predictability and increased legal certainty in the application of competition rules relating to services of general interest ...', and invited the Commission to report back on SGIs to the European Council at Laeken in December 2001.[24] The Commission subsequently submitted such a report, in which it finds many disadvantages in adopting a framework Directive.

Inter alia, it finds that:

> ... a framework Directive would necessarily be very general in substance and could not take account of the specificities that characterise each service of general interest. Such a Directive could therefore not replace sector-specific regulation and its added value in respect of sector-specific regulation would have to be examined. As a horizontal measure, the Directive could in general only set out minimum standards. In addition, a Directive should match the high level of our ambitions. The Commission will assess whether such a horizontal directive would be the right instrument or whether, given the differences in the structure and organisation of different services of general interest, a sector-specific approach combined with high standards of horizontal consumer protection is best suited for maintaining and developing high-quality services of general interest at the European level.[25]

The Commission concludes that it '... will examine the suggestion to consolidate and specify the principles on services of general interest underlying Article 16 of the Treaty in a framework Directive'.[26]

Also in the year 2001, the European Parliament explicitly called for a framework Directive.[27] In 2002, yet another example of how the idea of a framework

---

[23] Parliament, *Resolution on the communication from the Commission on services of general interest in Europe* (COM(96)0443 C4-0507/96), *OJ* C14, 19/01,1998, 74, Section 8.

[24] Commission, *Report to the Laeken European Council. Services of General Interest*, COM(2001) 598, Sections 5–6.

[25] Ibid., Section 51.

[26] Ibid., Section 53.

[27] More precisely, it: 'Calls on the Laeken European Council to support vis-à-vis the Commission and its proposal for a framework directive on the objectives and organisational arrangements of services of general interest based on Article 95 of the EC Treaty; this directive should create a legal framework which guarantees the availability of services of general interest to the public, particularly pursuant to Article 16 of the EC Treaty; Expects, therefore, the Commission to define in the framework directive the common principles on which the services of general interest are based at an appropriate tier of subsidiarity, to specify and define the common principles of democratic and transparent regulation, to ensure active involvement of citizens and users in the process of definition, evaluation and contract appraisal and to institutionalise a common pluralist appraisal procedure; Calls on the Commission to ensure consistency between the principles set out in its framework directive and the provisions governing specific industries already adopted ....' See Parliament, *European Parliament resolution on the Commission communication 'Services of General Interest in Europe'* (COM(2000) 580—C5-0399/2001—2001/2157(COS)), A5-0361/2001, 13.11.2001, *OJ* C140E/153, Sections 6–8.

Directive is still present in the political discourse may be found, this time by the Barcelona European Council, which states that:

> The integration of European networks and the opening of utility markets should take full account of the importance of quality public services. In this regard, the European Council underlines the importance for citizens, and for territorial and social cohesion, of access to services of general economic interest. In this context, the European Council asks the Commission to:—present its communication on evaluation methodology at the May Council and report to the Seville European Council on the state of work on the guidelines for State aids and if necessary propose a block exemption regulation in this area;—continue its examination with a view to consolidating and specifying the principles on services of general economic interest, which underlie Article 16 of the Treaty, in a proposal for a framework directive, while respecting the specificities of the different sectors involved and taking into account the provisions of Article 86 of the Treaty. The Commission will present a report by the end of the year.[28]

As a response to this request of the Barcelona European Council, the Commission prepared a short communication containing a status of the work on the examination of a proposal for a framework Directive on SGIs.[29] Here, the Commission explains that it finds it necessary to produce a Green Paper on SGIs, which will allow it to examine the question of a proposal for a framework Directive.[30] Thus, the feasibility and possible added value of a framework Directive should be the core subject for the paper[31] which should be reflected in the form of a consultation document.

In the Green Paper of 2003, the Commission outlines some of the advantages, which it associates with a general instrument:

> A general instrument could set out, clarify and consolidate the objectives and principles common to all or several types of services of general interest in fields of Community competence. Such an instrument could provide the basis for further sectoral legislation, which could implement the objectives set out in the framework instrument, thus simplifying and consolidating the internal market in this field. Consolidation of the Community "acquis" could be based on common elements of existing sector-specific legislation and would help to ensure overall consistency of approach across different services of general interest sectors. It could also have important symbolic value in that it would clearly demonstrate the Community's approach as well as the existence of a Community concept of services of general interest. Furthermore, consolidation could help the new Member States to develop their regulatory strategies in this area.[32]

The Commission is also concerned with certain disadvantages in this regard:

---

[28] Council, *Presidency Conclusions. Barcelona European Council 15 and 16 March 2002*, SN 100/1/02 REV 1, Section 42.

[29] Commission, *Communication from the Commission to the Council, the European Parliament, the Economic and Social Committee and the Committee of the regions on the Status of Work on the Examination of a Proposal for a Framework Directive on Services of General Interest*, COM(2002) 689.

[30] Ibid., Section 6.

[31] Ibid., Section 7.

[32] Commission, *Green Paper on Services of General Interest*, COM(2003) 270, Sections 38–39.

> However, such an approach would also have its limitations in that a framework instrument setting out common objectives and principles would be general in nature, as it would have to be based on the common denominator of different services with very different characteristics. If current levels of protection were to be maintained, it would still have to be complemented by sector-specific legislation, laying down more detailed provisions which take into account the specific characteristics of different services of general interest. Moreover, Article 16 does not provide a legal base for the adoption of a specific instrument. Other Treaty provisions could serve as a legal basis, depending on the content of the instrument. For example, Article 95 could be used, but a framework instrument based on this provision would have to be limited to services of general economic interest having an effect on intra-Community trade. This would mean that many important sectors would be excluded from the scope of the instrument because of their non-economic nature or because of their limited effect on trade. If Community legislation in such sectors is considered desirable, an amendment of the Treaty might be the best way of providing an appropriate legal basis.[33]

As regards its legal form, the Commission suggests that consolidation of common objectives and principles could be set out in a legislative instrument (that is, in a Directive or in a Regulation) or in a non-legislative instrument (that is, a recommendation, communication, guidelines, inter-institutional agreement).[34] On this basis, the Commission submits the following questions of relevance here for discussion:

> Is a general Community framework for services of general interest desirable? What would be its added value compared to existing sectoral legislation? Which sectors and which issues and rights should be covered? Which instrument should be used (e.g. directive, regulation, recommendation, communication, guidelines, inter-institutional agreement)?[35]

The reactions to the Green Paper and these particularly relevant questions have, not surprisingly, been mixed. Thus, the Commission has had to conclude that the views on the need for a general legal framework for SGIs have not converged during the debate so far and remain divided.[36] Some of the positive contributors view the establishment of a framework instrument as a tool to promote consistency and to clarify and consolidate the rules applicable to SGIs and the respective responsibilities of the Community and the Member States.[37] The added value of such a framework is also seen in increasing legal certainty and in strengthening the principle of subsidiarity, and the political and symbolic value is highlighted as a key element of the 'European social model'.[38] Some of the opposing contributors, among others, argue that the existing relevant Treaty provisions and the sector-specific regulation are sufficient and that a framework Directive would be too

---

[33] Ibid., Section 40.

[34] Ibid., Section 41.

[35] Ibid., Section 42.

[36] Commission, *Commission Staff Working Paper. Report on the Public Consultation on the Green Paper on Services of General Interest*, SEC(2004) 326, Section 4.3.1.

[37] Ibid., Section 4.3.1.1.

[38] Idem.

abstract and philosophical.[39] Also, it is pointed out that the legal base for a framework Directive is doubtful.[40]

The European Parliament's reaction to the Green Paper, which is expressed in a resolution from 2004, became a repetition of its: '… [call] for a legal framework to be drawn up under the co-decision procedure and respecting the subsidiarity principle, when the internal market and competition rules are being implemented'.[41] In addition, it, '… [calls] on the Commission to present a follow-up, by April 2004 at the latest, in order to draw the lessons from the Green Paper consultations and to clearly define its position on a possible legal framework'.[42]

In the White Paper from the Commission which followed in 2004, it is clear that the Commission has become quite sceptical regarding the idea of a possible framework instrument.[43] Parts of its central argumentation are the following:

> The Commission therefore considers appropriate not to proceed to submitting a proposal at this point in time but to re-examine the issue at a later stage. As part of this examination, the Commission would subject any legislative proposals to a prior extended impact assessment of its economic, social, and environmental implications [Footnote omitted]. As regards the calendar for such re-examination account may also be taken of the fact that the future entry into force of the Constitutional Treaty and of the proposed Article III-6 of the Constitution will bring another possible legal basis that would complement those already existing. The Commission considers appropriate to re-examine the issue once the Constitutional Treaty is in force. For the time being, the Commission will, as a general rule, pursue and develop its sectoral approach by proposing, where necessary and appropriate, sector-specific rules that allow account to be taken of the specific requirements and situations in each sector. However, without prejudice to existing sector-specific Community rules, a horizontal approach will be considered with regard to a number of specific issues, such as consumers' interests, the monitoring and evaluation of services of general interest, the application of state aid rules to financial compensation or the use of structural funds for the support of services of general interest. While the need for a framework instrument was an issue of considerable controversy, the necessity of ensuring the consistency and coherence of Community measures in the area of services of general interest was widely recognised in the public consultation. At the same time, it was stressed that it was essential for Community policies to respect and take account of the different characteristics of different services and of the diverse realities in the Member States. The Commission will step up its efforts to ensure full consistency of the Community's policies in the area of services of general interest and will look at full coherence of its sectoral policies with

---

[39] Ibid., Section 4.3.1.2.

[40] Idem.

[41] Parliament, *Services of general interest. European Parliament resolution on the Green Paper on services of general interest* (COM(2003) 270—2003/2152(INI)), 14.01.2004, P5_TA(2004) 0018, C92E/294, 16.04.2004, Section 5.

[42] Ibid., Section 6.

[43] Commission, *Communication from the Commission to the European Parliament, the Council, the European Economic and Social Committee and the Committee of the Regions. White Paper on services of general interest*, COM(2004) 374.

> regard to its general approach during the forthcoming reviews of the sectors concerned [Footnote omitted]. In addition, the Commission will review the situation of services of general interest in the European Union and the need for any horizontal measures in 2005. It intends to submit a report on its findings to the European Parliament, to the Council, to the European Economic and Social Committee and to the Committee of the Regions before the end of 2005.[44]

It becomes clear that the Commission had decided to await the future entry into force of the Reform Treaty, now the Treaty of Lisbon 2009.

Following this, the Parliament's Resolution on the Commission's White Paper took two years to adopt.[45] A key point is that the Parliament calls on the Commission to propose appropriate legal initiatives, as referred to in the resolution, and recalls that co-decision rights, where foreseen by the Treaty, should by fully exercised by all the parties involved in the field of SGIs and SGEIs.[46] It is noteworthy that this time the Parliament does not explicitly call for a framework Directive as such.

The last word from the Commission (so far) came at the end of 2007. After almost ten years of debate and several communications, the Commission decides to withdraw from previous intentions.[47] More precisely, it states:

> On the basis of the Protocol, and in line with Parliament's approach, the Commission will continue to consolidate the EU framework applicable to services of general interest, including for social and health services, providing concrete solutions for concrete problems where they exist. With progress made, attention should increasingly concentrate on the good transposition and application of EU rules, with greater emphasis on monitoring outcomes for the users and consumers, dissemination of information and exchange of practices, monitoring of enforcement and evaluation of performance. The Commission envisages a mix of sector-specific and issue-specific actions along the following three axes: [1. providing legal guidance on cross-cutting issues; 2. modernising and developing sector-specific policies; and 3. monitoring and evaluation].[48]

---

[44] Ibid., Section 4.1.

[45] Parliament, *Services of general interest. European Parliament resolution on the Commission White Paper on services of general interest (2006/2101(INI))*, P6_TA(2006)0380, 19.09.2006.

[46] Ibid., Section 31.

[47] Commission, *Communication from the Commission to the European Parliament, the Council, the European Economic and Social Committee and the Committee of the Regions. Accompanying the Communication on 'A single market for 21st century Europe'. Services of general interest, including social services of general interest: a new European commitment*, COM(2007) 725.

[48] Ibid., 11. See also 'Single Market Review Package strengthens support for consumers and small business', *Single Market Review*, No. 48, 2007, 10, where Barroso is said to have expressed that it will not be: '... feasible to propose a horizontal legislation regarding SGI, given the complexity of the matter and the large variety of different SGI it would need to cover. Furthermore, the Protocol agreed alongside the Treaty of Lisbon sets out the EU principles applicable to services of general interest and establishes a new, transparent and reliable framework at the level of the Treaty'.

As stated by several commentators, it appears somehow cynical that the Commission gave such a pride of place to the Lisbon Protocol even before it entered into force.[49]

The road taken so far regarding a possible legal framework has already been long and without concrete results. It has been demonstrated how the European Parliament originally actively expressed a desire for a Regulation in this field of law, but in its Resolution of 2006, it seemed reluctant to adopt this route in comparison to its original stance. On the contrary, the Commission seems to have been much more reluctant all the way and, in any case, now completely rejects the idea. It seems to prefer sector-specific regulation. The idea is probably still alive, as several organisations are very active in the field, including in particular PSE (the Socialist Group in the European Parliament), CEEP (European Centre of Enterprises with Public Participation and of Enterprises of General Economic Interest), CELSIG (European Liaison Committee on Services of General Interest), and ETUC (European Trade Union Confederation).[50] The latter organisation collects signatures to call on the Commission to propose European legislation on public services.[51]

In sum, the Commission has never been the *primus motor* in the process of setting up a legislative framework on SGEIs. In fact, it has, on a thin basis, ended up preventing the adoption of a legislative framework, to the frustration of some political actors. Whether this is a 'soft point' or not, will again depend upon the position of the commentator observing the process taken. Under all circumstances, it appears to be 'much ado about nothing'.[52]

---

[49] See for example, Damjanovic and De Witte 2009, 90, who argue that: 'The cynical element in the Commission's position lies in the fact that both the new competence in Article 14 TFEU and the new Lisbon Protocol were promoted by political actors who were concerned by the impact of negative integration of welfare services, but whereas Article 14 provides for a re-regulatory competence of the EU (to compensate for the effects of negative integration), the Protocol adopts a 'hands' off' approach, instructing the EU institutions to respect the policy autonomy of the Member States. The advocates of the existing negative integration approach, including the Commission, can therefore play out the Protocol against the second sentence of Article 14'.

[50] See for example, PSE, *Proposal for a Framework Directive on Services of General Economic Interest—May 2006. European Socials call for European Legal Framework for public services*, 30.05.2006; ETUC, *Statement adopted by the ETUC Executive Committee in their meeting held in Brussels on 06–07 June 2006. Towards a framework directive on services of general (economic) interest*; CELSIG, *Draft of Proposed Law on Services of General Economic Interest*, 28.06.2006; and CEEP, *CEEP Opinion: A European policy for services of general interest. Presentation of CEEP's initiative towards a European Framework on SGIs*, CEEP.2006/AVIS, 20.09.2006.

[51] See http://www.petitionpublicservice.eu/?utm_source=right&utm_medium=banner.

[52] For further discussion: Conseil Economique et Social 2008, pp. 42, 43; Van de Gronden 2009a, The EU and WTO Law on Free Trade in Services and the Public Interest, pp. 249–279; Van de Gronden 2009b, The Services Directive and Services of General (Economic) Interest; Krajewski 2008, 377–398; Rodrigues 2009; Szyszczak 2009; De Vries 2009, 139–158.

3.3.2 The Application of Soft Law

It has generally been stated in legal theory that a trend towards a '*softer*' model of European governance seems to exist through the use of soft law.[53] Also in the area of SGEIs, an increased amount of activity in this regard has taken place. In this section, reflections on different aspects of this development will be put forward in order to better understand the implications of the soft law approach in this particular area. In particular, the following three issues will be further discussed: 1. the importance of the different communications as 'law'; 2. the connection between the communications and 'hard law'; and 3. the implications of the soft law approach.

Regarding the first issue, it may be noted that some lawyers may deny that communications in general have a value as 'law'. In actual fact, some may claim that either a document is hard law or it is not law at all.[54] Although the concept of soft law may remain highly controversial to some, the discussion in Sect. 3.1 indicates that there may be certain political, and possibly even legal effects, which may arise from acts which on the surface are non-binding.

Senden distinguishes between three different categories of soft law instruments. The first of these is designated as '*preparatory and informative instruments*' which may include Green Papers, White Papers, action programmes, and informative communications.[55] It consists of instruments that are adopted with a view to the preparation of further Community law and policy and/or providing information on Community action.[56] The second category consists of the '*interpretative and decisional instruments*', which aim at providing guidance as to the interpretation and application of existing Community/EU law.[57] It may consist of the Commission's communications and notices, and also certain guidelines, codes and frameworks.[58] The third category covers a group of '*steering instruments*', and aim at establishing closer cooperation or even harmonisation between the Member States in a non-binding way.[59]

The instruments primarily under scrutiny here probably mainly contain traits belonging to the first category. However, when viewed together, they contain traits of the other categories. Senden finds that the first category might often not constitute soft law.[60] The reasons stated are, among others, mainly that they typically—but not always—do not lay down rules of conduct, at least not of a

[53] See for example, Cini 2000, 3.

[54] Ibid. at 4. See also Mörth 2005

[55] Senden 2004, 118.

[56] Ibid., 118.

[57] Ibid., 118.

[58] Ibid., 119.

[59] Ibid., 119.

[60] Ibid., for example, 118.

general, normative nature.[61] However, the communications under scrutiny here seem, when viewed in conjunction, to contain elements of general policy statements (and Commission discretion) on the one hand and probably legislation in a soft form on the other.[62] Thus, in my opinion they might have some legal impact, perhaps only indirectly, although it is difficult to concretise exactly where this begins and where it ends. Under all circumstances, it is a fact that legal doctrine makes references thereto, and at times overtake viewpoints such as definitions as expressions of the law. Hereby, *inter alia*, they may contribute to uniform thinking in different ways. It is a fact that the Advocates General and the General Court (the former Court of First Instance) may make explicit references to soft law.[63] Apparently, the European Court of Justice has not yet had the opportunity to make explicit reference to soft law in the field of SGEIs, but may do so implicitly. In other words, these communications are taken seriously by the legal and political community, and thus may be considered to have some kind of legal impact.

Regarding the second issue, that is the connection between the communications and 'hard law', it is noteworthy that soft law at times may serve the role of only temporarily being of importance. The metaphor of a 'stepping-stone' to hard law is a good way of describing this function.[64] In relation to the soft law scrutinised here, it is difficult to see the severe connection between the communications and the changes pursuant to actual, and potential, Treaty amendments. They might have happened anyhow, or they might even be seen as the Member States' reactions *against* the soft law initiatives by the Commission, perhaps fearing that the Commission might be using soft law as a stepping stone to hard law measures. Had the idea of a framework Directive (or equivalent legal instruments) become a reality, then a recognisable connection would have been visible in the Member States' reactions. However, the visions of a framework Directive (or a similar legal instrument) were never realised and (at present), the soft law may rather be viewed as a supplement to the limited hard law, with many deficiencies attached to it.

Finally, regarding the third issue, that is, other implications of the soft law approach, it may be emphasised that in legal theory, the use of soft law has been criticised because it may be an easier, speedier, and more flexible approach to implement obligations, than imposing the traditional hard legal obligations having to go through difficult democratic processes.[65] Cini has stated that probably the

---

[61] Ibid., for example, 219.

[62] See in this direction for example, Cini 2000, 4.

[63] See, for instance, General Court, Joined Cases T-309/04, T-317/04, T-329/04 and T-336/04, *TV 2/Danmark A/S*, et al. v. *the Commission of the European Communities* [2008] *ECR* II-2935; General Court, Case T-289/03, *British United Provident Association Ltd (BUPA)* v. *Commission of the European Communities* [2008] *ECR* II-2935; and Opinion of Advocate General Stix-Hackl delivered on 7 November 2002 in ECJ, Joined Cases C-34/01 to C-38/01, *Enirisorse SpA* v. *Ministero delle Finanze* [2003] *ECR* I-14203.

[64] See for example, Cini 2004, 25.

[65] Ibid., 4.

most damning criticism, despite the certain advantages, of soft law is that, it results in soft compliance:

> ... that is, as soft law is not legally binding, implementation must rest solely on the goodwill of those agreeing to and affected by it, which some might argue is a rather unstable foundation for policy consistency.[66]

Cini has argued that:

> ... when soft law is used, parliaments tend to be by-passed; its content is often vague and non-judiciable; it may be inconsistent with existing legislation; it tends to be inaccessible (opaque), with little scope for public input; and it can allow judges and/or administrators a dominant role in the making of policy.[67]

The problem may also be expressed as the existence of precarious tensions between the EU's commitment to the rule of law, on the one hand, and its regulatory practices on the other.[68]

Altogether, some may agree with Senden that certain advantages are connected with the use of soft law as it is considered to contribute to the effectiveness, legitimacy, and transparency of Community/EU action.[69] Indeed, this assertion holds a lot of truth. Yet, the dangers of application of soft law to the degree, and the way, it is used by the Commission may be criticised in itself. The Commission needs to exercise caution in the way in which soft law options are taken, when we take a general perspective of legitimacy, and not on the perspective of what the viewpoint of if, and how, SGEIs should be regulated in Europe.

3.3.3 The Approach to the Definition of Central Concepts

Concerning the definitions of central concepts, over the years the Commission, in particular, has demonstrated an interest in defining terms such as SGIs, SGEIs, public service, and universal service.[70] As explained in detail elsewhere, notably Chap. 7 by Davies and Szyszczak, this task has not necessarily been accomplished very carefully, and this will probably result in unexpected outcomes in future years, which may have an impact on the future organisation of national welfare states, and in connection therewith on the distribution of competences and the degree of EU-induced liberalisation.[71] The distinction between SGEIs and non-economic services of general interest appears to be a place where concrete activities cannot necessarily be situated, and where the Commission itself finds it

---

66 Ibid., 5.

67 Ibid. See also the discussions of Borrás and Conzelmann 2007, pp. 531–548.

68 See Joerges 2007, 5.

69 Senden 2004, 4.

70 See the 1996 Communication, supra n. 7.

71 See Neergaard 2009b, 17–50.

acceptable that the distinction is of a 'dynamic' character.[72] Also, regarding the concept of a 'universal service' the CFI/General Court has taken a different definition from that of the Commission.[73] Finally, it is worth mentioning that the issue of the placement of the competence to decide what constitutes a SGEI probably should be treated much more delicately than as suggested by the Commission.[74]

3.3.4 The Approach Concerning the Distribution of Competences

Concerning the distribution of competences, the picture is blurred and may be understood in the light of a kind of institutional power game between primarily the Commission, the Council, and the Parliament. The Commission has for instance (in 1996) stated that:

> Economic and social cohesion, harmonious urban and rural development, and environmental conservation are objectives of shared interest in Europe. In this context, general interest services share the same objectives as various other common policies introduced by the Community. This is why the Commission will be pushing ahead with those policies which are needed to get the most out of general interest services.... Making sure that everyone is provided with other general interest services, such as health, education, water, and housing, is a matter of national or regional responsibility. Nonetheless, there are ways in which the Community can help (cooperation, financial support, and coordination activities) and greater use should be made of them in connection with these services to promote equality of opportunity and to combat poverty and marginalization.[75]

Later, in 2000, it states that:

> In pursuing these aims, the Community takes due account of the principle of subsidiarity. Respect of this principle, in particular Member States' freedom to define what constitutes a service of general interest, requires a careful examination of the appropriate roles of the different levels of government in the regulation of such services. The Commission will further elaborate its position on the subject in the context of the forthcoming White Paper on Governance.... Both this political statement and the changes currently under way point to the need for a proactive stance on general interest services, which incorporates and goes beyond the approach based on the single market. In this vein, the Commission, in partnership with the national, regional, and local levels, will continue to promote a European perspective on general interest services for the benefit of citizens on three fronts: by making the most of market opening; by strengthening European coordination and solidarity; and by developing other Community contributions in support of services of general

---

[72] Ibid. In this regard, the *BUPA* case, supra n. 63 is of fundamental interest.

[73] Ibid.

[74] Ibid.

[75] 1996 Communication, supra n. 7, Sections 66 and 69.

interest. ...The Community involvement with services of general interest goes beyond developing the single market, including providing for instruments to ensure standards of quality, the coordination of regulators and the evaluation of operations. Other Community policy instruments and actions share the same objectives of consumer protection, economic, social and territorial cohesion, and help services of general economic interest in fulfilling their mission. Such contributions are meant to enhance, and by no means replace, the national, regional, and local roles in their respective fields ....[76]

In addition, it has, for example in 2003, argued that:

It is primarily for the competent national, regional, and local authorities to define, organise, finance and monitor services of general interest. The Community for its part has competencies in areas that are also relevant for services of general interest, such as: the internal market, competition and State aid, free movement, social policy, transport, environment, health, consumer policy, trans-European networks, industry, economic and social cohesion, research, trade and development co-operation, and taxation. The competencies and responsibilities conferred by the Treaty provide the Community with a whole range of means of action to ensure that every person in the European Union has access to high-quality services of general interest. Services of general interest linked to the function of welfare and social protection are clearly a matter of national, regional, and local responsibilities. Nevertheless, there is a recognised role for the Community in promoting co-operation and co-ordination in these areas. A particular concern for the Commission is promoting the co-operation by Member States in matters related to the modernisation of social protection systems.[77]

Furthermore, reference may be made to a statement put forward in 2004 that the division of tasks and powers between the Union and the Member States lead to a shared responsibility of the Union and the public authorities in the Member States but detailed definition of services to be provided and delivery of those services remain the responsibility of the Member States.[78]

The 2007 communication may be viewed as, perhaps implicitly, discussing the precarious issue of distribution of competences. The same ambiguity, as seen in

[76] 2000 Communication, Sections 55, 57, and 65.

[77] 2003 Communication, Section 31. Footnotes have been omitted from the quotation.

[78] 2004 Communication, 4. Also note that at 7, it is stated that: 'In the consultation it was highlighted that services of general interest should be organised and regulated as closely as possible to the citizens and that the principle of subsidiarity must be strictly respected. The Commission respects the essential role of the Member States and of regional and local authorities in the area of services of general interest. This role is reflected in the Community's policies on services of general interest, which are based on various degrees of action and the use of different instruments in line with the principle of subsidiarity. As in the past, the Commission intends, whenever required, to make proposals for sector-specific regulation only in areas that, like the large network industries, have a clear Europe-wide dimension and present a strong case for defining a European concept of general interest. Such Community regulation defines, as a general rule, only a regulatory framework that can be implemented and specified by the Member States, taking into account country-specific situations.' See also 17.

the earlier documents, may be observed.[79] Now the focus on social and health services has increased significantly.

The general picture gained is that it seems as if, on the one hand, the Commission wants to respect certain national competences, thereby probably expressing a respect of the principle of subsidiarity, yet, on the other hand, it seems to find 'a European perspective' on almost every kind of area. Thus, it is very difficult to detect where the Commission thinks the borderline lies between the EU and the Member State competences. Whether this is because the Commission has not wanted to define the borderline or whether it is because, it is not capable of doing so, or the borderline is not possible to see. However, both situations are in fact equally problematic and symptomatic of EU law at its present stage. Originally the Commission attempted to add the promotion of SGIs to the objectives of the Treaty. Most EU lawyers would realise the implications of what might seem to be a simple step. Some legal and political analysts might fear the initiation of a process of competences 'slipping away' from the Member States especially in relation to social services (as understood in the broadest terms). Thus, the role desired by the Commission and the role acceptable to the other actors in the power game of the EU is probably not identical and may to a large degree explain the political processes of these years where SGEIs have assumed a role in EU integration defined by soft law processes. This point of view is shared by Damjanovic and de Witte, who have pointed out that:

> Whether or not the Lisbon Treaty enters into force, it is likely that in the years to come the European Union will become ever more a 'multi-level welfare system' in which the states will continue to occupy a leading role in terms of organisation and funding of welfare services and in which the European Union will play a growing role in setting limits and providing incentives across a wide variety of welfare sectors. It is an open question in which direction this growing role of Europe will operate. Indeed, there is a discrepancy between the message conveyed by the Member State governments in the Lisbon Treaty (namely, that the European Union should essentially help the Member States to keep their welfare services operating in the way they wish) and the message conveyed in most of the European Commission's documents, namely that the provision of welfare services should be adapted to the requirements of market integration, in this field, will depend on the internal ideological battles within each institution (Commission, Council and Parliament) and on the power balance between those institutions.[80]

---

[79] See for instance the 2007 Communication, 9–10, where it is stated that: 'Services of general economic interest should be responsive and delivered as closely as possible to citizens and businesses. The action of the EU should respect the principles of subsidiarity and proportionality. The competent authorities of the Member States are free to define what they consider to be services of general economic interest and have broad discretion to decide how to organise, regulate, and finance these services, in accordance with EU law and within the limits of manifest error. In particular, the competition rules and the internal market rules do not apply to non-economic activities'.

[80] Damjanovic and De Witte 2009, 91–92.

3.3.5 The Approach Concerning the Identification of Clear Policies and Objectives Within an Overall Vision

Concerning the identification of clear policies and objectives within an overall vision, the Commission stated in the White Paper on European Governance that:

> Connecting the European Union to its citizens means identifying clear policies and objectives within an overall vision of where the Union is going. People need to understand better the political project which underpins the Union... Refocusing policies means that the Union should *identify more clearly its long-term objectives.*[81]

Over the years looking at the soft law on SGEIs it is not very easy to see what exactly it is that the Commission wants in this area as well as how the general principles are to be developed. Rather, one gets the impression of a rather controversial area, where the Commission changes its point of view from time to time. The following characterisation given by Temple Lang seems still to hold water:

> ... because Article 86 was potentially applicable to a diverse range of politically sensitive situations in different Member States, the Commission made very little use of Article 86 until the late 1980s, and the questions which arose were referred to the Court of Justice from national courts. These questions were answered without the Court or the Commission finding it necessary to formulate general principles. The result was to develop several legal rules on a case-by-case basis, which have not been explicitly related to one another, which overlap, and which have not clearly answered several foreseeable questions, which, due to accidents of litigation or to the prudence or tactics of plaintiffs, have not so far been raised. The nearest that the Commission has come to stating any comprehensive view was in the 1990s when, under French pressure, it produced several rather cautious Notices on 'services of general economic interest' under Article 86(2), which did little to clarify the overall legal position. The legal principles which have emerged have therefore never been authoritatively stated as a single set of rules in a clear conceptual framework.[82]

3.4 Conclusions

This chapter has primarily provided a critical scrutiny of the soft law of the Commission concerning SGEIs. *Inter alia,* it has been observed that although having had to launch the idea of a framework Directive (or similar legal instrument) the Commission has been reluctant towards the idea, and now it has dismissed the idea completely. The situation today is that when speaking of legislation, relevant Treaty provisions, and soft law co-exist, but still no 'in-between' layer in the shape of Directives (or the like) are to be found. In addition, it may be observed that regarding the soft points of the soft law, some

[81] Commission of the European Communities, *European Governance. A White Paper,* COM(2001) 428 at 28.

[82] See Temple Lang 2003, pp. 1–2.

do indeed seem to exist. Besides what has already been mentioned, it may be emphasised that the general impression is that increased legal certainty has not been the result of the use of soft law. Whether the use of soft law has led to increased effectiveness, legitimacy, and transparency of Community/EU action, may be questioned. Furthermore, the general principles to govern the area seem to be 'blowing in the wind', leaving the European Courts to develop the principles.

Finally, the greater use of soft law in itself may create and add to these problems. A lot of communications have been adopted, not necessarily with many concrete results. In other words, an overall approach to SGEIs has not yet been defined.

References

Borrás S, Conzelmann T (2007) Democracy, legitimacy and soft modes of governance in the EU: the empirical turn. J Eur Integr 29(5):531–548

Cini M (2000) From soft law to hard?: Discretion and rule-making in the Commission's state aid regime. Fielsole, EUI working papers RSC no. 35, European University Institute

Conseil Economique et Social (2008) Analysis of the implications of the Lisbon Treaty on services of general interest and proposals for implementation, Discussion Paper drawn up by European experts, 42–43

Damjanovic D, De Witte B (2009) Welfare integration through EU Law: the overall picture in the light of the Lisbon Treaty. In: Neergaard U et al (eds) Integrating welfare functions into EU law—from Rome to Lisbon. DJØF Publishing, Copenhagen

De Vries SA (2009) Harmonization of services of general economic interest: where there's a will there's a way. In: Van de Gronden J (ed) EU and WTO law on services. limits to the realization of general interest policies within the services markets? Wolters Kluwer, The Hague, pp 139–158

Joerges C (2007) Integration through de-legislation? An Irritated Heckler, European governance papers no. N-07-03, 5

Krajewski M (2008) Providing legal clarity and securing policy space for public services through a legal framework for services of general economic interest: squaring the circle? European Public Law 14:377–398

Mörth U (2005) Soft law and new modes of EU governance—a democratic problem? Paper presented in Darmstadt, November

Neergaard U (2008) Services of general (economic) interest and the services directive—what is left out, why and where to go? In: Neergaard U, Nielsen R, Roseberry LM (eds) The services directive—consequences for the welfare state and the European social model. DJØF Publishing, Copenhagen

Neergaard U (2009a) Services of general (economic) interest: what aims and values count? In: Neergaard U, Nielsen R, Roseberry LM (eds) Integrating welfare functions into EU law—from Rome to Lisbon. DJØF Publishing, Copenhagen

Neergaard U (2009b) Services of general economic interest: the nature of the beast. In: Krajewski M et al (eds) The changing legal framework of services of general interest in Europe—between competition and solidarity. TMC Asser Press, The Hague, pp 17–50

Rodrigues S (2009) Towards a general EC framework instrument related to SGEI? Political considerations and legal constraints. In: Krajewski M et al (eds) The changing legal framework of services of general interest—between competition and solidarity. TMC Asser Press, The Hague

Senden L (2004) Soft law in European Community law. Hart Publishing, Oxford, p 112

Senden L (2005a) Soft law and its implications for institutional balance in the EC. Utrecht Law Review, 1(1):79–99

Senden L (2005b) Soft law, self-regulation and co-regulation in European law: where do they meet? Electron J Comparative Law, 9(1):1–27

Szyszczak E (2007) The regulation of the state in competitive markets in the EU. Hart Publishing, Oxford, p 131 et seq

Szyszczak E (2009) Legal tools in the liberalisation of welfare markets. In: Neergaard U et al. (eds), Integrating welfare functions into EU law—from Rome to Lisbon, DJØF Publishing, Copenhagen, p 299 et seq

Temple Lang J (2003) European Union law rules on state measures restricting competition. Finnish Yearbook, 1–2

Van de Gronden J (2009a) The EU and WTO law on free trade in services and the public interest: towards a framework directive on services of general economic interest? In: Van de Gronden J (ed) EU and WTO law on services. Limits to the realization of general interest policies within the services markets? Wolters Kluwer, The Hague, pp 249–279

Van de Gronden J (2009b) The services directive and services of general (economic) interest. In: Krajewski M et al (eds) The changing legal framework of services of general interest—between competition and solidarity. TMC Asser Press, The Hague

Chapter 4
Article 106 TFEU is Dead. Long Live Article 106 TFEU!

Tarjei Bekkedal

Abstract This chapter raises the question of the purpose of Article 106 TFEU (ex Article 86 EC). Article 106(2) TFEU is traditionally seen as a derogation to the Treaty provisions and has an awkward role in the Treaty Chapter on competition. *Bekkedal* notes the conventional reading of the provision is that it is an autonomous exception to all of the Treaty provisions and is not confined to specific types of infringement of the TFEU. The conventional view also takes the position that Article 106(2) TFEU can be invoked by the Member States *and* undertakings. *Bekkedal*, in contrast, takes a radical view. He argues that Article 106(2) TFEU can only be invoked by *undertakings*. He makes the point that Article 106(2) TFEU should not be turned into a general clause in EU law because it should be an *exception* primarily targeted at economic objectives. In relation to the fundamental free movement provisions economic objectives are not, in principle, accepted as legitimate justifications to the free movement rules. *Bekkedal* also notes that the European Courts take a softer approach to the application of the principle of proportionality when applying Article 106(2) TFEU, whereas a classical application of the principle should be strict: 'a least restrictive alternative' assessment of the challenged restriction on competition and cross-border trade. If Article 106(2) TFEU is applied as a general clause with these softer standards for review, it could compromise the Internal Market project. *Bekkedal* finds a new role for Article 106 TFEU in that it could be considered as a value statement fulfilling the concept of a 'European Social Model.'

T. Bekkedal (✉)
Department of Private Law, University of Oslo, P.O. Box 6706 St. Olavs plass, 5 0130 Oslo, Norway
e-mail: tarjei.bekkedal@jus.uio.no

E. Szyszczak et al. (eds.), *Developments in Services of General Interest*, Legal Issues of Services of General Interest, DOI: 10.1007/978-90-6704-734-0_4,

Contents

4.1 Article 106 TFEU Revisited: Introduction and Outline

This contribution revisits a basic question: what is the scope of Article 106 TFEU in relation to the provision of services of general economic interest (SGEIs)? The answer to that question, as presented here, will contest the conventional view.

According to the conventional view, the exception in Article 106.2 TFEU may exempt the organisation and provision of SGEIs from the requirements of the Treaty, if the application of, for example, the fundamental freedom to provide services, the rules on competition, or the rules on State Aid will obstruct the performance of the operator of an indispensable service. Usually, the exception in Article 106.2 TFEU is described as autonomous, in the sense that it has a horizontal reach and is not confined to specific kinds of infringements. Consequently, according to the conventional view, it may be invoked by both undertakings and the Member States.

Article 106.1 TFEU is not expressly directed at SGEIs but at the entrustment of special or exclusive rights. Nevertheless, the entrustment of special or exclusive rights is quite a common technique for the realisation of SGEIs, typically to ensure that services are universally available. According to the conventional view, Article 106.1 TFEU may in that case make the Member States subject to the competition rules—which in their own capacity would only apply to undertakings. In the following, the application of Article 106.1 TFEU, read in conjunction with Article 102 TFEU, towards Member State regulation on SGEIs is referred to as 'the competition approach'.

The seed which initiates a broad re-elaboration of the conventional view is found in the recent practice of the ECJ. In *MOTOE*, the ECJ established that the exception in Article 106.2 TFEU can only be invoked by bodies which conduct activity *as an undertaking*.[1] In the judgments in *Asemfo* and *UPC*, the ECJ finally confirmed openly that Article 106.1 TFEU has no independent effect, in the sense that it must be read in conjunction with the relevant rules of the Treaty.[2]

This chapter will submit that the exception in Article 106.2 TFEU cannot be invoked to justify barriers to free movement (Sect. 4.2). Furthermore, it will be submitted that the competition approach towards the Member States' organisation of SGEIs on their own territory should, and is about to, be abandoned (Sects. 4.3 and 4.4). Together, these submissions leave no room for the application of Article 106.2 TFEU when cases which concern Member State regulation on SGEIs are handled in front of the Court. The application of Article 106.2 TFEU will be confined to issues which are handled by the Commission in the first instance, like the assessment of State Aid and the execution of the other powers enshrined in Article 106.3 TFEU.[3]

It should be emphasised that the constitutional importance of Article 106 TFEU with regard to SGEIs will not be contested. Section 4.5 of this chapter will try to sketch out how the *values* of Article 106 TFEU may be detached from the provision itself and reintegrated into the mandatory requirements doctrine, which forms an inherent part of the fundamental freedoms. This *new approach* will be described as one of transformation and transposition: The classical patterns of reasoning, which over time have been developed pursuant to Article 106.2 TFEU, are about to be redefined to suit the character of the fundamental freedoms and will thus reappear in a modified version. Article 14 TFEU may be seen as a catalyst in this regard. The provision confirms the constitutional importance of SGEIs and may encourage both a universal, and to some extent, holistic approach towards such services—to realise the vision of a European social model. The suggested approach rests on the citizen's *right* to access SGEIs—considered in tandem with the Charter of Fundamental Rights, Article 36—while free movement, competition or regulation are merely means to that end.

---

[1] ECJ, Case C-49/07 *MOTOE* [2008] *ECR* I-4863 para 46.

[2] ECJ, Case C-295/05 *Asemfo* [2007] *ECR* I-2999 para 40; ECJ, Case C-250/06 *UPC* [2007] *ECR* I-11135 para 15.

[3] The application of Article 106 TFEU by the Commission will not be discussed.

4.2 The Functioning and Scope of the Exception in Article 106.2 TFEU

4.2.1 Introduction

Section 4.2 contests the conventional view that the Member States can rely on the exception in Article 106.2 TFEU to justify barriers to free movement.[4] The reasons are twofold: first, the case law on Article 106.2 TFEU establishes a principal acceptance of justifications of an economic character,[5] while such justifications have been doctrinally rejected with regard to the fundamental freedoms.[6] Second, the reconciliation-test of Article 106.2 TFEU does, to some extent, deviate from the classical notion of proportionality which is inherent in the fundamental freedoms and the doctrine of mandatory requirements.[7]

The submission that Member States cannot invoke Article 106.2 TFEU to justify barriers to free movement gains support from the judgment in *MOTOE*, as the enactment of regulation is an act of authority which cannot be equated to the activities of an *undertaking*.[8] However, the *MOTOE* judgment will not be presented as the decisive argument against the conventional view, only as a confirmation of its mistaken propositions, whilst Article 106.2 TFEU is firstly considered as primarily a justification for objectives of an economic nature.

4.2.2 Primarily a Justification for Objectives of an Economic Nature

According to its wording, Article 106.2 TFEU is applicable to SGEIs. If that notion is understood to mark a difference from the more commonly used reference to the 'general interest', and if the exception is interpreted both literally and strictly, it may be argued that its scope is limited to objectives of an economic nature. The provision protects the public's economic interests with regard to the financing of society's *indispensable services*. Thus, it has formerly been argued that in its practical application, Article 106.2 TFEU is intrinsically linked to universal services, in their different market sectors, due to the very specific

[4] Numerous observers have held that Article 106.2 TFEU may serve as a justification for barriers to free movement. See for example Deringer 1964–1965, p. 138, Buendia Sierra 1999, Hatzopoulos 2000, pp. 75, 80–81, Maillo 2007, pp. 604–606, Neergaard 2007, p. 77, Szyszczak 2007, p. 217. Somewhat more reluctant, Snell 2005, p. 51.

[5] See Sect. 4.2.2 infra.

[6] Established doctrine since ECJ, Case 7/61 *Commission* v. *Italy* [1961] *ECR* 317 (at 329).

[7] See Sect. 4.2.3 infra.

[8] Supra n. 1. The literal reading of the provision is very clear in the opinion of AG Kokott, which the judgment explicitly refers to.

problems connected to the financing of such services (especially the risk of 'cream skimming').[9] Today however, that view is generally perceived as too formal.[10] In his seminal 1999 contribution, Buendia Sierra established that the exception in Article 106.2 TFEU accounts for objectives of both an economic and a non-economic nature. The protection of health was mentioned as an example of a legitimate concern—an example which we will return to, later.[11] Buendia Sierra admitted that the wording of Article 106.2 TFEU appeared to limit the scope of the exception to objectives of an economic character, but claimed that formal distinctions appeared to be 'groundless'—pointing to the fact that economic objectives must, in any case, promote some ultimate non-economic goal to be accepted. Admittedly, that submission is intuitively appealing. However, it may also be criticised.

It is worth recalling that the ECJ has consistently held that the exception in Article 106.2 TFEU is to be narrowly constructed.[12] To include objectives of a non-economic nature, is to take the opposite stance. Buendia Sierra's line of argument lacks appeal because it changes the character of Article 106.2 TFEU from a special exception into a general exception—and as we will return to, the ECJ does not seem to adhere to this idea.[13]

With regard to the mandatory requirements doctrine which forms an inherent part of the fundamental freedoms and protects the *general interest*, the ECJ has consistently held that considerations of an economic nature are generally not accepted.[14] Suffice to say, the distinction between economic and non-economic aims has not been regarded as 'groundless' with regard to the fundamental

---

[9] Wachsmann and Berrod 1994, p. 39.

[10] Hirsch et al. 2008, p. 1293.

[11] Buendia Sierra 1999, pp. 337–338. Probably, this has always been the main view, see, for example, Deringer 1968, pp. 246–247.

[12] See, e.g., ECJ, Case 127/73 *SABAM* [1974] *ECR* 313 para 19; ECJ, Case C-157/94 *Commission* v. *Netherlands* [1997] *ECR* I-5699, para 37 and ECJ, Case C-242/95 *GT-Link* [1997] *ECR* I-4449, para 50.

[13] See Sect. 4.2.4 infra.

[14] See, e.g., ECJ, Case 95/81 *Commission* v. *Italy* [1982] *ECR* 2187 para 27; ECJ, Case 238/82 *Duphar* [1984] *ECR* 523 para 23; ECJ, Case 288/83 *Commission* v. *Ireland* [1985] *ECR* 176 para 28; ECJ, Case 352/85 *Bond van Adverteerders* v. *Netherlands* [1988] *ECR* 2085 para 34; ECJ, Case C-288/89 *Gouda* v. *Commissariaat voor de Media* [1991] *ECR* I-4007 para 29; ECJ, Case C-324/93 *Evans Medical* [1995] *ECR* I-563 para 36; ECJ, Case C-484/93 *Svensson and Gustavsson* [1995] *ECR* I-3955 para 15; ECJ, Case C-120/95 *Decker* [1998] *ECR* I-1831 para 39; ECJ, Case C-398/95 *SETTG* [1997] *ECR* I-3091 para 23; ECJ, Case C-158/96 *Kohll* [1998] *ECR* I-1931 para 41; ECJ, Case C-264/96 *ICI* v. *Colmer* [1998] *ECR* I-4695 para 28; ECJ, Case C-224/97 *Ciola* [1999] *ECR* I-2517 para 16; ECJ, Case C-35/98 *Verkooijen* [2000] *ECR* I-4071 para 48; ECJ, Case C-254/98 *TK-Heimdienst* [2000] *ECR* I-151 para 33; ECJ, Case C-367/98 *Commission* v. *Portugal* [2002] *ECR* I-4731, para 52; ECJ, Case C-164/99 *Portugaia Construções* [2002] *ECR* I-787 para 26; ECJ, Case C-168/01 *Bosal* [2003] *ECR* I-9409 para 42; ECJ, Case C-388/01 *Commission* v. *Italy* [2003] *ECR* I-721 paras 19, 23 and ECJ, Case C-76/05 *Schwarz* [2007] *ECR* I-6849 para 77.

freedoms.[15] From an utterly material or pragmatic point of view that could, and probably would have to, be criticised. The State is not a business. It does not aim at a surplus, neither does it provide bonuses to its King or Queen or politicians. All incomes are spent for the betterment of its citizens. Hence for a State, *no objectives* are economic *in the end*. But that is not the point. The ECJ's rejection of economic objectives is better understood as a doctrinal proportionality test. The *least restrictive* way of handling budgetary concerns is generally through the tax system, not through specific regulation on the different economic sectors. This general economic logic may however be difficult to apply to some universal services, typically due to the risk of cream skimming. The very specific *economic logic* of such services may therefore make specifically constructed regulation *necessary*. In this particular regard, Article 106.2 TFEU has had an important role to play: to shelter SGEIs from detrimental competition from cherry pickers.

The only line of jurisprudence on the application of Article 106.2 TFEU that really deserves the description 'well established' is exactly the Court's approach to universal services in their different kinds. The objective of ensuring that providers of SGEIs enjoy economically acceptable conditions may justify limitations on competition—to secure the general availability of an alleged indispensable service.[16] The test is not strict as it does not require that the viability of the entrusted company is actually threatened.[17]

As we will return to later, it may seem that the Court *in fact* has accepted justifications with an economic objective on some occasions relating to the four freedoms and the mandatory requirements doctrine as well.[18] A distinct feature of Article 106.2 TFEU is that such objectives have been *openly* accepted *in principle*. This imposes on Article 106.2 TFEU, the character of being primarily a justification for economic objectives—relating to the provision of SGEIs.[19] Without elaborating the comparison further, it is worth noting that this is the main function of the exception in the field of State aid as well.

---

[15] A telling example is found in ECJ, Case C-385/99 *Müller-Fauré* [2003] *ECR* I-4509 paras 71–72 where the ECJ, contrary to Buendia Sierra's submission, emphasised the economic aims of the national regulation on access to medical and hospital services, even if intrinsically linked to the ultimate goal of health protection.

[16] See, e.g., ECJ, Case C-320/91 *Corbeau* [1993] *ECR* I-2533 paras 16–21; Case C-393/92 *Almelo* [1994] *ECR* I-1477 para 49; Joined Cases C-147 and 148/97 *Deutsche Post* and *Citicorp* [2000] *ECR* I-825 paras 49–52; Case C-340/99 *TNT-Traco* [2001] *ECR* I-4109 paras 53–55; Case C-475/99 *Ambulanz Glöckner* [2001] *ECR* I-8089 para 57; ECJ, Case C-162/06 *International Mail* [2007] *ECR* I-9911 paras 32–36.

[17] To this, see also Case C-67/96 *Albany* [1999] *ECR* I-5751 para 107 and Case C-157/94 *Commission* v. *Netherlands* [1997] *ECR* I-5699 para 52.

[18] See Sect. 4.2.4 infra.

[19] See also Hatzopoulos 2002, pp. 726–727.

4.2.3 Article 106.2 and the Fundamental Freedoms

The case law cited above concerns the competition approach where it is well-established that Member States may invoke the exception in Article 106.2 TFEU to justify prima facie violations of Article 106.1 TFEU, read in conjunction with Article 102 TFEU. Let us now turn to the more intriguing and important question. Can Member States invoke the exception in Article 106.2 TFEU to justify prima facie violations of the Treaty rules on free movement?

In the matter now discussed, the consistent interpretative guideline of the ECJ—that the exception is to be interpreted narrowly—becomes of vital importance. Surely, Article 106.2 TFEU is placed under the chapter 'Rules on Competition' Surely, the wording of the exception is first and foremost directed at the competition rules, and thus refers to 'undertakings' Applying Article 106.2 TFEU as an exception to the Treaty rules on the four freedoms does not appear to be a narrow construction, but the complete opposite. A wide interpretation would seem sensible if it was necessary to fill a gap, but the fundamental freedoms are well equipped with tailored exceptions—both the mandatory requirements doctrine and the written justifications. Article 106.2 TFEU does not fit in. Whether one agrees or disagrees that *only* objectives of an economic nature are relevant pursuant to the exception in Article 106.2 TFEU, it is at least well established that the exception will cover such objectives.[20] The consistent practice of the ECJ, that the Member States cannot (in principle) invoke arguments of an economic character to justify barriers to free movement would seem to be irrelevant, if the exception in Article 106.2 TFEU could serve to complement the mandatory requirements doctrine.

Buendia Sierra seems to couple a broad construction of the scope of the exception with a traditional and strict proportionality test, which will at the end of the day ensure a narrow application. According to Buendia Sierra, the proportionality test is fulfilled when the following three elements are proven: (1) that there is a causal relationship between the measure and the objective of general interest, (2) that the restrictions caused by the measure are justified by the benefits for the general interest, and (3) that the objective of general interest cannot be achieved through other *less restrictive means*.[21] However attractive this approach may appear on the theoretical level, it does not seem to work that way in practice. If Member States are allowed to invoke the exception in the first place, it may be fairly difficult to conduct a strict assessment of 'proportionality'.[22] A telling example is the judgment in *Commission* v. *Netherlands*. First, the Court repeated its well-established statement that Article 106.2 TFEU is to be interpreted narrowly. Thus, the Commission had contended that the Member State in question had to establish that there existed no other less restrictive means. The Court

---

[20] See Sect. 4.2.2 supra.

[21] Buendia Sierra 1999, p. 301.

[22] In a 2007 contribution Buendia Sierra too seems to point at this problem. Buendia Sierra 2007, p. 543.

however, expressed a different view, ruling that the burden of proof is not so extensive as to require the Member State to prove positively that no other conceivable measure can enable the entrusted tasks to be performed under the same conditions.[23]

As Baquero Cruz has shown in a very convincing contribution, the judgment in *Commission* v. *Netherlands* is no single example, but part of a broader and seemingly consistent picture.[24] Baquero Cruz concludes that the reconciliation-test applied by the Court 'does not impose on the decision-maker, the obligation to choose the option least restrictive of competition.'[25] That observation serves to confirm Baquero Cruz' submission that the reconciliation of interests induced by Article 106.2 TFEU, has autonomous features which make the label 'proportionality-test' quite unsuitable, if that notion is understood in its traditional sense. Let us investigate the constitutional backdrop of the observations Baquero Cruz presents, to provide a possible explanation for the reserved approach of the ECJ.

The content and functioning of Article 106.2 TFEU have primarily been clarified in cases which rest on the competition approach. From a constitutional point of view there is a remarkable difference between the rules on the four freedoms on the one hand and the competition rules on the other. The fundamental freedoms have the same constitutional character as traditional individual *liberties*—although their purpose may perhaps be of a more instrumental character: to establish a single market. Liberties protect some areas of private autonomy, but not private autonomy nor liberty as such. Liberties guarantee freedom from some restraints, but always in a defined sense (though not always clear), such as freedom of speech or freedom of movement across borders. Hence, one could say that the existence in the legal system of specific liberties is both a prerequisite for, and a confirmation of, the lawmakers' otherwise sovereign competence to issue restraints on liberty in the broad and undefined sense.

The competition rules do not have any similarities to liberties in the traditional sense—obviously because their main purpose is to prevent abuses from private companies in markets where competition is already presumed to exist. Basically, the competition rules establish *obligations not to*. If the obligation 'not to' is redefined and redirected towards the State, the competition rules may, however, establish some kind of right of *free competition*. If that latter notion is understood

---

[23] ECJ, Case C-157/94 *Commission* v. *Netherlands* [1997] *ECR* I-5699 para 58.

[24] Baquero Cruz 2005, pp. 187–197, making (in this regard) reference to ECJ, Case 155/73 *Sacchi* [1974] *ECR* 409; ECJ, Case 66/86 *Ahmed Saeed* [1989] *ECR* 803; ECJ, Case C-41/90 *Höfner* [1991] *ECR* I-1979; ECJ, Case C-320/91 *Corbeau* [1993] *ECR* I-2533; ECJ, Case C-393/92 *Almelo* [1994] *ECR* I-1477 and ECJ, Case C-67/96 *Albany* [1999] *ECR* I-5751.

[25] Baquero Cruz 2005, p. 196, confirming his foregoing thesis at 187: 'that the Court has never followed such an approach but a milder approach that entails a softer test'. The same conclusion is reached by Sauter 2008, pp. 186–188 and Stergiou 2008, p. 183. In the same direction, pointing at the different and softer assessment under Article 106.2 TFEU in comparison to the classical notion of proportionality, see Soriano 2003, p. 112. Flynn 1999, p. 193, makes a similar observation, noting that the ECJ has displayed a more reserved application of the competition rules since 1993. Contra, Davies 2009, p. 573.

as an ideal—a 'natural position' of no restraints—it equates to a protection of liberty in its broadest meaning. The constitutional problem is that courts never protect individual *liberty* in that broad material sense. Courts protect *liberty* in a formal way, through the principle of legality (viz. the formal notion of the Rule of Law)—as the law itself is the guardian of liberty. In addition, courts protect *liberties* in many different fields depending on which liberties the legal system contains. What constitutional courts do not do, is to consider—in a broader sense—how much freedom (e.g., freedom of competition) is enough freedom.

The traditional notion of proportionality, inherent in the four freedoms, should be strict, because there is a prima facie violation of true and explicit individual rights regarded by the legal system, which must be taken seriously. The notion of 'free competition' is much more blurred. If that notion is taken *too* seriously, i.e., if the classical proportionality-test is employed in the assessment pursuant to Article 106 TFEU, read in conjunction with the competition rules, that may entail a broad revision of the Member States' policy in the economic field.[26] In theory, adhering to neo-liberal arguments, there will always exist less restrictive means.[27] Such a broad revision may however seem unconstitutional and hence undemocratic. That can explain why the Court's approach has been more reserved in this regard, focusing first and foremost on whether the means actually chosen by the Member State seem to work. A central criterion is whether the public service provider is 'manifestly unable to satisfy demand'.[28] Indeed, that test does not reflect a classical notion of proportionality. Instead, it gives clear associations to the 'manifest error' test which the Court will resort to in situations where its control with other institutions is characterised by true deference—due to the political nature of their decisions. The answer to the question 'how much competition?' is to quite an extent, dependent on policy. If the purpose of the national regulatory framework is to make some SGEI available to the public, but the provider is still unable to satisfy demand, it would seem that the framework must suffer from some kind of manifest error. However, if that is the essence of the court-made test, pursuant to Article 106.2 TFEU, the assessment is not very strict.

We can extract two important conclusions from the foregoing elaboration. The first is that the traditional notion of proportionality cannot, and does not, count for the functioning of the exception in Article 106.2 TFEU. The second is that the Court's reserved application of that exception has probably had more to do with the less clearly-defined character of the competition rules than a true deference towards SGEIs. To put it differently: if Member State regulation which is intended to ensure the provision of SGEIs, encroach upon the *rules on the four freedoms*, it will not be unconstitutional to employ the traditional notion of proportionality. It does not

26 Reminding us of the Marenco/Pescatore polemic. See especially Marenco 1987, p. 420.

27 The basic neo-liberal norm is very simple and reads like this: 'The optimal allocation of recourses should be decided by the law of supply and demand.' However, that can hardly be transposed into a legal norm.

28 *Ambulanz Glöckner*, supra n. 16 para 62. Cf. Sect. 4.2.2 supra.

follow from the constitutional recognition of SGEIs that the seemingly softer test entailed by Article 106.2 TFEU must prevail in such situations. Quite to the contrary the traditional proportionality-test and its 'least restrictive requirement' have to be considered as an inherent feature of the protected rights, i.e., the fundamental freedoms.[29] That is not to say that market-interests must be given priority in such situations—as we know proportionality is a flexible tool. However, the mode of reconciliation is more fixed—having regard to the nature of the freedoms.

The conclusion of the arguments put forward so far is that Article 106.2 TFEU should not be allowed to serve as a justification for barriers to free movement. Thus, a restrictive interpretation of the exception should coincide with a restrictive scope of application. If the exception *is* brought forward, a restrictive interpretation on the level of assessment may, as we have seen, be difficult—running the risk of compromising the fundamental freedoms. If, in a specific case, the doctrine of mandatory requirements is not sufficient to save the day from the Member State's point of view, it would seem to be a very unhappy constitutional paradox if the exception in Article 106.2 TFEU provided a final bailout solution.[30] It is of course possible to deal with that problem by resorting to the traditional proportionality test under such circumstances, but then it is difficult to see why Article 106.2 TFEU should be applied in the first place. To pursue a kind of harmonisation will only do harm, neglecting the fact that Article 106.2 TFEU has a core area with a distinct character, and it may lead to confusion as to when these distinctive features prevail, and when the application of the exception is just copying other settled doctrines which already exist in their own capacity. Therefore, the exception in Article 106.2 TFEU should only be applied when its specific characteristics are essential to the assessment. In general, that will not be the case with regard to distortions to the fundamental freedoms. Hence the classical assessment of mandatory requirements coupled with the traditional proportionality-test should serve as the basis of reconciliation in such situations—not Article 106.2 TFEU.

4.2.4 The Case Law of the ECJ

4.2.4.1 Introduction: The 'Campus Oil' Judgment

Let us first make one thing clear: the case law where Member State regulation has been challenged pursuant to the competition approach, and where the Member

[29] On a general level, see Alexy 2002, pp. 66–69. More specifically see, for example, ECJ, Case C-169/91 *Council of Stoke-on Trent* v. *B & Q* [1992] *ECR* I-6635 para 15.

[30] In this regard it is proper to insist that the doctrine of mandatory requirements forms an inherent part of the freedoms. Hence, that doctrine must always be applied first, before turning to Article 106.2 TFEU which is a true exception. Then it becomes clear that the invocation of Article 106.2 TFEU will always, as also noted by van der Woude, lead to the problem of 'double justification'. Van der Woude 1991, p. 76. See also Davies 2009, pp. 563, 572.

States have been allowed to invoke Article 106.2 TFEU, has no bearing on the question of whether the Member States may invoke the exception in other regards, e.g., to justify prima facie violations of the fundamental freedoms. The exception is to be interpreted narrowly. A necessary implication is that the application of the exception must take due regard of the nature and purposes of the legal principles from which it may serve as an exception. Consequently, the exception is not as autonomous as it may appear. It seems impossible both to construe the exception narrowly *and* to let it form its own rule. The question of the applicability of Article 106.2 TFEU in *four freedom* cases must therefore be handled on its own premises.

Admittedly, in the case law of the ECJ, there are a few judgments which have involved the Treaty rules on the four freedoms, and where the exception in Article 106.2 TFEU has been applied. However, those cases share a common feature: Article 106.1 TFEU serves as the starting point, and the Member State is held responsible for violating *both* the competition rules and the Treaty rules on the four freedoms.[31] A separate section will be devoted to this special line of jurisprudence (Sect. 4.4 below). There are, however, no examples in the case law of the ECJ where Member State regulation has been assessed solely under the Treaty rules on the four freedoms, and where the exception in Article 106(2) TFEU has been applied. Quite to the contrary: in *Campus Oil* the ECJ emphasised that the exception could not exempt a Member State from the obligations arising from Article 34 TFEU, however, without stating any grounds for that finding.[32] That case is old, but as we shall see, the finding is that, it is still good law.

4.2.4.2 The Notion of 'Undertaking': The 'MOTOE' Judgment

The more recent judgment in *MOTOE* provides considerations of significant principal importance.[33] The private entity ELPA organised motorcycle-events, an activity which was found to be economic. Thus, in this capacity ELPA was considered to be an 'undertaking' pursuant to the competition rules. At the same time ELPA was vested with an exclusive right to authorise other undertakings to conduct similar activities. The two different functions were found to be incompatible as they created a conflict of interests contrary to Article 106.1 TFEU, read in conjunction with Article 102 TFEU. With regard to the application of the exception in Article 106.2 TFEU, Advocate General Kokott considered it to be of imperative importance to distinguish between ELPA's activities as an undertaking and its functions as a regulatory authority. With regard to the latter, which represented the problem, Article 106.2 TFEU was not applicable 'since the

[31] See, e.g., ECJ, Case C-179/90 *Merci* [1991] *ECR* I-5889; ECJ, Case C-266/96 *Corsica Ferries* [1998] *ECR* I-3949 and ECJ, Joined Cases C-147/97 and C-148/97 *Deutsche Post* [2000] *ECR* I-825.

[32] ECJ, Case 72/83 *Campus Oil* [1984] *ECR* 2727 para 19.

[33] Supra n. 1.

precondition for the application of that provision is the existence of a service, that is to say an economic activity *as an undertaking*.'[34] The ECJ came to the same finding and expressly referred to the Advocate General's elaboration.[35] The conclusion seems to reflect that the subjects referred to in Article 106.2 TFEU are 'undertakings', not public authorities.

Suffice to say, public authorities in the true sense never conduct economic activity, they just regulate it. Therefore, on the principal level, the *MOTOE* judgment provides a strong argument that lawmakers or regulators cannot invoke Article 106.2 TFEU when they operate as such. That observation is not at odds with the fact that the Member States have occasionally been allowed to invoke the exception in Article 106.2 TFEU in other regards, typically where the national regulatory framework on some SGEI has been challenged pursuant to Article 106.1 TFEU read in conjunction with Article 102 TFEU. In the majority of such cases there is a fundamental requirement that the behaviour of some private undertaking amounts to an abuse, and that the abuse may be *imputed* or traced back to the regulatory act of the State.[36] If that requirement is fulfilled, then the State is held responsible for *the act of the undertaking*—as the national regulatory framework left the latter with no choice on how to behave *commercially*. Naturally, if the State is held responsible for the commercial behaviour of an undertaking, pursuant to the competition rules, it must also be allowed to invoke exceptions which apply to undertakings, as Article 106.2 TFEU. However, if national regulations encroach upon the right to free movement, then there is no question of whether an act of an undertaking may be imputed to the State. If legal provisions establish a barrier to free movement, the public authorities of the State are *directly* responsible as such. To deny the invocation of Article 106.2 TFEU in that situation is nothing but taking the wording of Article 106.2 TFEU seriously—as it is an exception.[37]

4.2.4.3 The Case Law Concerning Monopolies in Goods

In his contribution Sierra argues that Article 106.2 TFEU may be invoked by the Member States, making reference to the judgments concerning the Dutch,

---

[34] Opinion of AG Kokott in *MOTOE*, supra n. 1, para 110 [emphasis added].

[35] *MOTOE*, supra n. 1 para 46.

[36] ECJ, Case C-323/93 *La Crespelle* [1994] *ECR* I-5077 para 18; ECJ, Case C-387/93 *Banchero* [1995] *ECR* I-4663, para 51; *Ambulanz Glöckner*, supra n. 16 para 39. See also Sect. 4.3.2 infra.

[37] Admittedly, as mentioned in supra n. 4, the mainstream view is that Member States can invoke the exception in all regards. That view traces long back, see, e.g., Page 1982, p. 27, who emphasises that both undertakings and Member States may benefit from the exception. However, it should be noted that the traditional view was also that Article 106.2 TFEU was an exception to Article 106.1 TFEU, and that the latter could never be used to strike down *general acts* (Page at 23). Thus, in practice, the functioning of Article 106.2 TFEU would be to justify what would otherwise connote to abuses.

Italian and French monopolies in the energy sector, dating back to 1997.[38] The jurisprudence of the ECJ concerning State monopolies of a commercial character, pursuant to Article 31 EC, does however seem to be of a very specific character. As we all know, the ECJ has always made it very clear that Article 31 refers to monopolies of *goods* only. Regarding *such monopolies*, the ECJ has accepted that Article 106.2 TFEU can be invoked as a justification for their very existence.[39] One possible explanation is the politically sensitive character of monopolies in goods, acknowledged explicitly by the fact of there being a *lex specialis* provision concerning such monopolies in the Treaty. The soft approach of Article 106.2 TFEU seem appropriate to that situation. In fact, in some of the early drafts on the Treaty, what we today know as Articles 37 TEU and 106 TFEU respectively, formed one single Article.

One should be extremely careful to draw general conclusions from the case law concerning monopolies in goods. If one conclusion is to be drawn, it might actually be that Article 106.2 TFEU is not relevant in other fields. It should be recalled that the ECJ has constructed the scope of Article 37 TFEU quite narrowly. In *Franzén* the ECJ drew a dividing line, stating that 'the effect on intra-Community trade of the other provisions of the domestic legislation which are separable from the operation of the monopoly although they have a bearing upon it' had to be examined with reference to Article 34 TFEU of the Treaty.[40] In the latter regard Article 106.2 TFEU was not applied. The same strict approach was followed in *Rosengren*. Swedish rules on imports of alcoholic beverages had the 'effect of channelling consumers who wish to acquire such beverages towards the monopoly.'[41] It is tempting to ask if that is not the entire purpose of the *existence* and *operation* of a monopoly, but the ECJ saw it differently, finding Article 37 TFEU to be irrelevant in this regard, resorting instead to Article 34 TFEU.[42]

The narrow interpretation of Article 37 TFEU makes the scope of the exception in Article 106.2 TFEU similarly narrow. It is submitted that this is intentional; otherwise there would seem to be no convincing explanation for the very careful elaboration made by the Court. Taken literally, the practice of the Court only prove the obvious, expressed by the ECJ in the *Hanner* judgment:

> … it is clear from the case law of the Court that Article [106.2 TFEU] may be relied upon to justify the grant by a Member State, to an undertaking entrusted with the operation of services of general economic interest, of exclusive rights *which are contrary to Article* [37.1 *TFEU*]…[43]

---

[38] Buendia Sierra 2007, p. 543, making reference to ECJ, Case C-157/94 *Commission* v. *Netherlands* [1997] *ECR* I-5699; ECJ, Case C-158/94 *Commission* v. *Italy* [1997] *ECR* I-5789 and ECJ, Case C-159/94 *Commissions* v. *France* [1997] *ECR* I-5815. In the same direction, see Stergiou 2008, p. 179.

[39] For another example see ECJ, Case C-438/02 *Hanner* [2005] *ECR* I-4551.

[40] ECJ, Case C-189/95 *Franzén* [1997] *ECR* I-5909 para 36.

[41] Case ECJ, C-170/04 *Rosengren* [2007] *ECR* I-4071 para 23.

[42] Op. cit. paras 24–27.

[43] *Hanner*, supra n. 39, para 47 [emphasis added].

The dividing line between regulation which secures the mere *existence* and *operation* of the monopoly, and other regulation with a possible negative impact on intra-EU trade is difficult to draw outside the field of goods. The application of Article 37 TFEU seems to correspond to the distinctions made in *Keck*, i.e., between selling arrangements and other regulation.[44] The reasoning in *Keck* has never been transposed to the other freedoms and it may seem that its distinctions are unsuitable outside the field of goods.[45] If that is correct, one may add that Article 106.2 TFEU seem to be unsuitable outside the very special and narrow category of 'monopolies in goods'.

4.2.4.4 Case Law Concerning the Health Sector: The Revealing Example

One of the most striking lines in the recent jurisprudence of the ECJ, that reveals a stark unwillingness to formally adhere to the exception in Article 106.2 TFEU in 'four freedom cases', starts with the *Decker* judgment.[46] The case concerned a prior authorisation requirement for the reimbursement of medical expenses incurred in another Member State—constituting a barrier to the free movement of goods pursuant to Article 34 TFEU. The ECJ repeated its consistent jurisprudence, confirming that aims of a purely economic nature cannot justify a restriction to the fundamental freedoms.[47] But it also made it clear that:

> However, it cannot be excluded that the risk of seriously undermining the financial balance of the social security system may constitute an overriding reason in the general interest capable of justifying a barrier of that kind.[48]

The statements in *Decker* seem to somewhat contradict themselves. As Snell puts it, the Court accepted an economic aim while claiming it was not doing so.[49] Admittedly, there is an obvious need to make sure that health services and other SGEIs can be provided under sound economic conditions. In fact, that is as we have seen accepted *in principal* in an established line of jurisprudence pursuant to Article 106.2 TFEU.[50] Therefore, it is not at all surprising that the Court has repeated its reasoning in *Decker* on later occasions, notably in the important and to some extent groundbreaking judgments in *Smits & Peerbooms*, *Müller-Fauré* and

---

[44] ECJ, Joined Cases C-267/91 and C-268/91 *Keck and Mithouard* [1993] *ECR* I-6097.
The point made becomes clearer if one compare with the judgments in *La Crespelle* and *Banchero*, supra n. 36.

[45] For some convincing arguments, see Hatzopoulos 2000, pp. 67–68.

[46] Supra n. 14. See also *Kohll*, supra n. 14, para 41.

[47] Formally, the *Decker* case does not alter the doctrinal rejection of economic aims, instead it has been taken as a confirmation, see, i.e., the reference made in *TK-Heimdienst*, supra n. 14, para 33.

[48] *Decker*, supra n. 14, para 39.

[49] Snell 2005, p. 43.

[50] See Sect. 4.2.2 supra.

Watts, all concerning the health sector.[51] The question is why the Court has not turned to the exception in Article 106.2 TFEU instead of constructing some kind of fiction under the mandatory requirements doctrine.

The Court's approach can be explained by two reasons. First, one must recall that, primarily, to define a service as an SGEI is considered to be a Member State competence.[52] That being so, and considering that economic aims are undoubtedly accepted under the exception in Article 106.2 TFEU, a broad interpretation of that exception would run a risk of *completely* undermining the consistent line of jurisprudence which makes it clear that economic aims cannot justify distortions to free movement. The fiction constructed by the Court will conserve the doctrinal rejection of economic aims, while *exceptionally* allowing them when they are of imperative importance—securing some ultimate non-economic aim.[53] Still it is clear that this represents something quite extraordinary.[54] The handling of the Court-made fiction is clearly the responsibility of the Court itself. Therefore, in a very complex field, which SGEIs rightly are considered to represent, the fiction under the mandatory requirements doctrine establishes some room for maneuver for the Court, which all in all can establish coherence without the risk of treading on Member State competences. This is a somewhat creative solution to the old debate of whether 'SGEIs' is an EU concept. The proponents of such a view had pointed to the danger of leaving the definition to the discretion of the Member States,[55] which is true enough. On the other hand, if the Court is to control more than a *manifest error* of definition, it will run the risk of engaging directly in the political discussions of the Member States. None of these rigid alternatives seem very attractive and the ECJ seems to have paved its own third way, steering clear of the pitfalls on both sides.

A second reason which might explain the subtlety is that the Court wants to stick to the traditional framework for reconciliation of interests in four freedom cases. As we have seen, the assessment pursuant to the exception in Article 106.2 TFEU does not seem to entail a 'least restrictive alternative test'.[56] Hence, the Court has made it quite clear that it is not necessary to prove that the survival of

---

[51] ECJ, Case C-157/99 *Smits & Peerbooms* [2001] *ECR* I-5473, para 72; ECJ, Case C-385/99 *Müller-Fauré* [2003] *ECR* I-4509, para 73; ECJ, Case C-372/04 *Watts* [2006] *ECR* I-4325, para 103. See also ECJ, Case C-444/05 *Stamatelaki* [2007] *ECR* I-3185, para 30.

[52] Communication from the Commission, *Services of general interest in Europe* (2001/C 17/04), para 22.

[53] To the latter requirement, see ECJ, Case C-324/93 *Evans Medical* [1995] *ECR* I-563 paras 36–37.

[54] Thus, the Court had no difficulty in rejecting that the cost of managing cultural assets (museums) could be considered a legitimate aim in ECJ, Case C-388/01 *Commission* v. *Italy* [2003] *ECR* I-721 para 22. Identically, regulation intended to preserve industrial peace in the Greek tourist industry, preventing adverse effects on that industry and ultimately on the economy as a whole was turned down in ECJ, Case C-398/95 *SETTG* [1997] *ECR* I-3091 para 23.

[55] See Buendia Sierra 1999, p. 279 et seq. for further references.

[56] See Sect. 4.2.3 supra.

the operator is in any way threatened to benefit from that exception. Conversely, the Court-made fiction in *Decker* and the following cases, seems to hold on to the traditional notion of strict necessity—requiring as we have seen that there is a risk of *seriously undermining* the financial balance of the system in question.[57] The practical implications of the latter requirement are important. A good example of the Courts nuanced approach is evident in *Müller-Fauré*. The Court found that the risk of seriously undermining the financial balance of the social security system could justify an authorisation requirement for *hospital treatment* abroad. However, such an arrangement was not accepted for *non-hospital treatment* abroad, where its removal was considered by the Court to have only limited budgetary impact.[58] It is submitted that such a distinction would have been very hard to draw had the Court instead resorted to the softer test pursuant to Article 106.2 TFEU.

It could be argued that the ECJ *is* treading on Member States' competences through its somewhat covert reasoning, keeping Article 106.2 TFEU in the dark, while employing (some of) its values only when it suits the Court. However, it does not follow from the wording of Article 106.2 TFEU that it can be brought forward by the Member States in four freedom cases at all. Therefore, the Court's technique does not take anything from the Member States—it gives. While evaluating the Court's reasoning, one must also bear in mind that its main duty is to ensure that law is observed. As emphasised in Sect. 4.2.3, the interpretation of Article 106.2 TFEU has more or less been ironed out in cases where Member State regulation has been challenged pursuant to the competition approach. Even though competition is regarded as a constitutional value, the competition rules do not establish any individual liberties in the true sense. The four freedoms should on the other hand be treated as individual rights and taken seriously. Hence, a stricter assessment is not only legitimate, it is also demanded.

4.2.5 Conclusions

The exception in Article 106.2 TFEU is directed at undertakings. Strictly interpreted, the exception may not be invoked by the Member States. Admittedly, it is settled case law that the exception will apply if Member State regulation is challenged pursuant to the competition approach: Article 106.1 TFEU read in conjunction with Article 102 TFEU. In that situation however, the behaviour of an undertaking is imputed to the State. A wide application of the competition rules corresponds with a wide application of the exception. If Member States are held responsible for the behaviour of undertakings, it seems necessary and logical to allow the invocation of any justification which is available to undertakings.

---

[57] If that requirement is not fulfilled, the Court will resort to the doctrinal rejection of economic aims. See, e.g., ECJ, Case C-109/04 *Kranemann* [2005] *ECR* I-2421 paras 31–35.

[58] *Müller-Fauré*, supra n. 15 paras 95–98.

Conversely, if Member State regulation violates the fundamental freedoms, the State is responsible as such, in their *public capacity*. Article 106.2 TFEU does not address that situation.

The case law of the ECJ seems to confirm the observations above. The ECJ has never treated Article 106.2 TFEU as a relevant exception in cases which solely concern the fundamental freedoms. That reluctance seems well-founded. The analysis of the case law on Article 106.2 TFEU revealed that the exception allows economic objectives as justifications for prima facie violations of the Treaty. To shelter public service providers from full competition to ensure their commercial viability is one thing, allowing the State, in its public capacity, to limit free movement due to budgetary constraints is quite another.

Furthermore, the reconciliation test inherent in Article 106.2 TFEU appears to be softer than the traditional proportionality test—which can be explained by the fact that competition is of a far more blurry and somewhat political nature in comparison to free movement. In cases which concern the fundamental freedoms, the Court should—and does also seem to—resort to the mandatory requirement doctrine and the traditional proportionality test. Article 106.2 TFEU is not applicable, but we have seen that the values of Article 106.2 TFEU are sometimes transposed and employed at the general level when they, according to the facts of the case, are of imperative importance. On some occasions, the Court has accepted economic justifications for barriers to free movement, without admitting it openly. To include some of the values of Article 106.2 TFEU in the doctrine of mandatory requirements does however seem to be fully legitimised by Article 14 TFEU as long as the balancing of interest and the mode of reconciliation take due regard of the nature of the fundamental freedoms. Of course, a covert reasoning may be more difficult to grasp in a concrete case than a more doctrinal approach, but it is easy to agree with Snell that this 'subtlety is desirable'.[59] On a general level, the Court's reasoning promotes constitutional coherence by establishing some flexible framework for reconciliation 'on the balance' which mirrors the nature of the fundamental freedoms and also takes due regard of the ultimate non-economic values.

4.3 Article 106 TFEU Read in Conjunction with the Competition Rules

4.3.1 Introduction

The hypothesis which will be tested is that the competition-approach does not add much as EU Law on the internal market stands today. If Member State regulation distorts competition, contrary to Article 106.1 TFEU, read in conjunction with

[59] Snell 2005, p. 55.

Article 102 TFEU, it will also in most imaginable situations amount to a restriction on free movement. If that is correct, the only thing the competition-approach really adds is the possibility for the Member States to invoke the exception in Article 106.2 TFEU. It will be submitted that the best way of respecting the interpretative guideline of the ECJ—that the exception in Article 106.2 TFEU is to be construed narrowly—is not to invoke the competition-approach either.[60]

This section will undertake a systematic analysis of Article 106.1 TFEU, to provide a constitutional explanation for its apparently diminishing importance in the case law of the ECJ. Then we will return to a more detailed analysis of the three main doctrines developed on the basis of Article 106.1 TFEU read in conjunction with Article 102 TFEU; the extension of the dominant position doctrine, the conflict of interests doctrine and the demand limitation doctrine.

4.3.2 The Diminishing Role of Article 106.1 TFEU in the Case Law of the ECJ

In *Asemfo* the ECJ concluded that:

> [i]t follows from the clear terms of Article 86(1) EC that it has no independent effect in the sense that it must be read in conjunction with the relevant rules of the Treaty.[61]

That finding has later been repeated in *UPC*.[62] The statement confirms that Article 106.1 TFEU is a mere reference provision. That conclusion is not revolutionary. Pappalardo made a similar submission as early as 1991.[63] However, Pappalardo's position was not at all uncontroversial. Through its clarification, the Court dismisses a more dynamic approach and brings a long debate on the proper interpretation of Article 106.1 TFEU to its end.

Article 106.1 TFEU has always been, and should probably still be, considered to express a special duty of loyalty addressed to the Member States. The long-standing question has been how far that obligation reaches. According to the grand-father judgment in *GB-INNO*, the Member States must not enact regulation that will deprive the competition rules of their *effectiveness*.[64] That statement is still good law, but its indefiniteness has always provoked more questions than answers. One possible interpretation has been that Member States must not enact regulation whose effects will encroach upon the objectives and purposes of the

[60] It should be noted that this seemingly unorthodox position was presented as the preferred approach by Van der Woude 1991, p. 76 as early as in 1991.

[61] *Asemfo*, supra n. 2, para 40. The Court's finding seems to deviate from the opinion presented by AG Geelhoed, paras 114, 121.

[62] *UPC*, supra n. 2 para 15. See also Opinion of Advocate General Jacobs in *Ambulanz Glöckner*, supra n. 16 para 88.

[63] Pappalardo 1991, p. 34.

[64] ECJ, Case 13/77 *GB-INNO* [1977] *ECR* 2115, paras 30–32.

competition rules (the *effet utile-approach*). Another and a more modest interpretation would be that Member States must not enact regulation which will lead to actual abuses from specific companies (the *behaviour-approach*).[65]

At first it seemed that the ECJ preferred a dynamic interpretation of Article 106.1 TFEU—the *effet utile-approach*. The judgment in *Corbeau* represents the most expansive and famous interpretation of the provision.[66] The judgment suffers from a lack of reasoning, but seemingly the ECJ considered the establishment of a dominant position as being contrary to the objectives of the competition rules per se—even if there was no actual abuse. Hence, the substantive part of the assessment would be that of justification, pursuant to Article 106.2 TFEU.

A first step-back, indicating a preference for the more modest *behaviour-approach*, appeared immediately afterwards and is well-known.[67] In the *La Crespelle* judgment, the Court ruled that the mere creation of a dominant position by the granting of an exclusive right within the meaning of Article 106.1 TFEU is not as such incompatible with Article 102 TFEU. A Member State contravenes the prohibitions contained in those two provisions only if, in merely exercising the exclusive right granted to it, the undertaking in question cannot avoid abusing its dominant position.[68]

The judgments in *Asemfo* and *UPC* are a second step-back. Probably, the concrete results in the two judgments were not dependent on the Court's reluctant interpretation of Article 106.1 TFEU. That part of the rulings has much more bearing in principle terms. The Court was not forced to take a clear stance, but it seems as if the ECJ wanted to lock a door—an action it seldom performs. Clearly, the Court prefers a literal reading, at the expense of a more dynamic interpretation of Article 106.1 TFEU. After the two judgments it will, on a principal level, be even more difficult than before to argue in favour of the *effet utile-approach*. On their own terms, the competition rules only prohibit abusive behaviour.

4.3.3 A Constitutional Explanation to the Court's Literal Interpretation of Article 106.1 TFEU

The choice between the modest behaviour approach and the more dynamic *effet utile-approach* is not exclusive to Article 106.1 TFEU. It should be recalled that, there the Court had used two different ways in which the Member States can be held responsible pursuant to the competition rules. The first is the combined

---

[65] For a more thorough description of the two alternative approaches, see Buendia Sierra 1999, p. 151 et seq., or Maillo 2007, p. 599 et seq.

[66] *Corbeau*, supra n. 16.

[67] On this see, Buendia Sierra 1999, p. 173 et seq., Maillo 2007, p. 603.

[68] *La Crespelle*, supra n. 36, para 18. See also *Banchero*, supra n. 36, para 51 and *Ambulanz Glöckner*, supra n. 16 para 39.

reading of the general duty of loyalty in what was Article 10 EC, and the competition rules—normally Article 81 EC (now Article 101 TFEU). This is referred to as the State Action doctrine.[69] The second way is Article 106.1 TFEU read in conjunction with the competition rules—normally Article 102 TFEU.

The alternative approaches were lively debated with regard to the State Action doctrine. In this regard the *behaviour-approach* must now be considered as settled case law.[70] Hence, as noted by Baquero Cruz, the State Action doctrine has been 'reduced to a rather marginal construction, dealing with very exceptional cases.'[71] It will typically apply where a Member State requires or favours the adoption of agreements, decisions or concerted practices contrary to Article 101 TFEU, or reinforces their effects. It has been submitted, however, that the Court's withdrawn application of the State Action doctrine has no bearing on the other path—the application of Article 106.1 TFEU read in conjunction with Article 102 TFEU.[72] I will not bring up the entire discussion here, but present a few remarks to explain why I disagree with that position.

The choice between the *effet utile-approach* and the *behaviour-approach* is better seen as an overarching constitutional dilemma rather than a mere doctrinal question—the latter allowing for different solutions with regard to different provisions of the Treaty, the former insisting on coherence. Whether Member States can be held responsible pursuant to the competition rules for enacting regulation that does not actually lead to abusive conduct from a specific company, but which may possibly create the same effects, is in all cases a question of competences.[73] It is hard to agree that the wording of Article 106 TFEU can make any difference because it is 'mainly about competition'.[74] The wording is notoriously unclear. In earlier days, Article 106.1 TFEU was understood by some observers to presuppose and thus legitimise special or exclusive rights by explicitly referring to them.[75] Considering the wording only, that is a perfectly viable interpretation. We can put it even simpler: considering the wording only, it makes perfect sense to submit that the purpose of Article 106 TFEU is to protect SGEIs from competition. Or, due to the unclear wording, one can resort to the neutral position as Marenco did. Some 25 years ago he analysed whether public undertakings where subject to the competition rules. His answer was in the affirmative, pointing to the fact that the

---

[69] See Szyszczak 2007, Chapter 2.

[70] This settlement was reached in ECJ, Cases C-2/91 *Meng* [1993] *ECR* I-5751; C-185/91*Reiff* [1993] *ECR* I-5801 and C-245/91 *Ohra* [1993] *ECR* I-5851 and is still valid law, see Joined Cases C-94/04 and C-204/04 *Cipolla* and *Macrino and Capodarte* [2006] *ECR* I-11421. For a precise elaboration of the judgments, see Reich 1994, p. 459. The most thorough analysis of the State Action doctrine is presented by Neergaard 1998.

[71] Baquero Cruz 2007, p. 556.

[72] Ibid. See also Baquero Cruz 2002, p. 130 and Buendia Sierra 1999, pp. 141–143 and 266-267.

[73] Neergaard 1998, pp. 321–322 rightly points to competence issues to explain the Courts reserved application of the State Action doctrine.

[74] Baquero Cruz 2002, p. 130. See also Baquero Cruz 2007, pp. 555–556.

[75] Van der Woude 1991, p. 69.

competition rules themselves do not qualify the notion of 'undertaking'. Hence, in their own terms and in their own capacity, the competition rules would apply to both public and private undertakings.[76] Marenco did not attach any significance to Article 106.1 TFEU in this matter, as the provision did 'not seem to help either way'.[77]

The point I would like to make is this: one cannot read anything out of the wording of Article 106 TFEU without interpreting it—and the interpretation should take constitutional considerations into account.[78] In this regard, one must recall the considerable constitutional difference between the rules on the four freedoms on the one hand and the competition rules on the other. As pointed out in Sect. 4.3.4: outside the field of liberties in the true sense, Constitutional Courts do not normally consider more broadly—how much freedom (i.e., freedom of competition) is enough freedom. So, if Article 106.1 TFEU is interpreted in a constitutional context it does not make sense to disregard the very reserved application of its twin brother—the State Action doctrine.[79]

On a principal level, the Court's literal reading of Article 106.1 TFEU in *Asemfo* and *UPC* coincides with the literal reading of Article 10 EC (repealed by the Treaty of Lisbon 2009 but replaced in substance by Article 4.3 TEU) and Article 101 TFEU—contrasting the dynamic interpretation, the Treaty's *liberties*—the four freedoms. It is submitted that *both* these lines of interpretation should be regarded as highly constitutional.[80] A dynamic interpretation of liberties is constitutional in the sense that it protects clearly established rights of individuals (freedom of movement) while also promoting the single market. A reluctant and literal reading of the competition rules (that is, with regard to Member State regulation) reflects that it is normally not for the courts to define the amount of individual freedom in a broad and undefined sense.

4.3.4 But What About Integration?

Dynamic interpretation has always been rooted in the integration-goal. If the interpretative approach towards Article 106.1 TFEU is literal—will that have an adverse effect on integration? The answer will be dependent on one's conception

---

[76] Marenco 1983, p. 497.

[77] Ibid., at 499.

[78] That approach gains support from ECJ, Case 283/81 *CILFIT* [1982] *ECR* 3415 para 20.

[79] On the connection between the two, see also Opinion of Advocate General Jacobs in *Albany*, supra n. 17, para 371.

[80] See in this regard opinion of Advocate General Teasauro in *Meng*, supra n. 70 para 29, pointing at some underlying 'normative aspect' to support a literal and thus not dynamic reading with regard to the State Action doctrine. Conversely, Baquero Cruz 2007, p. 585, equating dynamic interpretation and constitutional reasoning. But even if constitutional reasoning is often dynamic, it is not necessarily so. Constitutional considerations may also identify limits.

of 'integration'. Furthermore, it depends on whether the fundamental freedoms are a better tool to realise that present conception than the competition approach.

The Court-made doctrines on the competition approach stem from the early 1990s.[81] From a constitutional perspective it should be remembered that in 1992 the Maastricht Treaty introduced an adjustment to the basic principles of the EC Treaty, specifying that the activities of the Member States and the Community should include 'the adoption of an economic policy which is ... conducted in accordance with the principle of an open market economy with free competition.' The main focus of that period was to complete the internal market.[82] Integration was realised through the constitution of the marketplace. Thus, one possible conception of the EC Treaty could be that of an *economic constitution.* The competition rules were a handy tool to further the vision of a common marketplace at a time when the Treaty rules on the fundamental freedoms were not as mature and far-reaching as today.

Article 14 TFEU was introduced by the Amsterdam Treaty in 1997, after which the different courts made doctrines on the competition approach, have not been developed further. In 2009, the Lisbon Treaty established the new notion of a social market economy coupled with the moving of the reference to 'an open market economy with free competition' to a darker and less prosperous place in the TFEU.[83] The constitutional surroundings have been perfected. The tremendous success of the EC-project increases its impact on people's lives. It is no longer a union based on coal and steel. Therefore, the European citizen must be the target of the European project, and benefit from its achievements. With regard to SGEIs, that conception of integration is highlighted by the Charter of Fundamental Rights, Article 36, which reads:

> The Union recognises and respects access to services of general economic interest as provided for in national laws and practices, in accordance with the Treaties, in order to promote the social and territorial cohesion of the Union.

These observations themselves do not invalidate the competition approach towards SGEIs, but pave the way for other approaches if they fit better with the re-shaped conception of integration. The detrimental weakness of the competition approach is the impossibility of establishing a constitutional concept of sufficient competition which is workable when the vision of the legal system is somewhat more sophisticated than to establish as much competition as possible.

If we accept Prosser's observation, that '[m]arkets are never free, being constructed through, and dependent on, different kinds of legal (and social) structures',[84] it is also easy to agree with Odudu, that: 'the competition rules are simply

---

[81] As noted by Van der Woude 1991, a new era was introduced by the groundbreaking judgment in ECJ, Case C-202/88 *France* v. *Commission* [1991] *ECR* I-1223.

[82] A good description is provided by Flynn 1999.

[83] *OJ* 2007/C 306/49. The text of Article 4 EC shall become Article 119 TFEU.

[84] Prosser 2005, p. 1.

an inappropriate lens through which to view regulation.'[85] Taking the Member States' perspective it is certainly strange that the enactment of regulation, due to the limited reach of the notion of 'special or exclusive rights' in Article 106.1 TFEU, is not exposed to the competition rules in general, but mainly in situations where it composes the legal framework for SGEIs. With regard to such services concerns about competition might be said to have the least bearing, as they normally contain elements of solidarity.

These observations serve to emphasise that the competition approach presents the Court with great difficulties—not only in the concrete assessment but also on the normative level.[86] The question of how much competition has always been considered utterly political—especially when it comes to the (re)distribution of welfare.[87] And noteworthy, the more or less political question of how far the competition rules reach, is coupled with the exception in Article 106.2 TFEU which also has a political character.[88] The paragraph forms a part of the Commission competence enshrined in Article 106.3 TFEU. Thus, the Commission is the better or preferred institution to deal with Article 106 TFEU. Consequently the Court's control will normally be limited *if* the Commission has acted in the first instance.[89]

These arguments are not an attempt to shield the regulation of SGEIs from tight legal scrutiny. It is significantly important to control the use of special or exclusive rights to avoid a fragmentation of the market, as they amount to the most interventionist technique of realising national social policy. But consequently, it would also seem clear that the fundamental freedom to provide services, as it stands today, is both applicable and sufficient to secure the interests of the EU, by promoting equal opportunity and consequently a level playing field.[90] In fact, it is hard to see that competition rules really broaden the obligations of the Member States.[91] It is more difficult to ascertain an abuse rather than a restriction, and there is a risk that the competition approach is less efficient.

It is submitted that it would further the integration project, if the competition approach were to be abandoned, at least in the situation whereby Member State regulation also restricts free movement. The Court has not been unaware of the normative deficiencies of the competition approach—therefore it compensates through a quite generous application of the exception in Article 106.2 TFEU.

[85] Odudu 2006, p. 31.

[86] For further elaboration upon these difficulties, see Davies 2009, pp. 576–581.

[87] See on this issue Scharpf 2002, p. 645.

[88] Baquero Cruz 2005, p. 171.

[89] ECJ, Case T-106/95 *FSSA and others* v. *Commission* [1997] *ECR* II-299 paras 99, 100; ECJ, Case C-163/99 *Portugal* v. *Commission* [2001] *ECR* I-2613 paras 19, 20.

[90] As noted by Roth 2002, p. 14; 'The discrimination criterion corresponds to the *principle of undistorted competition* which is fundamental to the single market.'

[91] See also Davies 2009, pp. 556, 562.

Conversely, the four freedoms approach will entail a classical test of proportionality. The latter is a better guardian of integration.

Consequently, the application of Article 106.1 TFEU, read in conjunction with Article 102 TFEU must be extremely conscious of systematic and institutional considerations. Instead of developing different doctrines which define prima facie violations pursuant to the competition approach, and then turn to the exception in Article 106.2 TFEU, the whole assessment should be turned around. Considering the very specific characteristics of the exception in Article 106.2 TFEU, one must start by asking: what cases *should* be brought under the exception, *if any*? The answer to that question will define the proper area of Article 106.1 TFEU read in conjunction with Article 102 TFEU.[92] The following sections will explain the recent practice of the ECJ from that angle, to prove that the competition approach—just like the State Action doctrine—has been 'reduced to a rather marginal construction, dealing with very exceptional cases'.[93]

4.4 The Doctrines on Article 106.1 TFEU Read in Conjunction with Article 102 TFEU

4.4.1 The Extension of the Dominant Position Doctrine

The extension of the dominant position doctrine applies where a Member State vests a company which already holds a dominant position in one market, with special or exclusive rights on a neighbouring but separate market.[94] Even though the doctrine seems to be well-established and accepted in legal theory,[95] it has been applied by the ECJ in only a few cases.[96]

On a theoretical level the doctrine is interesting because it certainly has a potential for complementing the Treaty rules on the fundamental freedoms. According to the judgments in *Coname* and *Parking Brixen*, the award of special or exclusive rights (such as service concessions) will, in the absence of any transparency in the award process, be considered to be in breach of Articles 49 and

[92] This analytical approach is maybe unorthodox, but not new. The interpretation of Article 87.1 EC in ECJ, Case C-280/00 *Altmark* [2003] *ECR* I-7747 was to a great extent influenced by systematic considerations about the proper scope of the exception in Article 106.2 TFEU.

[93] Paraphrase of Baquero Cruz 2007.

[94] The landmark judgment is ECJ, Case C-18/88 *RTT* v. *GB-Inno BM* [1991] *ECR* I-5941.

[95] See Buendia Sierra 1999, p. 169 et seq.; Whish 2003, pp. 228–229, Maillo 2007, p. 602.

[96] A clear example is the *Ambulanz Glöckner* judgment, supra n. 16 para 43. Perhaps ECJ, Case C-203/96 *Dusseldorph* [1998] *ECR* I-4075 paras 61–63 should also be understood to employ the doctrine.

56 TFEU.[97] Normally therefore, the Member States are required to conduct a procedure of competitive tendering. However, even if the requirements which flow from the fundamental freedoms are fulfilled, it is of course imaginable that the winning company already holds a dominant position in another neighbouring market. Possibly then, a process which sits perfectly well with the Treaty rules on the four freedoms may nevertheless violate Article 106.1 TFEU, read in conjunction with Article 102 TFEU, *But*—it is also possible to consider the extension of the dominant position doctrine as a pragmatic and prescribed doctrine which the ECJ resorted to, *before* the application of the four freedoms was developed in such a sophisticated manner as today.

The extension of the dominant position doctrine has had a major impact on the telecommunications sector.[98] With the sector today being fully liberalised, it may seem that the ECJ is putting the extension of the dominant position doctrine to rest, on the same sector that once gave it birth. The *Connect Austria* case concerned the allocation of frequencies for mobile telephony.[99] The former Austrian telecommunications incumbent, Mobilkom, already held frequencies in the GSM 900 band, and was considered to have a dominant position in the national market for GSM telephony. Then, in addition, the company was awarded frequencies in the GSM 1800 band. It was disputed whether Mobilkom had paid a frequency fee in line with what its competitors had to bear. Clearly, if that was not the case, the award should be considered to be in breach of both the rules on the four freedoms and the state aid rules. Interestingly, however, the questions from the national court concerned the application of Article 106.1 TFEU, read in conjunction with Article 102 TFEU, supposedly due to the tradition of applying these provisions to the telecommunications sector. If the extension of the dominant position doctrine was still alive, it should in principle not be of decisive importance whether Mobilkom had paid the same fee as its competitors. The allocation of more frequencies could in all cases be said to extend or strengthen the company's dominant position. The ECJ, however, seemed to treat the extension of the dominant position doctrine as extinct. It ruled that the award of additional frequencies would be in breach of Article 106.1 TFEU read in conjunction with Article 102 TFEU if Mobilkom did not have to pay the same fee as other operators. Conversely, if the fee was fixed at a rate ensuring *equal opportunities*, the measure at hand would *not* be caught.[100] That finding seems like a mere reference to the Treaty rules on the four freedoms. The ECJ must of course ensure that the principle of equal treatment is observed, even in situations where national courts take no regard to the rules on the four freedoms, and base their questions solely on the competition approach.

---

[97] ECJ, Case C-231/03 *Coname* [2005] *ECR* I-7287; ECJ, Case C-458/03 *Parking Brixen* [2005] *ECR* I-8585.

[98] The Court has accepted the Commission's application of the doctrine in this regard, see ECJ, Joined Cases C-271/90, C-281/90 and C-289/90 *Spain, Belgium and Italy* v. *Commission* [1992] *ECR* I-5833 paras 36–38.

[99] ECJ, Case C-462/99 *Connect Austria* [2003] *ECR* I-5197.

[100] Ibid., paras 80–95.

The important tenet of the case is, however, that there does not seem to be anything more to the extension of the dominant position doctrine than would already follow from the rules on the four freedoms.

Preferably then, the award of new rights in their different kinds should be assessed solely on the basis of Articles 49 and 56 TFEU. In that case, as the Commission has also contended, the exception in Article 106.2 TFEU seems to be of no relevance.[101] During the award-process there will normally be no commercial behaviour on behalf of the undertaking which can be imputed to the State. As noted in Sect. 4.2.4.2, that link may seem to be a prerequisite if the State wants to invoke the exception in Article 106.2 TFEU as it, according to its wording, is directed at undertakings. The award process is of a purely regulative character, and as Barnard has pointed out, the requirements which have been derived from the fundamental freedoms may be seen as principles of good government.[102] Thus it would in any case seem difficult to construe how a formal requirement, like that of transparency, may have a negative impact on the performance of the preferred company.

4.4.2 The Conflict of Interests Doctrine: A Doctrine of Legal Capacity

The *ERT* judgment is often referred to as the leading precedent for the conflict of interests doctrine.[103] Greek law entrusted the national broadcasting company, *ERT*, with a monopoly to broadcast, *and* an exclusive right of transmission of other broadcasts, including broadcasts from other Member States. The ECJ ruled that such a situation would be in breach of Article 106.1 TFEU, where the rights were liable to create a situation in which *ERT* was *led to infringe* Article 102 TFEU by virtue of a discriminatory broadcasting policy favouring its own programs—*unless* the application of Article 102 TFEU would obstruct the performance of the particular tasks entrusted to the company.

Noteworthy, as Whish puts it, it was not necessary for *ERT* to have actually abused its dominant position, as long as the measures made this sufficiently likely.[104] To some, this may seem similar to an *effet utile-approach* towards the competition rules.[105] On further inspection, however, without denying the existence or importance of the conflicts of interests doctrine, it will be submitted that it

---

[101] SEC(2006) 516 Commission Staff Working Document, Annexes to the Communication from the Commission on social services of general interest in the European Union COM (2006) 177 final, 15.

[102] Barnard 2008, p. 355.

[103] ECJ, Case C-260/89 *ERT* [1991] *ECR* I-2925. See also ECJ, Case C-179/90 *Port of Genoa* [1991] *ECR* I-5889; ECJ, Case C-163/96 *Silvano Raso* [1998] *ECR* I-533, cf. Buendia Sierra 1999, p. 165 et seq., Maillo 2007, p. 599 et seq.

[104] Whish 2003, p. 228.

[105] Gyselen 2003, p. 77, Szyszczak 2007, p. 125.

should not at all be labelled a 'competition doctrine'. Therefore, it is also submitted that the exception in Article 106.2 TFEU is of no relevance either.

What the ECJ really feared in the *ERT* judgment was a potentially *discriminatory* broadcasting policy, encroaching on the basic principle of *equal opportunity* which arises from Article 56 TFEU.[106] That observation explains why no actual abuse was necessary. This led van der Woude to pose the well founded rhetorical question of why 'the Court still bothered to analyse these rights under Articles [102] and [106].'[107]

With regard to the fundamental freedoms it is clear that the Member States must establish a regulatory structure which both respects them, and also prevents obvious risks of violations. That point was spelled out much more elegantly in the later *Hanner* judgment.[108] The case concerned the Swedish monopoly on the retail sale of medicinal preparations ('Apoteket'). Even though a monopoly as such was justified it could not, in law or in fact, place goods from other Member States at a disadvantage, in comparison to trade in domestic goods. In this regard the Swedish regulation lacked structural safeguards—i.e., well-established, transparent procurement procedures to avoid discrimination. Thus, the ECJ found Article 37.1 TFEU to be infringed.[109] Interestingly, the Court noted '[a]ccordingly, it is unnecessary to deal with the second aspect, namely the question whether Apoteket does *in practice* place medicinal preparations from other Member States at a disadvantage.'[110] The latter finding makes it very clear that with regard to free movement, a lack of structural safeguards on behalf of the State, which creates a potential risk of discrimination, may in itself constitute an infringement.

The conflict of interests doctrine does not share much in common with 'competition law' in its true and original sense. The doctrine is not really about efficiency or freedom to compete. From an analytical point of view, it makes much more sense to treat the doctrine as a principle of good governance—more specifically as a doctrine of regulatory and legal capacity. The objectives of the doctrine have more in common with what one traditionally labels as rules on impartiality, rather than the objectives of the competition rules. The ECJ gave a fairly good description in the recent judgment in *MOTOE*, where the company's commercial exploitation of motorcycle events made it 'tantamount de facto' to also confer upon it, the regulatory power to authorise such events.[111]

While being increasingly common in sector-specific secondary regulation, the Treaty on the Functioning of the European Union itself suffers from an obvious lack of regulation on the important issue of legal and regulatory capacity. Since the

---

[106] *ERT*, supra n. 103 paras 19–26. As Hancher points to, the monopoly was not considered to be a problem as such. Hancher 1999, p. 722.

[107] Van der Woude 1991, p. 74.

[108] *Hanner*, supra n. 39.

[109] Ibid., para 44.

[110] Ibid., para 45 [emphasis added].

[111] *MOTOE*, supra n. 1 para 51.

market entails competition, it is from a pragmatic point of view, easy to understand why the ECJ sometimes resort to the competition rules to fill the gap and establish some basic principles of good governance. Thus the case law on the conflict of interests doctrine is better analysed in this broader context. Then, other decisions invoking quite different provisions of the Treaty other than Article 106.1 TFEU read in conjunction with Article 102 TFEU, can still be seen as part of the same doctrine. An interesting parallel is the Court's approach to Articles 10 and 81 EC which, not very surprisingly, fits the puzzle very well. As a supplement to the *behaviour-approach*, the Court has always made clear that the State Action doctrine will apply where a Member State 'divests its own rules of the character of legislation by delegating to private economic operators responsibility for taking decisions affecting the economic sphere.'[112] The above-mentioned *Hanner* decision can serve as another example. But the doctrine reaches further—and in my opinion even the judgments in *Viking* and *Laval* may be added to the picture.[113] As Azoulai points out, the Court was reluctant to entrust private organisations (trade unions) with the task of determining the nature of the public social order. He continues; 'Paradoxically—the state seems to be the only reference for the Court.'[114] However, viewed as a question of *legal authority*, it is, maybe not so paradoxical that only the State can function as the guarantor of the public interest.

The description of the conflicts of interests' doctrine, as a doctrine of legal capacity, indicates that the ECJ was wrong in the *ERT* judgment when it ruled that Article 106.2 TFEU could, in principle, justify the regulatory arrangement, if the application of Article 102 TFEU would obstruct the performance of the particular tasks entrusted to the company. If what we saw in its first appearance was not in fact a competition law doctrine, how can Article 106.2 TFEU serve as a justification? Or, to put it clearer: If what we saw was a principle of good governance, how can one possibly construe that this principle obstructs the performance of the company? In *Hanner*, the ECJ laconically ruled that there was no room for the exception: 'However, a sales regime of the kind at issue in the main proceedings … cannot be justified under Article [106.2 TFEU] in the absence of a selection system that excludes any discrimination against medicinal preparations from other Member States.'[115] That finding seems to be of relevance in all cases where the real problem is that the national regulatory regime is establishing some sort of conflict of interests, no matter whether the problem is tackled by the pragmatic use of Article 106.1 TFEU, read in conjunction with Article 102 TFEU, or some other Treaty provision.

---

[112] See, e.g., *Cipolla* and *Macrino and Capodarte*, supra n. 70 para 47.

[113] ECJ, Case C-341/05 *Laval* [2007] *ECR* I-11767 and ECJ, Case C-438/05 *Viking Line* [2007] *ECR* I-10779.

[114] Azoulai 2008, p. 1351.

[115] *Hanner*, supra n. 39 para 48. See also *MOTOE*, supra n. 1 paras 45–46 where Article 106.2 TFEU was found to be irrelevant to the case, as long as the performance of regulatory functions is not 'economic'.

4.4.3 The Demand Limitation Doctrine

The judgment in *Höfner* is the leading precedent for the *demand limitation doctrine*.[116] The German Federal Office for Employment was vested with exclusive rights of employment procurement. Hence, it was prohibited for everyone else to engage in employment activities. The ECJ ruled that the arrangement would be in breach of Article 106.1 TFEU if it created a situation where the agency could not avoid infringing Article 102 TFEU. Whether that was actually the situation was conditional on several requirements, most importantly that the agency had to be 'manifestly incapable of satisfying demand prevailing on the market for such activities.'[117]

With regard to the jurisprudence of the ECJ on Article 106.1 TFEU read in conjunction with Article 102 TFEU, the *demand limitation doctrine* is probably the most important. Nevertheless, as EU Law now stands, it is submitted that the fundamental freedoms should substitute the competition-approach even in cases where the demand limitation doctrine is, in principle, applicable.

One immediately striking feature is that the demand limitation criterion spelled out by the Court seems unnecessarily complex in comparison to the fundamental freedoms approach. Normally, an exclusive right for one privileged company will go hand in hand with a *prohibition* for other companies. A prohibition is a straightforward restriction to free movement. Of course in specific cases, as in *Höfner*, the assessment under the competition rules can be pretty straightforward as well, but that is not always the case.[118] Consider, as an example, the judgment in *Dusseldorp* where the ECJ ruled that:

> Article [106] of the ... Treaty, in conjunction with Article [102], precludes rules such as the Long-term Plan whereby a Member State requires undertakings to deliver their waste for recovery, such as oil filters, to a national undertaking on which it has conferred the exclusive right to incinerate dangerous waste unless the processing of their waste in another Member State is of a higher quality than that performed by that undertaking if, without any objective justification and without being necessary for the performance of a task in the general interest, those rules have the effect of favouring the national undertaking and increasing its dominant position.[119]

That finding entails an unduly complex evaluation for the national court. Astonishing then is the fact that, even if carried out correctly, it will still not achieve the goals of the single market. It seems clear that the regulation in *Dusseldorp* restricted free movement. Of course, that may in principle be justified with reference to the doctrine of mandatory requirements. However, even if it was proved that the market was being *efficient*, in spite of the fact that national

---

[116] *Höfner*, supra n. 24.

[117] Ibid., para 34.

[118] See ECJ, Case C-208/05 *ITC Innovative Technology* [2007] *ECR* I-181 para 52.

[119] ECJ, Case C-203/96 *Dusseldorph* [1998] *ECR* I-4075, operative part, para 2.

companies were favoured, that would simply be an irrelevant defense.[120] An important tenent of the rules on the four freedoms is that they do not presuppose any detailed analysis of the conditions in the market concerned.[121]

Compared to the rules on the four freedoms, the competition rules suffer from a lack of nuances, and simply do not reach far enough. As another example, consider the situation where there is sufficient justification (pursuant to the rules on the four freedoms) to vest some special or exclusive right to a privileged company. Clearly, the company itself cannot be accused of abusing its dominant position in the process of selecting the title holding company. Therefore, the award process must be assessed with the fundamental freedoms as its basis.[122]

On the other hand, it may be argued that Article 106.1 TFEU, read in conjunction with Article 102 TFEU can fill a loophole where there is no cross-border element—i.e., where national regulation restricts competition, but not free movement. This was actually the case in the *Höfner* judgment which, while often being analysed in principal terms, may also be viewed as an example of utter pragmatism. With regard to Article 56 TFEU, the Court remarked that the dispute concerned German regulation, and was between German parties only. Hence, the ECJ ruled that '[s]uch a situation displays no link with any of the situations envisaged by Community law.'[123] If that is true, it is highly questionable whether the competition rules legitimately can fill the 'gap'. Rather, the problem seems to be that the reach of Community law is not infinite—it stops somewhere—but somewhere the ECJ have yet to reach.

To some extent, the possible criticism presented above may be of historical interest only. The Court's assessment of the cross-border requirement in the *Höfner* judgment no longer seems to be good law—if, in fact, it ever was. If national regulation nationalises the market, it is quite foreseeable that disputes may be nationalised as well. That feature of national regulation should not at all prevent the application of the fundamental freedoms—quite to the contrary it represents the core problem. Therefore, there are strong reasons to embrace the development in more recent practice of the ECJ, where the Court focuses on the *hypothetical* intra-state element.[124] If such a hypothetical intra-state element exists, national actors too should be allowed to invoke the fundamental freedoms against their own State. That will increase the efficiency of EU Law—the most central rationale behind the doctrine of direct effect. Suffice to say, there existed a *hypothetical* intra-state element in *Höfner*. If there ever was a loophole, the Treaty rules on the four freedoms have filled it themselves.

---

120 See, e.g., ECJ, Case C-255/04 *Commission* v. *France* [2006] *ECR* I-5251 paras 28–29 and ECJ, Joined Cases C-338/04, C-359/04 and C-360/04 *Placanica* [2007] *ECR* I-1891 para 51.

121 See Davies 2003, p. 93 et seq.

122 See supra Sect. 4.2.3.

123 *Höfner*, supra n. 24 para 39.

124 See, e.g., ECJ, Case C-36/02 *Omega Spielhallen* [2004] *ECR* I-9609 and *Parking Brixen*, supra n. 97. On the latter see Hatzopoulos 2000, p. 93.

If the submissions presented so far are correct, the demand limitation doctrine, while having a clear existence on the theoretical level, does not have the potential to supplement the fundamental freedoms in any important ways. Instead, what it seems to add is a possibility for the Member States to invoke the exception in Article 106.2 TFEU. However, as argued in Sect. 4.2, the exception should be considered irrelevant in cases which also affect free movement. If that submission is correct, it is our duty to consider seriously when—and even if—the demand limitation doctrine should be invoked towards the Member States at all. A broad use of that legal basis will correspond to a broader application of the exception in Article 106.2 TFEU—contrary to the requirement of the ECJ that the exception is to be construed narrowly.

Some observers may find this way of seeing things illogical and even provocative. Admittedly, the regular assessment is to first apply the main rules, and then eventually the relevant exception. However, SGEIs raise unduly difficult problems and a linear approach is not sufficiently sophisticated to handle them. That is not to say that this contribution can present a full solution, but there are hints in the jurisprudence of the ECJ that can serve as a basis for a coherent approach.

Recently, the Court seems to have developed a certain reluctance when it comes to answering interpretative questions from national courts regarding the application of Article 106.1 TFEU read in conjunction with Article 102 TFEU. In a number of cases the ECJ has declared the questions inadmissible, pointing to the complexity of evaluation and a lack of sufficiently detailed market information.[125] True enough, the assessment is complex, but taken at face value, the line of argument put forward by the Court is not really convincing. When replying to interpretative questions, the ECJ assists national courts by describing how Community Law is to be understood. The application of the law, for example the concrete assessment of whether a company holds a dominant position, is the duty of the national court. The complexity of the final assessment did not seem to bother the ECJ in earlier days, i.e. in the mentioned *Dusseldorp* judgment. Therefore, the reluctance of the Court may imply a fiction. The Court seems to be maneuvering so as not to engage Article 106.1 TFEU read in conjunction with Article 102 TFEU, where it is more proper to solve the case on the basis of the four freedoms alone. That in turn will lead to a more diminishing use of the exception in Article 106.2 TFEU. That is not to say that the Court will never or should never apply the demand limitation doctrine. However, it is submitted that the Court should do this only where the case's characteristics suits the exception in Article 106.2 TFEU. As stated in Sect. 4.2.2 above, that requirement will typically be fulfilled when the case at hand concerns a universal service, and where the Member State's justification is directly aimed at securing the economy

[125] See, for example, ECJ, Case C-134/03 *Viacom* [2005] *ECR* I-1167, para 29; ECJ, Case C-451/03 *Ausiliari Dottori* [2006] *ECR* I-2941 para 26, and *Asemfo* supra n. 2 para 45.

of the privileged company. In other situations, the Court should resort to the new tendency of declaring the interpretative questions inadmissible.

The jurisprudence of the ECJ seems to be in line with the submission above. The last time the Court answered a question from a national court concerning the application of the demand limitation doctrine was the *Ambulanz Glöckner* judgment in 2001.[126] It is hard to see that the ECJ was provided with any more market information in this case, than in other cases where it has abstained from providing an answer. It is submitted that the true difference was that the *Ambulanz Glöckner* case concerned a classic universal service. The objective of the Member State regulation was to ensure that the service provider could run its business on economically acceptable conditions. Hence, the exception in Article 106.2 TFEU was suitable to the case—therefore it was proper for the ECJ to provide an answer to the interpretative question posed by the national court.

4.5 Article 106 TFEU and the European Social Model

4.5.1 Introduction

This section will sketch out a possible new approach towards SGEIs, which rests solely on the fundamental freedoms. Without denying the direct effect of Article 106 TFEU, it will be argued that the true importance of the provision appears when it is *not* given immediate application by the Court, but is instead considered as a value statement fulfilling the concept of a *European Social Model.* Importantly, that notion will not be understood in a material sense, i.e. as a conception of the 'European Welfare State'. Due to the limited scope of the EC Treaty, the limited competences enshrined in it, and the great differences between the national welfare systems of the Member States, a European social model can only be partial, not autonomous. Perhaps, it can be described more precisely as a system of 'bits and pieces', based on the existing social systems in the Member States, integrated by the principles of free movement and equal treatment and legitimised by the conception of a European citizen—with true rights of access to services, which the different Member States themselves have regarded as indispensable.

Schiek has described the European Social Model as polygamic, which means that social objectives must be considered as some kind of constitutional value, being part of—or having to be regarded when applying—the hard law of the Treaties.[127] The constitutional importance of SGEIs is confirmed by Article 14 TFEU. Buendia Sierra has submitted that Article 14 TFEU 'does not modify [Article 106.2 TFEU], but rather reaffirms the logic behind the provision.'[128]

[126] *Ambulanz Glöckner*, supra n. 16.

[127] Schiek 2008, p. 25.

[128] Buendia Sierra 1999, p. 313.

That may be so, but as noted by Szyszczak—even though Article 14 TFEU lacks direct effect, it has teleological value.[129] In other words, Article 14 TFEU has the potential of reaffirming the logic of Article 106.2 TFEU on the general level. Hence, the values of Article 106.2 TFEU may be seen as obligatory parts of a universal constitutional model of reasoning, in the reconciliation between Community principles and the social policies of the Member States.

The realisation of a European social model requires a specific sort of interaction, where the constituted model is regarded as integral to the different provisions by which it is constituted. Thus, the suggested approach may be described as holistic. It confirms the importance of SGEIs without letting Article 106.2 TFEU form its own autonomous rule. In cases which concern the fundamental freedoms, the values of Article 106.2 TFEU have to be taken into consideration, also regarding the citizens' right of access to SGEI, pursuant to the Charter of Fundamental Rights in the European Union, Article 36. However, the mode of reconciliation should be defined by the fundamental freedoms themselves, the mandatory requirements doctrine and the principle of proportionality, not the exception in Article 106.2 TFEU.

The approach which will be sketched out below, does not claim to present a complete description of the European Social Model. Its only ambition is to address one of its 'bits and pieces'—Article 106 TFEU. Speaking in practical terms, there are at least two important consequences of the suggested approach. Firstly, The constitutional force of Article 106.2 TFEU, read in conjunction with Article 14 TFEU, may influence the application of the mandatory requirements doctrine: Economic objectives may occasionally be accepted as justifications for barriers to free movement when they promote the provision of SGEIs—but not necessarily to such an extent that the application of the mandatory requirements doctrine is reduced to the mirror image of Article 106.2 TFEU. Secondly, with regard to the application of Article 106.1 TFEU read in conjunction with Article 102 TFEU, the most important doctrine has probably been that of *demand limitation*.[130] In short, the traditional conception of the competition approach reads like this: If a Member State reserves an economic activity for a privileged undertaking or a monopolist, it may amount to a violation of the competition rules if market-demand is not satisfied. Consequently that may establish a right for competitors to access the market.

Under a new approach, which is solely based on the fundamental freedoms, the old competition-doctrine of *demand limitation* will be transposed to a citizens' right to access SGEIs. That right, it will be submitted, is fundamental in the Dworkinian sense: if Member States restrict free movement to secure the provision of some SGEI, but are still unable to satisfy citizens' demand for the alleged indispensable service, mandatory requirements in the general interest will not be accepted as justifications.

---

[129] Szyszczak 2007, p. 220.

[130] *Höfner*, supra n. 24—cf. Sect. 4.4.3 supra.

4.5.2 The Transformation and Transposition of the Demand Limitation Doctrine

4.5.2.1 Introduction: A Right for Citizens

Let us recap a bit. In Sect. 4.2 it was submitted that the exception in Article 106.2 TFEU cannot justify distortions to free movement. On the other hand, it is clear from the case law of the ECJ that the Member States can invoke the exception with regard to the competition-approach and the doctrine of demand limitation.

With regard to the *demand limitation doctrine*, it was argued in Sect. 4.4.3 that all possible infringements would also be captured by the Treaty rules on the four freedoms. Hence, even if the features of a case make the competition-approach feasible, such cases may instead be assessed under the fundamental freedoms alone—to prevent the invocation of the exception in Article 106.2 TFEU.

Maybe it is not entirely precise to submit that the traditional demand limitation doctrine can in no way supplement the fundamental freedoms. Let us, as an example, consider the situation where a Member State establishes some kind of monopoly, or at least some kind of authorisation system in the field of gambling. Furthermore, let us presuppose that the system restricts free movement, but can be justified by some mandatory requirement.[131] Still, it would, in principle be possible to claim that such a system entails some sort of demand limitation in breach of Article 106.1 TFEU read in conjunction with Article 102 TFEU—in some situations that is the purpose of the system. Under such circumstances, it seems difficult for the Member States to invoke the exception in Article 106.2 TFEU. Clearly, gambling companies do not secure the common good, even though the regulation of gambling does. Gambling is not a SGEI.

However, it would seem quite paradoxical if the competition approach should lead to a result other than that which would follow from the rules on free movement in our example. Taken at face value, it would mean that the Member State regulation did not serve the common good after all, *or* imply that companies have a *right to compete* which overrides the common good. None of these alternatives seem sensible, and neither Article 106 TFEU nor the competition rules have been invoked in the numerous gambling cases before the Court.[132] Presumably, that is because the demand limitation doctrine does not at all entail some sort of right for companies—explained by the fact that the competition rules are not *liberties* in the true sense.[133] Instead it is submitted that the demand limitation doctrine entails a *right for citizens*—thus the doctrine protects *their interest*. That submission represents a restatement of the old doctrine whose correctness and

[131] See, e.g., ECJ, Case C-275/92 *Schindler* [1994] *ECR* I-1039 and ECJ, Case C-124/97 *Läärä* [1999] *ECR* I-6067.

[132] See, i.e., ECJ, Case C-243/01 *Gambelli* [2003] *ECR* I-13031, which according to paras 8 and 34 concerned special or exclusive rights. Still, Article 106 TFEU was not applied.

[133] Cf. Sect. 4.2.3 supra.

consequences we shall elaborate further. It will be argued that the doctrine of demand limitation may serve to nuance the proportionality test in all fields, establishing a citizen's right of access to SGEIs, thus preserving the European social model. Understood in that sense, the demand limitation doctrine has a universal character, independent of Article 106 TFEU.

4.5.2.2 The Transformation

Let us first scrutinise how the demand limitation doctrine was assessed by the ECJ in the *Ambulanz Glöckner* judgment—where it was introduced in the traditional way, by reference to Article 106.1 TFEU read in conjunction with Article 102 TFEU.[134] However, as we shall see, the approach of the ECJ was somewhat untraditional.

The case concerned exclusive rights for ambulance transport in the German region of Rheinland-Pfalz. The ECJ concluded that these rights would be contrary to Article 106.1 TFEU read in conjunction with Article 102 TFEU, if the entrusted company had a dominant position, and interestingly, if there was 'a sufficient degree of probability that national regulation actually prevented undertakings established in Member States other than the Member State in question from carrying out ambulance transport services there, or even from establishing themselves there.'[135] But the Court also found the objective of assuring the service provider's economical viability to be a relevant justification pursuant to the exception in Article 106.2 TFEU. The invocation of that justification was however made conditional, and would not be accepted if the medical aid organisations entrusted with the operation of the public emergency ambulance service were 'manifestly unable to satisfy demand in the area of emergency ambulance and patient transport services.'[136]

The ordering of the Court's findings in the *Ambulanz Glöckner* case deserves attention. First, the application of Article 106.1 TFEU read in conjunction with Article 102 TFEU was made dependent on the possibility of other companies to provide the same services, or establishing themselves in the same area. Therefore, as to the question of whether national regulation constituted a prima facie violation of the Treaty, the Court's reasoning relied to a very great extent, on a parallel to the fundamental freedoms, *not* a traditional demand limitation analysis.

Furthermore, the Court accepted justifications of an economic nature. Not until both the character of the infringement and the possible justification were established, was the question of demand limitation taken into consideration. The functioning of that test however was not to provide some additional arguments in a broad reconciliation assessment. Quite to the contrary, the rationale behind the

---

134 *Ambulanz Glöckner*, supra n. 16.

135 Ibid., para 66.

136 Ibid.

Court's requirement seems to be coarse-cut: It is hard to see how a Member State can justify distortions to the fundamental principles of the Treaty by reference to the importance of securing universal access to an indispensable service, if in fact not all citizens have access to it.

The observations presented above indicate that the demand limitation test introduces an additional factual requirement which may lead to a rejection of justifications which would otherwise, in the abstract, be legitimate. That will increase the impact of the Treaty principles, which may get a more absolute character. If it is proven that the regulatory efforts of the Member State fail to achieve their purpose, the likely result is that, the principles of free movement will prevail, and citizens' demand must then be served through the functioning of the market. That gives the refined doctrine of demand limitation, the character of being a right of access to SGEIs, protecting the interests of citizens. This understanding gains support from Article 36 in the Charter of Fundamental Rights in the European Union.

4.5.2.3 The Transposition

The *Ambulanz Glöckner* case concerned the classical situation of universal service. As the questions from the national court concerned Article 106.1 TFEU read in conjunction with Article 102 TFEU, it was quite easy for the ECJ to stick to the exception in Article 106.2 TFEU—which fitted the case.[137] But what if cases with similar characteristics are treated under the Treaty rules on the four freedoms?

As mentioned in Sect. 4.2, Article 106.2 TFEU should not be allowed to serve as an exception to the Treaty rules on the four freedoms. However, that does not exclude a more general application of a refined demand limitation doctrine, such as the one that appeared in *Ambulanz Glöckner*. If that doctrine is not in fact an application of the competition rules, but instead connotes a citizen's right of access to SGEIs, it should be of relevance in the assessment pursuant to the mandatory requirements doctrine as well. A universal approach is definitely supported by Article 14 TFEU. Seemingly, it is also confirmed in the practice of the ECJ.

In Sect. 4.2.4 above, we saw that in quite a few cases concerning national welfare systems, more specifically the right of cross-border hospital treatment, the Court did *in fact* recognise objectives of an economic nature as mandatory requirements, even though no references to Article 106.2 TFEU were made. Notably, that approach has been coupled with a demand limitation doctrine—still without any reference to Article 106 TFEU. While the Court, in *Smits & Peerbooms*, accepted that financial concerns could justify a requirement of prior authorisation for hospital treatment abroad, it also emphasised that the refusal of an application was dependent on the competent Member State being able to provide the *same or equally effective treatment without undue delay* from an

[137] Cf. Sect. 4.4.3 supra.

establishment with which the insured person's sickness insurance fund had contractual arrangements.[138] In other words, the barrier to free movement would not be justified unless patients demand was satisfied. That approach has later been repeated in various forms—the judgment in *Müller-Fauré* is especially illuminating. The Court repeated that the need to ensure the financial balance of the social security system, and the need of planning and rationalisation to avoid overcapacity, could justify a waiting list system and a requirement of prior authorisation for hospital treatment abroad.[139] However, the Court also clarified that if an authorisation was refused solely by referring to there being a waiting list, and without taking account of the medical situation of the patient, such considerations would seem to be *purely* economic, and hence unjustified.[140] This is a perfect example of how the fiction employed by the Court, while sometimes approving objectives of an economic character, also conserves the possibility of always retreating to the main rule—their illegitimacy.[141] In practical terms the implication seem to be that the assessment of necessity may be very strict. In support for such a strict approach, which may lead to a rejection of the justifications put forward by the Member State, the Court remarked that a waiting time which is 'too long or abnormal would be more likely *to restrict access* to balanced, high-quality hospital care.'[142] Therefore—if patients' access to a SGEI is not satisfied, the Court seems unwilling to accept that barriers to free movement can be justified, at least if the justification is economic in character.

The overriding character of the citizen's right to access was confirmed in *Watts*. Again the Court took as a starting point that, the need to ensure the financial balance of the social security system could constitute a legitimate consideration.[143] However, the strict necessity test entailed by the doctrinal disapproval of economic objectives, coupled with the demand limitation doctrine—understood as a citizens' right to access SGEIs—are the most interesting features of the case. Regarding the latter the Court stated that:

> … where the delay arising from such waiting lists appears to exceed in the individual case concerned, an acceptable period having regard to an objective medical assessment of all the circumstances of the situation and the clinical needs of the person concerned, the competent institution may not refuse the authorisation sought on the grounds of the existence of those waiting lists, an alleged distortion of the normal order of priorities linked to the relative urgency of the cases to be treated, the fact that the hospital treatment provided under the national system in question is free of charge, the duty to make available specific funds to reimburse the cost of treatment provided in another Member

---

138 *Smits & Peerbooms*, supra n. 51 para 103.

139 *Müller-Fauré*, supra n. 51, para 91.

140 Ibid., para 92.

141 Cf. Sect. 4.2.4.4 supra.

142 *Müller-Fauré*, supra n. 51 para 92 [emphasis added].

143 *Watts*, supra n. 51 paras 102–105.

State and/or a comparison between the cost of that treatment and that of equivalent treatment in the competent Member State.[144]

This finding implies that '[t]he fact that the cost of the hospital treatment envisaged in another Member State may be higher than it would have been had it been provided in a hospital covered by the national system in question, cannot in such a case be a legitimate ground for refusing authorisation.'[145] Equally where ancillary costs, such as travel and accommodation are covered where the treatment is provided in a national hospital, such costs must also be reimbursed if the patient travels abroad.[146] Thus, when there is an objective medical need, the citizens' right to free movement comes close to a trump.[147] If demand is not met, the Court seems unwilling to accept budgetary constraints, and will instead retreat to the traditional doctrine of the illegitimacy of economic objectives.

In this regard, the Court's approach seem to mirror the pattern of reasoning, developed pursuant to Article 106.2 TFEU—albeit transposed to the general level without mentioning the provision itself. Importantly though, behind all the subtlety, European citizens benefit from true welfare rights, stemming from the domestic sphere, being strengthened by EU Law, and gaining efficiency from the dynamics of the market.

4.6 Conclusions

Article 106 TFEU, read in conjunction with Article 14 TFEU, expresses a constitutional approval of the social importance of SGEIs. However, the application of the exception in Article 106.2 TFEU must also take sufficient regard to the fundamental principles of the market.

Section 4.2 concluded that the exception in Article 106.2 TFEU cannot be invoked by the Member States to justify barriers to free movement. That conclusion deviates from the nearly unanimous conventional view, but the latter is not supported by the practice of the ECJ, which, quite to the contrary, seems to confirm a narrow application of the exception.[148] There are two decisive arguments against turning Article 106.2 TFEU into a general clause:

(1) Article 106.2 TFEU should primarily be regarded as an exception directed at economic objectives, which the provision accepts as relevant *in principle*. With regard to the fundamental freedoms on the other hand, economic

144 Ibid., para 120, cf. also paras 129–131.

145 Ibid., para 73, cf. also paras 74, 64 and 148.

146 Ibid., paras 139–140.

147 In the same direction, however critical, Newdick 2006, p. 1657.

148 See Sect. 4.2.4 supra.

objectives are *in principle* not accepted as justifications for barriers to free movement.

(2) The reconciliation of interests pursuant to Article 106.2 TFEU deviates from the classical notion of proportionality which is inherent in the fundamental freedoms. While the classical proportionality test entails a 'least restrictive alternative' assessment, the reconciliation of interests pursuant to Article 106.2 TFEU is softer and more ad hoc based. Therefore, if Article 106.2 is turned into a general clause, and applied strictly on its own premises, it may compromise the fundamental freedoms.

Section 4.3 presented the main arguments against the competition-approach towards Member State regulation on SGEIs, based on the combined reading of Articles 106.1 TFEU and 102 TFEU. In most cases, the Treaty rules on the four freedoms appear to be the most efficient guarantor of the integration goal. From a practical point of view, it should also be emphasised that if a sector is so heavily regulated that Article 106.1 TFEU, read in conjunction with Article 102 TFEU may in principle be applicable, it is normally because concerns about solidarity or citizens' accessibility have been very prominent in the legislative process. Regarding the new notion of a 'social market economy' in the Lisbon Treaty, it would seem quite paradoxical if the functioning of Article 106.1 TFEU is to expose Member State regulation to the competition rules exactly in the quite limited number of situations where concerns about 'free competition' may seem to have the least bearing. Therefore, the fundamental freedoms should be considered to be the preferred legal basis to assess such cases, as they have the Member States as their natural subject. That in turn will also entail a more narrow use of the exception in Article 106.2 TFEU.

On the whole, the approach towards SGEIs that has been advocated in this contribution, reduces the immediate practical importance of Article 106 TFEU, but not its constitutional importance. From a constitutional perspective the essentials of the provision are its values, whose overarching character is confirmed by Article 14 TFEU, and also the Charter of Fundamental Rights in the European Union, Article 36. With regard to values, *generality* is a prerequisite to realising a European social model, an understanding which seems to influence the patterns of reasoning employed by the ECJ even in cases where Article 106.2 TFEU is not given immediate application. In Sect. 4.2.4, it was proven how the ECJ occasionally accepts economic justifications even with regard to the fundamental freedoms, if there is otherwise a *serious risk of undermining the financial balance* of a SGEI. In this regard, the approach of the ECJ mirrors the application of Article 106.2 TFEU, albeit somewhat modified. With regard to the nature of the fundamental principles involved, economic considerations are only accepted *in fact*, not in principle, which raise the bar and give the Court a strong grip over the assessment. In addition, 'the least restrictive' requirement is maintained, whereas the application of Article 106.2 TFEU on the other hand is not conditional on the viability of the entrusted company being actually threatened.

Section 4.5 proved how the ECJ, on a general level, seem to couple the acceptance of economic objectives with a demand limitation test. Whether Article 106.2 TFEU is applied or not, the invocation of economic aims as a justification for regulation on SGEIs will require that citizens' demand for an alleged indispensable service is met. In this respect, the approach of the Court seems to turn the traditional competition doctrine of *demand limitation* into a citizens' right of access to SGEIs. The transformation of the doctrine, and its transposition to the general level, is in line with the Commission's conception of the European Social Model:

> Europe is built on a set of values shared by all its societies, and combines the characteristics of democracy—human rights and institutions based on the rule of law—with those of an open economy underpinned by market forces, internal solidarity, and cohesion. These values include the access for all members of society to universal services or to services of general benefit, thus contributing to solidarity and equal treatment.[149]

It is noteworthy how the Commission in this statement links access to universal services with fundamental European values, mentioning them in the same breath as human rights. From an academic perspective one should always be a bit skeptical towards such formulations. Fine words may in the end be just that—words. In this case, however, the conception of the Commission seems to be confirmed by the ECJ, and is also supported by the Charter of Fundamental Rights, Article 36. If the Member States, in spite of regulation, are not able to satisfy demand for some allegedly important service, mandatory policy requirements cannot normally justify infringements to the fundamental freedoms. Either the Member State has to re-design its system, in order to make it function properly, or it must resort to the other mode of satisfying the general interest—that is, through the market. Conceived in this way, it can truly justify its association above with fundamental rights. According to Dworkin, a fundamental right in its true sense cannot be encroached upon by reference to public policy.[150] This is how the citizens' right to access universal service would seem to work in practice; if citizens' demand is not satisfied, the principles of the market will prevail.

Of course, the Court's approach may have consequences for national public policies. However, it does not interfere directly with those policies, but instead takes the priorities of the Member States as the starting point for the legal assessment, and is thus very principled. The idea of the European social model—emphasising that citizens must have access to universal services—legitimises that the citizen's right is intensively protected, on some occasions prevailing over the public concern of funding; hence giving the principles of free movement a character of being truly fundamental rights which benefit each and every individual European citizen.

---

[149] Commission Opinion. *Reinforcing Political Union and Preparing for Enlargement*, COM(96) 90, 28.08.1996 Section 8.

[150] Dworkin 1977, Chapter 7, esp. p. 192.

References

Alexy R (2002) A theory of constitutional rights. Oxford University Press, Oxford, pp 66–69
Azoulai L (2008) The court of justice and the social market economy: the emergence of an ideal and the conditions for its realization. CMLRev 45:133
Baquero Cruz J (2002) Between competition and free movement. Hart Publishing, Oxford, p 130
Baquero Cruz J (2005) Services of general interest and EC law. In: De Búrca G (ed) EU law and the welfare state. Oxford University Press, Oxford, p 16
Baquero Cruz J (2007) The state action doctrine. In: Amato G, Ehlerman C-D (eds) EC competition law: a critical assessment. Hart Publishing, Oxford, p 55
Barnard C (2008) Unravelling the services directive. CMLRev 45:323
Buendia Sierra JL (1999) Exclusive rights and state monopolies under EC law. Oxford University Press, Oxford p 292 et seq
Buendia Sierra JL (2007) An analysis of Article 86(2) EC. In: Rydelski MS (ed) The EC state aid regime: distortive effects of state aid on competition and trade. Cameron May, London, p 541
Davies G (2003) Nationality discrimination in the European internal market. Kluwer, The Hague p 93 et seq
Davies G (2009) Article 106 TFEU, the EC's economic approach to competition law, and the general interest. Eur Competition J 36:549
Deringer A (1964–1965) The interpretation of Article 90 (2) of the E.E.C. Treaty. CMLRev 2:129
Deringer A (1968) The competition law of the European economic community. Commerce Clearing House, New York, pp 246–247
Dworkin R (1977) Taking rights seriously. Harvard University Press, Cambridge (Chapter 7)
Flynn L (1999) Competition policy and public services in EC law after the Maastricht and Amsterdam Treaties. In: O'Keeffe D, Twomey P (eds) Legal issues of the Amsterdam Treaty. Hart Publishing, Oxford, p 185
Gyselen L (2003) Anti-competitive state measures under the EC Treaty: towards a substantive legality standard. ELRev Competition Law Checklist 55
Hancher L (1999) Community, state and market. In: Craig P, De Búrca G (eds) The evolution of EU law. Oxford University Press, Oxford, p 721
Hatzopoulos V (2000) Recent developments of the case law of the ECJ in the field of services. CMLRev 37:43
Hatzopoulos V (2002) Killing national health and insurance systems but healing patients? CMLRev 39:683
Hirsch G et al (2008) Competition law: European Community practice and procedure. Sweet & Maxwell, London, p 1293
Maillo J (2007) Services of general interest and EC competition law. In: Amato G, Ehlerman C-D (eds) EC competition law: a critical assessment. Hart, Oxford, p 591
Marenco G (1983) Public sector and Community law. CMLRev 20:495
Marenco G (1987) Competition between national economies and competition between businesses—a response to Judge Pescatore. Fordham Int Law J 10:420
Neergaard U (1998) Competition & Competences. DJØF Publishing, Copenhagen
Neergaard U (2007) Modernising Article 102 TFEU—with particular focus on public and otherwise privileged undertakings. Europarättslig Tidsskrift, p 54
Newdick C (2006) Citizenship, free movement and health care: cementing individual rights by corroding social solidarity. CMLRev 43:1645
Odudu O (2006) The boundaries of EC competition law. Oxford University Press, Oxford, p 31
Page AC (1982) Member States, public undertakings and Article 90. ELRev 7:19
Pappalardo A (1991) State measures and public undertakings: Article 90 of the EEC Treaty revisited. ECLRev 12:29
Prosser T (2005) The limits of competition law. Oxford University Press, Oxford, p 1
Reich N (1994) The 'November Revolution' of the European Court of Justice—Keck, Meng and Audi revisited. CMLRev 31:459

Roth WH (2002) The European Court of Justice's case law on freedom to provide services: Is Keck relevant? In: Andenas M, Roth WH (eds) Services and free movement in EU law. Oxford University Press, Oxford, p 1
Sauter W (2008) Services of general economic interest and universal service in EU law. ELRev 33:167
Scharpf FW (2002) The European social model. JCMS 40:645
Schiek D (2008) The European social model and the services directive. In: Neergaard U et al (eds) The services directive. DJØF Publishing, Copenhagen, p 25
Snell J (2005) Economic aims as justification for restrictions on free movement. In: Schrauwen A (ed) Rule of reason. Europa Law Publishing, Groningen, p 37
Soriano LM (2003) How proportionate should anti-competitive state intervention be. ELRev 28:112
Stergiou HM (2008) The increasing influence of primary EU law and EU public procurement law: must a concession to provide services of general economic interest be tendered? In: Van de Gronden J (ed) EU and WTO law on services: limits to the realization of general interest policies within the services markets. Kluwer Law International, Deventer
Szyszczak E (2007) The regulation of the state in competitive markets in the EU. Hart
Van der Woude M (1991) Article 90: competing for competence. ELRev 16:60
Wachsmann A, Berrod F (1994) Les criterès de justification des monopoles: un premier bilan après l'affaire Courbeau. Revue trimestrielle de droit européen 30:39
Whish R (2003) Competition law, 5th edn. LexisNexis, London

Chapter 5
The Definition of a 'Contract' Under Article 106 TFEU

Grith Skovgaard Ølykke

Abstract The fact that the public procurement Directives apply to contracts for the provision of SGEIs ensures transparency in the entrustment of SGEIs. This raises the question of whether the privileged rules of Article 106 TFEU apply alongside the specific public procurement rules, which are set out in secondary EU legislation. Looking at Article 106 TFEU through public procurement spectacles *Skovgaard Ølykke* identifies the determination of 'what is a contract' as a central issue for the application of the public procurement Directives. Where SGEIs are provided through in-house arrangements there will not be a 'contract' and where an SGEI is entrusted through a legislative act, this will also not satisfy the requirements of a 'contract'. A different set of problems arise where the entrustment of a SGEI take place by a service concession. The procurement Directives, subject service concessions to a special regime and service concessions are exempted from the Directives but under tight conditions. This raises the question as to whether Article 106(2) TFEU could be applied. Although this question has been debated in the academic literature, it has not been explicitly applied in litigation before the ECJ. However, *Skovgaard Ølykke* argues that in recent cases Article 106(2) TFEU could be the basis for the rulings, creating a new approach to contracts where SGEI are provided even where the *Teckal* criteria (see ECJ, Case C-84/03 *Commission* v. *Spain* [2005] *ECR* I-139, para 39; cf. ECJ, Case C-480/06 *Commission* v. *Germany* [2009] *ECR* I-4747) are not fulfilled. If this is the outcome of the case law, it gives a renewed role for Article 106(2) TFEU at a time when many commentators are questioning its continued existence in the TFEU.

Assistant Professor, Law Department, Copenhagen Business School, Frederiksberg, Denmark.

G. S. Ølykke (✉)
Juridisk Institut, Howitzvej 13, 3.sal, 2000 Frederiksberg, Denmark
e-mail: goe.jur@cbs.dk

E. Szyszczak et al. (eds.), *Developments in Services of General Interest*,
Legal Issues of Services of General Interest, DOI: 10.1007/978-90-6704-734-0_5,

Contents

5.1 Introduction

There is a sense of refuge when exclusive rights, Services of General Economic Interest (SGEIs) and Public Service Obligations (PSOs)/Universal Service Obligations (USOs) are mentioned; Member States have a *right* to grant, define, impose, entrust and assign.[1] It could be questioned whether this *right* is an unlimited carte blanche? Careful suggestions have been made that the new legislative power conferred on the Council and the Parliament in the second sentence of Article 14 of the Treaty of the Functioning of the European Union (TFEU)[2] could be used to provide a clear and transparent framework for the selection of undertakings entrusted with a Service of General Economic Interest (SGEIs).[3] However, the Commission has already held that the public procurement directives also apply for contracts for the provision of SGEIs in order to ensure transparency in the entrustment of SGEIs.[4]

In this contribution, it will be examined whether or not the privileges described in Article 106 TFEU (ex Article 86 TEC) are covered by the rules on public

[1] CFI, Case T-442/03 *SIC* [2008] *ECR* II-1161, para 145, where the CFI states that neither the wording of Article 86(2) EC (now Article 106(2) TFEU) nor case law requires a tendering procedure for the entrustment of a SGEI. See also Schnelle 2002, p. 202.

[2] *OJ* 2008 C 115/1.

[3] Sauter and Schepel 2009, p. 179.

[4] COM(2003) 270 final *Green paper on Services of General Interest*, para 81, COM(2004) 374 final, *White Paper on Services of General Interest*, at 15–16, and see also COM(2007) 725 final, *Services of general interest, including social services of general interest: a new European commitment*, at 4.

procurement, i.e., must the public procurement directives[5] or the public procurement specific interpretation of the rules of the Treaties (Treaty) be respected when exclusive rights are granted or the provision a Services of General Economic Interest (SGEI) is 'entrusted'?

Since the perspective in this book is on SGEIs, it is natural to take the starting point in what is now Article 106 TFEU (ex Article 86 TEC) and to put on the public procurement 'spectacles'. This contribution will look into one of the basic requirements for the public procurement directives to apply, namely the existence of a 'contract'.[6] Generally, nothing prevents public authorities from using their own resources to provide the various functions and services they are required to provide.[7] Therefore, an ample amount of case law exists concerning whether or not a specific relation between the contracting authority and a separate legal person providing, e.g., services, constitutes a 'contract'.

One line of that case law is particularly developed, namely the case law concerning so-called in-house providing, where the ECJ has taken a doctrinal approach and developed the *Teckal* criteria.[8] In order to fulfil the *Teckal* criteria, firstly, the contracting authority must exercise control over the provider which is similar to the control it exercises over its own departments; and, secondly, the provider must provide the essential part of its output to the controlling public authority. The case law of the ECJ has shown that the control, as well as the 'essential part of output', can be jointly held by several public authorities.[9] When the *Teckal* criteria are fulfilled, the relationship between the contracting authority and the provider is considered to be 'in-house provision', i.e., no 'contract' exists, thereby rendering the conduct of a public procurement procedure dispensable.[10]

A second line of that case law concerns imposition of obligations by a legislative act, and this line of case law will be analysed below. Moreover, the possible development of an exemption from the rules on public procurement concerning cooperation between public authorities for provision of public service tasks will be examined.

---

[5] Directive 2004/18/EC of the European Parliament and of the Council of 31 March 2004 on the coordination of procedures for the award of public works contracts, public supply contracts and public service contracts (henceforth: the 'Public Sector Directive'), *OJ* 2004 L 134/114 and Directive 2004/17/EC of the European Parliament and of the Council of 31 March 2004 coordinating the procurement procedures of entities operating in the water, energy, transport, and postal services sectors (henceforth: the 'Utilities Directive'), *OJ* 2004 L 134/1. Together the two directives are denominated the 'public procurement directives'.

[6] For a similar approach, see Drijber and Stergiou 2009 at 825–829; Sauter 2008 at 190, finds that the rules on public procurement generally apply to SGEIs, where third parties are chosen as providers (i.e., the provision is not in-house).

[7] ECJ, Case C-26/03 *Stadt Halle* [2005] *ECR* I-1, para 48.

[8] ECJ, Case C-107/98 *Teckal* [1999] *ECR* I-8121, paras 49–50.

[9] ECJ, Case C-340/04 *Carbotermo* [2006] *ECR* I-4137, paras 37 and 70.

[10] For the evolution of the in-house case law, see Caranta 2010, p. 13.

This contribution consists of three main parts: firstly, Article 106 TFEU (ex Article 86 TEC) is contemplated from a public procurement perspective, to identify possible 'contracts' (Sect. 5.2); secondly, Article 106(2) TFEU [ex Article 86(2) TEC] is considered as an exemption to the rules on public procurement (Sect. 5.3); and, lastly, conclusions are made (Sect. 5.4).

5.2 Article 106 TFEU (ex Article 86 TEC) and 'Contracts' in the Sense of the Public Procurement Directives

The definition of a 'contract' in the public procurement directives states[11]:

> "Public contracts" are contracts for pecuniary interest concluded in writing between one or more economic operators and one or more contracting authorities, and having as their object the execution of works, the supply of products or the provision of services within the meaning of this Directive.

In order for award of contracts to be within the scope of the public procurement directives, the contract must fulfil these criteria and the contract must have a value above the thresholds stipulated in the directives. However, the latter is less important, as the case law of the Court of Justice of the European Communities (ECJ) has shown that even contracts with a value below the thresholds,[12] and sometimes even contracts explicitly exempted from the public procurement directives,[13] cannot just be awarded directly to a preferred provider; the rules of the Treaties must be respected. In a public procurement context, the Treaties require, inter alia, transparency (some sort of publication) and non-discrimination on grounds of nationality.[14] Only where there is no cross-border interest in the award of the contract can 'contracts' outside the scope of the public procurement directives be directly awarded to a preferred contractor (subject to possible requirements under national public procurement regimes).[15] Henceforth, reference is made to the rules on public procurement to imply both sets of rules. There are of course exemptions to the public procurement directives, but it is outside the scope of this contribution to consider these exemptions.[16]

---

[11] Article 1(2)(a) of the Public Sector Directive and the parallel provision is Article 1(2)(a) of the Utilities Directive, which, however, does not define 'public contracts', but rather 'supply, works, and service contracts'.

[12] For example, ECJ, Case C-59/00 *Vestergaard* [2001] *ECR* I-9505.

[13] For example, ECJ, Case C-324/98 *Telaustria* [2000] *ECR* I-10745.

[14] See Commission Interpretative Communication on the Community law applicable to contract awards not or not fully subject to the provisions of the Public Procurement Directives, *OJ* 2006 C 179/2. Cf., Brown 2007, p. 1.

[15] Cf., Drijber and Stergiou 2009, pp. 811–815.

[16] Cf., Trepte 2007, pp. 239–256.

5.2.1 'Contracts' in Article 106(1) TFEU [ex Article 86(1) EC]

Article 106(1) TFEU [ex Article 86(1) EC] speaks, inter alia, of undertakings which have been granted special or exclusive rights.[17] Case law on Article 106(1) TFEU [ex Article 86(1) EC] has revealed that the 'measures' mentioned in that provision could be the special or exclusive rights themselves; i.e., also the granting of a new special or exclusive right, to a provider which has not previously held a special or an exclusive right constitutes a 'measure'.[18] Henceforth, only exclusive rights will be dealt with, as most case law deals with exclusive rights, but in principle the same applies for special rights. The Treaties do not contain any rules regarding the granting of exclusive rights. Nevertheless, it could be argued that Article 106(1) TFEU's [ex Article 86(1) TEC] requirement that all measures made in relation to undertakings which have been granted exclusive rights, must be compatible with the Treaties, include that the exclusive right must be granted in accordance with the rules on public procurement.[19] Article 3 of the Public Sector Directive mentions the granting of exclusive rights, but makes no reference as to how such rights should be granted.

The reason why the granting of exclusive rights is not explicitly regulated in the public procurement directives could be explained by the circumstance that exclusive rights are typically granted for the following two purposes: firstly, for compensation for a PSO (or USO) requiring uniform tariffs for the entire territory of the Member State (the exclusive right permits cross-subsidisation)[20]; or, secondly, as the basis of a concession (see further on service concessions Sect. 5.2.2.2 infra).[21] In both situations the exclusive right could be categorised as a type of pecuniary interest for the services to be carried out. This is probably where the

[17] Due to Article 345 TFEU (ex Article 295 TEC), public undertakings will not be considered specifically. However, it should be mentioned that contracts directly awarded (without a public procurement procedure) to public undertakings will often be argued to be in-house provision (see further Sect. 5.1 supra).

[18] Cf., Buendia Sierra 1999, pp. 135 and 138–139.

[19] See Joined Opinion of Advocate General Bot on 17 December 2009 concerning Cases C-203/08 (*Betfair*) and C-258/08 (*Ladbrokes*), para 154. From a different but obvious perspective, see Buendia Sierra 1999, p. 144, who argues that Article 86(1) TEC [now Article 106(1) TFEU] could be applied in conjunction with secondary legislation, e.g., the public procurement directives.

[20] As was seemingly the case in C-320/91 *Corbeau* [1993] *ECR* I-2533, paras 3 and 15 read in conjunction.

[21] For example, C-209/98 *Sydhavnens Sten &* Grus [2000] *ECR* I-3743, para 79, and the recent judgments in ECJ. Cases C-203/08 (Betfair), 3 June 2010, nyr, paras 46–47 and C-64/08 (Engelmann), 9 September 2010, nyr, paras 52–53, where the ECJ argues that the transparency obligations applicable to the award of service concessions should also apply to licensing systems with only one operator, inter alia, because the effect of such a licensing system is the same as the effect of a service concession. However, see also Drijber and Stergiou 2009, pp. 825–826, taking the standpoint that if the licensing system in question is comparable to the award of an exclusive right, no requirement to tender exists.

definition of a 'contract' in the public procurement Directives is not fulfilled[22]: an exclusive right is typically not granted in combination with a pecuniary interest; instead it is the pecuniary interest.

5.2.2 *'Contracts' in Article 106(2) TFEU*

Two different types of 'contracts' could be envisaged under Article 106(2) TFEU [ex Article 86(2) TEC]: firstly, the situation where a provider is 'entrusted' with the provision of a SGEI; and, secondly, the situation where particular tasks are 'assigned'.[23] Henceforth the 'particular tasks assigned' will be considered to be the same as PSOs (in the sense that PSOs are requirements from Member States regarding, inter alia, the scope, price or quality of a service).[24] This perception connects Article 106(2) TFEU [ex Article 86(2) TEC] and the *Altmark* test.[25]

Sauter proposes that SGEIs should be defined narrowly, as services, where the imposing of PSOs is necessary[26]:

> It appears consistent with the EU law principle of proportionality to limit the application of the SGEI concept to those cases where it is clear in advance that particular restrictions in relation to EU law obligations concerning free movement, competition, state aid and/or public procurement will be necessary (and therefore proportional) to enable the undertaking(s) charged with SGEI to provide those services, in the sense that they could not otherwise be provided to the requisite standard. Where this is not the case, reserving particular services to specific undertakings would simply not be necessary—and should therefore fail the proportionality standard that is explicitly included in Art. 86(2) EC.

It is clear from the wording of Article 106(2) TFEU [ex Article 86(2) TEC] that only providers of SGEIs to which PSOs have been 'assigned' could be exempted from the rules of the Treaties, as it is the importance of the fulfilment of the PSO which the provision protects. Therefore, application of Article 106(2) TFEU

---

22 For the same conclusion based on different arguments, see Drijber and Stergiou 2009, pp. 825–828.

23 Due to Article 345 TFEU (ex Article 295 EC), State monopolies of a commercial character will not be considered, however.

24 This perception is supported by COM(2003) 270 final, supra n. 4, para 17, COM(2004) 374 final, supra n. 4, 6, and Annex I at p. 22. The Commission also refers to 'the particular tasks of general interest' assigned to the providers of SGEIs; see COM(2007) 725 final, supra n. 4, at 6. Cf., Sauter 2008, p. 177, who argues that USOs is the main substantive content of SGEIs, but nevertheless, at 175 and 184, argues that PSOs is the core of SGEIs. PSO has been chosen over USO, because it appears the PSO is wider in scope than USO (where territorial coverage is an essential element, see Sauter 2008, pp. 176–177), and since PSO [in a wide sense, also covering USOs, it is submitted; cf., COM(2007) 725 final, at 6] is central for compensation according to the *Altmark* test, infra n. 25.

25 ECJ, C-280/00, *Altmark* [2003] *ECR* I-7747, paras 89–93.

26 Sauter 2008, p. 179. For a seemingly different opinion, see Buendia Sierra 2007, 593 at 627–630.

[ex Article 86(2) TEC] is only relevant to the situations mentioned by Sauter in the recited paragraph, regardless of the more specific definition of SGEIs.

From the perspective of the rules on public procurement, even if the Member States have a right to define SGEIs (political discretion/choice), does that imply that they can also (freely) decide to whom they 'entrust' the provision of SGEIs and to whom they 'assign' PSOs? The answer to this leads to a circular reasoning: a service can only be a SGEI, if it has been 'entrusted' to a specific undertaking but in order to be a SGEI, a PSO must be 'assigned' leading to the result that PSOs related to the specific SGEI can only be 'assigned' to the undertaking 'entrusted' with the provision of this specific SGEI.[27]

Another interpretation could be that PSOs could be 'assigned' to different providers, but Article 106(2) TEFU [ex Article 86(2) TEC] would only make exemption for providers which were also 'entrusted' with the provision of a SGEI. However, such an interpretation would contradict the finding above, i.e., it is the PSO which is protected.

An alternative and more desirable interpretation is that even though the wording of the provision mentions both 'entrustment' and 'assignment' these two seemingly separate formal requirements could be fulfilled contemporarily; i.e., the 'entrustment' of a SGEI implies the 'assignment' of a PSO or vice versa. This interpretation could explain case law where focus on the PSO, rather than on the 'entrustment' of the SGEI,[28] and will be the point of departure for the analysis below.[29] An examination of case law, on the basis of the criterion that the

---

[27] This seems to have been the case in C-159/94 *Commission* v. *France* [1997] *ECR* I-5815, para 66, where, however, the award of the concession was not an issue.

[28] See, for example, ECJ, Case C-127/73 *SABAM* [1974] *ECR* 313, paras 22–23, where the assignment of (particular) task(s) seems important to the ECJ; ECJ, Case C-258/78 *L.C. Nungesser* [1982] *ECR* 2015, para 9, and ECJ, Case C-66/86 *Ahmed Saeed* [1989] *ECR* 803, para 55; ECJ, Case C-320/91 *Corbeau* [1993] *ECR* I-2533, para 15, where the ECJ only mentions 'entrustment', but nevertheless elaborates on the PSO involved (the ECJ is emphasising the content of the PSOs in a manner suggesting that the SGEI is the PSO); ECJ, Case C-159/94 *Commission* v. *France* [1997] *ECR* I-5815, where paras 72–89 contain a thorough discussion of which PSOs were imposed on the provider of the SGEI; ECJ, Case C-266/96 *Corsica Ferries* [1998] *ECR* I-3949, para 45 (the reference to safety in port waters); ECJ, Joined Cases C-147 and 148/97 *Deutsche Post* [2000] *ECR* I-825, paras 43–45; ECJ, Case C-53/00 *Ferring* [2001] *ECR* I-9067, paras 7, 31 and 32; ECJ, Case 340/99 *TNT Traco* [2001] *ECR* I-4109, para 53; ECJ, Case C-457/99 *Ambulanz Glöckner* [2001] *ECR* I-8089, para 55 and ECJ, Joined Cases C-83, 93 and 94/01P *La Poste* [2003] *ECR* I-6993, para 34; CFI, Case T-289/03 *BUPA* [2008] *ECR* II-81, paras 161–162, where the CFI accepts the argument of the parties that a SGEI is the same as a PSO. Moreover, see Community framework for State aid in the form of public service compensation, *OJ* 2005 C 297/4, para 12, where the first requirement for the act entrusting a provider with the provision of a SGEI is '(a) the precise nature and duration of public service obligations'.

[29] Along the same lines, see Szyszczak 2007, p. 211, Sauter and Schepel 2009, p. 168, and 'Services of General Economic Interest—Opinion Prepared by the State Aid Group of EAGCP' (2006), available at http://ec.europa.eu/competition/state_aid/studies_reports/studies_reports.html#studies, 2 and 3.

'entrustment' of a SGEI/PSO should be at least peripherally assessed by the ECJ, otherwise the judgment was left out, discloses that the Member States seem to prefer 'entrustment' by legislation,[30] or by concession[31]; both of these forms of 'entrustment' have been accepted by the ECJ.[32]

It is indisputable that the SGEI/PSO must be 'entrusted' by an act of public authority[33]; i.e., the public authority must act in its exercise of public authority function.[34] Moreover, the PSO must be linked to the subject-matter of the SGEI and should contribute to satisfying that interest.[35] The requirement that a SGEI/PSO should be 'entrusted', could therefore be seen as a means, firstly, to avoid circumvention,[36] i.e., not all services qualify for exemption under Article 106(2) [ex Article 86(2) TEC]—the SGEI/PSO must pursue specific ends, i.e., contribute

[30] For examples of 'entrustment' by legislation, see, e.g., ECJ, Case C-41/90 *Höfner* [1991] *ECR* I-1979, para 24; ECJ, Case C-157/94 *Commission* v. *the Netherlands* [1997] *ECR* I-5699, para 45; ECJ, Joined Cases C-147-148/97 *Deutsche Post* [2000] *ECR* I-825, para 45; ECJ, Case C-340/99 *TNT Traco* [2001] *ECR* I-4109, para 3 and ECJ, Case C-220/06 *Correos* [2007] *ECR* I-12175, para 79.

[31] For examples of 'entrustment' by concession, see ECJ, Case C-393/92 *Almelo* [1994] *ECR* I-1477, para 31, where the concession was granted by a measure of public law; ECJ, Case C-159/94 *Commission* v. *France* [1997] *ECR* I-5815, para 66, and implicitly ECJ, C-209/98 *Sydhavnens Sten & Grus* [2000] *ECR* I-3743, paras 17, 71 and 79 read in conjunction.

[32] See ECJ, Case C-30/87 *Bodson* [1988] *ECR* I-2479, para 18 where the concessions at issue were described as '… *contracts … concluded between communes acting in their capacity as public authorities* and undertakings entrusted with the operation of a public service…' [emphasis added].

[33] ECJ, Case C-127/73 *SABAM* [1974] *ECR* 51, para 20; ECJ, Case C-172/80 *Züchner* [1981] *ECR* 2021, para 7 and ECJ, Case C-66/86 *Ahmed Saeed* [1989] *ECR* I-803, para 55. However, see the Opinion of Advocate General Léger on 10 July 2001 concerning ECJ, Case C-309/99 *Wouters*, para 160, for the point that the ECJ has mitigated the requirement relating to the existence of a formal act of the public authorities.

[34] See also Buendia Sierra 2007, p. 630, who seems to attribute significant weight to the formal public/private law distinction: '…, if a public entity enters into a contract governed by private law with an undertaking for the purpose of carrying out of an economic activity it is not, by definition, acting in the exercise of public authority *functions*.' It is submitted that a distinction needs to be made between the decision to provide a specific SGEI/PSO, the choice of in-house/ex-house and the actual 'entrustment' of a SGEI/PSO (by legislative act/concession) to a third party. At least the first mentioned is an act of public authority, since it is a political choice of what services to provide. It can also be argued that the 'entrustment' of a SGEI/PSO by legislative act is exercise of public authority. See Sect. 5.3 infra on cooperation between public authorities to ensure the provision of public services which they are obliged ('entrusted') to provide by legislation.

[35] ECJ, Case C-159/94 *Commission* v. *France* [1997] *ECR* I-5815, para 68.

[36] Cf., Buendia Sierra 2007, p. 629.

to acknowledged national policies[37]; and, secondly, to distinguish SGEIs/PSOs from sector regulation.[38]

5.2.2.1 'Entrustment'/'Assignment' by Legislative Act

'Entrustment' by legislation is only relevant where the SGEI sector has not been liberalised at EU level, as sector regulation provides for possible ways of 'entrusting' the provision of SGEIs/PSOs, e.g., the rules on public procurement.[39]

It is not obvious that the 'entrustment' of the provision of a SGEI/PSO by a legislative act is a 'contract' in the sense of the rules on public procurement, as it seemingly does not live up to the basic requirement of the 'contract' being entered into by the parties (a contracting authority and a third party). Three recent cases decided in the context of claims regarding the rules on public procurement are of relevance here.

In *Asemfo*, it appears that the absence of 'contracts' due to the relevant legislative set-up was of major importance.[40] Briefly stated, in *Asemfo* the legal framework applicable to the public undertaking Transformación Agraria SA (Tragsa) stipulated that Tragsa was required to carry out various services for the public authorities at their request, within the timeframe stipulated by the public authority and at a tariff fixed by regulation. Advocate General Geelhoed concluded that the statutory regime governing a public undertaking like Tragsa would have to be stipulated to comply with the case law on in-house provision.[41] The ECJ seems to argue two ways: firstly, the relationship between Tragsa and the public authorities was not contractual[42]; and, secondly, the criteria for in-house provision were fulfilled, with regard to the public authorities holding shares in Tragsa.[43] Regarding the first argument, the ECJ stated[44]:

[37] Sauter 2008, p. 184, links the 'entrustment' requirement to the proportionality test (necessity test) in Article 106(2) TFEU [ex Article 86(2) TEC].

[38] ECJ, Case C-7/82 *GVL* v. *Commission* [1983] *ECR* 483, para 32. Seemingly contrary, see the CFI's ruling in Case T-289/03 *BUPA* [2008] *ECR* II-81, para 182 in conjunction with para 196, where the provision of private medical insurance was regulated, but seemingly no provider was required to supply the insurances. The CFI defined the legislation as an 'act of public authority', but denied that the legislation was a regulation or an authorisation of the providers of private medical insurances; see para 182.

[39] For examples, see Drijber and Stergiou 2009, p. 842–843.

[40] ECJ, Case C-295/05 *Asemfo* [2007] *ECR* I-2999, para 60.

[41] Opinion of Advocate General Geelhoed on 28 September 2006 concerning C-295/05 (*Asemfo*), para 97.

[42] *Asemfo*, paras 54 and 60.

[43] *Asemfo*, paras 57–58 and 61 in conjunction with paras 63–64, where the ECJ, however, did not distinguish between services carried out for shareholders and non-shareholders.

[44] *Asemfo*, para 54.

> It must be observed that, if, which it is for the referring court to establish, Tragsa has no choice, either as to the acceptance of a demand made by the competent authorities in question, or as to the tariff for its services, the requirement for the application of the directives concerned relating to the existence of a contract is not met.

Seemingly, where the legislative regime applicable requires the provider to carry out the orders given by (specified) public authorities, at a tariff fixed by the public authorities, the relationship is not a 'contract' in the sense of the rules on public procurement. It should be noted that the national legislation in question explicitly stated that the relationship between Tragsa and the public authorities should be considered instrumental and not contractual.[45]

Approximately 8 months later, the ECJ elaborated on the above in *Correos*.[46] In *Correos*, Spain claimed that a Cooperation Agreement directly awarded to the universal postal service provider (Correos) by a ministry was not a 'contract', because Correos was an instrument of the Spanish State and was unable to refuse to enter into the Cooperation Agreement[47]; hereby Spain was implicitly referring to *Asemfo*. The ECJ underlined that the ruling in *Asemfo* was confined to the specific circumstances of that case,[48] and it qualified (or generalised) the findings in *Asemfo* to the following[49]:

> It is only if the agreement between Correos and the Ministerio were in actual fact a *unilateral administrative measure solely creating obligations for Correos—and as such a measure departing significantly from the normal conditions of a commercial offer made by that company* [emphasis added], a matter which is for the [national court] to establish—that it would have to be held that there is no contract and that, consequently, [the public procurement directive] could not apply.
>
> In the course of that examination, the [national court] will have to consider, in particular, *whether Correos is able to negotiate with the Ministerio, the actual content of the services it has to provide and the tariffs to be applied to those services and whether* [emphasis added], as regards non-reserved services, *the company can free itself from obligations arising under the Cooperation Agreement, by giving notice as provided for in that agreement* [emphasis added].

It should be noted that in *Correos*, an agreement was made, contrary to what was the case in *Asemfo*. In the recited paragraphs, the ECJ stated that the agreement would only cease to be a 'contract' if it were a 'unilateral administrative measure'; in other words it considered when an agreement is a 'legislative act' rather than a 'contract'. Thus, the attributes mentioned in the recited paragraphs are characteristic for legislative acts, which is the kind of 'entrustment' considered in this section. Where 'entrustment' is made by a legislative act, it will therefore normally not be a contract. The approach taken by the ECJ in *Correos* seem to indicate that a case-by-case assessment will be adopted by the ECJ.

---

45 *Asemfo*, para 51.

46 ECJ, Case C-220/06 *Correos* [2007] *ECR* I-12175.

47 *Correos*, para 49.

48 *Correos*, para 52.

49 *Correos*, para 54.

On the same day as *Correos* was decided by the First Chamber of the ECJ, *Commission* v. *Ireland* was decided by the Grand Chamber.[50] The set-up in the national legislation was perhaps unusual, in the way that the health board was seemingly responsible for the provision of ambulance services (and could have provided them itself), whereas the local authority concerned could choose to provide the services. Hence, the health board contributed economically to the provision of the ambulance services provided by the local authority.[51] It was undisputed that no written contract was made between the parties (only a draft agreement concerning the health board's financial contributions existed).[52] The ECJ found that[53]:

> … it is conceivable that DCC [the local authority] provides such services to the public in the exercise of its own powers derived directly from statute, and applying its own funds, although it is paid a contribution by the Authority for that purpose, covering part of the costs of those services.

The ECJ declared that under these circumstances, the Commission had not lifted the burden of proof required to establish that a public contract had been awarded.[54] In this way, the ECJ rejected the Commission's claim that where no contract exists in writing, the public procurement specific interpretation of the Treaty should be applied, a claim which had been accepted by the Advocate General.[55] The ECJ instead focussed on the existence of a 'contract' and found that a 'contract' does not exist where the service is provided under statutory powers vested on the provider, even though a contracting authority (public authority) contributes to the coverage of the costs of providing the services.

The examined case law shows a tendency towards formality in the assessment, rendering 'entrustment' by a national legislative act outside the scope of the rules on public procurement, where the ECJ usually prefers effects based assessments; i.e., are the effects of the legislative set-up similar to those of a contractual relation?[56] However, this conclusion is not clear-cut as *Correos* shows signs of a case-by-case assessment; the ECJ may wish to assess whether the legislative act has a character of a contract, in the sense of the rules on public procurement. In this context, it should be noted that when remuneration or compensation for the provision of PSOs is taking place (i.e., a pecuniary interest is at stake), the transaction may be subject to the rules on State aid. A special regime has emerged on

---

[50] ECJ, Case C-532/03 *Commission* v. *Ireland* [2007] *ECR* I-11353.

[51] *Commission* v. *Ireland*, paras 5–6.

[52] *Commission* v. *Ireland*, para 15.

[53] *Commission* v. *Ireland*, para 35.

[54] *Commission* v. *Ireland*, para 36.

[55] *Commission* v. *Ireland*, para 15 and opinion of Advocate General Stix-Hackl on 14 September 2006 concerning C-532/03 (*Commission* v. *Ireland*).

[56] Cf., Opinion of Advocate General Geelhoed on 28 September 2006 concerning C-295/05 (*Asemfo*), para 58.

assessment of compensation for PSOs, namely the so-called *Altmark* test.[57] Where compensation is paid according to the accumulative conditions in the *Altmark* test, the notification requirement for State aid does not apply.[58] Case law from the ECJ has shown that the *Altmark* test should be taken literally and is not easily fulfilled.[59] It is submitted that, probably, the simplest way of complying with the *Altmark* test would be by awarding the SGEI/PSO through public procurement.[60] Where (part of) the pecuniary interest is an exclusive right, Article 106(1) TFEU [ex Article 86(1) TEC] and its necessity (proportionality) assessment may apply in conjunction with other Articles of the Treaties.

5.2.2.2 'Entrustment'/'Assignment' by Concession

Whereas 'entrustment' by legislation does not obviously exhibit the characteristics needed for the 'act of public authority' to resemble a 'contract' in the sense of the rules on public procurement, such characteristics are present in the case of 'entrustment' by service concession.[61] Where the service concession is remunerated by an exclusive right, the public procurement procedure would probably pivot around the quality of the services in combination with extra financing possibly needed.[62]

Since service concessions have a special status in the public procurement regime, a few comments should be made on SGEIs/PSOs and service concessions. Awards of service concessions are exempted from the public procurement directives,[63] but such exemption requires a specific assessment of whether or not the contract in question is indeed a service concession. Under the rules on public procurement, the essential characteristics of a service concession are that the contract confers a risk on the provider and that the remuneration (at least partially) is paid by users of the service.[64] It could be argued that the transfer of risk in concessions to provide a SGEI/PSO would in many cases be negligible,[65] due to the presumed inelastic demand for such services, coupled with the exemption from the rules of the Treaties, where this is necessary in order to ensure that the

[57] C-280/00 *Altmark* [2003] *ECR* I-7747, paras 89–93.

[58] Article 108(3) TFEU [ex Article 88(3) TEC]. For critique, see, e.g., Nicolaides 2003, p. 561.

[59] ECJ, Joined Cases C-34-38/01 *Enirisorse* [2003] *ECR* I-14243, paras 31–40 and ECJ, Case C-451/03 *ADC Servizi* [2006] *ECR* I-2941, paras 59–68.

[60] See also Müller 2009, p. 40.

[61] On the concept of a 'concession', see, e.g., Neergaard 2005, p. 141.

[62] See also supra n. 21 on licensing schemes, exclusive rights and service concessions.

[63] Article 17 of the Public Sector Directive, and Article 18 of the Public Utilities Directive.

[64] See Neergaard 2005, p. 176; Trepte 2007, pp. 205–206, and for a discussion of recent case law on the concept of a concession, see Kotsonis 2010.

[65] For a discussion of the necessary element of risk, see Kotsonis 2010.

SGEI/PSO can be provided under economically acceptable conditions.[66] However, the purpose of this contribution is not to discuss the concept of a concession, so it will merely be emphasised that where the 'entrustment' is made by concession (or contract, which, as argued, is possibly more likely) the public authority entrusting the SGEI/PSO must adhere to the rules on public procurement.[67]

5.3 Article 106(2) TFEU [ex Article 86(2) TEC] as an Exemption from the Rules on Public Procurement

Even though the possibility of exemption from the rules on public procurement on the basis of Article 106(2) TFEU [ex Article 86(2) TEC] has seemingly not been extensively debated in academic literature,[68] the argument that Article 106(2) TFEU (then Article 86(2) TEC) should provide an exemption from the rules on public procurement has from time to time found its way into public procurement proceedings.[69] So far, the ECJ has explicitly considered arguments based on Article 106(2) TFEU in a public procurement context. In Commission v. Germany, paras 126–129, the argument based on Article 106(2) TFEU was rightly rejected due to obvious absence of necessity. Nevertheless, it is submitted that Article 106(2) TFEU could be the implicit basis on which recent case law in the field of public procurement rests.

The first case of interest is *Commission* v. *Spain* concerning Spanish public procurement law which provided for an exemption from the rules on public procurement for all inter-administrative agreements; that is, cooperation agreements between public authorities and public bodies.[70] The ECJ held that the *Teckal* criteria had to be applied to inter-administrative agreements (otherwise) covered by the rules on public procurement.[71]

---

66 ECJ, Case C-320/91 *Corbeau* [1993] *ECR* I-2533, para 16 read in conjunction with para 19; ECJ, Case C-209/98 *Sydhavnens Sten & Grus* [2000] *ECR* I-3743, para 77, and ECJ, Case C-475/99 *Ambulanz Glöckner* [2001] *ECR* I-8089, para 57.

67 It could be mentioned that in *Sydhavnens Sten & Grus*, the contracting authority advertised the 'contract' in a press release to attract interested business partners (concessionaires), see ECJ, Case C-209/98 *Sydhavnens Sten & Grus* [2000] *ECR* I-3743, para 24, even though the circumstances of the case took place prior to ECJ, Case C-324/98 *Telaustria* [2000] *ECR* I-10745, where the ECJ underlined the transparency obligations derived from the EC Treaty (now EU and EFU Treaties); see para 62.

68 However, see Sauter 2008, p. 178; Stergiou 2008, pp. 178–180, and Drijber and Stergiou 2009, pp. 833–834.

69 For recent examples, see, for example, ECJ, Case C-532/03 *Commission* v. *Italy* [2007] *ECR* I-11353, para 26 and ECJ, Case C-480/06 *Commission* v. *Germany* [2009] I-nyr, para 28.

70 ECJ, Case C-84/03 *Commission* v. *Spain* [2005] *ECR* I-139, para 9.

71 *Commission* v. *Spain*, paras 39–40.

The second case of interest is *Commission* v. *Germany* concerning disposal of waste, and the construction of an incineration plant to fulfil this task.[72] The Commission's action, and therefore the judgment, was explicitly limited to the contract between the city of Hamburg and four Landkreise (administrative districts), and did therefore not concern possible 'contracts' between the city of Hamburg and a private party for the construction and operation of the incineration plant.[73] In order for the plant to function on favourable economic conditions (presumably for the operator of the plant, but this is not specified), the city of Hamburg contracted with four Landkreise (administrative districts) to ensure inflow of the optimal amounts of waste for the plants.[74] In the contracts between the city of Hamburg and the four Landkreise, the city of Hamburg reserved a part of the new incineration plant's capacity to the Landkreise, in return for remuneration of operating costs (transferred directly to the operator of the plant) and for access to unused landfill areas in the four Landkreise. The Commission claimed that the contract should have been tendered.

The ECJ initially ruled out the use of the *Teckal* in-house criteria: the Landkreise did not exercise any control in the sense of the first *Teckal* criterion (see Sect. 5.1 supra).[75] The approach taken in *Commission* v. *Germany* therefore constitutes a new line of argumentation. The ECJ argued in the following way[76]:

> It must nevertheless be observed that the contract at issue *establishes cooperation between local authorities with the aim of ensuring that a public task that they all have to perform, namely waste disposal, is carried out* [emphasis added]...
>
> In addition, it is common ground that *the contract* [emphasis added] between Stadtreinigung Hamburg and the Landkreise concerned must be analysed as the culmination of a process of inter-municipal cooperation between the parties thereto and that it *contains requirements to ensure that the task of waste disposal is carried out. The purpose of that contract is to enable the City of Hamburg to build and operate a waste treatment facility under the most favourable economic conditions owing to the waste contributions from the neighbouring Landkreise, making it possible for a capacity of 320,000 tonnes per annum to be attained* [emphasis added]. For that reason, the construction of that facility was decided upon and undertaken only after the four Landkreise concerned had agreed to use the facility and entered into commitments to that effect.

With regard to this argumentation and to the case in its entirety, the following comments could be made.

Firstly, it is submitted that the contract did not concern the provision of services as such; rather it concerned the financing of the new incineration plant. In order for the plant to operate efficiently, under the most economically favourable conditions, it had to operate at a capacity of 320,000 tons. Under the contract, the Landkreise committed to collectively supplying 120,000 tons of waste for incineration and

---

72 ECJ, Case C-480/06 *Commission* v. *Germany* [2009] I-nyr.

73 *Commission* v. *Germany*, paras 31 and 36.

74 *Commission* v. *Germany*, para 38.

75 *Commission* v. *Germany*, para 36.

76 ECJ, Case C-480/06 *Commission* v. *Germany* [2009] I-nyr, paras 37–38.

without this commitment, the city of Hamburg would not have initiated the construction of the incineration plant. The point to be made is that the argumentation recited above is rather similar to that employed in Article 106(2) TFEU (Article 86(2) TEC) cases; especially in *Sydhavnens Sten & Grus*, where an exclusive right to collect certain kinds of waste for recycling was considered necessary by the ECJ in order for the new plant to operate under economically acceptable conditions.[77] The contract in *Commission* v. *Germany* is not very different as it achieves the same aim of efficient operation as the exclusive right did in *Sydhavnens Sten & Grus*, it just had another form. On this basis, it could possibly be argued that the agreement did not fulfil the condition that a 'contract' must concern the provision of works, goods or services, in order for the award to be covered by the rules of public procurement.

Secondly, and along the same lines, the ECJ also seemingly argued that there was no pecuniary interest in the contract, since the city of Hamburg transferred all the Landkreises' payments to the operator of the plant.[78] Hence, the ECJ could also in this way have found that the contract was not a 'contract' under the rules on public procurement. On the basis of the recent case law referred to above, where the ECJ has focussed on the existence of a 'contract' (Sect. 5.2.2.1 supra), this could have been an obvious route for the ECJ to take. Possibly, the solution was less desirable for the ECJ, as this could have necessitated taking into account the issue of the city of Hamburg's involvement with the private operator of the plant (an issue which the judgment, as mentioned, was explicitly delimited from considering) and the payments for landfill capacity.[79]

Thirdly, the ECJ (and the Commission; see para 46) had several times mentioned the 'public task', 'public service objective' and 'legal obligation' which the contract should ensure fulfilment of, namely the disposal of waste.[80] It could be considered whether the contract at issue was a 'normal' service contract or it was a contract for ensuring the SGEI/PSO consisting of incineration of waste?[81] Admittedly, the ECJ did not use the SGEI/PSO terminology in *Commission* v. *Germany*, but Article 86(2) TEC (now Article 106(2) TFEU) was relied upon by Germany.[82] The collection and treatment of different types of waste has previously been considered a SGEI/PSO by the ECJ under specific circumstances.[83] From another perspective, it could be asked whether the subject of the contract mattered

---

[77] Compare *Commission* v. *Germany*, para 38 and ECJ, Case C-209/98 *Sydhavnens Sten & Grus* [2000] *ECR* I-3743, paras 77–78.

[78] *Commission* v. *Germany*, ibid., para 43.

[79] *Commission* v. *Germany*, para 16.

[80] *Commission* v. *Germany*, paras 37, 38, 41 and 42.

[81] Cf., *Commission* v. *Germany*, para 44: 'It thus appears that the contract in question forms both the basis and the legal framework for the future construction and operation of a facility intended to perform a *public service, namely thermal incineration of waste…*' [emphasis added].

[82] *Commission* v. *Germany*, para 28.

[83] ECJ, Case C-203/96 *Dusseldorph* [1998] *ECR* I-4075, para 67 (implicitly) and ECJ, Case C-209/98 *Sydhavnens Sten & Grus* [2000] *ECR* I-3743, para 75. Cf., Buendia Sierra 2007, p. 630.

in the specific case. In other words: would the ECJ have ruled differently had the contract concerned, for example, software? *Commission* v. *Germany* (II) was also a case on cooperation between public entities (The Central Data Office of the German federal state Baden-Württemberg and the Institute for local-authority data-processing in the German federal state of Bavaria), concerning a contract for development of software for motor vehicle registration.[84] The substance of the judgment concerned the use of the negotiated procedure without notice. The outcome of *Commission* v. *Germany* (II) was that Germany had failed to fulfil its obligations under the relevant public procurement directive. Neither the *Teckal* criteria (possibly because they were not fulfilled) nor the argumentation concerning cooperation between public authorities in *Commission* v. *Germany* were pleaded by Germany or assessed *ex officio* by the ECJ. Otting and Sormani-Bastian draw parallels to *Commission* v. *Germany* and they find that the reason for the different outcomes of the cases is the different aims of the contracts[85]:

> Consequently, it is the authors' view that different treatment seems to lie in the fact that contracts between public authorities which have as their object the provision of services usually offered in the market or the supply of market products usually offered in the market, and which involve the offering of services to another contracting authority in the same way as to any other private economic operator, cannot justify any exemption.

The interpretation offered by Otting and Sormani-Bastian must be understood as referring to the type of services concerned.

It could be considered whether the difference between the two cases rests on the fact that the public entities in *Commission* v. *Germany* acted in their role as public authorities, seeking to ensure the provision of certain services, whereas, even though the Central Data Office of the German federal state Baden-Württemberg, is certainly a public authority, possibly acting in that role when it decided to purchase software, the Institute for local-authority data-processing in the German federal state of Bavaria was *not* acting as public authority when it agreed to supply the software. Probably, the Institute for local-authority data-processing in the German federal state of Bavaria could not be characterised as a public undertaking, as, seemingly, it did not act in on the market but only supplied public authorities with software[86]; however, it was a public entity, and presumably a contracting authority. This interpretation could embrace *Commission* v. *Spain* (see supra), where the ECJ denied that all agreements between public authorities another

---

[84] ECJ, Case C-275/08 *Commission* v. *Germany* (II) [2009] I-nyr. The case is only accessible in German and French. However, see Otting and Sormani-Bastian 2010, where the facts are mentioned in detail.

[85] Otting and Sormani-Bastian 2010, NA63.

[86] Cf. Buendia Sierra 1999, p. 42. The public entity delivering the software was in the application described as: '...ha[ving a] legal personality under public law, and was established with the particular purpose to coordinate and promote electronic data-processing in public administration in the interests of the general public.' See action brought on 24 June 2008—*Commission of the European Communities* v. *Federal Republic of Germany* (Case C-275/08) (2008/C 223/44), *OJ* 2008 C 223/28.

public authorities/public bodies could be exempted from the rules on public procurement.

Combining the findings above, and along the lines of the interpretation offered by Otting and Sormani-Bastian, it is proposed that *Commission* v. *Germany* may imply that where the contract is entered into by two or more public authorities acting in that capacity in order to ensure the provision of a SGEI/PSO,[87] which they are under a legislative obligation to provide, the contract is not covered by the rules on public procurement.[88]

On the basis of the above, it seems like the ECJ is opening up to cooperation between public authorities, also where the *Teckal* criteria are not fulfilled. It is proposed that the ECJ has been inspired by the principles underlying Article 106(2) TFEU [ex Article 86(2) TEC], and possibly that it is only the cooperation between public authorities for the provision of SGEIs/PSOs which is exempted. Time will show.

5.4 Conclusions

It has been the purpose of the analysis in this contribution to form some general ideas by taking an integrated perspective on Article 106(2) TFEU [ex Article 86(2) TEC] and the rules on public procurement. SGEIs/PSOs will probably often be provided through in-house arrangements, and are thereby outside the scope of the rules on public procurement, because no 'contract' is present. Even where SGEIs/PSOs are 'entrusted' to third parties, it is often effectuated by a legislative act, not obviously exposing the attributes characterising a 'contract' in the sense of the rules on public procurement. However, it is conceivable that the ECJ will take a case-by-case approach examining the character of the legislative act before it decides whether or not it is a 'contract' in the sense of the rules on public procurement.

It appears that an exemption from the rules on public procurement is emerging for contracts between public authorities ensuring the fulfilment of general interest objectives, even where the *Teckal* criteria for establishing in-house provision are not fulfilled. It has been argued that this exemption could be inspired by the principles underlying Article 106(2) TFEU [ex Article 86(2) TEC], but further case law is needed to clarify and substantiate this hypothesis.

---

[87] See also argument made supra n. 34.

[88] For alternative interpretations, see Treumer 2010, pp. 175–176, arguing that the ECJ was inspired by French case law, Pedersen and Olsson 2010, pp. 41–45, for an interpretation on the basis of the legal framework of inter-muncipality coorperation (i.e., legal entity v. contract).

References

Brown A (2007) Seeing through transparency: the requirement to advertise public contracts and concessions under the EC treaty. Public Procure Law Rev, 1

Buendia Sierra JL (1999) Exclusive rights and state monopolies under EC law—Article 86 (formerly Article 90) of the EC treaty, Oxford University Press, Oxford

Buendia Sierra JL (2007) Article 86—exclusive rights and other anti-competitive state measures. In: Faull J, Nikpay A (eds) The EC law of competition, 2nd edn. Oxford University Press, Oxford

Caranta R (2010) The In-house providing: the law as it stands in the EU. In: Comba M, Treumer S (eds) The in-house providing in European law, DJØF Publishing, Copenhagen, p 13

Drijber B, Stergiou H (2009) Public procurement law and internal market law. CMLRev 46(3):805

Kotsonis T (2010) The role of risk in defining a services concession contract: wasser—und Abwasserzwekverband Gotha und Landkreisgemeinden (WAZV Gotha) v Eurawasser Aufbereitungs—und Entsorgungsgesellschaft mbH (C-206/08) (WAZV). Public Procure Law Rev, NA4

Müller T (2009) Efficiency control in state aid and the power of Member States to define SGEIs. Eur State Aid Law Q 9(1):39

Neergaard U (2005) The Concept of concession in EU public procurement law versus EU competition law and national law. In: Nielsen R, Treumer S (eds) The new EU public procurement directives, DJØF Publishing, Copenhagen, p 141

Nicolaides P (2003) Compensation for public service obligations: the floodgates of state aid? Eur compét Law Rev 24(11):56

Otting O, Sormani-Bastian L (2010) A review procedure before the national courts is not relevant for declaring a failure to fulfil an obligation under the treaty: a note on commission v Germany (C-275/08). Public Procure Law Rev NA59

Pedersen K, Olsson E (2010) Commission v Germany—a new approach to in-house providing? Public Procure Law Rev 33

Sauter W (2008) Services of general economic interest and universal service in EU law. ELRev 33(2):167

Sauter W, Schepel H (2009) State and market in european union law, Cambridge University Press, Cambridge

Schnelle U (2002) Unconditional and non-discriminatory bidding procedures in EC state aid surveillance over public services. Eur State Aid Law Q 2(2):195

Stergiou H (2008) The increasing influence of primary EU law on EU public procurement law: must a concession to provide services of general economic interest be tendered? In: Van de Gronden J (ed) EU and WTO law on services: limits to the realization of general interest policies within the services markets, Kluwer, Deventer

Szyszczak E (2007) The regulation of the state in competitive markets in the EU, Hart Publishing, Oxford

Trepte P (2007) Public procurement in the EU—a practitioners guide, 2nd edn. Oxford University Press, Oxford

Treumer S (2010) In-house providing in Denmark. In: Comba M, Treumer S (eds) The In-House Providing in European Law, DJØF Publishing, Copenhagen, 165

Part II
New Legal Issues

Chapter 6
Social Services of General Interest and EU Law

Johan W. van de Gronden

Abstract This paper explores the impact of EU law on Social Services of General Interest (SSGI) such as social housing. At first sight one could argue that it is for the Member States to regulate these services and that EU law does not play a significant role in this respect. However, it is apparent from the case law of the ECJ that many SSGI constitute economic activities and fall, therefore, within the ambit of the Treaty provisions on free movement and competition. Hence, EU Institutions, especially the ECJ and the Commission, have the opportunity to influence the provisions of SSGI. How do they make use of this opportunity? Attention is paid to both case law of the ECJ and the soft law approach of the Commission.

Contents

J. W. van de Gronden (✉)
Department of International and European Law, Radboud University Nijmegen, P.O. Box 9049, 6500 KK Nijmegen, The Netherlands
e-mail: J.vandeGronden@jur.ru.nl

E. Szyszczak et al. (eds.), *Developments in Services of General Interest*, Legal Issues of Services of General Interest, DOI: 10.1007/978-90-6704-734-0_6,

6.1 Introduction

The Commission has issued several documents on Social Services of General Interest (SSGI),[1] revealing that EU law influences social policy measures of the Member States. Although the EU has only limited powers in the field of social policy, the EU Internal Market and competition rules affect the way social services are offered in the Member States. It is a well-known fact that the EU Courts interpret the Treaty provisions on the fundamental freedoms and competition extensively. As a result social services cannot escape from the applicability of these provisions. Then again, the provisions of significant social services should be protected from adverse effects that may result from the application of the 'market rules' laid down in the Treaty. No wonder that the Commission has started to develop a policy on SSGI.

This chapter explores how EU law affects the Member States' competences to regulate SSGI.[2] In particular, it examines the extent to which the EU Internal Market and competition rules force Member States to open up various branches of SSGI and/or to what extent the provision of SSGI must be made subject to market forces. This chapter sketches the main contours of the delicate interplay between the EU Internal Market and competition rules and SSGI.

The plan of the chapter is as follows. In Sect. 6.2, SSGI are defined. Subsequently the impact of the EU Internal Market law (the free movement rules and harmonisation measures such as the Services Directive) will be discussed. Then, attention will be paid to competition law. Furthermore, the soft law documents of the Commission regarding SSGI will be touched upon. Finally, some conclusions will be drawn.

6.2 What are Social Services of General Interest?

What are SSGI? To start with, SSGI in the sense of the present chapter do not relate to health services, as the EU is developing a special framework for the latter.[3] Following the Commission approach[4] this paper considers the following services as SSGI:

---

[1] These documents will be discussed in Sect. 6.5.

[2] This chapter will not examine how national labour law is influenced by the Treaty provisions on free movement. After all, SSGI concern services that, although being of a social nature, are provided to the citizens of the EU Member States, whereas labour law aims at creating rights and obligations for employees and does not, as a consequence, regulate the provision of special services. On the impact of the EU free movement rules on labour law, see for example, Prechal and De Vries 2009 and Barnard 2006.

[3] At the time of writing, the Commission proposal for the Directive on the application of patients' rights in cross-border health care, COM(2008) 414 final, was subject to a (complicated) negotiation process.

[4] This approach is laid down in the soft law documents of the Commission discussed in Sect. 6.5 of the present paper.

(1) statutory and complementary social security schemes; and
(2) other essential services 'provided directly to the person'.[5]

The first category of SSGI covers the main risks of life such as those related to ageing and unemployment. The second category of SSGI aims at facilitating social inclusion and safeguarding fundamental rights.[6] An important example of such services is social housing (the availability of cheaper housing through rents or construction loans).[7] From the outset it is clear that the provision of social housing services is capable of integrating certain groups into society.

It should be stressed that under EU law, SSGI are not a legally distinct category service within Services of General Interest. The term SSGI is used only in policy documents of the Commission and not in primary and secondary EU law. Treaty provisions do not mention SSGI and EU harmonisation measures such as the Services Directive do not pay attention to these services. A distinction must be made between SSGI of an *economic* nature (SSGI constituting economic activities) and SSGI of a *non-economic* nature (SSGI constituting non-economic activities).[8] According to settled case law of the ECJ, every entity engaged in economic activities is an undertaking within the meaning of EU competition law.[9] Offering of goods and services in a market is regarded as an economic activity.[10] The ECJ deploys a comparable test in free movement cases. Services that are normally provided for economic consideration are services in the sense of Article 56 TFEU (ex Article 49 EC).[11] Irrespective of whether social services are qualified as SSGI by a Member State, these services constitute economic activities, if they meet the requirements set by the ECJ. Below, it is explained how the concept of economic activities is applied in free movement (Sect. 6.3) and competition law (Sect. 6.4).

---

[5] See, inter alia, Communication from the Commission. Implementing the Community Lisbon Programme: Social services of general interest in the European Union, COM(2006) 177 final, 4.

[6] Ibid.

[7] Cf., *Commission Staff Working Document, annexes to the Communication from the Commission on Social services of general interest in the EU*, SEC(2006) 516, 18.

[8] See Neergaard 2009, p. 32.

[9] See, for example, ECJ, Case C-41/90, *Höfner* [1991] *ECR* I-1979.

[10] ECJ, Case 118/85 *Commission* v. *Italy* [1987] *ECR* 2599.

[11] See, for example, ECJ, Case C-158/96 *Kohll* [1998] *ECR* I-1931; ECJ, Case C-120/95 *Decker* [1998] *ECR* I-1831; ECJ, Case C-157/99 *Smits en Peerbooms* [2001] *ECR* I-5473; ECJ, Case C-385/99 *Müller-Fauré* [2003] *ECR* I-4509 and ECJ, Case C-372/04 *Watts* [2006] *ECR* I-4325.

6.3 Free Movement and Social Services of General Interest

Two categories of SSGI should be distinguished: social security schemes and social services provided directly to the person. In this section the relationship between social security schemes and the EU free movement rules will be discussed first. Then, attention will be paid to the impact of these rules on the other social services. Subsequently, the consequences that EU harmonisation measures may have on the provision of SSGI will be examined.

6.3.1 Social Security Schemes and Free Movement

In *Freskot*[12] the ECJ had to decide on the applicability of the free movement rules to social security schemes. At issue was a Greek social security scheme in agriculture. Farmers established in Greece were subject to a compulsory insurance against damage caused by natural risks. The farmers were obliged to pay contributions, by which the body implementing this social security schemes, ELGA, was financed. The ECJ was asked to decide whether the services provided by ELGA did fall within the ambit of Article 56 TFEU (ex Article 49 EC). The Court held that this was not the case, as the characteristics of the contribution, including its rates, were determined by the national legislature, and the benefits, provided by ELGA, were framed in national legislation in such a way as to apply equally to all operators in agriculture.[13]

Remarkably, the analysis of the ECJ did not stop here. The Court continued by stating that it should be examined whether the implementation of the Greek scheme would give rise to a restriction of the freedom of insurers established in other Member States. In so far as the compulsory insurance scheme covers insurable risks, it might constitute a restriction of the free movement of services.[14] Insurance companies established in other Member States were hindered from offering their insurance services in Greece. In the view of the writer of this chapter, these considerations put forward by the ECJ in *Freskot* imply that compulsory affiliation to a social security scheme concerning insurable risks is likely to result in restrictions on the free movement of services, as foreign insurers are prevented from providing similar services to enterprises or other entities that are subject to this compulsory affiliation. It is surprising that in legal doctrine, not much attention is paid to the *Freskot* ruling. The consequences of the ECJ's broad reading of the free movement rules in this case are that in social security scheme cases, the scope of the Treaty provisions is extended beyond the concept of economic activities. As soon as a Member State introduces a social security scheme that covers insurable

[12] ECJ, Case C-355/00 *Freskot* [2003] *ECR* I-5263.

[13] See paras 57 en 58 of *Freskot*.

[14] See para 63 of *Freskot*.

risks (from the perspective of a foreign insurance company), it is forced to design this scheme in line with the Treaty provisions on free movement. In this regard it should be noted that a restriction of the free movement of services (caused by a social security scheme) may be justifiable in the light of the exceptions laid down in the Treaty (especially Article 52 TFEU (ex Article 46 EC)) or as developed in the case law of the ECJ[15] (overriding requirements of general interest, also referred to as 'Rule of Reason').[16] In *Freskot* the ECJ held that the Greek compulsory insurance scheme was justified by the Rule of Reason, because it pursued an objective of social policy. It was thought that the cover provided by this scheme was limited to the necessary minimum and that, as a result, Greek farmers were at liberty to supplement this cover by taking out additional policies.[17] It was not entirely clear whether the cover provided by the compulsory scheme did go beyond what is necessary. The ECJ stated that the national court had to investigate whether '... the financing of ELGA and, therefore, its primarily social objective would be compromised if Greek farmers were allowed to take out insurance policies with private insurers ...'.[18] Consequently, the Greek scheme was not proportionate if it covered too many risks in the light of the social task assigned to ELGA. Hence, national social security schemes covering insurable risks are justifiable as long as the risks they cover are closely related to the social task of the managing bodies concerned. The cover of these schemes may not be dissociable from the essential functions of this task.

The approach developed by the ECJ in *Freskot* was confirmed by the *Kattner Stahlbau*[19] judgment. The latter concerned a German statutory insurance scheme against accidents at work and occupational diseases. In this case not only the German government but also the Commission contended that the introduction of compulsory affiliation to a social security scheme concerning accidents at work and occupational diseases belong to the sole competences of the Member States and do not fall within the scope of the fundamental freedoms. This contention was rejected by the ECJ. It held that Member States must comply with the Treaty provisions on free movement in designing social security schemes.[20] Moreover, in its view, the scheme at issue restricted the free movement of services, because it covered risks that also might be the subject of insurance contracts of private companies established in other Member States.[21] In other words, the German scheme at issue covered insurable risks and as a result it did not only fall within the

[15] This exception was acknowledged by the ECJ in Case 120/78 *Cassis de Dijon* [1979] *ECR* 649.

[16] See, for example, Mortelmans 2008, p. 59.

[17] See para 70 of the judgment in *Freskot*.

[18] See para 71 of *Freskot*.

[19] ECJ, Case C-350/07, *Kattner Stahlbau* v. *Maschinenbau- und Metall- Berufsgenossenschaft* [2009] *ECR* I-1513.

[20] See para 74 of *Kattner Stahlbau*.

[21] See para 82 of *Kattner Stahlbau*.

ambit of Article 56 TFEU (ex Article 49 EC) but it was also caught by the prohibition laid down in this Treaty provision. As in *Freskot*, the mere existence of insurable risks entails the applicability of the Treaty provisions on free movement of services and, virtually, automatically the violation of the prohibition of Article 56 TFEU (ex Article 49 EC). Nevertheless, the German scheme could be justified by the Rule of Reason provided that the principle of proportionality was met. The ECJ explicitly put forward that the minimal cover provided by the social security scheme at stake, which enables the affiliated undertakings to top up their cover by taking out supplementary insurance, is a factor in favour of the proportionality of this scheme.[22] So, if the German scheme provided for the cover of risks that are not necessary for the performance of the social task assigned to the managing bodies concerned, it is not in accordance with the principle of proportionality. It was for the national (referring) Court to apply this proportionality test. Then again, it must be noted that due account had to be taken of the requirements of financial equilibrium. The fair chance exists that commercially oriented private companies will deploy themselves to the most profitable activities, that is, the insurance of young and healthy employers, leaving the bad risks to the managing bodies entrusted with the performance of a social task, if the cover provided by these bodies is too minimal.[23] This problem of cherry picking may be solved by extending this cover to risks that are not strictly related to the social objectives at issue, which is in line with the principle of solidarity.

It is apparent from the foregoing discussion that Member States must take due account of the fundamental freedoms in designing social security schemes. In so far as these schemes cover insurable risks, they must be in accordance with the principle of proportionality. Especially, the national legislature must ensure that the cover is limited to what is necessary. However, in this respect considerations related to problems of cherry picking may justify a somewhat extended scope of the cover provided.

So far, attention has only been paid to statutory social security schemes by the ECJ in its free movement case law. As far as the writer of this chapter is aware, the ECJ has not handed down any judgments regarding free movement and *complementary* social security schemes. However, it may be derived from the above-analysis that the Member States enjoy less powers in regulating complementary schemes than in regulating statutory schemes. It may be assumed that complementary schemes relate to insurable risks, as these services may be offered in the market. Furthermore, the provision of services by entities managing these schemes is not connected with the essential features of social objectives. As a result, compulsory affiliation to complementary schemes is regarded to be in violation of Article 56 TFEU, and it is even questionable whether an exception may be invoked.

---

[22] See para 89 of *Kattner Stahlbau*.

[23] See para 90 of *Kattner Stahlbau*.

The analysis has focussed on the obstacles that commercial (service) providers ('supply side') have to cope with in their attempt to compete with national social security schemes. Social security schemes may also prevent beneficiaries ('demand side') from moving to other Member States. Of special interest is the question whether beneficiaries who cannot exercise the rights conferred upon workers by the Treaty may invoke EU law. After all, in many cases persons depending on social security benefits for their living are not able to derive rights from their (former) status of worker. At this stage of the analysis the concept of European Citizenship comes into play. Can such beneficiaries rely upon the Treaty provisions on European Citizenship if they are not entitled to social security benefits, solely due to the fact they have moved from one Member State to another Member State? This intriguing question was at issue in the case *Chamier-Glisczinski*.[24] Although one would have expected a firm decision against the background of the progressive free movement judgments delivered in other social security cases, the ECJ shied away from interpreting the Treaty provisions on European Citizenship expansively in *Chamier-Glisczinski*. It held that disparities between social security schemes do not in themselves constitute an infringement of Article 21 TFEU (ex Article 18 EC). As long as the differences in the two schemes of the Member States concerned cannot be considered to be the cause of discrimination, this Treaty provision is not violated. Consequently, the Treaty provisions on free movement that lack an economic dimension, that is, the EU rules of European Citizenship, are not capable of breaking open national social security schemes, which stands in sharp contrast with the 'regular' free movement rules.

6.3.2 *Other Social Services and Free Movement*

The second category SSGI concerns services directly provided to the person. If they are normally provided for remuneration, these activities constitute services within the meaning of Article 56 TFEU. As a result, national laws governing these services must be in conformity with Articles 56 TFEU et seq., if these laws are capable of affecting the temporary provision of services by providers established in other Member States. Article 49-55 TFEU are relevant, in so far as these national laws affect the permanent provision of services by providers coming from another Member State.

6.3.2.1 General Remarks

The current case law of the ECJ on free movement and social services (directly provided to the person) is pretty diverse. In well-known cases of *Humbel*[25] and

[24] ECJ, Case C-208/07 *von Chamier-Glisczinski* [2009] *ECR* I-6095.

[25] ECJ, Case 263/86 *Humbel* [1988] *ECR* 5365.

Wirth[26] the ECJ held that services provided under the national education system cannot be regarded as services within the meaning of the Treaty provisions on free movement because by organising this system the State '... is fulfilling its duties towards its own population in the social, cultural, and educational fields.'[27] Furthermore, it is of importance that such a system is mainly financed by public means and not by the recipients of the educational services. Consequently, educational services provided in a traditional and public framework fall outside the scope of the free movement rules.[28] If commercial mechanisms are introduced into the way education is offered to, for example students, the national laws governing the educational organisation fall within the scope of the fundamental freedoms and must be line with these freedoms.[29]

Social care for elderly people is regarded as a service within the meaning of the free movement rules according to the ECJ in *Sodemare*.[30] The reasoning for the applicability of these rules was rather disappointing, as the ECJ only put forward that a company from Luxembourg attempted to pursue activities on a stable and continuous basis in the economic life of Italy. In any event, the aim of this company was to provide social services to elderly persons on a profit-making basis, which was not allowed under Italian law. The ECJ held that the non-profit condition laid down in Italian law was not contrary to the Treaty provisions on the freedom of establishment, as the implementation of the services provided to elderly people was based on the principle of solidarity. The ECJ took into account that this condition ensures that decisions taken by the providers of the services concerned are not influenced by the need to seek profit but by considerations related to social objectives. Furthermore, the present stage of the European integration process does not preclude Member States from making the provision of

---

[26] ECJ, Case C-109/92 *Wirth* [1993] *ECR* I-6447.

[27] See para 18 of *Humbel*.

[28] A Member State is not allowed to grant its citizens tax facilities that only apply to educational services provided in the Member State concerned and not in other Member States. In ECJ, Case C-76/05 *Schwarz and Gootjes—Schwarz* [2007] I-6849 and ECJ, Case C-318/05 *Commission* v. *Germany* [2007] *ECR* I-6957 the ECJ held that the Treaty provisions on free movement and on European Citizenship are violated if national legislation confers upon taxpayers, a right to a reduction in income tax by allowing them to claim the payment of school fees to certain private schools established in national territory, but excludes such rights in relation to school fees paid to a private school established in other Member States. These rulings, however, do not call into question the non-economic nature of the educational services concerned, because the point of departure was not the service provider but the service recipient (and tax payer). Cf. also Case C-56/09 *Emiliano Zanotti*, 20 May 2010, n.y.r.

[29] ECJ, Case C-153/02 *Neri* [2003] *ECR* I-13555.

[30] ECJ, Case C-70/95 *Sodemare* [1997] *ECR* I-3395.

social welfare services, such as care for elderly people, subject to a non-profit condition, as long as this condition is applied in a non-discriminatory way.[31]

6.3.2.2 *Sint Servatius*: The Facts

In *Sint Servatius*, the ECJ addressed the role that EU free movement law plays in social housing for the first time. This case concerned a preliminary reference made by the administrative court of the Dutch Council of State (*Afdeling Bestuursrechtspraak van de Raad van State*). Sint Servatius, a Dutch social housing company established in Maastricht, decided to start a commercial housing project in Liège (Belgium). The Minister of Housing decided not to approve this project, since it was at odds with the social tasks assigned to Sint Servatius. According to Dutch law, the special tasks assigned to social housing companies concern activities carried out in the Netherlands and, in principle, the implementation of these tasks must, as a consequence, be confined to the Dutch territory. In turn, Sint Servatius started a procedure in order to annul this decision and claimed that the Minister of Housing violated the EU rules on the free movement of capital by preventing Sint Servatius from investing in the housing market of another Member State. Remarkably, in reaction to this point of view the Minister of Housing contended that she was not allowed to approve the investments of Sint Servatius on the Belgian market, as this company is financed by public means, which enables it to get loans at favourable rates. This would lead to an infringement of the Treaty provisions on state aid in the view of the Minister.

6.3.2.3 *Sint Servatius*: The ECJ's Decision

It was clear from the outset that in the *Sint Servatius* case many complicated issues of EU law were at hand. No wonder that the Dutch Council of State decided to send an impressive amount of preliminary questions (over 10 questions) to the ECJ. However, the judgment that the ECJ handed down in fall 2009[32] turned out to be a disappointment. Although the pattern of the first part of the ruling is in line with long-standing case law, the second part of the ruling fails to address all of the important issues raised by the Council of State.

As expected, the ECJ started with pointing out that the Dutch measure at stake constituted a restriction of free movement of capital, as it submitted cross-border property investment projects of housing corporations to a prior administrative authorisation procedure, in which these corporations must demonstrate that the

---

[31] In legal doctrine it is argued that judgments such as *Sodemare* show that the ECJ is prepared to uphold obvious restrictions on the basis that profit making could interfere with the provision of social services to persons who are depending on these services. See Hancher and Sauter 2010, p. 120.

[32] ECJ, Case C-567/07 *Sint Servatius* [2009] ECR I-9021.

investments concerned are in the interests of housing in the Netherlands. The ECJ moved on by contending that overriding requirements of general interest (the Rule of Reason) accommodate objectives of social housing policy and are, therefore, capable of justifying restrictions to free movement. However, in the present case the ECJ feared that the conditions governing the exercise of the Dutch authorities' powers to clear cross-border housing investments were not well-defined. If the discretion that public authorities enjoy in exercising their powers was unlimited, the principle of proportionality was not met. It was for the referring national court to determine this matter. So far, so good, one would say.

However, the ECJ refused to examine whether the concept of Services of General Economic Interest (SGEI) was capable of justifying restrictions of free movement of (in this case) capital caused by national social housing laws. It stated that the prior authorisation scheme at stake did not concern special or exclusive rights granted to corporations such as Sint Servatius, rather the national proceedings were about the lawfulness of a restriction to which social housing companies are subject.[33]

This point of view is hard to understand. Admittedly, the cross-border investments of Sint Servatius concerned commercial activities and were not related to the core business of social housing corporations. However, the Dutch Minister of Housing feared that the involvement in these commercial practices would prevent Sint Servatius from adequately performing the social tasks entrusted to this social housing corporation. Hence, the ECJ was called upon to make clear whether the concept of SGEI is capable of addressing problems resulting from conflicting interests of undertakings entrusted with special tasks. In this chapter it is outlined how the ECJ forces Member States to depart from a strong divide between core social services and services that may be made subject to market forces. But in *Sint Servatius* the ECJ failed to explain *how* the concept of a SGEI could help them to make a sharp distinction between both groups of services in an adequate way. This is a missed opportunity.

Further, the ECJ refused to examine whether allowing Sint Servatius to make cross-border housing investments could lead to violations of the Treaty provisions on state aid. This refusal is closely related to its position on the (ir)relevance of Article 106(2) TFEU: in both matters, the ECJ was not prepared to pay due consideration to the intertwined relationship between the social housing services and the commercial housing projects of Sint Servatius. However, it could not definitely be ruled out that Sint Servatius would reallocate the funding received for its social housing task to its commercial cross-border housing projects. In other words, Sint Servatius's practices could have led to conflicts of interests, in that in terms of financial resources this corporation would have given priority to its commercial activities. It is astonishing that the ECJ did not care about these problems at all in *Sint Servatius*, whereas, as will be outlined below, in other EU state aid cases Member States were obliged to require that social housing

[33] See point 46 of the judgment in *Sint Servatius*.

corporations, being engaged in both social and commercial activities, have a system of separate accounts.

6.3.2.4 Issues Open to Debate: SGEI and Free Movement

By refusing to answer the preliminary questions on the concept of SGEI, the ECJ has not addressed the issue as to whether Article 106(2) TFEU may be regarded as an exception in free movement cases. This is a contentious issue, discussed in Chap. 4 by Bekkedal. However, according to this Treaty provision undertakings, entrusted with the operation of SGEI are only subjected to the rules contained in the Treaty, in particular those on competition, in so far as the compliance with these provisions does not obstruct the special task assigned to them. Consequently, from the wording of Article 106(2) TFEU it could be derived that this Treaty provision allows Member States to derogate not only from the competition rules but also from other rules, including the free movement provisions. Furthermore, it is apparent from the ECJ's case law that Article 106(2) TFEU may be applied in cases involving free movement matters.[34]

In the view of the writer of this chapter, the concept of SGEI laid down in Article 106(2) TFEU is perfectly suited for accommodating considerations related to SSGI in free movement cases. In the discussion above, it is pointed out that in cases concerning social security schemes, the free movement of services may be restricted due to problems of cherry picking (*Kattner Stahlbau*). It is settled case law of the ECJ that Article 106(2) TFEU may be invoked if, without restricting competition, undertakings entrusted with a special task cannot perform this task under economically acceptable circumstances.[35] The condition of economically acceptable circumstances is closely related to problems of cherry picking. After all, by emphasising the economically acceptable circumstances, the ECJ protects undertakings having a SGEI mission against enterprises that are mainly occupied with services under the most profitable circumstances.[36] Exactly the same problem was at stake in *Kattner Stahlbau,* where a public body managing an insurance scheme against accidents at work and occupational diseases was protected from competition on the part of commercial insurance companies. Furthermore, in its landmark decision *Corbeau* (already mentioned) the ECJ specified that the exclusion of competition is not justified for services that are dissociable from the essential functions of the special task concerned.[37] A similar point of view was taken by the ECJ in *Freskot* where the Greek social security scheme at issue was

---

[34] See for instance: ECJ, Case C-266/96 *Corsica Ferries France* [1998] *ECR* I-3949 and ECJ, Case C-157/94 *Commission* v. *The Netherlands* [1997] *ECR* I-5699.

[35] See ECJ, Case C-320/91 *Corbeau* [1993] *ECR* I-2533, para 16.

[36] Cf. paras 17 and 18 of the *Corbeau* judgment.

[37] See para 19 of the *Corbeau* judgment.

justifiable in so far as it covered the risks that are not dissociable from the essential functions of the task assigned to the body managing this scheme.

Further, by refusing to apply Article 106(2) TFEU in *Sint Servatius*, the ECJ missed the opportunity to give guidance on the issue of the margin of appreciation. In its preliminary reference, the Dutch Council of State had explicitly asked whether a Member State has a wide margin of discretion in determining the scale of the SGEI concerned and the manner in which that interest is promoted. Furthermore, it wanted to know whether the fact that the EU has only limited powers in the social housing sector (if any), is of relevance in this respect. Unfortunately, these questions remain unanswered. However, it must be noted that in competition law cases the ECJ bases its proportionality test on the test of economically acceptable circumstances.[38] This approach is not as strict as the test of the less restrictive means, which is usually deployed in free movement cases in which it is scrutinised whether the conditions of the Rule of Reason or Treaty exceptions such as Article 52 TFEU (ex Article 46 EC) are met.[39] After all, it is not necessary under the *Corbeau* standard to prove that the undertaking entrusted with a SGEI mission can only survive if it is allowed to restrict competition. Unsurprisingly, in legal literature, it is argued that the ECJ does not strictly construe the exception contained in Article 106(2) TFEU.[40] All in all, it remains to be seen whether Member States have more leeway in regulating SSGI under Article 106 (2) TFEU than under the traditional free movement exceptions. Hopefully, the ECJ will shed more light on this matter in the near future.

6.3.2.5 Litigation in Market-Oriented SSGI Schemes

At the end of the discussion of the *Sint Servatius* case, it must be pointed out that this case illustrates that a Member State that introduces competition elements into its SSGI schemes may encounter problems resulting from undertakings (sometimes as in *Sint Servatius*—entrusted with a special social task) pursuing commercial activities in other Member States. Due to the market oriented setting of the SSGI schemes created by the Member States concerned, these companies are encouraged to be increasingly involved in commercial projects. At the moment that public authorities prevent these operators from undertaking such projects they may be tempted to invoke the Treaty provisions on free movement *vis-à-vis* the state in order to break away from the system. It goes without saying that this development is a significant challenge for both the Member States and the EU Institutions (for example the Commission, ECJ) in finding ways of dealing with these problems and, especially, methods of balancing the objectives of free competition and social policy.

---

[38] See para 16 of the *Corbeau* judgment.

[39] See for example, Buendia Sierra 1999, pp. 319, 320.

[40] See for example Baquero Cruz 2005, pp. 193–198 and Cicoria 2006, p. 179.

6.3.3 Harmonisation and SSGI

As the EU is not competent to harmonise social security schemes and other social services, no EU legislation that explicitly deals with SSGI is in place. However, some EU Directives and Regulations could affect the competence of the Member States to regulate these matters. Therefore, some attention needs to be paid to the impact harmonisation may have on the provision of SSGI. Due to space constraints, only a few EU Directives can be discussed. It should be noted that the Social Security Regulation[41] will not be analysed here, since this piece of EU legislation aims at promoting the free movement of persons by coordinating social security schemes and not by harmonising them.

Of great importance are the Insurance Directives. A Member State may decide to privatise the implementation of a social security scheme, which implies that the modelling of such a market-oriented scheme must be in line with the applicable Non-life Insurance directives. Admittedly, pursuant to Article 2(1)(d) of the First Non-life Insurance Directive[42] insurance schemes forming part of a statutory system of social security of a Member State do not fall within the ambit if the Non-life Directives. Unsurprisingly, social security schemes that are (virtually) only based on the principle of proportionality are not covered by these Directives according to the ECJ.[43] However, in establishing the applicability of the Non-life Insurance Directives, the ECJ focuses on the substantive and constituent elements of a given insurance system and not on the formal place that such a system has in national law. Thus the ECJ ruled that the Belgian disability insurance schemes did fall within the scope of the Directive because these schemes were offered by insurers at their own risk.[44] This conclusion was not called into question by the fact that according to Belgian law, this insurance system was regarded as a social security scheme. This finding did not entail that the Belgian legislature was not entitled to impose obligations upon the insurers concerned, since in Article 55 of the Third Non-life Insurance Directive[45] an exception for compulsory insurance against accidents at work is contained. A similar exception for health care insurance is laid down in Article 54 of this Directive. In any event, it is clear that

[41] See Regulation 883/2004 of the European Parliament and of the Council on the coordination of social security systems, *OJ* 2004 L166/1, which have repealed Regulation 1408/71 of the Council on the application of social security schemes to employed persons and their families moving within the Community, *OJ* 1971 L149/2. However, the latter remains in force for a limited number of purposes related, for example, to agreements concluded with Switzerland.

[42] First Council Directive (73/239) on the coordination of laws, regulations and administrative provisions relating to the taking-up and pursuit of the business of direct insurance other than life assurance, *OJ* 1973 L228/3.

[43] See ECJ, Case C-238/94 *Garcia* [1996] *ECR* I-1673 and the *Freskot* case.

[44] ECJ, Case C-206/98 *Commission* v. *Belgium* [2000] *ECR* I-3509.

[45] Third Council Directive (92/49) on the coordination of laws, regulations, and administrative provisions relating to direct insurance other than life assurance and amending Directives 73/239/EEC and 88/357/EEC, *OJ* 1992 L 228/1.

Member States that privatise social security schemes must take due account of the obligations that are imposed upon them by the Non-life Insurance Directives.

As for social services provided directly to the person, the Services Directive[46] is of relevance. It must be pointed out that this Directive carves out several social services such as social housing and child care. These social services are excluded in so far as they '... are provided by the State, by providers mandated by the State or by charities recognised as such by the State ...' It is not clear what is meant by 'mandated by the State': it is uncertain to what extent the private provision of the social services concerned benefit from this exclusion.[47] In the future, this issue needs to be clarified. Taken all together, it cannot be excluded that some SSGI that seem to fall outside of the scope of the Services Directive on first sight, will turn out to be covered by this piece of EU legislation due to a narrow interpretation of the 'carve-out provisions' of this Directive given by the ECJ in future cases.[48]

National laws governing social services that are not exempted from the scope of the Directive must, of course, comply with the provisions thereof. In this regard, however, it should be noted that Article 17 of the Services Directive exempts all SGEI from the obligation of the Member States to respect the freedom of providers to provide services laid down in Article 16. Member States may circumvent one of the core directive provisions by designating social services as SGEI. In other words, by modelling social services as SSGI in the sense that they constitute SGEI, Member States can escape the impact that Article 16 may have on their competences to regulate these services.[49]

Last but not least, European public procurement law may also come into play. If a public authority decides to externalise the provision of SSGI, the Directive for the award of public works contracts, public supply contracts, and public service contracts[50] could be applicable. A public authority could conclude a public service contract with a provider, which means it pays this provider a fixed remuneration. In that case, the Directive is applicable, provided that certain thresholds are met, and as a result the award of the contract should be made subject to the (limited) procedure that applies to Annex II B services.[51] However, if the public authority

---

46 Directive 2006/123 of the European Parliament and of the Council of 12 December 2006 on services in the internal market, *OJ* 2006 L 376/36.

47 Barnard 2008, p. 341.

48 Interestingly, Nistor argues that particular national health care laws may be caught by the Services Directive, as they are not related to services directly provided to patients. See Nistor 2009, p. 331 and 332.

49 See Van de Gronden 2009, pp. 248–250.

50 Directive 2004/18 on the coordination of procedures for the award of public works contracts, public supply contracts, and public service contracts, *OJ* 2004 L134/114.

51 See Commission Staff Working Document of 20 November 2007, *Frequently asked questions concerning the application of public procurement rules to social services of general interest*, SEC(2007) 1514, 7.

externalises the provision of a SSGI by granting a service concession, the Directive is not applicable pursuant to Article 1(4).[52] In this regard, it should be noted that apart from the public procurement rules laid down in secondary legislation, Member States should also observe the EU principles of primary law such as the principle of transparency, equal treatment, and non-discrimination,[53] which are derived from the Treaty provisions on free movement.[54] All in all, European public procurement law could prevent Member States from awarding a SSGI task to the provider of their reference. It should be noted that the need to provide SGEI does not automatically lead to the non-applicability of the EU public procurement rules. If compliance with these rules is not be liable to prevent the accomplishment of SGEI tasks, the Member State concerned is oblige to follow the procedures prescribed by EU public procurement law.[55]

The analysis carried out above shows that it cannot be ruled out that harmonisation measures taken by the EU legislature may interfere with the powers of the Member States to regulate SSGI. However, the discussion of the Insurance Directives and the Services Directive makes it clear that explicit provisions dealing with the special position of SSGI could prevent the proper provision of these services from being put under pressure. Hence, paying due attention to the special position of social services during the process of drafting secondary EU legislation seems to be indicated. By so doing, the EU legislature is able to ensure that the provision of these services will not be put at stake.

6.4 Competition Law and SSGI

The competition rules contained in the Treaty only apply to undertakings. It is settled case law that every entity engaged in economic activities is an undertaking and addressee of these rules.[56] Economic activities are defined as the offering of goods or services on the market.[57]

---

52 See Commission Staff Working Document of 20 November 2007 'Frequently asked questions concerning the application of public procurement rules to social services of general interest', SEC(2007) 1514, 8.

53 See about this matter: Drijber and Stergiou 2009, p. 805 et seq.

54 See for example, ECJ, Case C-231/01 *Coname* [2005] *ECR* I-7287. It is apparent from cases such as ECJ, Case C-507/03 *Commission* v. *Ireland* [2007] *ECR* I-9777 that these principles also apply to Annex IIB services.

55 See ECJ, Case C-160/08 *Commission* v. *Germany*, 29 April 2010, n.y.r.

56 ECJ, Case C-41/90 *Höfner* [1991] *ECR* I-1979.

57 ECJ, Case 118/85 *Commission* v. *Italy* [1987] *ECR* 2599.

6.4.1 Competition Law and Social Security Schemes

6.4.1.1 General Remarks

In several cases, the ECJ has examined whether the bodies managing social security schemes are engaged in economic activities. From this case law it could be derived that in social security cases, the ECJ has developed an approach that departs from the question of how significant is the role of the principle of solidarity.[58] It scrutinises how much room the national legislature leaves, for competition in the implementation of the social security scheme concerned and focuses on the role the solidarity principle plays.[59] If it finds that the principle of solidarity is predominant, the activities concerned are not regarded as economic. In various cases the ECJ considered it of great importance that a social security scheme operated on a redistributive basis,[60] that the rates were determined by law and that thc benefits are also determined by national legislation (mechanical implementation of the rules). In these cases, it was assumed that the systcm of social security was almost completely based on the solidarity principle and, as a result, the implementing bodies were not considered to be undertakings.[61] In this regard it is remarkable that in the cases of *Freskot* and *Kattner Stahlbau*, where the ECJ progressively extended the scope of the EU free movement regime to insurable risks, the principle of solidarity played a decisive role in applying the concept of undertaking to the managing bodies concerned. It was examined with great care whether the implementation of their social tasks was mainly based on the principle of proportionality.[62] In *Kattner Stahlbau*, the ECJ paid attention to the supervision mechanisms of the State as well.[63] It is striking that the ECJ finally decided that the managing bodies concerned were not engaged in economic activities and that, therefore, competition law was not applicable, whereas at the same time it held that the free movement rules did apply.[64] Consequently, these judgments show that scope of free movement is broader than the scope of competition law.[65] The free movement rules are capable of breaking open social security schemes, whereas the role of competition law is limited in this respect.

---

58 See Buendia Sierra 1999, p. 52 et seq.

59 See Hatzopoulos 2002, p. 710 et seq.

60 Cf. Sauter and Schepel 2009, p. 89.

61 See ECJ, Joined Cases C-159/91 and C-160/91 *Poucet and Pistre* [1993] *ECR* I-637 and ECJ, Case C-218/00 *Cisal* (2002) *ECR* I-691.

62 See paras 76–79 of *Freskot* and paras 44–59 of *Kattner Stahlbau*.

63 See paras 60–68 of *Kattner Stahlbau*.

64 See Sect. 6.3.1 supra.

65 See also Szyszczak 2009, p. 210.

In the light of the foregoing it may be argued that the majority of the statutory social security schemes do not fall within the ambit of competition law. After all, it may be expected that with regard to the majority of the statutory schemes, the benefits granted by these schemes and the rates of the contributions that must be paid by the affiliated person are determined by national law, which is regarded as an expression of solidarity in the case law of the ECJ. In the view of the writer of this chapter, the situation is different, when the national legislature introduces elements of competition into a statutory scheme. For example, in the Netherlands basic health care schemes are managed by private insurance companies. Since they may be for profit and are capable of influencing the benefits granted to insured persons and the rate of the contributions to be paid by the affiliated persons, the Commission decided that private insurance companies are undertakings within the meaning of European competition law.[66]

What is the point of view of the ECJ on complementary social security schemes? Against the background of the case law on statutory schemes it is not surprising that in the view of the ECJ, complementary schemes amount to economic activities because, next to solidarity, elements of competition play a role in implementing these schemes. For example, in the *Brentjens* cases[67] it was pointed out that the Dutch pension schemes at stake were based on the principle of capitalisation, which means that the level of benefits largely depends on the financial results of the investments made by the managing organisation. Furthermore, it turned out that life insurance companies in certain circumstances were also entitled to offer competing products. In these circumstances the bodies managing the Dutch complementary pension schemes must be regarded as undertakings.[68] Hence, competition law is applicable if the national legislator in designing a social security system has opted for a mix between competition and solidarity.

As a consequence, the policies carried out by bodies managing complementary schemes must be in accordance with the EU competition rules. However, these policies may be at odds with the principles of free competition. Therefore, the concept of SGEI, as laid down in Article 106(2) TFEU, may be very helpful in order to solve these tensions. For example, pursuant to the provisions of Dutch law applicable in the *Brentjens* cases (already mentioned), the complementary pension schemes may only be offered by special institutions assigned with this task by the State (*bedrijfstakpensioenfondsen*) in certain industry sectors. So, exclusive rights to provide these services were created, which resulted in a violation of European competition law (Article 106(1) in conjunction with Article 102 TFEU). However,

---

66 See the Decision of the Commission of 22 December 2005 on the introduction of a risk equalisation system in the Dutch Health Insurance, N541/2004 and N542/2004—C (2005) 1329 fin.

67 ECJ, Case C-67/96 *Albany* [1999] *ECR* I-5751; ECJ, Joined Cases C-115/97, C-116/97 and C-117/97 *Brentjens* [1999] *ECR* I-6025 and ECJ, Case C-219/97 *Drijvende Bokken* [1999] *ECR* I-6121.

68 A similar approach was deployed by the ECJ, Case C-244/94 *FFSA* (1995) *ECR* I-4015.

the ECJ ruled that these exclusive rights were justifiable in the light of Article 106(2) TFEU, to protect the viability of industry sector pension schemes which could not be offered under economically acceptable conditions if low risk profiles left the scheme, which would leave the pension funds with high risk profiles only. In other words: the concept of SGEI contained in Article 106(2) TFEU enables the Member State to model complementary social security schemes in such a way that problems of cherry picking are addressed, even if this leads to restriction of competition. The ECJ's interpretation of Article 106(2) TFEU is tailored to address the problems of cherry picking and it is clear that these problems occur frequently in social security cases.

6.4.1.2 State Aid and Social Security Schemes

It should be noted that the concept of SGEI is also of great importance in State aid matters. In many cases Member States do not only confer special tasks (and rights) on bodies managing (complementary) social security schemes but also transfer financial resources to them. It goes without saying that this could entail state aid problems, as Article 107(1) TFEU precludes Member States from granting state aid to undertakings that distort competition on the Internal Market and influence intra-Community trade. In *Altmark*[69] the ECJ held that compensation granted by the State with a view to the performance of Public Service Obligation (PSO) does not constitute State aid, in so far as the following conditions are fulfilled: (1) the undertaking is charged with the execution of a clearly defined PSO, (2) the parameters of the amount of the compensation are established in an objective and transparent way, (3) the compensation goes not beyond what is necessary, and (4) in the case of absence of public procurement of the contract concerned, the amount of the compensation is determined on the basis of the expenses a well-run undertaking would have incurred.[70] The great advantage of the *Altmark* approach is that the compensatory measure at hand does not need to be notified to the Commission, as it does not constitute state aid within the meaning of Article 107(1) TFEU. What is more, it is not subject to the famous standstill provision, which may force Member States to recover illegal state aid from the companies involved.[71] Although *Altmark* does not give a carte blanche to Member States, it does extend the Member States' powers to finance PSO.[72]

---

[69] ECJ, Case C-280/00 *Altmark* [2003] *ECR* I-7747.

[70] See paras 88–93 of *Altmark*.

[71] See for instance Case C-39/94 *La Poste* [1996] *ECR* I-3547.

[72] See Fiedziuk 2010, p. 280.

So far, the *Altmark* approach has only been applied in cases on health insurance[73] and not in (other) social security cases where a SSGI may be at issue.[74] As health care falls outside the scope of the present paper, because health care services are not regarded to be SSGI, this case law will not be elaborated on.[75] In this respect, however, it should be noted that the EU Institutions that took the decisions in these health care cases (the (then) CFI and the Commission) gave the Member States considerable leeway in financing a PSO.[76] In any event, the competent social security authorities of the Member States should be aware of the state aid problems that the transfer of financial means to managing bodies may cause. This implies that they have to model this transfer in such a way that the national social security schemes may benefit from the *Altmark* approach. Moreover, case law of the ECJ on this issue should be awaited. The concept of PSO may inspire the EU Courts, and in their slipstream the Commission, to further develop the concept of SSGI and to integrate PSO consideration into the constituent elements of this concept.

It is apparent from the *Freskot* case that apart from the transfer of financial resources to managing bodies, other State aid problems may occur. In *Freskot* the question was raised whether the compulsory social security scheme may confer benefits on the companies that are covered thereunder.[77] The ECJ put forward the argument that such benefits could entail State aid but it should be scrutinised whether in the absence of compulsory cover the agriculture enterprises concerned could have obtained cover from private insurers, to what extent the contributions correspond to the actual economic costs of the provided benefits and whether these benefits satisfy the condition of selectivity.[78] Unfortunately, the national referring judge did not provide the ECJ with the necessary information to address these questions, and as a result the ECJ did not give any answers with regard to the state aid questions. Nevertheless, the ECJ did give some guidance by considering that the benefits granted by the scheme at issue to the Greek agriculture enterprises may be justified in the light of the social objective of protecting these enterprises against the natural risks to which they are exposed.[79] In this writer's view, these

---

[73] See Case T-289/03 *British United Provident Association* (*BUPA*) [2008] *ECR* II-81 and the decision of the Commission of 22 December 2005 on the introduction of a risk equalisation system in the Dutch Health Insurance, N541/2004 and N542/2004—C (2005) 1329 fin.

[74] The *Altmark* approach is applied to other services than SSGI. In General Court, Case T-222/04, *Italy* v. *Commission* [2009] *ECR* II-1877, the CFI (now the General Court) held, that compensatory measures taken in order to finance public utility services cannot benefit from this approach, if the applicable national laws confine themselves to stating that the activities pursued are in public economic interest without clearly setting out what special service should be provided by a particular corporation.

[75] On this matter, see, for example, Van de Gronden 2009–2010, p. 5 et seq. and Sauter 2009, p. 269 et seq.

[76] See Van de Gronden 2008, pp. 754–757.

[77] See para 82 of *Freskot*.

[78] See paras 84 and 85 of *Freskot*.

[79] See para 86 of *Freskot*.

considerations could be brought into relation to the *Altmark* approach. However, further case law should be awaited and it remains to be seen to what extent the ECJ will be prepared to integrate PSO with the concept of SSGI.

6.4.2 Competition Law and Other Social Services

6.4.2.1 General Remarks

In several cases, the ECJ has decided that organisations providing social services directly to the person are engaged in economic activities. For example, in the famous *Höfner* case the Court decided that job placement services are economic activities and, as a result, institutions offering these services are undertakings within the meaning of EU competition law, even if these institutions are public authorities within the meaning of national law; this decision was confirmed by the ECJ in *Job Centre.*[80] The main reason for this finding is that employment procurement has not always been carried out by public institutions, and, what is probably more important, it is not necessary that such services are offered by public authorities.[81] It could be argued that social services provided to the person that can be offered on the market, are economic activities regardless of the way they are designed by the Member States (private or public law). In these cases, the ECJ does not pay much attention to the role that the principle of solidarity plays. This implies that many social services (provided directly to the person) constitute economic activities in the sense of European competition law.

This conclusion is endorsed by a Decision that the Commission took with regard to an Irish social housing case.[82] In Ireland municipalities carry out social housing activities by offering cheaper housing conditions through rents and construction loan to certain consumers. The Commission pointed out that, by doing so, the municipalities are in competition with other housing companies and, are therefore, engaged in economic activities. Irrespective of the fact that municipalities are bodies of public law and offer social housing service on the basis of the solidarity principle, they are considered to be undertakings within the meaning of competition law.

If the EU, Courts and the Commission further build upon this line of reasoning, it may be expected that many social services (directly provided to the person) constitute economic activities. After all, many of these services may be offered on the market. Possibly, this conclusion does not hold true for fundamental educational services offered by primary and secondary school organisations, by colleges of higher education and universities. It could be argued that these services are of

[80] ECJ, Case C-55/96 Job Centre [1997] *ECR* I-7119.

[81] See para 22 of *Höfner* and para 22 of *Job Centre*.

[82] See the Decision of the Commission of 3 July 2001 in Case N 209/2001—Ireland, SG (2001) D/289528.

(semi-)collective nature (in so far as they relate to the duties of the government '... towards its own population in the social, cultural, and educational fields...'[83]), which implies that they cannot be offered on the market. It goes without saying that educational services provided (by for example universities) in a market oriented context do constitute economic activities, because these services can be provided in competition with commercial operators.

What does the applicability of the Treaty provisions on competition entail? Social housing companies, institutions providing job placement services, etc., have to comply with the cartel prohibition (laid down in Article 101 TFEU) and the prohibition on the abuse of a dominant position (as contained in Article 102 TFEU). Furthermore, mergers between these organisations having an Internal Market dimension in the sense of the Merger Control Regulation[84] must be notified to the Commission, whereas in many occasions medium sized mergers (without an Internal Market dimension) must be approved by the competent national competition authority, as many Member States have aligned their merger control rules with European competition law.

Last but not least, it should be pointed out that State interventions regarding these social services must be in conformity with the EU regime on the State aid and competition law (Article 106(1) EC, Article 4(3) TEU in conjunction with Article 101–102 TFEU and Articles 107–109 TFEU). Due to space constraints, this contribution will further focus on the Treaty provisions on state aid (Articles 107–109 TFEU), as many social services are financed by public means, which could give rise to state aid problems.

6.4.2.2 State Aid and Social Services Directly Provided to the Person

As a result of the *Altmark* ruling, in 2005 the Commission took a Decision (based on Article 86(3) EC, now Article 106(3) TFEU), in which the SGEI conditions are tailored to, inter alia, social housing companies.[85] If the *Altmark* conditions are not fulfilled and, as a result, the compensation given to a social housing institution does not constitute PSO, this compensation could benefit from the exemption laid down in the 2005 Decision of the Commission. This means that it does not need to be notified to the Commission, in the same way that compensatory measures fulfilling the *Altmark* conditions do not have to be notified. The exemption of the Decision is applicable, if a SGEI mission is entrusted by way of one or more

---

[83] See para 18 of *Humbel*, supra n. 25.

[84] Council Regulation 139/2004 of 20 January 2004 on the control of concentrations between undertakings (the EC Merger Regulation), *OJ* 2004 L24/1.

[85] See the Decision of the Commission of 28 November 2005 on the application of Article 86(2) of the EC Treaty (now Article 106(2) TFEU) to State aid in the form of public service-compensation granted to certain undertakings entrusted with the operation of services of general economic interest, *OJ* 2005 L312/67. In this regard, it should be noted that the term 'Decision' is misleading, as this official act provides general rules on matters of SGEI.

official acts of public authorities and the amount of the transfer of money does not exceed what is necessary for the performance of this special task.

It should be noted that from the outset that it is not clear *what* the additional value of this Decision is in comparison with *Altmark*. Similar conditions as outlined in the 2005 Decision play a role in the PSO context of *Altmark* as well. Possibly, a Member State could rely upon this Decision in order to justify a compensatory measure that do not meet the fourth Altmark criterion (the amount of the compensation does not exceed the costs of a well-run company). It is expected that the Commission will publish its review on the 2005 Decision in the course of 2010.[86] Hopefully the matter related to the fourth *Altmark* condition will be addressed in this review.[87]

In any event, it is clear that in EU law, the special task carried out by social housing companies is acknowledged and that this special task is capable of justifying the funding of these companies by the State. However, it is very important that Member States explicitly entrust social housing companies with the operation of SGEI missions. By doing so, they ensure that the PSO approach laid down in *Altmark* and the 2005 Commission Decision can be invoked. In other words, Member States must develop an explicit SGEI policy that outlines which social services are essential and constitute SGEI. Such a policy may contribute to the further development of SSGI in the EU. The following dispute between the Netherlands and the Commission on the financing of social housing activities shows what might happen if Member States fail to come up with explicit policy measures towards SGEI and social services.

In 2005, the Commission sent a letter to the Dutch government stating that compensation granted to social housing companies was not in line with the EU rules on state aid.[88] It was of the opinion that the SGEI mission concerned was not clearly defined. The activities of the social housing enterprises were not restricted to specific low-income groups or households but also encompassed services provided to high-income groups. The Commission clarified its point of view by explaining that social housing companies should base their activities on a clear and transparent division between their social tasks (newly built houses for low-income groups) and commercial housing services.[89] It goes without saying that only social tasks may be financed by public means.

[86] Cf., Article 9 of the Decision of the Commission of 28 November 2005 on the application of Article 86(2) of the EC Treaty (now Article 106(2) TFEU) to State aid in the form of public service-compensation.

[87] Also the Monti Report, which was recently published in order to revitalise the EU's Single Market Strategy, claims that clarifying the conditions for compensating public services obligations is necessary, in particular to ensure that citizens have access to basic financial services. See Monti 2010, pp. 74, 75. http://ec.europa.eu/bepa/pdf/monti_report_final_10_05_2010_en.pdf.

[88] See State aid E 2/2005 (EX-NN 93/02)—Financiering van woningcorporaties—Nederland, 18 July 2005.

[89] Bange corporaties, Financieel Dagblad of 7 September 2005.

The lack of a clear definition of the SGEI missions concerned, created a Dutch State aid problem in social housing.[90] Unsurprisingly, the Dutch Minister of Housing has promised the Commission to improve the financial transparency and to oblige social housing companies to introduce a system of separate accounts.[91] Furthermore, the commitment was made to change the Dutch laws on social housing in such a way that they will provide, inter alia, that 90% of the dwellings in each social housing company must be rented to a pre-defined target group of less advantaged persons.[92]

In December 2009, the Commission adopted a Decision on these new Dutch laws[93] and put forward that the clear definition of the target group (persons having an income below 33,000 euro per year) adequately addressed the problems outlined in its letter of 2005. The definition of the SGEI deployed in the (proposed) Dutch social housing laws clearly delimits the scope of the activities to socially less advantaged households and were, therefore, acceptable in the Commission's view.[94] Furthermore, the Commission was not opposed to the practice of renting out 10% of the dwellings to higher income groups, as this practice contributes to '… social mixity and social cohesion …' in cities and towns in the Netherlands[95] (it prevents some neighbourhoods from being populated solely by low income groups). Eventually, in 2009—after being involved in a heated debate with the Dutch authorities for over 4 years—the Commission approved the system of social housing on the basis of Article 106(2) TFEU, as this system will be made subject to a significant reform leading to a strong divide between the core social housing activities and other activities (of a commercial nature). On top of this, in its 2009 Decision, the Commission also approved aid for declining urban areas proposed by the Dutch authorities in order to improve the quality of life in the most deprived urban areas. The Commission found (again) that this aid was justifiable in the light of Article 106(2) TFEU.[96] Although the Dutch state aid measures were cleared, the Commission Decision was appealed against as it was believed that the Commission has not the authority to intervene with national policies on social housing and Services of General (Economic) Interest.[97] In this interesting and principal case the General Court, and possibly the European Court of Justice on appeal, will have the opportunity to shed light on the relationship between the EU state aid rules and social housing.

---

[90] See De Vries and Lavrijsen 2009, p. 408.

[91] See the letter of the Minister of Housing of 13 September 2005, Woningcorporaties, Kamerstukken II (official parliamentary documents), 29 453, nr. 20.

[92] See Commission Decision in Cases No. E 2/2005 and N 642/2009 (The Netherlands, Existing and special project aid to housing corporations) of 15 December 2009, at point 41.

[93] Ibid.

[94] See Commission Decision in Cases No E 2/2005 and N 642/2009 (The Netherlands, Existing and special project aid to housing corporations) of 15 December 2009, at points 56 and 57.

[95] Ibid., at point 58.

[96] Ibid., at points 92–102.

[97] This appeal is registered as General Court, Case T-201/10, Case T-202/10 and Case T-203/10.

In an Irish case on social housing the process of approving the State aid at stake went much smoother.[98] At issue was a financial system that was operated in order to finance social housing activities. The Housing Finance Agency (HFA) raised funds at favourable rates on the capital market and, subsequently, transferred these funds to the authorities that provided social housing services to the most socially disadvantaged households. The task assigned to HFA may be supported by a state guarantee. As already mentioned, the social housing authorities were considered as undertakings within the meaning of EU competition law. They benefited from the funding raised by the HFA that in turn was supported by State guarantees. As a consequence, the Irish system concerned constituted state aid. However, the measure was justified because the housing corporations involved were entrusted with the operation of a SGEI. The Commission considered that the beneficiaries of the Irish scheme were socially disadvantaged households. Furthermore, the condition of entrustment was met, as the tasks of HFA were set out clearly in Irish legislation. Unlike the (old) Dutch system that was targeted by the Commission in 2005, the Irish measures financing social housing were based on clearly defined SGEI missions.

In this writer's view, the fact that social housing services were only provided to low-income households was of great importance. In this regard the EFTA case on the Icelandic Housing Financing Fund is of relevance. In this case, the EFTA surveillance authority was of the opinion that the State aid measures concerned were not justifiable, although the social housing services that were financed by these measures might be regarded as SGEI.[99] These measures did not pursue a sufficiently restricted social objective, because all households (low-income and high income groups) could benefit from the scheme concerned.

These cases show that the concept of SGEI plays an important role in bringing the funding of social housing activities in line with EU law. So, Member States that model these activities as SGEI may fairly assume that national measures aimed at financing these activities will be compatible with EU law. However, it is of great importance that the group of beneficiaries is restricted to low-income households and does not encompass wealthy people.

6.5 Soft Law: Communications from the Commission

In the light of the case law analysed in the previous sections it is not a surprising that the Commission noted in its White Paper on SGEI of 2004 that, although the SSGI belong to the competences of the Member States, EU law has an impact on the

[98] Decision of the Commission in case State aid N 209/2001—Ireland, Guarantee for borrowings of the Housing Finance Agency, 3 July 2001.

[99] See the decision of the EFTA surveillance authority in case No 406/08/COL to initiate the formal investigation procedure with regard to the relief of the Icelandic Housing Financing Fund from payment of a State guarantee premium, 27 June 2008.

instruments for their delivery and financing.[100] On the one hand, the Commission contended that the special features of SSGI should be fully recognised. On the other hand it was put forward that the distinction between missions and instruments needs to be clarified in order to assist Member States which make use of market-based systems in order to deliver social services.[101] On top of this, the Commission put forward that in future communications the development of social services will be described and monitored in close cooperation with the Member States.[102]

In 2006, the Commission issued its first Communication dedicated to SSGI.[103] This Communication recognises the special characteristics of SSGI by stressing, inter alia, that they operate on the basis of the solidarity principle, that they aim to protect the most vulnerable, that they are not for profit and that they are strongly rooted in (local) cultural traditions.[104] However, it is striking that in the view of the Commission, the fact that the provision of SSGI increasingly fall under the EU rules on the Internal Market and competition is '... a sign of the trend towards modernising social services, via greater transparency and greater effectiveness in organisation and financing.'[105] In other words: the introduction of competition elements into various national SSGI schemes is supported by EU law and should even be regarded as a manifestation of modernisation of social policy. Furthermore, in the 2006 Communication the application of the EU Internal Market and competition rules to SSGI is briefly touched upon.[106]

In order to monitor the developments with regard to SSGI, the Commission commissioned a study. According to this study, social services have been expanding and this expansion was accompanied by the introduction of new steering mechanisms that are, inter alia, market-oriented.[107] The study also contends that the way EU Internal Market and competition law should be applied to SSGI is frequently misperceived in many Member States, and that therefore EU action in the form of advancing monitoring and documentation of good practices may be very helpful.[108] As a result of this study, Member States and stakeholders

---

[100] See the Communication from the Commission of 12 May 2004, White Paper on Services of General Interest, COM(2004) 374 final, 16. See Chap. 3 by Neergaard.

[101] Ibid.

[102] See the Communication from the Commission of 12 May 2004, *White Paper on Services of General Interest*, COM(2004) 374 final, 17.

[103] Communication from the Commission of 26 April 2006. *Implementing the Community Lisbon programme: Social services of general interest in the European Union*, SEC(2006) 516.

[104] Ibid., at 4 and 5.

[105] Ibid., at 6.

[106] A comprehensive discussion of the interplay between SSGI and these EU rules can be found in the Commission *Staff Working Document accompanying the 2006 Communication on SSGI*, COM(2006) 177 final.

[107] Study on Social and Health Services of General Interest in the European Union, by Manfred Huber, Mathias Maucher, Barbara Sak, Prepared for DG Employment, Social Affairs and Equal Opportunities, DG EMPL/E/4, VC/2006/0131, 5.

[108] Ibid., 6.

were asked to give their views on the relationship between SSGI and EU law. The feedback report showed that the majority of the respondents were not in favour of the adoption of binding European laws on SSGI.[109] However, monitoring and coordination[110] by the EU was welcomed.[111]

In 2007, in the slipstream of the launch of its policy for 'a single market for 21st century Europe', the Commission issued a new Communication that, inter alia, dealt with SSGI.[112] In this Communication the applicability of the internal market and competition rules to, inter alia, SSGI is discussed. According to the Commission, only services provided for remuneration (services having an economic character) are caught by the free movement rules.[113] However, this point of view is not supported by the analysis carried out in Sect. 6.3 of this chapter. This section pointed out that according to the case law of the ECJ insurable services, even those provided in a state-regulated context, fall within the scope of the Treaty provisions on free movement. So, the scope of the fundamental freedoms is broader than assumed by the Commission. In its 2007 Communication, the Commission again recognised the special nature of SSGI and stressed once more the point that the provision of these services is subject to a modernisation process.[114] In this process market considerations and compliance with the EU rules on the internal market and competition play an important role. Furthermore, the Commission has put forward that it wants to contribute to the development of a methodology to set, monitor, and evaluate quality standards.[115] Apart from this, the Commission will support 'cross-European bottom-up initiatives' aimed at developing these (voluntary) standards and exchanging good practices.[116] Interestingly, the Commission stated that the Protocol on Services of General Interest annexed to the Treaty of Lisbon 2009 will serve as a bench mark for reviewing EU and national actions regarding SGEI.[117] So, since 1 December 2009 (the date the Treaty of Lisbon entered into force) EU principles of primary law governing SGEI including SSGI are in place. The Commission kept its promise with regard to its monitoring commitments and published its first biennial report on SSGI in 2008.[118] Once

---

[109] Feedback report to the 2006 questionnaire of the Social Protection Committee (available at: http://ec.europa.eu/employment_social/spsi/docs/social_protection/2008/feedback_report_final_en.pdf), 15.

[110] It was explicitly put forward that the Open Method of Coordination could contribute to the field of SSGI and the focus should be on the exchange of good practices.

[111] Feedback report to the 2006 questionnaire of the Social Protection Committee, 17.

[112] Communication from the Commission of 20 November 2007, *Services of general interest, including social services of general interest: a new European commitment.*

[113] Ibid., 5.

[114] Ibid., 7 and 8.

[115] Ibid., 13.

[116] Ibid.

[117] Ibid., 9.

[118] Commission Staff Working Document, *Biennial Report on social services of general interest*, SEC(2008) 2179/2.

again, in this report attention was paid to the modernisation process of SSGI and the need to clarify the consequences that the EU Internal Market and competition rules have for SSGI.

In this regard it should be noted that in 2007 the Commission also issued two Frequently Asked Question (FAQ) documents. The first FAQ document relates to public service compensations[119] and the second FAQ document concerns issues of public procurement and SSGI.[120] The aim of these documents is to give guidance to the Member States' competent authorities on how to deal with state aid and public procurement matters in relation to SSGI. The guidance given by the Commission was evaluated by the Social Protection Committee. It turned out that the FAQ documents are generally welcome but the evaluation report also specifies various questions which should be taken into account when the Commission updates these FAQs.[121]

The recent Monti Report acknowledges that it is for the Member States to ensure that SSGI are provided but claims that the EU can 'assist Member States in modernising these services and adapting them to a changing environment and to the evolving needs of citizens regarding their scope and quality.'[122] This Report also points to the modernisation process to which SSGI have been subject to over the last two decades. Interestingly, the Monti Report does not only pay attention to 'traditional SSGI' but also points to services to which citizens should have access in modern society, such as basic banking services and access to broadband Internet connection.[123] It is even proposed to make the State aid and public procurement rules more flexible with a view on these essential services. At the writing of this chapter the official reaction of the Commission to this Report was not available.

It is apparent from the analysis carried out above that a red thread running through the Commission's soft law approach towards SSGI is that the provision of these services is subject to a modernisation process. An important aspect of this process is the introduction of market-driven elements into SSGI schemes. It is this writer's view that the Commission appreciates this aspect of the SSGI modernisation process, as it considers the application of the EU Internal Market and competition rules to SSGI as a significant manifestation of this process. Consequently, it may be assumed that future Member State action aiming at liberalising

---

[119] Commission Staff Working Document of 20 November 2007, *Frequently asked questions in relation with Commission Decision of 28 November 2005 on the application of Article 86(2) of the EC Treaty to State aid in the form of public service compensation granted to undertaking entrusted with the operation of services of general economic interest, and of the Community Framework for State aid in the form of public service compensation*, SEC(2007) 1516.

[120] Commission Staff Working Document of 20 November 2007, Ibid.

[121] See the Operational Conclusions of the Social Protection Committee on the application of Community rules to SSGI, SPC 2008/17-final, 21.

[122] See *A New Strategy for the Single Market. At the Services of Europe's Economy and Society, Report the President of the European Commission by Mario Monti*, 9 May 2010, 73. Available at: http://ec.europa.eu/bepa/pdf/monti_report_final_10_05_2010_en.pdf.

[123] See the Monti Report, supra n. 122, at 75 and 76.

and privatising SSGI schemes will be welcomed by the Commission.[124] Furthermore, the Commission refrains from proposing legally binding European laws for SSGI but it does continue issuing all kinds of soft law documents and setting up voluntary cooperation frameworks. By doing so, the Commission is influencing the way SSGI are modelled and provided in the Member States.

6.6 Conclusions

The Treaty provisions on free movement are capable of opening up national social security systems, as far as these systems concern insurable risks. The *Freskot* and *Kattner Stahlbau* cases show that the distinction between non-economic and economic activities is not a clear dividing line for applying these rules to social security schemes. In contrast, competition rules such as the Treaty provisions on state aid are only of relevance if the social security scheme at hand operates on a mix of solidarity and competition elements. If this is the case, the funding of the managing bodies concerned could be questionable in the light of the EU State aid rules. However, like the funding of social services directly provided to the person, the concepts of PSO and SGEI may help the Member States in designing a 'EU law compatible policy' of transferring financial resources to these managing bodies.

The diverging ways of applying the free movement and competition rules to SSGI could even give rise to tensions. Above it is argued that compulsory affiliation to complementary schemes may be at odds with the free movement rules. But in the *Brentjens* case law, the compulsory affiliation to the Dutch complementary pension schemes was not in violation of the applicable competition rules.

The key to reconciling these conflicting findings might be the concept of SGEI. It is argued that the exception of Article 106(2) TFEU gives more leeway for Member States to regulate SGEI than the traditional free movement exceptions do. The restriction of competition that was at stake in *Brentjens* was justified by Article 106(2) TFEU. Probably, a similar restriction of free movement could also be justifiable in the light of this Treaty provision. In this regard it should be noted that the insertion of Article 16 into the EC Treaty, now Article 14 TFEU, according to which the proper provision of SGEI should be ensured, shows a shift from a market-centred approach to an approach in which social values also are of importance.[125] Furthermore, it should be pointed out that according to Article 36 of the Charter on Fundamental Rights of the EU[126] the EU should recognise and respect access to SGEI. Against this background, it is a pity that in the *Sint Servatius* case, which concerned the relationship between social housing services and free movement, the ECJ failed to clarify the role Article 106(2) TFEU may

124 See also Karayigit 2009, p. 581.

125 See Prosser 2005, p. 553.

126 *OJ* 2000 C 364/1.

play in national SSGI policies. The constitutional dimension of this Treaty provision and its significance for SSGI were not elaborated in the case.

It is clear that the issue of dissociablility of the non-essential services from essential social services plays an important role in the case law of the ECJ. National SSGI policies leading to restrictions in the provision of 'dissociable services' are regarded to be incompatible with EU law in many of the ECJ judgments. It could be argued that the Commission has further built on this finding of the ECJ in its soft law documents. The introduction of competition elements is regarded by this EU institution as a manifestation of the modernisation process of SSGI. The Commission further encourages the Member States to design their SSGI schemes in a clear and transparent way.

What are the future prospects of the SSGI in the EU? In this writer's view, rethinking this concept is of eminent importance. Admittedly, the term SSGI could give rise to conceptual confusion,[127] but it is also capable of solving problems that occur in legal practice. Member States can protect social services from adverse effects resulting from the application of the EU Internal Market and competition rules by designating these services as SGEI. This means that a constituent component of SSGI should be the entrustment of a special task by the State. After all, the requirement of entrustment is an essential condition for relying upon the concept of SGEI as laid down in Article 106(2) TFEU and for relying upon the *Altmark* approach (PSO). So, social services constituting economic activities must be modelled as SGEI in so far as they are regarded by the Member States to be of special interest for their citizens. This means that SSGI should be designed in a clear and transparent way. By doing so, the Member States make clear which services should be provided on the market and which services, being SSGI, should be protected from market forces. In this regard the protecting measures of the Member States should be confined to what is necessary for the fulfilment of the social objectives concerned.

To conclude, it seems inevitable that elements of competition will be introduced into schemes for the provision of services that now have a social dimension in many Member States. EU law will force Member States to reconsider the designs of these schemes. It may be assumed that in the future national policies aimed at protecting essential social services will only be successful if Member States transform these essential services into SSGI, in the sense that these services are SGEI. Hence, the future development of essential social services depends largely on the way Member States make a distinction between essential social services (SSGI) and other services.

[127] See Krajewski 2008, p. 386.

References

Baquero Cruz J (2005) Beyond competition: services of general interest and European Community Law. In: De Búrca G (ed) EU law and the welfare state. In search of solidarity. Oxford University Press, Oxford, pp 193–198

Barnard C (2006) EC employment law. Oxford University Press, Oxford

Barnard C (2008) Unravelling the Services Directive. CMLRev 45:341

Buendia Sierra JL (1999) Exclusive rights and state monopolies under EC law. Article 86 (Former Article 90) of the EC Treaty. Oxford University Press, Oxford

Cicoria C (2006) Non-profit organizations facing competition. The application of United States, European and German Competition Law to not-for-profit entities. Peter Lang Publishing, Frankfurt am Main

De Vries SA, Lavrijsen S (2009) Netherlands. In: Krajewski M, Neergaard U, Van de Gronden JW (eds) The changing framework for services of general interest in Europe. Between competition and solidarity. T.M.C. Asser Press, The Hague, p 408

Drijber BJ, Stergiou H (2009) Public procurement law and internal market law. CMLRev 46:805

Fiedziuk N (2010) Towards a more refined economic approach to services of general interest. Eur Public Law 16:280

Hancher L, Sauter W (2010) One step beyond? From Sodemare to DocMorris: the EU's freedom of establishment case law concerning healthcare. CMLRev 47:120

Hatzopoulos VG (2002) Killing national health and insurance systems but healing patients? The European market for health care services after the judgments of the ECJ in Vanbraekel and Peerbooms. CMLRev 39:710

Karayigit MT (2009) The notion of services of general economic interest revisted. Eur Public Law 15:581

Krajewski M (2008) Providing legal clarity and securing policy space for public services through a legal framework for services of general economic interest: squaring the circle? Eur Public Law 14:386

Monti M (2010) A new strategy for the single market. At the service of Europe's economy and society. Report to the President of the European Commission by Monti M, 9 May 2010, 74 and 75. http://ec.europa.eu/bepa/pdf/monti_report_final_10_05_2010_en.pdf

Mortelmans KJM (2008) Chapter VIII The functioning of the internal market: the freedoms. In: McDonnell A, Kapteyn PJG, Mortelmans KJM, Timmermans CWA (eds) The law of the European Union and the European Communities. Kluwer International, Alphen aan den Rijn, p 59

Neergaard U (2009) Services of general economic interest: the nature of the beast. In: Krajewski M, Neergaard U, Van de Gronden JW (eds) The changing legal framework for services of general interest in Europe. T.M.C. Asser Press, The Hague, p 32

Nistor L (2009) Public services and the European Union. A study of the impact of community law on health care. Dissertation, Health Insurance and Educational Services, Groningen

Prechal S, De Vries SA (2009) Seamless web of judicial protection in the internal market. Eur Law Rev 51:5

Prosser T (2005) Competition law and public services: from single market to citizenship rights? Eur Public Law 11:553

Sauter W (2009) Case comment on Case T-289/03, British United Provident Association. CMLRev 43:269

Sauter W, Schepel H (2009) State and market in European Union law. The public and private spheres of the internal market before the EU Courts. Cambridge University Press, Cambridge

Szyszczak E (2009) Modernising healthcare: pilgrimage for the Holy Grail? In: Krajewski M, Neergaard U, Van de Gronden JW (eds) The changing legal framework for services of general interest in Europe. T.M.C. Asser Press, The Hague, p 210

Van de Gronden JW (2008) Cross-border health care in the EU and the organization of the national health care systems of the Member States: the dynamics resulting from the European Court of Justice's Decisions on free movement and competition law. Wisconsin Int Law J 26

Van de Gronden JW (2009a) The Services Directive and services of general (economic) interest. In: Krajewski M, Neergaard U, Van de Gronden JW (eds) The changing legal framework for services of general interest in Europe. T.M.C. Asser Press, The Hague, pp 248–250

Van de Gronden JW (2009–2010) Financing health care in EU Law: Do the European state aid rules write out an effective prescription for integrating competition law with health care? The Competition Law Rev 6(1):5

Chapter 7
Universal Service Obligations: Fulfilling New Generations of Services of General Economic Interest

Jim Davies and Erika Szyszczak

Abstract This chapter charts the development of universal service obligations (USOs) in the EU liberalisation programme. *Davies and Szyszczak* see an expanding role for the concept of USOs in the future development of the EU, from a social perspective as well as a commercial perspective. The authors note that whereas a Member State has a wide competence to define a SGEI, this is no longer the case when a USO is found in liberalising legislation. The authors question whether the use of USOs is a temporary device and whether USOs will survive if, and when, there is full market liberalisation of a sector. Their chapter charts the various stages of the evolution of an EU concept of a USO and their analysis concludes that far from the gradual demise of the USO in the liberalisation process, they see the concept changing, evolving and expanding in its role of protecting the consumer–citizen interest in the Internal Market. A second focus of this chapter is to place the consumer–citizen at the heart of the USO. While academics have argued that USOs have a role to play in protecting the *vulnerable* consumer contributing to the evolution of a *social* European private law Davies and Szyszczak argue that USOs have a much wider remit in contributing not only to the inclusiveness of EU society but also the *effectiveness* of the benefits brought by an Internal Market. They argue that by placing the consumer–citizen of EU law at the heart of a complex web of networked relationships several new issues emerge of governance of the processes and outcomes through which consumer, competition and integration issues are mediated.

J. Davies (✉)
Department of Law, School of Social Sciences, The University of Northampton, Park Campus, Boughton Green Road, Northampton, NN2 7AL, UK
e-mail: jim.davies@northampton.ac.uk

E. Szyszczak
University of Leicester, Barrister, Littleton Chambers, London, LE1 7RH, UK
e-mail: ems11@le.ac.uk

E. Szyszczak et al. (eds.), *Developments in Services of General Interest*,
Legal Issues of Services of General Interest, DOI: 10.1007/978-90-6704-734-0_7,

Contents

7.1 Introduction

The aim of this chapter is to trace the evolution of the universal service concepts found in EU regulation and to (re)-locate the role of the consumer as a central actor in the regulation of universal service obligations (USOs) in the liberalisation process. Our reasons for doing this are because USOs represent a Europeanisation of the traditional public services [or as they are re-named in EU law services of general (economic) interest]. A study of universal obligations allows an inquiry as to how far, and in what form, can the traditional public services be regulated at the EU level and also retain the capacity to evolve and adapt to new technology and consumer demands.

A second reason for this chapter is to revisit the classical view of USOs as focussed upon the vulnerable consumer and creating a new triangular relationship with the State. Our analysis is that USOs create a new paradigm of consumer rights. The relationships which have emerged involve not only complex triangular relationships between the consumer–provider–State but also give rise to complex networks of multi-dimensional and multi-level economic and political relationships.

In order to analyse these developments the chapter is organised as follows. After this Introduction, Sect. 7.2 examines the political and economic reasons for developing ideas of USOs in EU law. Section 7.3 identifies the generic understandings of USOs. Section 7.4 examines the evolution of public service obligations and the move away from simple triangular relationships between the State–provider–consumer to examine a more complex triangle geometry and the emergence of networks. Section 7.5 then raises issues on the governance and regulation of USOs. Finally, Sect. 7.6 draws some conclusions as to whether USOs will continue to exist in EU law and the challenges which face them with new technology creating convergence between different sectors.

7.2 The Political and Economic Reasons for EU Universal Service Obligations

Writing in May 2010 Mario Monti states:

> In order to be able to effectively participate in the single market citizens need access to a number of basic services of general economic interest, in particular in the area of network industries, such as postal services, transport services or telecommunication services. In the network industries, market opening at EU level has therefore always been accompanied by measures ensuring that a universal service continued to be provided.[1]

However, earlier when introducing the section of his Report '3.3 Social services in the single market' Monti describes the place of public services within the single market as 'a persistent irritant'.[2] Uncertainty over the survival of basic essential public services in liberalised markets led the Member States to include positive references to their existence in the central EU Treaty provisions. The concern to maintain relationships with vulnerable consumers was matched with other concerns of the Member States involving the role of public services in social, economic, and regional cohesion within the Member States. As Chap. 2 by Bauby shows, Article 14 TFEU reinforces the crucial role that services of general economic interest (SGEI) play in territorial and social cohesion within the Member States and the EU and at the same time modernises the old Article 16 EC by providing a legal base for the regulation of SGEIs at the EU level, despite a lack of competence to do so, either as an aim or as an objective of the EU. Protocol 26 on Services of General Interest to the Treaty of Lisbon 2009 reinforces the role of subsidiarity and diversity in developing the delivery of SGEIs in the EU and re-affirms the Member States' competence to deliver and organise non-economic services of general interest.

Article 36 of Charter of Fundamental Rights of the European Union, found in Chapter IV entitled 'Solidarity', also recognises *access* to SGEIs 'as provided for in national laws and practices' as part of the promotion of social and territorial cohesion in the EU. Other aspects of the Charter build upon economic and social rights found in national constitutions and international, and regional human rights, and economic and social rights' documents. These provisions complement the role of Article 106(2) TFEU in providing a shield from the full force of the economic (or 'market') rules of the TFEU for SGEIs where these rules would obstruct or hinder the SGEI tasks assigned to undertakings.

Historically, the ring-fencing of SGEIs in the interpretation of Article 106 (2) TFEU allowed the Member States to demand special rules for SGEIs in the liberalisation programmes of telecommunications, postal services, and utilities which swept across the EU in the 1990s through the definition and special protection of USOs in EU legislation.[3] The more challenges that were made to State monopolies,

---

1 Monti 2010, p. 74.

2 Ibid., at p.73.

3 See Szyszczak 2001; Neergaard 2008.

the more the Commission used soft governances processes to link the old world of public services to the new world of SGEIs and USOs. As Neergaard shows:

> ... the impression may be gained that 'services of general economic interest' are such services which are subject to 'USOs', such as the obligation to provide a certain service throughout the territory at affordable tariffs and on similar quality conditions, irrespective of the profitability of the individual operations.[4]

Similarly Neergaard cites the ECJ's concurrence with this view from its ruling in *Almelo*[5] and also the report from the Conseil Economique et Social and the Opinion issued by the State Aid Group of EAGCP,[6] as taking the same view.[7] The Commission also sees linkages between SGEIs and USOs in its Communication, *Opportunities, access and solidarity: towards a new social vision for twenty-firstcentury Europe*.[8]

Academic authors have also argued that universal services should coincide with SGEIs.[9] However, as Neergaard concludes where universal services are present there is also a strong indication that this will be a SGEI but it is not the only, or decisive, test.[10]

Recognising that USOs were essential *commercial* activities which are not necessarily responsive to normal market conditions was an important step in the mediation of State responsibility for universal services and the supply of these services in liberalised markets. The use of market discipline or 'marketisation' of essential services was seen to contribute to efficiency, affordability and choice. This was a policy approach which was a central element in the new public management: the promotion of consumer sovereignty. However, by so doing, the Member States agreed to the Europeanisation of these services, through their definition in EU legislation, setting the parameters for compensation mechanisms for the delivery of USOs by State and non-State bodies and by the creation of new sets of consumer rights where the central premises of the delivery of the USO were not met.[11]

---

[4] Neergaard 2009, p. 39, citing as an example Commission, *Communication from the Commission. Services of General Interest in Europe* COM(2000) 580, 19 January 2001 and the *Commission Green Paper on Services of General Interest*, COM(2003) 270.

[5] ECJ, Case C-393/92 *Municipality of Almeloand Others* v. *Energiebedrijf IJsselmij* [1994] *ECR* I-1477, paras 47–48.

[6] *Analysis of the Implications of the Lisbon Treaty on Services of General Interest and Proposals for Implementation.*

[7] Discussion Paper drawn up by European Experts 2008, pp. 41–42, looking at the application of the concept of SGEIs for liberalising network industries.

[8] COM(2007) 726 at p.10.

[9] See for example, Sauter 2008, p. 179.

[10] Neergaard 2009, p. 44.

[11] Contrast with SGEIs where the Member States retain competence to define a SGEI and have some leeway in the funding arrangements provided that they follow the conditions in ECJ, Case C-280/00 *Altmark* [2003] *ECR* I-7747 or satisfy the proportionality of the funding to the Commission.

The regulation of the liberalisation processes in the EU was intended as an interim step, with a desired move towards fully competitive markets. This raised the question of what would be the future role of USOs and how would they be reconciled with competitive markets?

7.3 Generic Definitions and Understanding of Universal Service Obligations

The two terms, 'public service obligation' and 'USO', are used inter-changeability but they have a different genealogy. The General Court in *BUPA*[12] accepted the parties' submission that in *Altmark*[13] a public service obligation corresponds with a 'service of general economic interest', as understood under Article 106(2) TFEU. Indeed in 1957 the drafters of the original Treaty of Rome 1957 took the bold step of re-inventing public services in a new European language of 'services of general economic interest', a concept unknown in the legal, political or scientific languages of the Member States in 1957.[14]

Public service obligations are obligations which the State has chosen to create in defining the kind and coverage of certain public services within its territory. In contrast, in this chapter, we are focusing upon a narrow definition of USOs as defined in the sectoral liberalisation legislation of the EU. This is because we see the terminology of USOs as a significant move at the EU-level to depart not only from ideas of 'public' service obligations but also its own terminology of 'services of general economic interest'. Universal services signify that certain services are available to all but can be provided by either the public bodies owned and regulated by the State or non-State bodies or a hybrid of public and private provision. This neutrality in ownership and provision is significant in the over-arching EU policy of liberalisation and the creation of consumer sovereignty. Universal service obligations also create a grass-roots consumer responsiveness model in that consumers, as citizens, have a right to choose high quality, reliable, and continuous services. In the liberalised network industries public USOs establish a compensatory basis for the provision of services on social or broad economic need that would otherwise lack commercial viability but also do more: they create a *range* of consumer rights. Significantly, they create rights to access to information from providers and regulators contributing to a more sophisticated notion of a 'consumer–citizen' in EU law.[15]

---

[12] CFI/GC, Case T- 289/03 *BUPA* [2008] *ECR* II-741.

[13] ECJ, Case C-280/00 *Altmark* [2003] *ECR* I-7747.

[14] See Chap. 2 by Bauby. For a discussion of the different historical, political, and cultural influences on the evolution of public services in Europe see Prosser 2005.

[15] Davies 2010.

Universal service obligations are defined in the *Communication From the Commission Services of General Interest in Europe* in 2001 as:

> Universal service, in particular the definition of specific USOs is a key accompaniment to market liberalisation of service sectors such as telecommunications in the European Union. The definition and guarantee of universal service ensures that the continuous accessibility and quality of established services is maintained for all users and consumers during the process of passing from monopoly provision to openly competitive markets. Universal service, within an environment of open and competitive telecommunications markets, is defined as the minimum set of services of specified quality to which all users and consumers have access in the light of specific national conditions, at an affordable price.[16]

This is essentially explaining the over-arching normative approach to USOs, focusing upon *what they do*, rather than their content. In the liberalisation Directives the specific detail is left to sectoral legislation and a margin of discretion is left for the Member States to adapt the USO to local needs.

Szyszczak argues that the use of USOs in liberalised markets is double-edged: the use of USOs to protect essential public services in the liberalisation processes serve as a reminder of the limits of the market to guarantee the public interest values, but also as an indicator of how the market can improve the quality of these values.[17]

Some of the criticisms of using State monopolies came from their inability to deliver sufficiently high quality public services and to adapt to changing consumer needs and demands. Thus in addition to the idea of universality in coverage of universal services the liberalisation programmes also focused attention on quality, continuity of supply, access, affordability and consumer protection issues. This linkage between universality as well as other consumer interests was not accepted by some theorists as being naturally progressive. In addition to confusing public and private law obligations, confusion is created by shifting a former field of activities belonging to politics to economics.[18] Teubner describes the new role for the providers of universal obligations as a strange phenomenon whereby arcane principles discarded from medieval law obligations are suddenly transposed into the private law relationships of competitive markets.[19]

Universal service obligations are envisaged as having a role to play in the redistributive tasks of the State, allowing for wealthier providers and consumers to cross-subsidise poorer consumers of public services. Liberalisation is portrayed as engaging consumers by allowing consumers greater choice over services and goods, and places consumers in a better legal position to assert their rights on the *quality* of what were once perceived to be public services. This is achieved through a focus on transparency and empowering the consumer through information.

---

[16] *OJ* 2001 C 17/4, 19 January 2001, Annex II, p. 23.

[17] Szyszczak 2007, p. 243.

[18] Micklitz 2009, p. 10.

[19] Teubner 1998, p. 411.

A central outcome in the liberalisation process is to place the consumer at the epicentre of a system of complex networks. This aspect of liberalisation has been ignored in the various analyses of the dynamics of liberalisation and USOs.

Micklitz has argued '... that the EU rules on universal services contain the nucleus of an emerging social European private law.'[20] His argument is that USOs were used to prevent social exclusion as State monopolies delivering basic services were privatised. Thus the role of USOs was to '... guarantee the supply of these services to those who lack the resources to buy them at the market price.'[21] However, the role of universal services in providing protection for vulnerable consumers is seen as flawed because its focus is upon a second generation of social law in the form of consumer rights. This critique is seen in the analysis which examines the creation of a consumer-citizenship role for citizens within a fundamental rights context.[22] It is argued that for citizens many of the rights attaching to 'universal' service obligation are contingent upon *access* to a first generation of *social* rights: owning, or having access to property in order to enjoy telecommunications, postal and utility services.

If we look more closely at the content and scope of USOs we see that the role of USOs extends beyond the protection of the vulnerable consumer to playing a bigger role in social, regional and territorial cohesion and the concept is used to assuage fears of the Member States that their role in providing for, protecting, and developing the general interest is limited where core services necessary for the general interest are taken away from State control.

Our analysis of USOs shows that over time different generations of USOs have developed and that the concept has evolved into a normative status, capable of adaptation to new technological and social demands. Rather than retreating in a competitive market place the concepts have evolved into new forms of fundamental and consumer-citizenship rights as Member States have linked the evolution of USOs with developments in technology. There has been a focus on the content and delivery of public service obligations and USOs, particularly in terms of sector specific content and their delivery at national level.

What interests us is understanding the development of USOs in such a way that we can consider what, if any, core aspects can be identified, what their scope may be, and what the next stage in the evolution of USOs may look like. Already at the EU level, we can see the development of multi-layered obligations and the sectoral influences of the market or technology on the nature of USOs. We also observe consumer, fundamental rights, and citizenship rights emerging as core ideas in the development and evolution of USOs.

---

[20] Micklitz 2009, p. 1.

[21] Ibid.

[22] Szyszczak 2009a, b.

7.4 The Evolution of Universal and Public Service Obligations

In this part of the chapter we show how different generations of USOs have emerged in the liberalised sectors.

7.4.1 Developing the Model: The Telecoms Sector and Universal Service Obligations

Early USOs were about *access*, essentially concerned with providing a service to consumers and users within geographical areas where there could be no commercial advantage. Beginning in the telecoms sector, USOs introduced the concept of splitting the *content* of services away from the physical network infrastructure and creating new wholesale markets as delivery streams for providing consumers and end users with *choice*. The development of USOs has been through EU legislation, hard law, and soft law communications, and is notable by the very sparse litigation in the area. Thus the concepts are legislative concepts, with only minor input from judicial interpretative sources.

The telecommunications terminal equipment market was the first to experience EU legislative USOs through which the Member States were to ensure equality of access in which consumers were to be given a free choice between the various types of equipment available.[23] Sectoral liberalisation was to be promoted through the withdrawal of any existing special or exclusive rights to provide terminal equipment and provisions to ensure that economic operators had the right to import, market, connect, bring into service and maintain terminal equipment, subject to independent regulatory type-approval for technical specification.[24] This legislative foray into the design of EU-wide liberalised and regulated markets was merely a first step, soon to be followed by reinforcement of the provisions for full mutual recognition of type-approval for terminal equipment[25] and the ECJ's endorsement of the regulatory independence aspect of the liberalised market model.[26]

During the first half of the 1990s, the telecom sector liberalisation measures spread rapidly beyond the terminal equipment market to provide for harmonised conditions for open and efficient access to telecoms networks and telecoms

---

[23] Directive 88/301/EEC of 16 May 1988 on competition in the markets in telecommunications terminal equipment, *OJ* 1998 L 131/73, and particularly recital 2 of the Preamble.

[24] Ibid., Articles 2, 3 and 6.

[25] Directive 91/263/EEC of 29 April 1991 on the approximation of the laws of the Member States concerning telecommunications terminal equipment, including the mutual recognition of their conformity, *OJ* 1991 L 128/1.

[26] ECJ, Case C-221-94 *Commission* v. *Luxemburg* [1996] *ECR* I-5669, para 21.

services,[27] harmonised and liberalised markets in satellite equipment and services[28] and the removal of restrictions limiting the provision of cable TV services.[29] The Full Competition Directive of 1996 brought an end to the special or exclusive rights that had ensured the initial financial stability of telecom network operators in developing a *geographic* universal service and connection to *any* service provider upon request within a reasonable period of time.[30] Network investment and technological development had brought geographic coverage and digitalisation to a number of Member States and the on-going heavy investment programmes, optic fibre-coverage, and network penetration were expected to improve significantly in the other Member States in the following years.[31] Universal service coverage at an affordable price, as the tenet of PSO's in the Open Network and Universal Service Directive, was accompanied by a particular geographic and *social* obligation to maintain affordability 'for users in rural or high cost areas and for vulnerable groups of users such as the elderly, those with disabilities or those with special social needs.'[32] To that end, Member States were to be able to provide for special or targeted tariff schemes with, *inter alia,* price capping or geographical averaging until competition was able to provide effective price control.[33]

The culmination of this first phase in the development of the USO model came with the much discussed Universal Services Directive in which the model was identified as dynamic and responsive to technological change. The first recital in the Preamble identified that:

> [t]he liberalisation of the telecommunications sector and increasing competition and choice for communications services go hand in hand with parallel action to create a harmonised regulatory framework which secures the delivery of universal service. The concept of universal service should evolve to reflect advances in technology, market developments, and changes in user demand. The regulatory framework established for the

---

[27] Directive 90/387/EEC of 28 June 1990 on the establishment of the internal market for telecommunications services through the implementation of open network provision, *OJ* 1990 L 192/1.

[28] Directive 94/46/EC of 13 October 1994 amending Directive 88/301/EEC and Directive 90/388/EEC in particular with regard to satellite communications, *OJ* 1994 L 268/15.

[29] Directive 95/51/EC of 18 October 1995 amending Directive 90/388/EEC with regard to the abolition of the restrictions on the use of cable television networks for the provision of already liberalized telecommunications services,*OJ 1*995 L 256/49.

[30] Directive 96/19/EC of 13 March 1996 amending Directive 90/388/EEC with regard to the implementation of full competition in telecommunications markets, *OJ* 1996 L 074/13, recital 4 of the preamble. Special or exclusive rights for the provision of voice telephony had hitherto been maintained by Article 2 of Directive 90/388/EEC on competition in the markets for telecommunications services, *OJ* 1990 L 192/10. .

[31] Ibid.

[32] Directive 98/10/EC on the application of open network provision (ONP) to voice telephony and on universal service for telecommunications in a competitive environment, *OJ* 1998 L 101/24, Article 3(1).

[33] Ibid.

> full liberalisation of the telecommunications market in 1998 in the Community defined the *minimum* scope of USOs and established rules for its costing and financing.[34]

It was a model that, at a minimum, defined universal service as a product available to all, independent of geography and at an affordable price.[35] A product that was to be provided in a regulated, and competitive market[36] with quality of service and reporting obligations placed on service providers,[37] together with financial transparency,[38] special measures to ensure access and affordability to the disabled and those end users identified as having low incomes or special social needs[39] and with provisions made for transparent, simple and inexpensive consumer complaints processes.[40]

7.4.2 The Model Applied: First Generation Obligations Extended to Other Market Sectors

The liberalisation of the telecom sector in the late 1980s, was a key turning point in the realisation that consumers wanted *choice* in the provision of essential services. The approach in the telecom sector saw different obligations relating to different aspects of the telecom business introduced on a step by step basis as a mechanism for eventually providing a geographical universal service network and an open access model that brought a competitive environment to service content. It was only after a number of years of developing the model that a review and restatement of the nature of the public service obligation (PSO) saw the notion of geographic universality introduced in 1997. In the same year, many aspects of the model were applied to postal services.[41]

The developmental initiative of maintaining special or exclusive rights during the early stages of liberalisation that had been used in the telecom sector were, within price, and weight limits, repeated in the postal sector for 'the clearance, sorting, transport, and delivery of items of domestic correspondence, whether by accelerated delivery or not.'[42] As with telecoms, the Postal Services Directive provided for the creation of independent national regulatory

[34] Directive 2002/22/EC on universal service and users' rights relating to electronic communications networks and services (Universal Service Directive), *OJ* 2002 L 108/51 [emphasis added].

[35] Ibid., Article 3.

[36] Ibid., Article 17.

[37] Ibid., Article 11 and Annex III.

[38] Ibid., Articles 13, 14 and 17(4).

[39] Ibid., Articles 7 and 9(3).

[40] Ibid., Article 34.

[41] Directive 97/67/EC on common rules for the development of the internal market of Community postal services and the improvement of quality of service, *OJ* 1998 L 15/14.

[42] Ibid., Article 7(1).

authorities,[43] competition of the non-reserved services relating to domestic correspondence,[44] quality of service obligations,[45] financial transparency,[46] and provisions made for transparent, simple and inexpensive consumer complaints processes.[47] Minimum harmonisation of universal quality of service obligations for the postal sector were set out in Article 3 and Articles 16–18 of the Directive with a standard formula for monitoring the routing time for end to end delivery for cross-border mail provided for in an Annex.

The next sector to be liberalised was postal services. The Postal Competition Directive of 2002 provided for reductions, to take effect in 2003 and 2006, of the price and weight limits that applied to the special or exclusive rights attached to items of domestic correspondence.[48] The objective was the 'gradual and controlled opening of the letters market to competition which allows all universal service providers sufficient time to put in place the further measures of modernisation and restructuring required to ensure their long-term viability under the new market conditions.'[49] The final removal of special or exclusive rights in the postal sector came with the 2008 Full Market Opening Directive that acknowledged that the:

> … progressive and gradual opening of postal markets to competition has provided universal service providers with sufficient time to put in place the necessary modernisation and restructuring measures required to ensure their long-term viability under new market conditions, and enabled Member States to adapt their regulatory systems to a more open environment.[50]

Again, the legislative model for USOs was reinforced with the 2008 Directive that elaborated the scope of independent national regulatory authorities, the gradual opening of markets to full competition, the setting of quality standards for universal service provision and the creation of a system to ensure compliance with those standards, financial transparency and provisions made for transparent, simple and inexpensive consumer complaints processes.[51]

With the passing of time, similar obligations have been applied to the gas and electricity utilities but it is only in the telecoms, posts, and electricity sectors that we find the obligation for a *universal* service offering. There is no such obligation with regard to retail gas services where the sector has, since its second legislative

---

[43] Ibid., Articles 1 and 22.

[44] Ibid., recital 39 of the Preamble with Article 22.

[45] Ibid., Articles 16, 17 and 18.

[46] Ibid., Articles 12–15.

[47] Ibid., Article 19.

[48] Directive 2002/39/EC amending Directive 97/67/EC with regard to the further opening to competition of Community postal services, *OJ* 2002 L 176/21, Article 1(1).

[49] Ibid., recital 14 of the Preamble.

[50] Directive 2008/6/EC amending Directive 97/67/EC with regard to the full accomplishment of the internal market of Community postal services, *OJ* 2008 L 052/3, recital 12 of the preamble and Article 1(8).

[51] Ibid., Article 1.

package, been organised on the basis of *public service obligations* and *consumer protection*.[52] The Common Rules Directive of the second legislative package for the internal electricity market[53] identifies that the retail electricity sector is also organised on the basis of PSOs and *consumer protection* with provision for universal service extended specifically to all household customers and 'where Member States deem it appropriate, small Enterprises... with fewer than 50 occupied persons and an annual turnover or balance sheet not exceeding EUR 10 million.' We return to these distinctions concerning the nature of PSO's and USOs, and to the association of PSOs with consumer protection, shortly, but first highlight those aspects of our *first generation* USO model that both reappear and are developed in the common rules of the energy sector.

The first generation USO model has developed from the rules attached to the telecoms Terminal Equipment Directive of 1988 into a relatively standard design embracing common components. Primary among these components is the obligation placed on Member States to establish competent, independent *national regulatory authorities* (NRAs) that have developed from the independent body merely responsible for type approval in the 1988 Directive[54] to the regulatory authorities of the first decade of the twenty-first century. These are regulatory authorities with diverse responsibilities for ensuring non-discrimination, effective competition, and efficient functioning of the market. The key areas of responsibility for the NRAs begin with the monitoring in their respective industry sectors of the capacity and interconnection in open networks; transparent accounting; tariff calculations; adherence to the competition rules; quality of service parameters; sectoral development within the context of the internal market and consumer complaints processes.

With Member States obliged to develop independent NRAs, increasingly detailed operational obligations have been placed on the service providers to meet and publish quality of service measures and to provide transparent complaints processes as a consumer right. The most recent obligations in the telecoms and the electricity sector call for service providers to provide tariff options to consumers that meet special social needs or provide special measures for disabled end-users. This is an important development because new sets of triangular relationships emerge with distinctive rights enforceable through legal processes. These we would term 'consumer-citizenship rights' and can be viewed as part of a new process of creating and delivering a European-level and a European-wide social model which extend the consumer role, not merely through the application of a developing rights agenda, but also through a greater agency role in sectoral

---

[52] Directive 2003/55/EC concerning common rules for the internal market in natural gas and repealing Directive 98/30/EC, *OJ* 2003 L 176/57, Article 3.

[53] Directive 2003/54/EC concerning common rules for the internal market in electricity and repealing Directive 96/92/EC, *OJ* 2003 L 176/37.

[54] Directive 88/301/EEC of 16 May 1988 on competition in the markets in telecommunications terminal equipment, *OJ* 1998 L 131/73, Article 6.

governance structures that are, or at least as the early indications suggest, evolving to provide platforms of voice and influence for consumer input into policy processes.

At the EU level, and with a sector specific architecture similar to that described elsewhere for the networks and structures of European consumer policy governance more generally,[55] the Council of European Energy Regulators (CEER) and the European Regulators Group for Electricity and Gas (ERGEG) were established to facilitate cooperation between the national regulatory agencies (NRAs) directly, and between the NRAs and the Commission. In a joint commentary from CEER and ERGEG, they identify that the aim 'is to create a stable and coherent climate for investment in an efficient integrated grid and, to deliver *open and competitive single EU markets in* gas and electricity *in the consumer interest.*'[56] Their factsheet summarises the consumer specific provisions of the *third* legislative package for energy[57] as including: a new *consumer forum* that is intended to stimulate the creation of a truly liberalised retail market and is positioned as analogous to the Florence (electricity) and Madrid (gas) forums that were established to promote market opening and competition through an informal EU level framework for the discussion of issues and the exchange of experience.[58] Based on these intentions, the new forum is to 'focus on specific retail issues… [in which] it should serve as a platform for all stakeholders to promote the establishment of an EU wide retail market' and provide guidance to assist Member States and the regulatory authorities in establishing clear, and gradually harmonising, market rules on competition in the retail market.[59]

Called the 'Citizens' Energy Forum', this new body is chaired by the Commission and attended by national and European consumer associations, representatives of the Member States, national energy regulators, and representatives from the electricity and gas industries. At its meetings in October 2008 and September 2009, in London, the Forum has debated, in detail, the changing role of the regulator and the increasing role of consumers in the new legislation, and has progressed a range of issues in the consumer interest. The Forum has identified 'the limited extent to which European citizens, and in some cases Member States,

---

[55] Davies 2009, p. 245.

[56] ERGEG and CEER, '3rd energy package and creating an effective EU Agency (ACER) in the consumer's interest' (2008) Fact Sheet Reference No. FS-08-01, Available at: http://www.energy-regulators.eu/portal/page/portal/EER_HOME/EER_PUBLICATIONS/NEWS_ARCHIVE/FS-08-01_CEER-ERGEG_EnergyAgency_2008-02-20.pdf (last accessed on 25 June 2010).

[57] Comprising, Regulation (EC) No 713/2009 establishing an Agency for the Cooperation of Energy Regulators; Regulation (EC) No 714/2009 on conditions for access to the network for cross-border exchanges in electricity; Regulation (EC) No 715/2009 on conditions for access to the natural gas transmission networks; Directive 2009/72/EC concerning common rules for the internal market in electricity, and Directive 2009/73/EC concerning common rules for the internal market in natural gas.

[58] Commission (EC), 'Draft proposal for a Directive concerning common rules for the internal market in electricity' (Communication) COM (2007) 528 final, 19 September 2007, 18.

[59] Ibid.

understood how European legislation protects their rights.'[60] The response has been to facilitate the provision of accurate and practical *information* about local or regional retail markets through a 'Checklist' relating to energy consumer rights.[61] Significantly, the Forum also suggests that:

> [i]nformation for consumers is not enough to ensure their active participation in the market... [that] consumers must be put back in the driving seat with regard to the development of retail markets so that they are sufficiently empowered to make markets deliver concrete benefits.[62]

The rhetorical structure of the energy Directives suggests USOs can be defined as a special sub-set or application of public service obligations in which all consumers enjoy a right to access the service at 'a specified quality within their territory at reasonable, easily, and clearly comparable and transparent prices' and in which the Member State may appoint a supplier of last resort.[63] This is a sector specific right to a universal service as one component in a set of public service obligations that have developed a consumer protection, rather than consumer access, character that we suggest can be catalogued as a *second generation* of public service obligations.

7.4.3 A Second Generation of Public Service Obligations

The second generation of PSOs are multi-layered, placing operational obligations on service providers, through the Member States, to provide transparent, quality of service performance information. They have developed from initiatives aimed at opening national markets in services of general economic interest with new objectives directed at the continuation of cross-border market consolidation and elimination of residual competitive barriers. The 2009 Energy Directives highlight these developments providing for the promotion of regional cooperation in which Member States are obliged to facilitate the creation of a competitive internal market and foster 'the consistency of their legal, regulatory and technical

60 Press Release, 'Citizens' Energy Forum', MEMO/09/429, 30 September 2009, http://europa.eu/rapid/pressReleasesAction.do?reference=MEMO/09/429&format=HTML&aged=0&language=EN&guiLanguage=fr (last accessed on 25 June 2010) at p. 2.

61 Directive 2009/73/EC concerning common rules for the internal market in natural gas, Article 3(12) and Directive 2009/72/EC concerning common rules for the internal market in electricity, Article 3(16).

62 Press Release, 'Citizens' Energy Forum', MEMO/09/429, 30 September 2009, http://europa.eu/rapid/pressReleasesAction.do?reference=MEMO/09/429&format=HTML&aged=0&language=EN&guiLanguage=fr (last accessed on 25 June 2010) at p. 2.

63 Directive 2009/72/EC concerning common rules for the internal market in electricity, Article 3(3).

framework.'[64] Whilst the scope of PSOs has been extended from regulatory oversight of market opening at national level to one at the level of a fully integrated internal market, the development of associated consumer protection measures introduced by these most recent Energy Directives, further, and incongruously extends other aspects of the regulatory role in the direction of protective consumer agency.

With an emphasis on security of supply, the right to a universal supply of electricity at a reasonable, easy and clearly comparable, transparent and non-discriminatory price is coupled, in both the electricity and gas sectors with an increased range of PSOs that take the form of reinforced consumer rights and better enforcement. The role of regulators is considerably extended through new duties requiring them to ensure that consumer protection measures are enforced and that customers benefit through the efficient functioning of their national market. Regulators will be involved in ensuring that the consumer has prompt access to their consumption data, and in monitoring the level, and effectiveness of market opening through the active monitoring of switching rates, complaints, and any distortion or restriction of competition in the retail market.[65] The Directives of this third legislative package oblige the Member States to ensure that a single point of contact be established to provide consumers with all necessary information concerning their rights[66]; to ensure that an independent mechanism such as an energy ombudsman or a consumer body is in place for the efficient treatment of complaints and out-of-court dispute settlements[67]; and to define vulnerable consumers and may refer to those suffering energy poverty, a definition that may also refer to the prohibition of disconnection at critical times.[68] As with their predecessors, the new energy sector Directives also contain specific consumer protection measures in an Annex: but measures that are reinforced here with new provisions providing consumers with the right to be properly informed of actual electricity consumption and costs, frequently enough to enable them *to regulate their own electricity consumption* and the right to a *good standard* of complaint handling by their energy service provider in which the consumer must be informed of the appropriate procedures.[69] Changes, it is argued, that will strengthen the normative base for consumer-citizenship practice and, to a degree, stimulate features of consumer motivation and capability that will promote increased consumer agency in the energy markets.

---

[64] Directive 2009/72/EC concerning common rules for the internal market in electricity, Article 6 and, similarly Directive 2009/73/EC concerning common rules for the internal market in natural gas, Article 7.

[65] Directive 2009/72/EC concerning common rules for the internal market in electricity, Article 37(p) and (j); Directive 2009/73/EC concerning common rules for the internal market in natural gas, Article 41 (q) and (j).

[66] Ibid., Articles 3(12) and 3(9) respectively.

[67] Ibid., Articles 3(13) and 3(9) respectively.

[68] Ibid., Articles 3(7) and 3(3) respectively.

[69] Ibid., respectively Annex 1(i) and Annex 1(f) of both Directives [emphasis added].

This development of a consumer rights focus to PSOs in services of general economic interest is taken even further in the Consumer Rights and Privacy Directive of November 2009.[70] This latest legislative development introduces a number of amendments, *inter alia*, to the Universal Services Directive that obliges Member States to ensure: an equivalence of access, choice, and information to disabled consumers and end users[71]; the right to a clear, comprehensive and easily accessible contract meeting a minimum of specified requirements[72]; consumer involvement in the setting, by the regulator, of service provider performance targets[73]; the right to withdraw from a contract without penalty upon notice from the service provider of any modification to contractual conditions[74]; the respect of fundamental rights and freedoms as defined in Article 6 of the European Convention for the Protection of Human Rights and Fundamental Freedoms[75]; the promotion of access to services of social value including the missing children hotline number[76]; ease of switching supplier[77] and as far as possible, that NRAs take account of, amongst others, the views of consumers, and disabled consumers through the establishment of a consultation mechanism that should include a consumer consultation body independent of the NRA.[78]

Taken together, this latest generation of Services of General Economic Interest measures highlight a set of PSOs that provide for market monitoring, fundamental rights, and social needs. They require transparency of quality and cost information and the structural development of consumer interfaces with the market. If this range of provisions is taken to represent the parameters the EU is using to define PSOs, then it would appear that a core set of PSOs have evolved that can be listed as:

- The measurement of the level and effectiveness of market opening through the active monitoring of switching rates, complaints, and any distortion or restriction of competition in the retail market.
- Provision of mechanisms for consumer consultation.

---

70 Directive 2009/136/EC amending Directive 2002/22/EC on universal service and users' rights relating to electronic communications networks and services, Directive 2002/58/EC concerning the processing of personal data and the protection of privacy in the electronic communications sector and Regulation (EC) No 2006/2004 on cooperation between national authorities responsible for the enforcement of consumer protection laws (Text with EEA relevance), *OJ* 2009 L 337/11.

71 Directive 2002/22/EC on universal service and users' rights relating to electronic communications networks and services (Universal Service Directive), *OJ* 2002 L 108/51, Articles 1(1), 6(1), 7(1), 21(3)(f), 23(a)(1), 26(4), 27(a)(2) and 31(1), as amended.

72 Ibid., Article 20(1), as amended.

73 Ibid., Articles 11(4) and 22(3), as amended.

74 Ibid., Article 20(2), as amended.

75 Ibid., Article 1(3), as amended.

76 Ibid., Article 27(a), as amended.

77 Ibid., Article 30(4), (5) and (6), as amended.

78 Ibid., Article 33(1) as amended, together with Recital 49 of Directive 2009/136/EC.

- Provision of consumer information concerning their rights through a single point of contact.
- The right to a good standard of complaint handling by the service provider in which the consumer must be informed of the appropriate procedures.
- The right to a transparent description of tariffs and the services offered so that consumers are able to make choices between providers.
- The right to published and comparable supply time, and quality of service measurements.
- The fundamental right to privacy with respect to the processing of personal data.
- Access and affordability provisions for vulnerable and disabled consumers.
- An independent mechanism such as an ombudsman or independent consumer body is established for the efficient treatment of complaints and out-of-court dispute settlements.

7.5 Governance and Regulatory Issues

Although individual market sectors attract different approaches to universal or public service obligations the core of normative ideas we see associated with the developing definitions of USOs have brought a number of advantages. They have helped to facilitate a degree of cross-border trade and introduced or developed a number of basic rights. There are also limitations. The minimum harmonisation approach has seen regulatory fragmentation at the national level where regulatory bodies may vary significantly in terms of competences, independence, and financial and human resources. These are obstacles that have been seen as barriers to the development of pan-European services. Some of these obstacles may be addressed by placing the role of the consumer at the heart of the system of networks and network governance which have been created.

7.5.1 Triangular Relationships: Triangle Geometry

The classic model of drawing the regulatory relationships in the liberalisation process is that of a simple triangle (Fig. 7.1). The State is the regulator of the new provider–consumer relationship. This conceptual approach is developed by Teubner[79] and is followed in other writings.[80] This simple triangle analysis ignores the dynamic regulatory role of the EU, which we would argue, should add a complementary, second, triangle of relationships: the EU–Member State–provider/user dynamic. The intervention of the EU provides not only the legal basis of the

[79] Teubner 2000.

[80] See for example, Micklitz 2009.

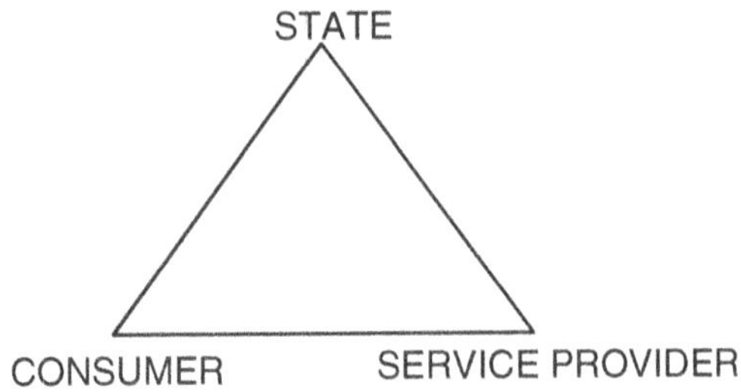

Fig. 7.1 Classic model of liberalisation relationships

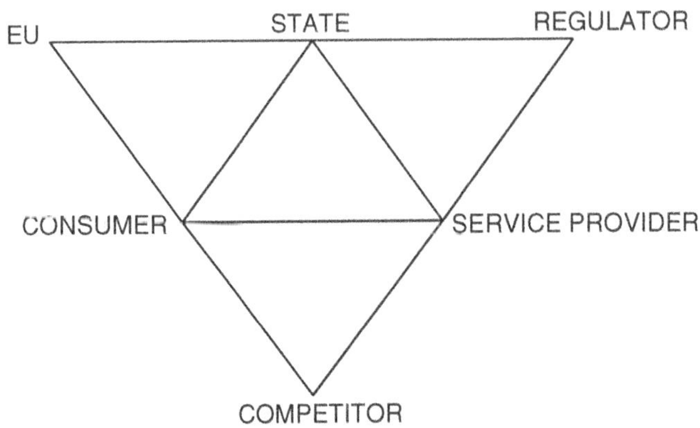

Fig. 7.2 Developed model of liberalisation relationships

content of the USO, but also the private law means for the consumer to enforce the legal obligations Fig. 7.1.

The triangular relationship between the State–the service provider–the user (consumer) has been used to explain the decentralisation of resource allocation and increased efficiency, balanced alongside the role of the State in intervening in the regulation of liberalised services and goods, in order to ensure that a collective welfare can be maintained where the services involved are not normally commercially viable. But this limited analysis of the dynamics of liberalised markets uses only a triangular relationship at the level of the State–the provider–the user (consumer) and ignores other dynamic relationships involved with USOs. We argue that even if we remain with the relationships at the State level, USOs require regulatory independence creating a further, third, triangle involving independent regulators Fig. 7.2.[81]

Finally, and to add symmetry, but also to reflect the idea of consumer choice as an obligation, we can add a fourth triangle to represent the day to day market relationships between the consumer, the supplier and any competitors. Even so, the visualisation and description of these relationships is this way does not capture the

[81] Thatcher and Coen 2008, p. 31.

dynamics of the regulation and role of PSOs in liberalised markets. To this end a more fluid description appears necessary.

Prior to the mid 1980s the traditional simple bilateral private law relationship, based on freedom to contract between the customer and the merchant, had been complicated. In those sectors that were subject to liberalisation, the incumbent service provider was obliged to contract with the customer and the legal relationship between the State monopoly and the customer switched to a public law setting in which price was often determined by political subsidy. Privatisation and liberalisation introduced new dynamics into the customer/service provider relationship. Privatisation brought with it the concept of the USO that reached 'beyond the limits set to the freedom of contract via standard terms legislation.'[82] It introduced a guarantee of 'access to all, irrespective of the economic, social or geographical situation, at a specified quality and an affordable price.'[83]

Where privatisation was accompanied by rules to prevent social exclusion, liberalisation introduced competition to and *choice* of service provider. The essential nature of this marketisation of public services attracted an amalgam of developing normative processes and the hybridisation of public and private law in the sector specific regulation discussed above in Sect. 7.3. This is a regulatory framework in which the Commission expresses an aspiration for an active and participatory consumer citizenship practice with the regulatory agencies acting in part as 'representatives' of the consumer–citizen interest alongside consumer organisations and other influential bodies of civil society. The Commission recognises that for consumers to take up their rights often requires the existence of independent regulators with appropriate staff, and clearly defined powers and duties. These include powers of sanction that include the ability to monitor the transposition and enforcement of public and universal service provisions. The Commission is also positively supporting the development of networks of consumer organisations, both sector specific and general *and* at both national and EU level.[84] Consumer organisations that also support the exercise of consumer rights and provide the consumer with:

- Support in pursuing individual issues and complaints;
- Proactive consumer watchdog agencies;
- Political lobbying agencies in consumer matters;
- Cross-border consumer dispute resolution bodies;
- Policy influencing representative associations of consumer groups.

These are organisations of civil society that complement the national enforcement and regulatory public agencies. Together, this network of agencies provides for the representation and active participation of consumers in the definition and evaluation of services; the availability of appropriate redress and compensation

[82] Micklitz 2009, p. 11.

[83] Szyszczak 2007, pp. 244–245.

[84] See Davies 2009.

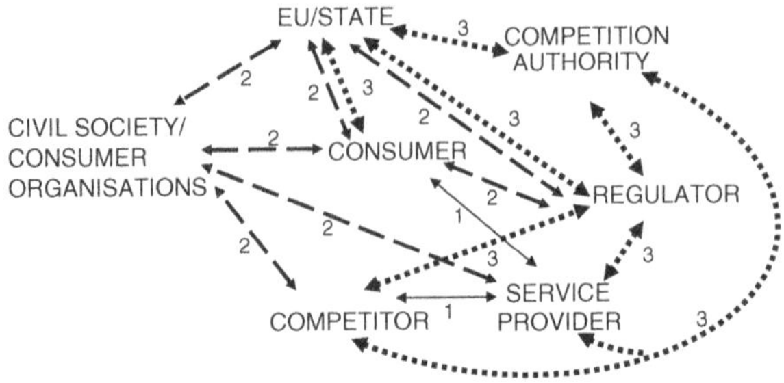

Fig. 7.3 Functional model of liberalisation relationships

mechanisms, and for a review of the consumer protection and support framework to reflect new social, technological and economic developments.[85] Yet, there is no legal obligation in the secondary legislation for the regulatory agencies to uphold the rights of consumer citizens, although there is a gradual movement of EU secondary law into that direction which might overcome the discrepancies between the role and function of the regulatory agencies in the Member States.[86]

When analysing the policy of the EU in relation to PSOs, the consumer can be considered as a node within a network of legal and quasi-legal relationships. Whilst any node in such a network may be assessed in relation to all the other nodes that make up that network we have, as a reflection of our assertions that PSOs contain elements of fundamental rights and social needs for individuals, placed the consumer at the heart of this network that we have depicted in Fig. 7.3. If we take the consumer market as a whole, not just the liberalised services of general interest, what we now see are the remains of the *private law* relationships between the consumer and the service provider and in the normal commercial relationships between competitors on the same market, indicated by the arrows numbered 1 in Fig. 7.3. The *public law* areas of consumer protection and market regulation now define the legal relationships between the statutory market actors and those undertakings providing the services that comprise the market: relationships that we have indicated by the arrows numbered 3 in Fig. 7.3.

To complete this network model, structures of new governance, indicated here with arrows numbered 2, provide channels through which organisations, and structures of civil society have developed to influence the market by offering consumers' informational support, through pursuing soft law solutions and consumer watchdog activities, and by providing consumers the voice and influence to shape policy at the national and EU levels.

---

[85] Commission (EC), 'Services of general interest, including social services of general interest: a new European commitment' (Communication) COM(2007) 725 final, 20 November 2007, pp. 10–11 [emphasis added].

[86] Micklitz 2009, p. 16.

7.6 Conclusions: Will there be Future Generations of Universal Service Obligations?

Article 3 TEU states that the Union shall establish, *inter alia*, 'a highly competitive social market'. There is much debate as to what shape the future EU highly competitive social market will look like. It may appear hazardous to predict the content of this new mix of law, politics, and economics but the way this will take shape may be more predictable.[87] Universal service obligations would be a useful vehicle to create competitive markets with a social dimension. The Monti Report 2010 addressed the use of USOs as an element of the new strategy for the single (internal) market, making a concrete proposal for using Article 14 TFEU as the legal base for a extension of USOs to the provision of broadband access.[88] It is also worth recalling that Article 1 of Protocol No. 26 annexed to the TFEU and the TEU states a modern role for SGEIs which embrace aspects of universal service concepts:

> *Article 1*
> The shared values of the Union in respect of services of general economic interest within the meaning of Article 14 of the Treaty on the Functioning of the European Union include in particular:

- The essential role and the wide discretion of national, regional, and local authorities in providing, commissioning and organising services of general economic interest as closely as possible to the needs of the users;
- The diversity between various services of general economic interest and the differences in the needs and preferences of users that may result from different geographical, social or cultural situations;
- A high level of quality, safety and affordability, equal treatment, and the promotion of universal access and of user rights.

Our research shows that USOs exist in an evolving environment but there are indicators that we can identify to give us clues as to what the next generation of USOs may look like and, learning from experience, question how cautious should we be with some of the Commission's proposals for change?

From our analysis of USOs our conclusion is that far from the gradual demise of the USO in the liberalisation process, we see the concept changing and evolving, and expanding in its role of protecting the consumer–citizen interest in the Internal Market. Universal services evolve within the framework of each sector as technology advances, but also new concepts emerge. The focus of the EU has been on network services but societal changes also drive new consumer demands and necessities. One example is the decline of cash-based transactions with the move towards banking services for a range of payment mechanisms, including the

---

87 See for example, Van de Gronden and Szyszczak 2011, where the role of solidarity is analysed to cement the tensions between national health care systems and the emerging EU regulation of many health care issues.

88 Monti 2010, p. 75.

payment of social security. Thus ownership of a bank account has become a prerequisite of economic engagement in the EU and a symbol of exclusion where access to banking services is not available.[89] In health care, tensions exist between national, solidarity-based health care systems based on providing a universal health service and the fact that with rising costs and more demands placed on providing high quality immediate health care, are forcing the Member States to transfer costs away from the tax payer by greater privatisation of health care provision. The EU has not been able to develop a satisfactory response to this new mix of public and private provision when applying the competition rules to health care undertakings. One solution would be to develop concepts of USOs which could be ring-fenced from the full application of the market rules.[90]

From our analysis we can define some basic questions to be addressed in future provision of USOs. Are USOs necessary? How will they be defined? How will they be funded?' What new questions should we be asking about USOs, given the evolution in the scope and application of these ideas already seen in the EU? In response to the last question we can ask if the processes through which USOs emerge are responsive enough to technological changes which have accelerated as a result of liberalisation and privatisation processes. For example, in the telecoms sector there is a rapid convergence between telephony, internet broadcasting, and multimedia technologies. Without adapting to these technological changes the use of USOs attached to old technology can leave vulnerable users socially excluded. In the postal sector, can the USO connected to 'snail mail' continue to be a USO when faster and more efficient means of sending 'mail' and texts have replaced letter-writing? The application of technological developments also affects the convergence of service offerings between previously distinct sectors. For example, in the future, what can we expect from the roll-out of smart metering technology that draws together digital communications and energy services and that will, in time, give consumers new levels of control and choice over their energy usage that they will exercise through their broadband internet service?[91] This new technology may affect wider concerns over privacy and data protection. Thus an unknown factor is what will consumer expectations of better quality, technological innovation and more efficient services have on the market? And how will the State and the market respond?

[89] Again in Monti 2010, p. 75, a proposal is made for a proposal, possibly using Article 14 TFEU as the legal base, for a regulation ensuring that all citizens are entitled to a number of basic banking services.

[90] See Szyszczak 2009, p. 191.

[91] Art. 3(11), Dir. 2009/72/EC concerning common rules for the internal market in electricity and repealing Directive 2003/54/EC (hereafter, E-directive) and Art. 3(8), Dir. 2009/73/EC concerning common rules for the internal market in natural gas and repealing Directive 2003/55/EC.

References

Davies J (2009) Entrenchment of new governance in consumer policy formulation: a platform for European consumer citizenship practice? J Consum Policy 33:245
Davies J (2011) The Consumer Citizen in European Law and Policy, Palgrave Macmillan
Micklitz H-W (2009) Universal services: nucleus for a social European private law, EUI Work Paper Law 12:10
Monti M (2010) A new strategy for the single market. At the service of Europe's economy and society. Report to the President of the Commission José Manuel Barroso ('The Monti report') 9 May 2010, p 74
Neergaard U (2008) Services of general (economic) interest and the services directive—what is left out, why and where to go? In: Neergaard U, Nielsen R, Roseberry L (eds) The services directive, consequences for the welfare state in the European social model, DJØF Publishing, Copenhagen
Neergaard U (2009) Services of general economic interest: the nature of the beast. In: Krajewski M, Neergaard U, Van de Gronden J (eds) The changing legal framework for services of general interest in Europe, TMC Asser Press, The Hague, p 17
Prosser T (2005) The limits of competition law. OUP, Oxford
Sauter W (2008) Services of general economic interest and universal service in EU law. ELRev 33.2:179
Szyszczak E (2001) The provision of public services in competitive markets. Yearb Eur Law, 35
Szyszczak E (2007) The regulation of the state in competitive markets in the EU. Hart, Oxford, p 243
Szyszczak E (2009a) Modernising healthcare: pilgrimage for the Holy Grail? In: Krajewski M, Neergaard U, Van de Gronden J (eds) The changing legal framework for services of general interest in Europe, TMC Asser Press, The Hague, p 191
Szyszczak E (2009b) Legal tools in the liberalisation of welfare markets. In: Nielsen R et al (eds) Integrating welfare functions into EU law—from Rome to Lisbon. DJØF Pub. Copenhagen
Szyszczak E (2011) Patients' rights: a lost cause or missed opportunity? In: Van de Gronden J, Szyszczak E, Neergaard U, Krajewski M (eds) Health care and EU law. TMC Asser Press, The Hague
Teubner G (1998) After privatisation? the many autonomies of private law. Curr Leg Probl 51:393
Teubner G (2000) After privatisation?—the many autonomies of private law. In: Wilhelmsson T, Hurri S (eds) From dissonance to sense: welfare state expectations, privatisation and private law. Ashgate, Farnham
Thatcher M, Coen D (2008) Reshaping European regulatory space: an analysis. West Eur Polit 31
Van de Gronden J, Szyszczak E (2011) Conclusions. In: Van de Gronden J, Szyszczak E, Neergaard U, Krajewski M (eds) Health care and EU law. TMC Asser Press, The Hague

Chapter 8
Public Service Obligations: Protection of Public Service Values in a National and European Context

Martin Hennig

Abstract Terms such as 'services in the general interest' and 'services of general economic interest' have received a lot of attention from legal scholars and other practitioners of law during the course of the last decade. The same amount of attention has not been paid to the term 'public service obligations', which represents a common mechanism for the realisation of services of general economic interest throughout the Member States of the European Union. However, the term 'public service obligation' is not a thoroughly defined concept of law within the European Union and its legal framework. In this chapter, the term is traced back to its origins in French and Anglo-Saxon public administrative law and it is explained, how it is interpreted and applied in the context of EU law. Special focus is placed on the single provision dealing explicitly with public service obligations which can be found in the Treaty on the Functioning of the European Union namely Article 93 on State aid in EU transport law.

Contents

M. Hennig (✉)
University of Tromsø, 9037, Tromsø, Norway
e-mail: martin.hennig@uit.no

E. Szyszczak et al. (eds.), *Developments in Services of General Interest*, Legal Issues of Services of General Interest, DOI: 10.1007/978-90-6704-734-0_8,

8.1 Introduction

A general feature in all Member States is that, at some level, states assume responsibility for securing the provision of public services to their citizens.[1] These activities of the state share the common denominator that they are regarded as being in the general public interest within their national borders.[2] States can either ensure the provision of such services themselves or entrust their provision to external operators, either public or private, which are not considered to be emanations of the state.[3] Regardless of how public services are provided, states must have the regulatory means to be able to make sure that the services for which they are responsible, fulfil both quantitative and qualitative requirements laid down in national law or deriving from political promise or expectation. A common method applied by public authorities for ensuring the realisation of high standard public services is through the imposition of general interest requirements on service providers. This regulatory mechanism is within EU terminology referred to as 'public service obligations'.

When Member States introduce competition to markets which were previously operated by the public sector or subject to exclusive rights (monopoly), it is important to create a regulatory regime capable of ensuring that service providers fulfil the social policies which the states or their respective public authorities are committed to provide to citizens.

Besides securing the actual provision of a service to citizens, public service obligations can be used by public authorities as instruments to ensure the provision of high quality services by imposing requirements relating to security of supply, regularity, quality and price of supplies, and environmental protection.[4] Hence, public authorities possess an important regulatory tool, which can be applied in order to shape or form the content or quantity of the activities falling within the remit of their responsibility.

For these reasons, public service obligations have served as important protective instruments in the process of liberalisation in Europe. Over the course of the last decades, European countries have initiated comprehensive reforms, especially in the utilities sectors, introducing competition in regulated sectors.[5] The driving

---

[1] See Malaret Garcia 1998, pp. 57–82; Loughlin 2003, pp. 7–12 and Odudu 2006, p. 46.

[2] Malaret Garcia 1998, p. 57.

[3] Freedland 1998, pp. 2–5.

[4] See for example, Article 1(e) and para 17 of the Preamble to Regulation (EC) No 1370/2007 of the European Parliament and of the Council of 23 October 2007 on public passenger transport services by rail and by road, and repealing Council Regulations (EEC) Nos 1191/69 and 1107/70, *OJ* L 315/1 and similar provisions both in Article 3 of the Directive 2003/54/EC of the European Parliament and of the Council of 26 June 2003 concerning common rules for the internal market in electricity and repealing Directive 96/92/EC, *OJ* L 176/37 and Directive 2003/55/EC of the European Parliament and of the Council of 26 June 2003 concerning common rules for the internal market in natural gas and repealing Directive 98/30/EC, *OJ* L 176/57.

[5] Defeuilley 1999, pp. 25–27.

elements behind the opening of markets to competition are based on the idea that private ownership is supposed to be superior to public, and promotion of competitive forces is expected to raise efficiency and enhance protection of consumers' interests.[6]

Nevertheless, the introduction of competition does not necessarily guarantee adequate public service provision. Where market forces rule, market players are primarily concerned with profit and have little or no incentive to pursue social considerations. In competitive markets, there is always the risk of *cherry picking* and *social dumping*. Cherry picking occurs when profit seeking draws operators to the lucrative and fast growing markets, thus refusing to offer services or offering services at higher prices on unprofitable markets or in scarcely populated areas. Social dumping, the other undesired effect of competition, can occur when service providers encourage low income customers to exclude themselves from the market by requiring the payment of high deposits, prepayment, and disconnection.[7]

The concept of public service enjoys different levels of protection in different Member States. As will become apparent, in France, public services (*les services publics*) are afforded constitutional protection both in terms of reservation of ownership as well as substantive criteria relating to the content of the services. In the United Kingdom on the other hand, the concept of public service does not enjoy the same well developed general legal principles about the concept of public service.[8] These differences in the legal status of public services may help explain why the two Member States organise their public service provision in different ways. It is attempted to demonstrate that in France, public authorities need to take into consideration criteria such as continuity, equality, and adaptability of service. For this reason, when French public authorities design public service contracts or licence agreements, they must be certain that the public service obligations imposed on service providers are in accordance with their constitutional requirements. Conversely, in the United Kingdom, public authorities and public service operators are not under the same constitutional commitment to adhere to general public service principles. Thus, service providers are not weighed down with additional constitutional requirements and interpret their obligations as precise commitments.[9]

The purpose of this chapter is twofold. Firstly, a closer look will be taken at the evolution of the concept of public service obligations in France and the United Kingdom. For the purposes of making sense of the term, its constituent elements will be analysed separately in a comparison between French and UK public administrative law. Since all public service obligations involve the performance of a 'public service' it is essential to conduct an analysis of national conceptions of 'public service' and how the authorities manage them by imposing obligations

[6] Ibid., p. 26.

[7] Ibid., p. 28.

[8] Prosser 2005, at p. 96.

[9] Ibid., addressing the situation among UK public utilities, p. 30.

upon service providers. Having reviewed national practice, it will be attempted to compare the national understanding and use of the terms 'public service' and 'public service obligations' to those employed in EU law. In this regard, it will also be asked how the national ideas of 'public service' relate to the EU law creation 'services of general interest' which is now made part of the European legal vocabulary through the Protocol on services of general interest which is annexed to the TEU and the Treaty on the Functioning of the European Union (TFEU).

Having placed the concept of public service obligations in a larger national and EU law context, focus will shift towards the use of the term in the TFEU. It is submitted that the use of the term 'public service' in the primary legislation of the TFEU causes semantic confusion. It is further discussed whether the concept of public service found in the TFEU holds the same meaning as 'services of general interest'. Drawing on this discussion, it is questioned whether the creation of legal terms such as 'services of general interest,' benefits or undermines the goal of promoting the shared values upon which Union membership is based.

8.2 Public Service Obligations: From a National to a European Legal Concept

8.2.1 Public Service Obligations: Protection of Public Services in France

France is frequently cited as a representative of what can be described as a *Continental* concept of public service. Public service regimes in Continental European countries share certain similar traits, such as constitutional or legal protection of public services and well developed general principles about the meaning of public service.[10] However, it is not the purpose of this chapter to synthesise these similarities on a European-wide scale. Instead, this chapter is confined to demonstrating how public authorities exercise control over public services. It starts off by examining what the French notion of 'service public' entails and showing how the public administration imposes special obligations on the selected operators of essential services.

As pointed out by Malaret Garcia, legal scholars are in agreement that the French concept of 'service public' is used with at least two distinct meanings.[11] The first meaning of the term is *organic*, referring to the institutional structure of the administrative apparatus of local or central government, that is, the public service sector itself. The second meaning of the term is not concerned with

[10] Prosser 2005 at p. 96.

[11] Malaret Garcia 1998, p. 62. See also Scott 2000, at p. 312.

describing the personnel side of public administration, but refers to the material legal principles which apply to the provision of public services. When describing the concept of 'service public' from a material perspective, focus is directed at the actual activities performed, asking whether they are tasks of general interest falling within the responsibility of the state. The French 'service public' must be viewed from an institutional as well as a functional perspective, thus making a distinction between the actual public service providers, as well as recognising the criteria which apply to the provision of public services.

Public services viewed from a functional perspective can explain how public services can be performed by bodies which are not part of the state or governed by public law. Since public services are activities, it is not indispensable to entrust their operation to companies outside the public sector. As pointed out by Fournier, in France, for instance, the task of passenger transport by train is regarded as a 'service public' which is entrusted to the SNCF (the French railways). However, from an institutional perspective, the SNCF does not belong to the public service sector.[12]

Defining exactly what constitutes a 'service public' is no simple task. First of all, not all activities of general interest are public services. For instance, the general provision of food, which under all circumstances would amount to an activity in the general interest, is, except in times of crisis, left to private initiative and has for that reason not been considered a 'service public'.[13] Initially, the French state was only preoccupied with functions of sovereignty such as justice, police, and tax collection—known as the 'Etat gendarme', but has over the course of the last centuries grown to include welfare activities such as education, public works, health, employment, urban development, and transport.[14]

It is thus relevant to ask which activities are considered 'services publics' and who determines their public service nature? According to Malaret Garcia, the answer to the first part of the question is that the determination of the 'service public' characteristics of an activity must be drawn up objectively.[15] She arrives at this argument by referring to the work of Duguit who stated that a public service is[16]:

> ... any activity that has to be governmentally regulated and controlled because it is indispensable to the realization and development of social interdependence and is of a nature such that it cannot be fully assured save by governmental intervention.

As explained by Prosser, the trademark of 'service public' reflects state concern for social solidarity and social cohesion, making the concept 'essentially

---

[12] Fournier 1993, pp. 13–61.

[13] See Fournier 2010 Public Services available at Embassy of France in Washington, available at http://www.info-france-usa.org/spip.php?article641, last accessed 30 November 2010.

[14] Ibid.

[15] Malaret Garcia 1998, p. 64, see in particular fn. 27.

[16] Ibid.

non-economic and distributive in nature'.[17] Activities displaying these characteristics will be classified as 'services publics' and subjected to a special legal regime based on principles of continuity, equality among users, adaptability of service. These substantive requirements were initially developed by Professor Rolland in the 1930s and are to a varying degree applicable to all public services.[18] In recent years; however, Rolland's laws have been supplemented by new rules established by Parliament, including provisions relating to quality of service and transparency, and are not universally applied to all public services.[19]

Given the importance of 'services publics', the French government, or part of its public administration, assumes responsibility for the provision of such services. As pointed out by *Malaret Garcia*, the 'service public' is 'an activity with respect to which the public administration fulfils a fundamental role'. However, the importance of such activities does not require the public administration to provide the activities directly, but must somehow assume responsibility for their provision to citizens. In doing so, the state or the responsible public authority must establish the framework and instruments necessary for guaranteeing their distribution.[20]

Thus, having established a framework and necessary instruments for providing public services to citizens, the French public administration possesses the necessary tools for imposing obligations on service providers. With the regulatory framework in place, a link between the public administration and the service provider is created, enabling the public administration to impose obligations related to the content, price, quality, and frequency of the activities to be provided to citizens.[21] The necessity of establishing such a regulatory framework is not only based on the duty upon the public administration to fulfil the public service requirements deriving from the 'Rolland's laws', but such a framework also provides a special apparatus of regulation of the economic and social functioning of the activity concerned.[22]

8.2.2 Public Service Obligations: Protection of Public Services in the United Kingdom

As distinct from France, in the United Kingdom there is no recognition of public services at the level of constitutional principle. Although public services lack constitutional protection or a general legal foundation developed in case law, this is not to say that they have been left unsheltered from the market forces.

---

[17] Prosser 2005 at p. 103.

[18] Malaret Garcia 1998, pp. 65–69 and Prosser 2005 at pp. 102–106.

[19] Scott 2000, p. 312.

[20] Malaret Garcia 1998, pp. 62–63.

[21] Ibid., p. 63.

[22] See generally, Freedland 1998, pp. 2–5.

The common law doctrine of 'common callings', which is the precursor of the 'essential facilities' doctrine secures public access to important facilities such as docks and harbours and prevent owners (often monopolies) from engaging in abuse of dominance and restricting output.[23] Another type of protection came through political means. From the 1940s nationalisation of public utilities offered protection of public service goals by the minister, through the role of the board of the industry and through the representation of consumers by consumer councils and consultative mechanisms.[24]

In light of the privatisation of public services in the 1980 and 1990s, regulatory authorities were created which supervised both the completion of competition on markets as well as vesting the regulatory authorities with regulatory powers in order to acheive public service goals.[25] However, the UK Government did not embody principles of public service in law, the exception being the creation of regulators of public utilities with specific provisions intended to serve public goals. These particular public service goals were in turn often laid down as public service obligations in licences (or authorisations) awarded to public utilities.[26]

In the United Kingdom, there is a long tradition of subjecting public utilities to 'universal service obligations'.[27] In general EU law, the principle of universality covers a set of obligations relating to access to essential facilities and the imposition of obligations on service providers to offer defined services according to specified conditions, including complete territorial coverage and at reasonable prices.[28] Nevertheless, as pointed out in the 2007 Communication from the Commission, these universal obligations are a minimum set of rights and obligations which can be further developed at national level.[29] However, in the United Kingdom, little development of universal service obligations beyond the minimum standards occurred.

The reasons for the lack of further development of the principle of universality may be explained by the fact that the United Kingdom, unlike France, lacks a well-developed public service doctrine. As explained in Sect. 8.2.1, in France, public services enjoy constitutional protection and activities classified as 'services publics' are subject to requirements of continuity, equality, and adaptability of service. In the United Kingdom, this general legal backdrop is missing. Instead, as pointed out by Defeuilley, in the wake of the introduction of competition, the 'principle of universality has been translated in precise commitments (quality and performance

[23] Prosser 2005 at 39–40, However, as pointed out by Scott, the common law doctrine of common callings has been virtually obliterated by over a century of sector specific legislation in the UK, although it is still remembered in the US under the duties of 'common carriage', Scott 2000, pp. 312–313.

[24] Prosser 2005, pp. 41–42.

[25] Ibid., pp. 44–45.

[26] Ibid., pp. 68–69.

[27] Rawnsley and Lazar 1999, pp. 182–183. See Chap. 7 by Davies and Szyszczak.

[28] COM(2007) 725, p. 10.

[29] Ibid.

standards, complaints procedures, access to information), whose scope and limits vary from one industry to another'.[30] Therefore, it is possible that UK public utilities and public service providers in general, do not feel obliged to take on a broad concept of public services similar to that adopted in France. In turn, service providers, who do not wish to expand their public service commitments more than necessary, interpret their public service obligations narrowly.

Consequently, a narrow interpretation of public service obligations and a strong focus on competition can have negative effects upon technological choice. As pointed out by *Defeuilley*, [i]n a competitive environment, public utilities tend to adopt least-cost available techniques considering neither their social effects (externalities), nor their ability to match future evolution'.[31] However, the preference for competition over social policy is not solely to blame on UK public utilities and profit seeking behaviour. Another element to be taken into consideration is the fact that UK public utilities have been placed in an unstable regulatory environment.[32] Public utilities, when exposed to changing public duties and confronted with new market entrants, respond by adopting a short-term perspective concentrating of producing high profit and giving low priority to long-term investments.[33]

However, in France, both public authorities and service operators adopt long-term perspectives for the purposes of providing public services. The constitutional backdrop placing both public authorities and service providers under an obligation to adhere to the principles of continuity, equality, and adaptability, has resulted in a more stable regulatory environment. The substantive content of public service obligations is less likely to change overnight, thus making long-term planning a less risky venture than in the United Kingdom.

8.2.3 Public Service Obligations: Protection of Services of General Interest Under EU Law

8.2.3.1 Introduction

As demonstrated in Sects. 8.2.1 and 8.2.2, Member States can protect their public service values by imposing different obligations on service providers. The level of commitment and devotion by service providers to ensure the fulfilment of these obligations is influenced by the legal status of public services in national legal systems, the degree of competition on markets and the duration of the contract concluded with the awarding authorities.

---

[30] Defeuilley 1999, pp. 27–28.

[31] Ibid., p. 28.

[32] Ibid., p. 34.

[33] Ibid., p. 35.

Unlike Member States, which impose requirements on service providers in order to fulfil a public service mission within the borders of their territory, protection of services of general interest under EU law has a supranational perspective. Firstly, EU law determines the scope of application of the rules on competition to services of general interest.[34] Member States must not award exclusive rights which can lead to an abuse of a dominant position.[35] However, where market intervention is necessary in order to ensure the provision of the public service task entrusted to the service provider, State measures in breach of the competition rules can be justified through the derogatory mechanism provided in Article 106(2) TFEU.

Secondly, the rules laid down in Article 14 TFEU, Article 36 of the Charter on Fundamental Rights and the new addition of the Protocol on Services of General Interest, places the EU under a duty to respect and to ensure the completion of the shared values inherent in services of general interest. These values are precisely what public service obligations are intended to secure, thus placing the EU under a duty to make sure that its legal framework allows for their realisation under EU law.

In order to avoid confusion between a structural and an organic understanding of the term 'public service', the EU legislature makes use of the terms 'services of general interest' and 'services of general economic interest'.[36] As explained by Supiot, in an organic sense, the term public service 'designates a service provided by or under the authority of the State (as is the case, for instance, with public enterprises charged with responsibility for providing a service to the public)'.[37] Another reason for steering clear of the term 'public service' is that 'services of general economic interest' is an EU law concept which does not correspond to the different national concepts employed in all Member States.[38]

It would be acceptable to submit that the concept of 'services of general interest' is *functional*. Whereas an organic concept would be limited to those services provided by the state or emanations of the state, a functional concept

---

[34] For a particularly interesting discussion of what constitutes 'economic activity' and the scope of application of the rules on free movement and competition, see Odudu 2006, pp. 23–56.

[35] Article 106(1) TFEU cf. Articles 101 and 102 TFEU, for an extensive analysis see Buendia Sierra 1999.

[36] See COM(96) 443, 2 and COM(2003) 270, *Green Paper on Services of General Interest*, pp. 6–7. The term'services of general economic interest' can be found in TFEU Articles 106(3), 14, and in the Charter of Fundamental Rights of the European Union Article 36, see Neergaard 2009 who explains thoroughly how these terms are used in a EU law context. In the Protocol on services of general interest, both the terms 'services of general interest' and 'services of general economic interest' are employed, for a particularly interesting discussion of the this protocol, see D. Damjanovic and De Witte 2009 at p. 53.

[37] Supiot 1998, p. 161.

[38] Buendia Sierra 1999, pp. 279–280.

refers to the importance of the provision of certain services to the benefit of society.[39] By drawing attention away from the structure under which a service is performed, and instead focusing on the indispensable nature of the service to society, the concept steers clear of the public/private divide which is capable of depriving EU law of its efficiency. The creation of functional concepts is an approach which is also embraced by the Court of Justice in the field of free movement[40] and in competition law.[41]

Whereas it is true that the concept of 'services of general interest' is functional for the purpose of discarding the public/private law divide, the functionality of the concept is not without its limitations. A completely functional conception of 'services of general interest' would be extendable to all services or activities in society which are indispensable to citizens, not only those endorsed or secured by the State. Yet, the European conception of 'services of general interest' seems to be confined to certain essential activities which are either provided by the State itself or to activities provided through private initiative where the State acts as a guarantor of their provision.

It is difficult to imagine an activity, which is not endorsed by a Member State, being classified as a 'service of general interest'. This necessary link between the State and the provision of the service is evident in Article 106(2) which states that undertakings 'entrusted' with particular tasks may be exempted from the rules contained in the Treaties, in particular the rules on competition. This link, confining 'services of general economic interest' to activities backed by State initiative was confirmed in *BRT-II*,[42] in which the Court made clear that:

> 20. Private undertakings may come under that provision, but they must be entrusted with the operation of services of general economic interest by an *act of the public authority*.
>
> 21. This emerges clearly from the fact that the reference to 'particular tasks assigned to them' applies also to undertakings having the character of a revenue-producing monopoly.

---

[39] Morris 2000, p. 171.

[40] See ECJ, Case 149/79 *Commission* v. *Belgium* [1980] *ECR* 3881, concerning the ambit of Member State discretion to reserve certain posts within the public service sector to nationals. The Court of Justice limited the scope of the 'public service exception' in Article 45(4) TFEU (ex Article 39(4) EC) to those posts which involved 'direct or indirect participation in the exercise of powers conferred by public law and duties designed to safeguard the general interests of the State or of other public authorities', para 10. By focusing on the nature of the disputed posts, the approach of the Court can be described as 'functional' as opposed to an 'institutional' or 'organic' test, which would depend on the way in which posts were classified under national law, see Arnull 1999, p. 372.

[41] In ECJ, Case C-41/1990 *Klaus Höfner and Fritz Elser* v. *Macrotron GmbH* [1991] *ECR* I-1979, the Court displayed its affinity for efficient application of Union competition law by defining the concept of 'undertakings' in Article 101(1) TFEU in functional terms. The functionality of the test is apparent in paragraph 21 where the Court defines undertakings as 'every entity engaged in an economic activity, regardless of the legal status of the entity and the way in which it is financed', see also Odudu 2006, p. 24.

[42] ECJ Case 127/73 *BRT II* [1974] *ECR* 318, paras 20 and 21.

The necessary link between State and 'services of general interest' makes it difficult to comprehend exactly why the EU lawmakers felt the need to set this concept apart from the more understandable and well-known term 'public service'. Certainly, a distinction should be drawn between economic and non-economic services, but the former category could rather be classified as 'industrial and commercial public services', thus avoiding the current incomprehensible terminology.[43]

The TEU and TFEU contain no legal definition of the concept of 'public service obligations'. However, the European Commission in its *White Paper on Services of General Interest* in 2004, gives a useful description of the term which encapsulates the concept in a EU law perspective[44]:

> The term public service obligations is used in the White Paper. It refers to specific requirements that are imposed by public authorities on the provider of the service in order to ensure that certain public interest objectives are met, for instance, in the matter of air, rail and road transport, and energy. These obligations can be applied at Community, national or regional level.

It is unlikely that the EU will make an attempt at capturing the essence of the concept of 'public service obligations' in a legal definition in its Treaties. It would most likely be counterproductive to try to define once and for all the various requirements imposed on service providers given the task of ensuring public interest objectives on behalf of public authorities. This submission is supported by the statement of the European Parliament which considered that[45]:

> … it is neither possible nor relevant for common definitions of services of general interest, or of the public-service obligations resulting from them, to be drawn up, and that an eventual framework instrument would be much too general in nature to provide added value, and may risk jeopardising the continuous development of services of general interest.

It is noticeable that in an EU law context, public service obligations are instruments which can be employed by public authorities to impose requirements on service providers. However, the use of the term 'public service obligations' is reserved to the imposition of requirements, related to the realisation or protection of 'services of general interest'.

EU law does not contain an exhaustive list of the criteria qualifying as 'specific requirements' which public authorities may impose on service providers. However, it seems apparent that it is futile to speak of 'public service obligations' outside situations in which public authorities are dealing with the realisation of a service of general interest. This use of the term excludes requirements which are

---

43 See Supiot, who compares the European concept of 'services of general economic interest' to traditional 'industrial and commercial public services' performed by private law organisations in France, Supiot 1998, p. 161.

44 *White Paper on Services of General Interest*, COM(2004) 374 final, p. 23.

45 European Parliament Resolution on the Green Paper on services of general interest, 14.01.2004, (T5-0018/2004).

unrelated to general interest objectives laid down in contract or legal provision from being labelled ‘public service obligations’. Thus, a service requirement can only be characterised as a public service obligation if it imposes on the provider one or more of the elements included in the Union concept of service of general interest. In the 2003 *Commission Green Paper on Services of General Interest* these elements include in particular values and goals recognised by the European Union as a whole such as universal service, continuity, quality of service, affordability, and user and consumer protection.[46]

As shown in Sect. 8.2.1, the French qualification of the concept of ‘service public’, reserves the use of the term to those services designated as public services by the state or competent public authorities. A similar system of qualification is thus emerging in EU law. Even though Member States are free to create their own services of general interest, a Europe-wide concept inevitably presupposes ‘European recognition’ of the shared values deserving the status of ‘service of general interest’.

8.2.3.2 Article 93 TFEU: The Provision That the World Forgot About

As explained in Sect. 8.2.3.1 the European Commission and the European Parliament show preference towards the use of the term ‘service of general (economic) interest’ over ‘public service’. It is unquestionable that the term ‘services of general interest’ has come to stay, and its authority as a legal concept has been confirmed by the fairly recent inclusion of Article 14 to the TFEU, Article 36 of the Charter on Fundamental Rights and Protocol 26 on services of general interest.[47]

Nevertheless, the TFEU is not without reference to the expression ‘public service’. As opposed to Article 45(4) TFEU,[48] Article 93 TFEU contains a functional concept of ‘public service’, allowing Member States to protect public

---

[46] COM(2003) 270, paras 49–63.

[47] However, it must be pointed out that Article 14 TFEU and Article 36 of the Charter on Fundamental Rights refer to ‘services of general economic interest’, whereas the concept ‘services of general interest’ was for the first time mentioned in Protocol 26 on Services of General Interest which entered into force 1 December 2009.

[48] Article 45(4) TFEU includes derogation from the freedom of movement of workers, providing that Member States in certain cases may reserve ‘employment in the public service’ to its own nationals. It is clear from the wording of Article 45(4) that this derogation provides a possibility for Member States to subject entire public sectors to a nationality criterion. However, a purely structural interpretation of the term would enable Member States to determine at will, the post covered by the exception. For this reason, the institutional approach to this derogation was rejected and instead a functional approach limitation to the exception was adopted, taking into account the tasks and responsibilities of each post (ECJ, Case C-173/93 *Commission* v. *Belgium* [1997] *ECR* I-3207, para 27). The rejection of an institutional approach to this provision by the Court of Justice has fittingly been described by Sauter and Schepel as ‘… functionalism within the institutional category of State-employed workers’, Sauter and Schepel 2009, pp. 62–63.

service values through financing of measures intended to facilitate the 'needs of coordination of transport'[49] or the process whereby the state or public authorities compensate operators for the cost of providing services which the undertakings are required to perform by law or acts of public authority.[50] Article 93 TFEU reads:

> Aids shall be compatible with this Treaty if they meet the needs of coordination of transport or if they represent reimbursement for the discharge of certain obligations inherent in the concept of a public service.

There is no obvious explanation to why this provision makes use of the term 'public service'. It is tempting to ask whether the values 'inherent in the concept of a public service' differ from the values inherent in the concept of 'services of general interest'? The answer to this question is unmistakably no. It is clear that the two terms mean exactly the same thing. The similar meaning of the terms is reflected in the circular, definition of 'public service obligations' in Regulation 1370/2007 on public passenger transport by road and rail Article 1(e) which states that:

> 'public service obligations' means a requirement defined or determined by a competent authority in order to ensure public passenger transport services in the general interest that an operator, if it were considering its own commercial interests, would not assume or would not assume to the same extent or under the same conditions without reward.

It seems that the EU legislators are reluctant to remove completely the well-established terms 'public service' and 'public service obligations' from their legal vocabulary. For instance, if the EU were to get rid of all reference to 'public service' in their legal framework, it would end up with incomprehensible constructions of 'Eurospeak' such as 'service of general interest obligation' or 'service of general economic interest obligation'.[51]

It is questionable whether the creation of the term 'services of general interest' has enhanced clarity concerning the shared values among Member States. Criticising EU legal terminology might be considered by some as quibbling over semantics. Nevertheless, the European legislators should be mindful of creating new legal concepts which blur rather than bring out the underlying values inherent in the concept of public service.

---

49 The European Courts have not defined precisely what aids meeting 'the needs if coordination of transport' means, see Greaves 2000, p. 20.

50 Ibid.

51 The European Federation of Public Service Unions (EPSU) abstains from the use of the terms 'service of general interest' and 'services of general economic interest' referring to such constructions as 'Eurospeak', see http://www.epsu.org/spip.php?page=recherche&recherche=eurospeak&x=0&y=0. The ECJ has also demonstrated its fondness for the term 'public service obligations', see ECJ, Case C-280/00 *Altmark* [2003] *ECR* I-7747. Notice should be taken that the term 'service of general interest obligation' has indeed been used by the Commission, see Commission of the European Communities, Communication from the Commission, Services of general interest in Europe, 20.09.2000, COM(2000) 580 (2001/C17/04), 19 January 2001, Section 14.

8.3 Conclusion

Imposition of obligations on service providers has proved to constitute a useful tool for Member States in terms of complying with their duty to supply essential services to citizens. Each Member State has its own national concept of 'public service' which makes it difficult to capture this concept in an all embracing definition. In the wake of liberalisation of service provision, the historical background and legal status of public services has led to different national legal frameworks for imposing public service obligations on service providers. In this article, it has been demonstrated that in French public administrative law 'les services publics' enjoy constitutional protection and a general awareness of the duty placed upon public authorities and service providers to respect the principles of continuity, equality among users, adaptability of service. This legal basis protecting the substantive character of public services has led to stable conditions and legal certainty for service providers. The use of long time contracts has enabled public authorities and service providers to develop public service obligations in a steady environment which has resulted in an adaptable system responding to the changing needs of society.

In the United Kingdom, public services do not enjoy the same constitutional status as in France. Public service values have been protected through political rather that legal mechanisms. However, especially the public utilities have been subjected to extensive sector specific regulation. It is submitted that the lack of protection of public service values at constitutional level has been among the reasons why public service obligations are interpreted by the utilities as specific requirements rather than general overarching duties.

Under EU law, 'services of general interest', that is public services in the language of the EU, are afforded protection from both the rules of free movement and competition through different juridical techniques. The EU has also committed itself and its Member States to protect the shared values inherent in the concept of 'services of general interest' through recognition of common values such as universal service, continuity, quality of service, affordability and, user and consumer protection. This recognition of shared values is influenced particularly by the French and Continental tradition. The mechanism enabling public authorities in Member States to impose public service obligations on service providers is recognised in EU utilities regulation, and serves the purpose of harmonising certain shared values.

However, it is submitted that the replacement of the term 'public service' for the new creation 'service of general interest' undermines the mission of protecting common shared values in the EU. This confusion created by terminology is highlighted by the fact that the TFEU and sector specific regulation still contain reference to the term 'public service'. In this regard, it can be asked whether the EU should abandon their newly invented legal terms or stick with the well established and easily understood concept of 'public service' which can be found in Article 93 TFEU.

Acknowledgment I would especially like to thank my colleagues at the University of Tromsø for their insightful comments on an early draft of this chapter.

References

Arnull A (1999) The European union and its court of justice, 1st edn. Oxford University Press, Oxford

Buendia Sierra JL (1999) Exclusive rights and state monopolies under EC law: article 86 (formerly article 90) of the EC treaty. Oxford University Press, Oxford

Damjanovic D, De Witte B (2009) Welfare integration through EU law: the overall picture in the light of the Lisbon Treaty'. In: Neergaard U et al (eds) Integrating welfare functions into EU law—From Rome to Lisbon. DJOF Publishing, Copenhagen

Defeuilley C (1999) Competition and public service obligations: regulatory rules and industries games. Ann Pub Co-op Econ 70(1):25–48

Fournier J (1993) Le Train, l'Europe et le service public, Jacob O, Paris, 13–61

Fournier J (2010) Public services available at embassy of France in Washington. http://www.info-france-usa.org/spip.php?article641, Accessed 30 November 2010

Freedland M (1998) Law, public services, and citizenship—new domains, new regimes? In: Freedland M, Sciarra S (eds) Public services and citizenship in European law: public and labour law perspectives. Clarendon Press, Oxford

Greaves R (2000) EC transport law. Pearson Education Limited, Essex

Loughlin M (2003) The idea of public law. Oxford University Press, Oxford

Malaret Garcia E (1998) Public services, public functions, and guarantees of the rights of citizens: unchanging needs in a changed context. In: Freedland M, Sciarra S (eds) Public services and citizenship in European law: public and labour law perspectives. Clarendon Press, Oxford, pp 57–82

Morris GS (2000) Employment in public services: the case for special treatment. J Leg Stud 20(2):167–183

Neergaard U (2009) Services of general economic interest: the nature of the beast. In: Krajewski et al (eds) The changing legal framework for services of general interest in Europe. T.M.C. Asser Press, The Hague

Odudu O (2006) The boundaries of EC competition law: the scope of article 81. Oxford University Press, Oxford

Prosser T (2005) The limits of competition law: markets and public services. Oxford University Press, Oxford

Rawnsley D, Lazar N (1999) Managing the universal service obligation. In: Crew MA, Kleindorfer PR (eds) Emerging competition in postal and delivery services. Kluwer Academic Publishers, Boston, pp 182–183

Sauter W, Schepel H (2009) State and market in European union law: the public and private spheres of the internal market before the EU courts. Cambridge University Press, Cambridge

Scott C (2000) Services of general interest in the European union: matching values to regulatory technique. Eur Law J 6:310–325

Supiot A (1998) Employment, citizenship, and services of general public interest. In: Freedland M, Sciarra S (eds). Public services and citizenship in european law: public and labour law perspectives, Clarendon Press, Oxford, 161

Part III
Global Issues

Chapter 9
Public Private Partnerships and Government Services in Least Developed Countries: Regulatory Paradoxes

Priscilla Schwartz

Abstract This chapter discusses the regulatory paradoxes that emerge as public–private partnerships (PPP) that are used to supply traditional government services in least developed countries (LDCs). PPP were first developed in industrialised States to improve the quality and economic efficiency of public services in industrialised countries using market based solutions. They have become more important as governments have attempted to keep public spending under control and a general reluctance of electorates to pay higher taxes for public services. In LDCs, the issue is different: governments frequently do not have the funds to develop and maintain public services. The United Nations has endorsed the use of PPP (as a means of realising the Millennium Development Goals) that benefits the public and delivers economic development and an improvement in the quality of life. Gradually a revolution has taken place with use of private capital harnessed to deliver public services and infrastructure projects. As *Schwartz* points out, there appears an inherent conflict between the *commercial* interest underpinning PPP for social services, especially health care, and the goals of a public policy. Both goals seem irreconcilable. Yet these solutions have been transplanted to LDCs to ensure that basic social services are provided. *Schwartz* takes as a case study, the use of PPP in delivering health care services in Sierra Leone offering an analytical model to identify the concept of PPP in a developmental context of government health services in LDCs. *Schwartz* is able to offer a model which allows for the possibility of using PPPs for facilitating increased aid flows for funding a technical solution to problems encountered in health care systems in LDCs. She concludes by stating

P. Schwartz (✉)
School of Law, University of Leicester, University Road, LE1 7RH Leicester, UK
e-mail: ps162@le.ac.uk

E. Szyszczak et al. (eds.), *Developments in Services of General Interest*,
Legal Issues of Services of General Interest, DOI: 10.1007/978-90-6704-734-0_9,

that whatever model is adopted LDC should retain the autonomy to choose the right regulatory mechanisms and provide the institutional capacity to meet the health challenges they face.

Contents

'Let those who have less in life have more in law'
Ramon Magsaysay
(President of the Philippines, 1953–1957)

9.1 Introduction

The public private partnership (PPP) doctrine was conceived out of the need to ensure economic efficiency and to improve the quality of public services in developed countries. The underlying rationale is that efficiency in the management of public services will be enhanced through collaboration between public and private entities including, some interaction between their distinct legal and regulatory framework and using market-based solutions. The doctrine has its roots in the policy of liberalisation of services markets which was championed mainly by the developed countries through the global trading system and anchored by the influence of private transnational corporations (TNCs) over the economic activities and relations of states.

The TNC according to Cutler, acquire a specific structure of authority and hegemony which couples with the dominance of liberalism to entrench 'global political authority'; and such authority is made effective due to the strategic location of the private TNC at the nexus between economics and politics, private and public activities, and local and global political economies.[1] This 'global political authority' deeply implicates the TNC in undermining the role of the state especially in its effort to direct the process of development through distinctions of the public and private divide. The wave of the British experiment with large-scale privatisation programmes in the early 1980s altered the respective roles of the public and private sector worldwide as it encouraged private firms in productive activities that were traditionally owned and managed by the state.[2]

In the special case of the LDCs,[3] however, privatisation evolved mainly through pressure from the international donor agencies (where aid has been conditional on privatisation) and from domestic capital market interests at the expense of transparency.[4] Infrastructure development and extractive industries were initial targets for private sector involvement.

Today the PPP concept re-brands the privatisation agenda in an aggressive bid to ensure predominant private sector participation especially of the private TNC in government services primarily to entrench the policy of market liberalisation and to complement the trend of economic globalisation. We are warned that *laizer-faire* liberalism is not the spontaneous automatic expression of economic facts; but a political programme of deliberate policy designed to change the state's leading personnel and the economic programme of the state itself.[5] This is true in the case of the role of the State, in the health sector.

Health and social services have long been considered the direct responsibility of a country's government. In many countries medical services are operated on a non-market basis and are considered by many to be a national public good and therefore not appropriate for commercialisation. Current state practice, however, shows that numerous countries now employ institutional approaches and regulatory regimes that structure health care with stronger market orientation thus widening the space for increased private participation.[6] Yet the term PPP bears no certain legal definition. It is usually used in reference to the legal regime of a given partnership, the institutional framework governing PPP operations and the regulatory conditions that border partnership interests. The prevailing policy objectives driving PPP include the creation of an enabling business environment, the promotion of innovation, competition, and social regulation, and to ensure

---

1 Cutler 1999, p. 66.

2 United Nations ST (1997) p. 3.

3 Reference to LDC depicts as a special group of states characterised by a low income level and structural impediments to growth, and requiring special measures for dealing with those problems. This designation is based on a simple set of criteria (per capita gross domestic product (GDP), share of manufacturing in GDP and adult literacy; see Handbook on the Least Developed Country Category 2008 (accessed July 2009).

4 United Nations ST (1997) p. 5.

5 Supra n. 2.

6 International Trade Centre (ITC) Business Briefing Trade Policy: WTO Services—'Service Sector: Health related and Social Services' (ITC Business Briefing) available at: http://www.intracen.org/btp/wtn/newsletters/2010/services12.htm (last accessed 02/04/10).

international cooperation on these; work force development and risk-sharing with the private sector (through venture capital investment) are recent additions.[7] Invariably an effective regulatory framework and substantial state action is required to implement these objectives. Within this market centred rationale, embedded legal uncertainty and regulatory conundrum, PPP is widely promoted as a development tool that could ensure basic health and social services in LDCs.

But the state of most LDC health sectors including Sierra Leone is deplorable. Inadequate government health infrastructure, poor primary health care service conditions, the prevalence of diseases, unemployment, and poverty paint a grim picture for competitive marketing of LDC health services. More particularly, sub-Saharan Africa is furthest behind on almost all of the health related Millennium Development Goals (MDGs) and is losing ground in obtaining more funds for disease prevention, access to affordable drugs for treatment, and increased aid to build functioning public health systems to administer these.[8] It is in recognition of this grim peculiarity of LDC health sector challenges that this article advocates and scopes a *developmental context* of health services delivery for LDCs. The context represents primarily a pursuit of policy objective for the promotion of affordable, accessible, and universal health care services, as a public purpose for which the government is to provide, facilitate, and regulate in the interest of its people.

Under the principles of the UNICEF/WHO Alma-Ata Declaration, the provision of such health care should be 'at a cost that the community and the country can afford to maintain at every stage of their development in the spirit of self-reliance and self-determination.'[9] Over the years however, the LDC governments have relied on official financial flows including loans, grants, export credits, and publicly guaranteed debt to fulfil this public purpose. But the trend of decline in the official flows to LDC and the substantial increase in unofficial 'private for-profit' finance and other private cross-border giving noted by Harford et al. contorts the performance of this function.[10]

Ultimately, at the turn of the century, concerns over the high rate of communicable and deadly diseases and the need to ensure global health security paved the way for a reconditioning of the LDC health objectives as a global agenda to be addressed in a '*global partnership*'. Under this partnership, the global community' with the cooperation of pharmaceutical companies assume responsibility

[7] See Trubek 2009, p. 31.

[8] UNICEF 2008 (accessed 8/05/09); also The International Development Research Centre 'Privatization, Liberalization and GATS' (The IDRC) available at http://www.idrc.ca/en/ev-67858-201-1-DO_TOPIC.html (last accessed 06/03/10) 9.

[9] UNICEF/WHO Declaration of Alma-Ata International Conference on Primary Health Care, Alma-Ata, USSR, 6–12 September (1978) para 6 (Alma Declaration).

[10] Harford et al. 2005, pp. 1–2; unofficial flows include foreign direct investment, migrant workers' remittances, portfolio equity flows, grants from NGOs, and loans without a sovereign guarantee. Other giving includes foundations, corporations, religious groups, and membership-based NGOs.

particularly for reducing child mortality, improving maternal health, combating HIV/Aids, malaria, and other diseases.[11] Action on the explicit and specific commitments to establish a global fund on AIDS, TB, and malaria (on an initial pledge $1.3 billion) evidences in the GFATM.[12] This globalisation of partnership introduces the doctrine of PPP in LDC health delivery systems in a transformational way that blurs the distinction between the traditional economic orientated PPP and the developmental context of PPP in LDCs.

This chapter discusses the doctrine of PPP and its application to LDCs health delivery systems especially through the lens of Sierra Leone's health sector. It examines different types of PPP arrangements under broad categories namely: international trade and economic partnerships, global health partnerships, development PPP, and domestic health initiatives to illustrate the practice of respective health PPP. It examines the regulatory problems engendered by complex system of PPP arrangements and questions the appropriateness of marketing 'public–private for profit partnerships' as a development mechanism for delivery of health services in poor countries. It proposes a *developmental context* of PPP and recommends a pro-active role for LDC governments in regulating development partnerships as vital for achieving their public health goals. The following section, presents an analyses of the various permutations of PPP in aid of extrapolating if any, a *developmental context* of health services applicable to LDCs.

9.1.1 The Doctrine of Public–Private Partnership

The United Kingdom Private Finance Initiative of the 1990s attempted a systemic programme for PPP that was focussed on limiting public expenditure. Much later, emphasis was placed on public purchases of quality services and risk allocation. Under EU law, PPP enjoys prominence through concepts of SGI and SGEI,[13] and shaped by EU policy on competitive tendering of public works and services. Yet the term remains undefined and there is no specific system governing PPP.[14]

---

[11] UN Millennium Development Goals (MDGs) available at http://www.un.org/millennium goals/goals.html# (last accessed 07/08/08).

[12] The IDRC, supra n. 8 at 9 Note that the generic commitments on a key role for strong national health systems in the delivery of effective prevention, treatment and care, and in improving access to essential health services and commodities without discrimination continues on the low end of the total budget of ODA support for health.

[13] A SGI is a non-economic service which is not traded on the market and in which users and their requirements are the main focus of public action) and SGEI is an economic service that operates in a market environment). EC Commission, *Services of general interest in Europe* (2001/C 17/04) EN *OJ* (2001) C 17/7.

[14] EC Initiative on Public Private Partnerships and Community Law on Public Procurement and Concessions. http://ec.europa.eu/internal_market/publicprocurement/ppp_en.htm (EC PPP Initiative) (accessed 08/04/09).

In general, the term refers to forms of cooperation between public authorities and the *world of business* which aim to ensure the funding, construction, renovation, management or maintenance of an infrastructure, or the provision of a service.[15] According to the then Commissioner for Internal Market and Services, it is still unclear how the existing 'patchwork quilt' of rules should apply to PPP.[16] He also notes the difficulty in developing a coherent framework that provides the public and the private side with legal certainty and to facilitate institutional framework within which PPP can work most efficiently.[17]

The UN Study Group Report defines PPP as implying 'a common understanding of shared goals, a willingness to repartition responsibilities for their achievement, a continuing public–private dialogue on what needs to be done to promote their realisation, and a supportive policy and institutional framework.'[18] According to the United States National Council for PPP, the concept refers to contractual relations between a public agency and a private sector entity for the purpose of sharing skills, assets, risks, and rewards potential of each sector in the delivery of service or facility for the use of the general public.[19] From the United States perspective, PPP does not represent 'corporate philanthropy' or 'charity work' to help poor nations but forms a cooperative alliance that can *benefit business* and the society in which the business operates.[20]

The African Union (AU) and its New Partnership for African Development (NEPAD) agency, view PPP as a means to 'achieving economic transformation in Africa by working closely together with the private sector in utilising respective core competencies to form synergies and achieve results collectively.'[21] PPP is also having a role in increasing public financing for the provision of basic infrastructure, for example, roads, energy, and water supplies and advancing the African Agenda under WTO and EPAs.

In other forums, however, a social dimension of PPP is shaping what is described as 'public-social-private partnerships' (PSPP). This concept derives from the inapplicability of business and profit led PPP model to fulfil public aims such as the common good and welfare.[22] PSPP covers, cooperation models

---

[15] Ibid. [emphasis added].

[16] McCreevy 2005 (accessed 08/04/09).

[17] Ibid.

[18] United Nations ST (1997) p. 2.

[19] National Council for Public Private Partnerships: 'How Partners Work' http://www.ncppp.org/howpart/index.shtml# (NC/PPP) (last accessed 06/04/09).

[20] Green 2008 (last accessed 06/04/09).

[21] Declaration The African Private Sector Forum: 22–23 January (2008) Addis Ababa, Ethiopia p.4; also NEPAD Business Group: AU pursues stronger public–private sector partnership June (2004) available at http://www.commit4africa.org/declaration/assembly-african-union-12th-ordinary-session-addis-ababa (last accessed 06/04/09).

[22] 'Public/social/private partnerships are methods of co-operation between private and government bodies' available at: http://www.answers.com/topic/public-social-private-partnership#From_PPP_to_PSPP (PSPP) (accessed 28/05/09).

between participants that are not only agencies of the state and private enterprises (as in PPP), but also social enterprises and social economic organisations.[23] The goal of PSPP financing tool is the servicing of social protection and supporting interests and activities for the improvement of opportunities for disadvantaged people or groups.[24] PSPP models should only be supported by the state in cases where they serve the long-term social needs of disadvantaged members of society. 'This responsibility belongs to the state and the state only.'[25]

The forgoing permutations of PPP are split on emphasis between business orientation of the PP concept and the developmental. The UN and PSPP descriptions represent a more cohesive framework and approach to PPP from which the *developmental context* of LDC health services could construct. The commonality of partnership goals, the recognition of other social private partners, the strategic partitioning of health responsibilities by the state, and a supportive institutional framework that allows for policy considerations of the state and continuing dialogue on implementation of social goals, frames the *developmental context* of health services in LDCs, that is the promotion of affordable, accessible, and universal health care services to citizens as a public purpose which the government is to provide, facilitate, and regulate.

The following section will illustrate the various partnership models that can be derived from health and social services in order to present a context of practical application of the various permutations of the PPP doctrine discussed above.

9.1.2 Partnering Models for Health Facility and Services

There are several models of partnering mechanisms for engaging private sector participation especially in public hospitals, health centres or clinics. The discernible models include facility arrangements involving construction, ownership type, management, operation and maintenance, and other financing agreements. These are notably:

(a) *Build-Own-Operate* (*BOO*)—private firm builds, owns, and operates a public hospital;
(b) *Build-Operate-Transfer* (*BOT* or *BTO*)—a private partner builds and operates the hospital facility (contract or franchise) and transfers it to the public agency after a period of time;
(c) *Buy-Build-Operate* (*BBO*) *or Lease-Develop-Operate* (*LDO*)—a form of asset sale (or lease) in which a private operator invests capital to rehabilitate or expand existing facility and operates it under contract with the public agency;

[23] Ibid.

[24] Ibid.

[25] Ibid.

(d) *Design-Build-Maintain (DBM)*—private partner designs, constructs, and has responsibility for maintenance of the facility; but ownership of asset remains with the public agency;
(e) *Purchase-Leaseback*—the private firm finances and builds a new public hospital then leases it back to the government;
(f) *Contract Services for Operations, Maintenance and/or Management*—transactions involving private management of a public hospital, out sourcing support services (clinical, non-clinical, and specialised), procurement of labour, medicine, equipment; and technical expertise. Also *collocation agreements* in which a private wing is located within or beside a public hospital;
(g) *Tax-Exempt Lease*—a public partner finances capital assets or facilities by borrowing funds from a private investor or financial institution. The private partner generally acquires title to the asset, but then transfers it to the public partner;
(h) *Developer Finance*—the private party finances the construction or expansion of a public facility in exchange for the right to build a profitable facility at the site and receive future income from user fees (residential homes, commercial stores, or industrial);
(i) *Turnkey Model*—the private developer commits to build the facility for a fixed price and absorbs the construction risk of meeting that price commitment;
(j) *Free entry model*—where qualified private providers are allowed to freely enter and exit the health care market without establishing a contractual relationship with the government. Other applicable regulatory instruments for ensuring safety and minimum quality of care include: licensing, certification, and accreditation. Government might also use financial and other incentives (taxes, subsidies, and training opportunities) to influence the behaviour of private providers.[26]
(k) *'Institutionalised PPPs'*—arrangements 'outsourcing of public tasks, which involves the creation of public service undertakings held jointly by both a public and private partner.'[27]

Traditionally, health and social services are generally considered to be a national public good for which a country's government must have direct responsibility to provide and operate on a non-market basis. In other cases, these services are delivered by both private and public suppliers, often done on behalf of the government and not on a commercial basis per se.[28] This element of non-commercialisation or marketability of such services is an attribute of the *developmental context* of health services that is applicable to LDCs and which could

[26] See generally, Taylor and Blair 2002; Marek et al. 2003; NC/PPP supra n. 19.
[27] McCreevy 2005.
[28] ITC Business Briefing, supra n. 6.

potentially ensure accessibility of a government's citizens to essential health services without discrimination.

The permutations of PPP doctrine which emphasise the business environment over the social element including a focus on cost and economic efficiency, explains why regulatory regimes in numerous countries have been moving in the direction of stronger market orientation.[29] This trend opens space for increased private participation of domestic as well as foreign providers in public health care delivery through one or more of the partnering models outlined above. The International trade Centre identifies three types of institutional approaches to how health care is structured along market oriented partnerships especially in OECD countries and in other economically advanced developing countries.[30] These are:

- *Reimbursement systems*: here the patient pays for the service supply (retroactively) and is then reimbursed by his insurer or the insurer makes the payment directly[31];
- *Contract systems*: here, a compulsory insurance is normally provided by a limited number of public or non-profit agencies and an agreement establishes the terms and conditions of cooperation between consumers and the specified health care providers[32];
- *Integrated health systems*: Here medical personnel and other health care spending are normally funded and controlled by one single institution which usually is the government.

The PPP partnering models for engaging private sector participation in public oriented health systems (be it in the form of facility, management or financing agreements), are clearly representative of the EU, US and AU permutations of PPP. These models generally tend to emphasis the business environment of health service transactions over the social element. They advocate cooperation only between public agencies and private enterprises with a focus on infrastructure, cost, and efficiency. This dimension undermines the UN and PSPP view of PPP, which as observed earlier, represent a more cohesive framework and approach to PPP from which the developmental context of LDC health services could construct. The developmental context recognises the role of other social private partners, the duty of the state to strategically partition health responsibilities, and the importance of having a supportive institutional framework that would allow for policy considerations of the state and continuing dialogue on implementation of health and social goals. This dimension has the potential to promote affordable,

[29] Ibid.

[30] Ibid.

[31] This system caters for multiple providers usually private insurance companies thus providing the patient a wide scope for selecting the preferred health care providers and the service supply.

[32] Under contract systems hospitals are usually funded on the basis of per diem rates or fees per case or service and may be subject to budget caps. People tend to be invariably restricted to a preselected range of hospitals, while others allow for treatment by additional providers similar to the reimbursement system.

accessible and universal health care services to citizens as a public purpose for which the government is to provide, facilitate and regulate.

9.1.3 Partnering Models and Sierra Leone's Primary Health Care Facility

How do the various partnering models apply to Sierra Leone's primary health care facility services (PHC/FS)? First there is an estimated total number of eight hundred and ninety-eight PHC/FS including hospitals, community health clinics (CHC), and maternal child health clinics (MCHC) and posts scattered around twelve districts in the provinces and the Western Area and Urban including Freetown, the capital.[33] Each provincial district has at least one (not more than two) government hospital in terms of ownership and management. There are twelve private hospitals in six districts which operate independent from government; eight of these are mission hospitals and four are industrial hospitals including the diamond mining company facility.[34]

The Western Area has two government hospitals while Western Urban (Freetown) has ten government hospitals and thirty-nine private and industrial hospitals. Most of the private facilities are owned (by medical practitioners) and managed privately. Three of the ten government facilities are in some form of PPP arrangement. For example, the Choithrams Memorial Hospital represents a Model (d) *Design-Build-Maintain* (*DBM*) arrangement—Choithrams designed and constructed the facility and has responsibility for the maintenance of the facility but ownership of asset remains with the public agency. There are foreign Indian doctors operating in the Choithrams hospital. Also, a variant of Model (f)—*Collocation Agreements* exist between the GOSL, the UNAMSIL Mission (a UN agency) and the hospital management. The GOSL is currently negotiating another 'collocation agreement' between Choithrams hospital and the Italian NGO Clinic 'Emergency Life Support for War Victims'.[35]

There is future potential for adapting a blend of PPP health facility Models (c), (f) and (g) under terms of a recent World Bank IDA Grant. The grant is for the restoration of the essential functions of health care delivery system and for strengthening both public and private health sector capacities, in order to improve the efficiency of

---

[33] Two hundred and fourteen of these facilities, (mainly CHC and MCHC) are not functioning and an estimated 100 need rehabilitation.

[34] Directorate of PHC, *The Primary Health Care Hand Book Policy* Ministry of Health and Sanitation, (MOH/SL): Freetown, SL, May 2007 (PHC Handbook).

[35] See MOHS/SL *A Handbook of Health NGOs, Donors and other Partners in Sierra Leone*, MOHS Youyi Building Freetown, Sierra Leone January (2008). (Donor Handbook) Also, Fofana Ibrahim L, Liaison Officer for Donor Relations, MOHS/SL—Comments from Interview held on 23/04/09 at the MOHS Youyi Building Freetown, Sierra Leone.

the health sector.[36] The provisions include, inter alia, rehabilitation of selected hospitals and health centres and acquisition of clinical and related services, the procurement of goods and works through competitive bidding, including through '*direct contracting and procurement from United Nations Agencies*'.[37] Other policy conditions attached to the grant requires the GOSL to enhance private sector participation in the delivery of quality health services through, inter alia, 'contracting out' services and provision of incentives to potential private sector entities.

In the *developmental context* of LDC health services, appropriate health infrastructure and effective facility management is vital in ensuring affordable and universal access for all social groups. But how can one reconcile the concept of 'economic efficiency' with 'equity' in PPP? How do the various PPP health facility models appreciate the concept of universal access and affordability in a poor country lacking national health insurance or mandatory employer insurance schemes? In fact a UN report cautions that the economic rebalancing that is necessary under transition to PPP can undermine the basic political and economic goal of most governments: that is, the provision of basic needs to the lowest income Groups.[38] The transition could also place new resource and skills demands on government agencies and risk conflict in the application of rules.

What the discourse suggests is that the inception of health facility PPP models in LDCs contemplates fundamental complexities and critical policy issues. In particular how to ensure universal and affordable health care to an uninsured population in a *public–private-for-profit-partnership*. What will be the cost to government employing incentive systems, exclusivity privileges, and tax exemptions to facilitate such access? What will be the effect on competition and the private sector enhancement on already struggling public health services? In my view, serious consideration should be given to developing a national health insurance scheme. In the interim however, LDC governments would need to assess the appropriateness of legal instrument, regulatory mechanism, and institutional framework in their collaboration with private health services suppliers.

9.2 International Cooperation: Trade and Other Economic Arrangements

The role and nature of PPP in international cooperation of states for pursuit of LDC health objectives is quite complex. First, it does not immediately translate the private component of PPP. Second, there is a dichotomy between interstate

---

[36] Health Sector Reconstruction And Development Project: Grant Number H289—SL Financing Agreement (Amending And Restating Development Grant Agreement) Between Republic Of Sierra Leone And International Development Association Dated July 11, 2007 (World Bank/SL HSRD Project (2007).

[37] Ibid. [emphasis added].

[38] United Nations ST (1997) p. 4.

cooperation in multilateral and regional institutional settings on the one hand and in bilateral context. Then there is the component of global cooperation on health issues which is more inclusive, encouraging variety of public–private entities to collaborate on the achievement of universal health goals or on issues within respective mandates at domestic level. Also, the legal arrangement that may govern each strand is not always certain, and is largely policy driven or based on broadly stated principles or other 'soft law'. The following section discusses selected cooperation models under PPP in relation to the WTO rules, particularly the GATS and TRIPS agreements on the one hand and that of international and global partnerships.

9.2.1 PPP and WTO Rules

Cooperation on international trade is important for health service delivery in LDCs. For example, most LDC WTO member governments lack manufacturing capacity of essential medical products. The context of globalisation of partnerships would require the setting up of foreign companies or organisation across borders for the supply of health service either on a commercial or non-commercial basis. Similarly, WTO LDC members would need to access medical technology to facilitate better health conditions for their peoples. The WTO General Agreement for Trade in Services (GATS) and the Agreement on Trade Related Intellectual Property Rights (TRIPS) can ensure these transactions within prescribed rules, general principles, and special policy considerations under the WTO framework. This section examines the context of PPP in the relevant WTO agreements especially its role in enhancing health development goals as a governmental purpose in LDCs.

9.2.1.1 The Services Agreement (GATS)

The GATS agreement constitutes the legal framework through which WTO Members could progressively liberalise trade in services including health-related services. The prevailing perception is that the GATS is primarily a vehicle for the expansion of business opportunities for TNC, which 'locks in' existing service privatisation and liberalisation policies in order to secure and entrench pro-competitive policies in areas that have been autonomously liberalised.[39] The key concern is that GATS will unavoidably lead to increased privatisation of essential public services as health care, although the joint WHO and WTO publication assures us that '… all the WTO agreements explicitly allow governments to take measures to restrict trade in pursuing national health policy objective.'[40]

---

[39] The IDRC supra n. 8.

[40] ITC Business Briefing supra n. 6.

It is argued that the liberalisation of health services could facilitate the introduction of new private resources that could support the public health system in developing countries and provide new and more efficient management techniques including for medical professionals.[41] David Woodward maintains that the distinctive features of the market for health services, particularly in developing countries, means that the 'benefits of trade' argument is not applicable and that GATS policy seriously constrains health policy.[42] Concerns remain over the fact that private investments in health services would emphasise those services for which a market exists and therefore likely to be concentrated in services for the affluent.[43] Such investments which focus on increased income uneasily aligns with health services where the goal is not increased income but equitable access to quality services, including by those who may not be able to purchase traded services. These concerns warrant an examination of the nature of GATS influence on PPP and the impact on LDC developmental context of health services.

Health services applicable under the GATS agreement are classified under two main categories namely[44]:

- *hospital, social, and other health services* (for example, health services delivered under the supervision of doctors, residential health facilities, and ambulance services) and
- *professional services* (for example, medical, dental and veterinary services, and the services provided by nurses, midwives etc.)

Article 19(2) GATS explicitly provides that liberalisation must take place with due respect for national policy objectives and the level of development of individual WTO members. The extent to which the health sector of an individual country is liberalised, allowing for increased involvement of the private sector in public health services in particular, will depend on the nature of commitments made in its schedule defining the level of trading rights that are guaranteed under the GATS. Pursuant to Articles 15 and 16 of the Agreement, commitments are made in terms of 'market access' (opening the market to foreign providers) and 'national treatment' (treating foreign providers the same as domestic providers). These commitments could be effected with respect to any combination of the four modes of 'supply of services'[45] namely cross-border supply, consumption abroad, commercial presence and presence of natural persons[46]:

---

[41] The IDRC supra n. 8.

[42] Woodward 2005, pp. 511–534.

[43] The IDRC supra n. 8.

[44] See 'Health and Social Services' available at: http://www.wto.org/english/tratop_e/serv_e/health_social_e/health_social_e.htm (last accessed 04/03/09).

[45] This includes the production, distribution, marketing, sale and delivery of a service: Article 28.

[46] GATS Article 2 (a)–(d).

- The *cross-border supply* mode involves the delivery of health services from the territory of one Member State in the territory of another Member State[47]: (for example, include internet consultation, 'tele-health' services, diagnosis, treatment medical claims processing, medical records transcription services, shipment of laboratory samples, and medical education);
- The *consumption abroad* mode, known in health parlance as 'health or medical tourism' caters for incidents when patients seek treatment abroad especially when such treatment may be unavailable in the home country or where it is more affordable in another country (for example, patient medical care or to undergo surgery);
- The *commercial presence* mode governs the supply of health services in one Member State, through investment by foreigners (natural persons, companies or a firm) in the territory of another Member State. Such investment could be for the provision of health insurance, establishment of private hospitals, clinics, treatment centres other health operations (like technical assistants), or management contracts for such facilities, whether they are public, or private;
- The *presence of natural persons* mode covers the temporary movement of health professionals from one country to another. This category will include medical specialists (doctors, nurses, or dentists) moving to a foreign country on a temporary basis to provide expertise to a hospital or medical services provider.[48]

The GATS agreement allows WTO Members to choose which service sectors to open up to trade and foreign competition and by which specific mode of service supply. Under the provisions of Article 27(a), the GATS will apply where member governments, institute measures[49] that 'affect' trade in health services relating to any of the four supply modes explained above.[50] Second, pursuant to Article I: 3(b) and (c), GATS will apply where such measures relate to the provision of health and social services that are not in the 'exercise of government authority' because they are supplied on commercial and competitive basis. Similarly, the rules on specific commitment (Articles 2, 16 and 17) are not applicable to measures governing procurement by governmental agencies of services for a governmental purposes, provided that such services or their supply are not purchased

[47] In other words suppliers and consumers are located in different countries.

[48] Note that under the Annex on Movement of Natural Persons, Members remain free to apply measures regarding citizenship, residence or employment on a permanent basis.

[49] These could be in the form of 'a law, regulation, rule, procedure, decision, administrative action, or any other form.'

[50] GATS Article 28: 'measures by Members affecting trade in services' include measures in respect of: (i) the purchase, payment or use of a service; (ii) the access to and use of, in connection with the supply of a service, services which are required by those Members to be offered to the public generally; (iii) the presence, including commercial presence, of persons of a Member for the supply of a service in the territory of another Member. Other measures or policies that may not be affected by specific commitments include non-discriminatory domestic regulations (for example, standards, licensing requirements); non- discriminatory subsidies; export-related measures (for example, promotion and restriction) and visa requirements.

with a view for commercial resale or with a view to use in the supply of services for commercial sale.[51] Accordingly, the GATS contain a government 'carve out' that seek to ensure governments' ability to set and implement public health measures or policies (including through PPP arrangement) that are non-commercial or non-competitive in nature.

The GATS recognises that increasing participation of developing countries in world trade shall be facilitated through negotiated specific commitments for the strengthening of their domestic services capacity and its efficiency, and competitiveness, inter alia, through access to technology on a commercial basis. This consideration accentuates the market oriented dimension of health services that potentially overrides the government 'carve out' for provision of public health services. However, the GATS recognises the serious difficulty facing LDC in accepting negotiated, specific commitments in view of their special economic situation and their development, trade and financial needs.[52]

9.2.1.2 The GATS, PPP Concept and LDC Health Services

What the above analysis so far suggests in the context of the applicability of the PPP concept and related partnering models is that the GATS classification of supply modes could basically cover PPP facility, management and financial services models outlined above including the institutional approaches operative in the models of reimbursement, contracts and integrated systems. PPP under the GATS Agreement would apply where health and social services are provided by both private and public suppliers through various legal forms of collaborative partnerships. In other words, the private foreign supplier could be sole provider of health services on behalf of the government (monopolies or exclusive suppliers) either on a commercial or none commercial basis. However the requirement of non-commercialisation (non-profitability) and non-competitiveness is the fundamental *caveat* that must inform any PPP arrangement for supply of health service especially where the purpose is to facilitate the *developmental context* of health services.

Problems could arise as to the classification of social services that could be provided by private organisations on behalf of government on a part commercial and part aid funded/charity basis which may be necessary for ensuring the developmental context of health services especially in LDC. In other words, since most countries allow some commercial or competitive provision of virtually all public services the caveat may not adequately shield government measures for

---

[51] See GATS Article 13(1). Other measures or policies not affected by specific commitments include non-discriminatory domestic regulations (for example, standards and licensing requirements); non- discriminatory subsidies; export-related measures (for example, promotion and restriction); and visa requirements.

[52] GATS Article 4(1)(a) and (3).

public health from a trade challenge. In fact it becomes difficult in particular cases to determine what is excluded from the category of social services.

Notwithstanding the forgoing anomaly, LDC members could be able to form PPP for the supply of Health services through the various supply modes such as foreign medical professionals, patients, technical assistants, or the foreign ownership or management of hospitals, clinics or office within their territory or of WTO Member States.[53] Over half a dozen sub-Saharan African countries have committed to full liberalisation of several modes of medical and dental services, including provisions for private foreign investment, with only one such country having made any GATS commitments involving specialised medical services.[54] It could be possible under GATS for such LDC members to institute health services PPP within the commercial and market orientated framework. But they may need to circumvent the obligation requiring them to give like foreign health services or service providers in their country equal treatment as that afforded to the foreign PPP service providers in their countries; or to make available to other foreign health service providers the same privileges enjoyed by domestic health service suppliers.[55]

LDC member governments may avoid this obligation by stipulating conditions and limitations they wish to maintain in the sector to regulate participation within their PPP policy preference.[56] They would also be required to publish promptly all measures taken in respect of the PPP arrangement pertaining to or affecting the operation of the GATS and should notify the Council for Trade in Services of all related legal or regulatory changes.[57] More importantly, LDC members may even choose not to schedule their health sector at all and so operate their PPPs outside WTO rules[58]; or they could invoke the special LDC 'needs' consideration principle, or the GATS policy exceptions for protection of human health especially given the prevalence of diseases in most LDC.[59]

It may be that LDC members have undertaken the WTO-type commitments in other economic partnership arrangements governed by different regimes. Even in this case, as noted by Adlung and Carzaniga, GATS Article 5:3 offers several elements of flexibility to developing countries participating in EIAs.[60] For instance, the prohibition of new or more discriminatory measures is to be applied

---

[53] See GATS Article 1:2(c); Article 28(d) and Article 28(m)(ii); also, see generally, Smith et al. 2008, pp. 437–446; Adlung 2005, p. 11.

[54] Note that these countries have made these GATS commitments with fewer limitations than those defined by the already well-developed EC 12 members. See generally GATS Schedules; and The IDRC, supra n. 8, pp. 7–8.

[55] GATS Article 2.1; (The Non-discrimination—MFN Principle); Article 16 and 17 (Market Access and National treatment specific obligations as inscribed in members' Schedules).

[56] GATS Article 20.

[57] GATS Article 3 (Transparency obligation).

[58] GATS Article 5 (Economic integration).

[59] GATS Preamble (paras 3–6) and also Article 4 and Article 14.

[60] Adlung and Carzaniga 2009, p. 8.

in accordance with the level of development of the countries concerned both overall and in individual sectors.[61] At another level, LDC members may be able to take policy measures to form a non-commercial and non-competitive *developmental context* PPP with a foreign health services supplier for the purpose of providing or facilitating universal and affordable health services to their citizens. Such arrangement will be exempt from the scope of the GATS entirely, on the basis that the particular health service is supplied in the exercise of 'governmental authority' and is 'supplied neither on a commercial basis, nor in competition with one or more service suppliers.'[62] Invariably, as Adlung and Mattoo clearly suggest, 'there are virtually no policy regimes that would be GATS- inconsistent per se, or at least, that could not be accommodated under the exceptional provisions.'[63]

Sierra Leone has market access limitations in relation to all sectors in its schedules including Health services in terms of the 'commercial presence' mode of service supply. It requires that foreign service providers incorporate or establish the business locally in accordance with the relevant provisions of Sierra Leone laws and, where applicable, regulations particularly with respect to land and building acquisition, lease or rental. It maintains no market access and national treatment limitation over its health sectors other than (in context of professional services) that commercial presence must take the form of partnership.[64] The foreign ventures shall have to be competitive and registered institutions in their own countries. This limitation requiring competitive foreign ventures (albeit in own countries) could potentially affect the non-commercial and non-competitive *developmental context* of PPP that could be possible. Such discrepancies highlight PPP regulatory paradoxes. It also lends validity to scholars who question whether measures that may uneasily sit between public and private law obligations and having a 'mixed regulatory/commercial character' are measures for the GATS.[65]

The TRIPS Agreement

The TRIPS Agreement regulates intellectual property rights (IPR) protection within the WTO free trade agenda. It recognises the *private* nature of IPR on the one hand, and the *public* element underlying policy objectives of national IPR systems especially the developmental and technological. The Agreement aims

---

[61] Ibid.

[62] Articles 1:3(b) and (c). For scholarly literature on the definition of 'government service', including perspectives on whether GATS impinge on the ability of government to provide vital social services and possible policy choices open to WTO members in the area of services regulation see Krajewski 2003; Adlung 2005; Smith et al. 2008; Adlung and Carzaniga 2009; Adlung and Carzaniga 2001, 352 et seq.; David 2004.

[63] Adlung and Mattoo 2008; Adlung 2005; Adlung and Carzaniga 2009, p. 8.

[64] WTO Schedule of Commitments.

[65] Lang 2004, p. 813.

to address the difficulty in finding harmonised standards for protection and enforcement of IPRs and to ensure a balance between private rights and public obligations. As a basic principle, WTO TRIPS seeks to ameliorate the impact of enhanced protection of IPR on social and economic welfare by allowing its members to adopt measures necessary to protect public health and nutrition and to promote the public interest in sectors of vital importance to their socio-economic and technological development.[66]

Prior to the TRIPS agreement, the issue of intellectual property did not affect the manner in which developing countries and LDC could obtain essential medicines (on or off patents) since the process depended much on their procurement methods, local production capabilities, public health policies and general financial resources.[67] But the TRIPS regime by Article 28 provides exclusive rights for the inventor as an incentive for innovation with limited exceptions for consumers to use such inventions. For many LDC however, innovation gains could never fully compensate for the intellectual property rights monopoly-related losses[68] (including harm to global access to legally, affordable essential medicines). However, the TRIPS Agreement and other initiatives taken by the WTO members for the protection of public health provide some flexible mechanisms by which developing countries and LDCs could access essential pharmaceutical products easier.

One such mechanism is Article 6 which allows WTO Members to set own policies concerning the 'exhaustion' of IPR and also to create their parallel imports system within the chosen policy.[69] International exhaustion occurs when national law allows importation of an IPR protected product without the authorisation of the patent holder, after that product has been legally sold more cheaply in a foreign market.[70] This mechanism allows developing countries to search the global market place for pharmaceutical products that are priced lower than that available in the home market. In this regard, whether or not LDCs have the capability to manufacture medicines they could access essential drugs by parallel importation.

Another provision in aid of LDC access to pharmaceutical products under the TRIPS Agreement is Article 30 which allows for exception to the exclusive right of patent-holders 'provided that such exceptions do not unreasonably conflict with a normal exploitation of the patent and do not unreasonably prejudice the legitimate interests of the patent owner, taking account of the legitimate interests of third parties.' This provision encounters certain difficulties in that the conditions do not set clear boundaries on what are to be considered permissible exceptions.

---

[66] TRIPS Articles 7 and 8.

[67] Abbott and Reichman 2007, p. 927.

[68] Messerlin 2005, pp. 1198–1200 (accessed 04/04/09).

[69] See generally Matthews 2005, p. 420; Paas 2009, p. 609; Watson 2009, 154 et seq. See also Tuosto 2004.

[70] This is usually possible especially with pharmaceutical product markets where TNC engage in the practice of differential pricing of their products across the different markets.

A further flexibility derives from Article 31, which provides for *'other use'*[71] of the subject-matter of a patent 'without authorisation of the right holder' where such use relate to compulsory licensing, government use and in addressing restrictive business practices. The compulsory licensing system under that provision gives WTO members the right to authorise the use of a patented invention by manufacturers other than the patent right-holder. The use of compulsory licences could lead to a lower cost of drug than the equivalent patented products whose price in the regular market may be too high. The effect of this provision is at the core of the balance of rights between the largely market oriented and profit driven private pharmaceutical industries and the developing country efforts to provide cheap generic medicine for their populations.

The provision however lists series of conditions that must be met for issuing a compulsory license. For instance under Article 31(f) the licensees could only use the patented invention for the benefit of their own domestic market. This condition affects LDC countries which have no potential to support manufacturing in the pharmaceutical sector under compulsory license.[72] The WTO Members, sought to overcome this obstacle in 2001, by adopting the Doha Declaration[73] which clarifies the role of compulsory licences. Paragraph 5(b) of the Declaration affirms the right of WTO Member States to grant compulsory licenses and the freedom to determine the grounds upon which such licenses are granted. In effect, other than conditions of national emergency, public non commercial use and anti-competitive practices, (which are included in Article 31), the members could obtain the licenses on the basis of any public health situation; and they reserve the right to decide the kind of situations they will classify as a national emergency or circumstance of extreme urgency.[74]

Similarly by an Implementation Decision adopted as on 30 August 2003, the WTO Members waive the Article 31(f) obligation under the compulsory licenses to allow manufacturing countries to export generic medicines to other countries if the exported medicines meet the public health needs of the countries importing them. The importing country must clearly state the exact amount of medicines they intend to purchase and the pharmaceutical companies should employ specific labelling, packaging, and marketing mechanisms, to ensure that the companies will only export the designated medicines to countries that obtain the compulsory licenses.[75]

[71] 'Other use' refers specifically to use other than that allowed under Article 30 and includes use by the government or third parties authorised by the government.

[72] Note that under this article, exportation countries could not sell their products that made under the compulsory license to other countries more than what should be supplied in the domestic market. See Abbott 2002, p. 499.

[73] See Declaration on the TRIPS Agreement and Public Health, WTO Ministerial Conference, Fourth Session, Doha, Adopted on 14 November 2001, WT/MIN(01)/DEC/2.

[74] TRIPS Article 31(b) and (k); Haochen 2004, p. 137.

[75] On the implications of the application of the Decision, see Paas 2009, pp. 612–613.

9.2.1.3 The TRIPS, PPP Concept and LDC Health Services

What emerges from the WTO developing members' commitment to ensure protection and enforcement of nearly all forms of IPR[76] of their developed counterparts, who are predominantly IPR-holders, is a sort of 'thy-brother's-keeper' partnership which could pose challenges particularly for LDCs. The foregoing analysis undoubtedly show that the WTO rules on TRIPS hold profound implications for the concept of PPP both from a context of 'public private for profit partnerships' and from the non-commercial and non-competitive developmental context PPP. The latter context will invariably represent a PPP for a government purpose to provide or facilitate, inter alia, accessible and affordable pharmaceutical products, and health technology for their citizens on a non-commercial basis. But the LDC governments would need to collaborate with the private sector on their approach to medicines or medical technology, where they desire to use the TRIPS flexibility provisions to overcome IPR constraints.

Similarly, cooperation and collaboration would be required between WTO developed country governments and their private enterprises on the one hand and LDC governments on the other, for the purpose of addressing public health problems afflicting many LDCs, especially those resulting from HIV/AIDS, tuberculosis, malaria, and other epidemics. The Doha Declaration stresses the need for the TRIPS Agreement to be part of the wider national and international action to address these problems.[77] That Declaration and subsequent Decisions pave the way for a new kind of PPP arrangement that potentially reposition economic interests of the developed countries and rebalances the rights of their pharmaceutical industries in order to address public health challenges facing LDCs.

Such partnership derives not from the traditional PPP models with its market based underpinnings, but from the pursuit of shared goals of addressing LDC public health needs through cooperation between the public and private entities. Under this partnership, the LDC are accorded waivers and dispensations including grace periods from patent protection. For example the poorest countries are not obliged to implement, apply, or enforce the TRIPS obligations on patents before 2016, instead of the originally scheduled date of 2005. Developed members also commit to provide incentives to their enterprises and institutions to promote and encourage technology transfer to the LDC members pursuant to Article 66.2.[78]

[76] Including over knowledge, research and development of health related technology, patented pharmaceutical products and processes, medical/clinical procedures.

[77] The Doha Declaration supra n. 73 paras 2 and 7.

[78] Decision on Least-Developed Country Members—Obligations Under Article 70.9 of the TRIPS Agreement with Respect to Pharmaceutical Products (8 July 2002); Decision on the Extension of the Transition Period under Article 66.1 of the TRIPS Agreement for Least-Developed Country Members for Certain Obligations with Respect to Pharmaceutical Products; and Decision on Implementation of paragraph 6 of the Doha Declaration on the TRIPS Agreement and public health (30 August 2003); paragraph 7 = all available at http://www.wto.org/english/tratop_e/trips_e/pharmpatent_e.htm (last accessed 8/05/09).

More recently, the Paragraph 6 system (established under the General Council Decision of August 2003) was given effect for the first time in September 2008 to ship generic medicines from Canada to treat HIV/AIDS patients in Rwanda.[79] It is alleged that access to medicines has improved through a major reduction of prices enhanced by international funding.[80] It is schemes like this, which underscore Tuosto's laud for the benefits of making available medicines to LDC otherwise than through the transfer of technology or foreign investment.[81] But caution should be exercised in over-emphasising the benefits of drug availability in the LDC outside local production capacities and not down play other important domestic policy tools (like direct investment and industrialisation) which are necessary to pursue health goals within a broader economic development agenda. As Andrew Lang effectively puts it, a distinction ought to be made between accounts of the social impacts of international trade itself and the analysis of the impact of international trade regime on the policies making purposes of its members—demarcating social from political impact of trade regimes.[82] This suggestion is useful for navigating the cross-road between the TRIPS agreement and the economic activities that impact LDC public health challenges.

What is clear from this analysis of the TRIPS Agreement in relation to the concept of PPP and the implications for public health in poor countries is a bias in favour of private involvement in public health service provision predominantly on a commercial platform, but also from a cooperative and collaborative framework that will allow LDC to meet precarious health challenges. There are also so many conditions to the WTO solutions which seek to ensure that the TRIPS flexibility provisions do protect public health as oppose to the pursuit of industrial and commercial policy objectives. But the prevalence of these conditions seed some doubt over their effective implementation. This scepticism is further compounded by the practice of bilateral trade agreements between developed and developing countries which tend to impose stronger provisions and additional limitations than those available under the TRIPS and de facto could make the use of the WTO flexibilities more difficult.[83] These short comings no doubt influenced calls for the millennium development strategy which combines 'trade and aid for development' on the rationale that the TRIPs provisions should be complemented by aid in the form of subsidised purchases of essential medicines.

Ultimately, it seems that what started off as a predictable rule-based WTO/TRIPS and public health issue has transformed, whether by design, coincidence or unforeseeable consequence, into an international and global public–private policy

---

[79] Pascal 2008. WTO News: Speeches at http://www.wto.org/english/news_e/sppl_e/sppl111_e.htm (accessed 08/03/2009).

[80] Ibid.

[81] Tuosto 2004, p. 542.

[82] Lang 2007, at pp. 345–346.

[83] For example the US uses bilateral pressure under Section 301 to address exhaustion issues; see Messerlin 2005, pp. 198–200.

issue, that is fanned by a cosy alliance of political, economic and moral considerations, and operative outside the remit of rules, rights and responsibilities. The important question now is: whether the anomaly and regulatory paradox of the *global partnerships for health* have a 'collocation agreement' with the WTO, or is it to be explained simply as the practice for the WTO to support the political policy objectives agreed upon by its members?

9.2.2 International and Global Health Partnerships

International and global partnerships on health (IHPs) have the objective of addressing constraints to the health MDGs. They ensure international cooperation and collective responsibility for achieving the MDGs and translating such cooperation into action. IHPs facilitate increase in aid flows or alternative source of health financing that is channelled through the 'Global Fund' that was set up with express purpose of raising money from governments, private individuals, and the corporate sector. This global responsibility essentially necessitates cooperation, collaboration, and coordination between wide variety of public and private actors in partnerships at varying levels of interests and engagement. In this section I examine relevant IHPs and their activities in LDCs.

The main IHP initiatives are: The *Global Fund to Fight AIDS, Tuberculosis, and Malaria* (GFATM); The *Global Alliance for Vaccines and Immunisation* (GAVI); The World Bank *Multi-Country HIV/AIDS Program* (MAP); The United States *President's Emergency Plan for AIDS Relief* (PEPFAR); The *Roll Back Malaria, initiative* (WHO/RBM); the *Stop Tuberculosis Partnership*; Research and development PPPs; and *Initiative on Public–Private Partnerships for Health* (IPPPH).[84]

The GAVI Alliance is an example of 'spaghetti bowl' of PPP cocktail. In the mix are:

- Developed country donors—ensure that health receives an adequate proportion of ODA and also contribute to technical and policy expertise;
- Developing country governments—recipients of Aids vaccines;
- International organisations—(WHO and UNICEF) support countries in their application for GAVI funds, including monitoring of GAVI-related immunisation activities;
- Research and technical health institutes—who provide technical staff for operations and help build capacity for research and development;

[84] See generally Eldis 'Health and development Information Team' (Eldis HAI Team) available at: http://www.eldis.org/go/topics/resource-guides/health-systems/global-initiatives-and-public-private-partnerships/public-private-partnerships—Information on all the relevant initiatives can be accessed through this site. (last accessed 04/06/09).

- International financiers (World Bank)—expanding its loans and credits in support of immunisation and enhancing its policy dialogue with ministries of finance, health, and other partners to recognise the value of immunisation and new vaccine development;
- Industrialised country vaccine industry[85]—ensures pool of global expertise for development and distribution of new and under-used vaccines and accessibility to vaccines especially for children of poorest people and countries;
- Developing country vaccine industry—through DCVMN[86]—shape a broader, healthier global vaccine market and to improve vaccine affordability;
- Private sector philanthropists (The Gates Foundation) and civil society organisations.[87]

Several innovative mechanisms continue to inform international IHP under the GAVI.[88] Under the Advanced Market Commitment (AMC) mechanism for example, donors commit money as incentives to vaccine makers in order to guarantee the price of vaccines once they have been developed. Companies that participate in an AMC make legally binding commitments to supply the vaccines at lower and sustainable prices after donor funds made available for the initial fixed price, are spent.[89] As observed by Micklewright and Wright, 'Health looks especially attractive to large donor looking for a problem that can be solved by funding a 'technical' solution.'[90]

Then there is the so-called 'ethical investment' for health development goals. HSBC, in collaboration with the International Finance Facility for Immunisation (IFFIm), the GAVI Alliance and the World Bank, have designed the innovative Vaccine Investment Plan.[91] The initiative ensures that the IFFIm bonds are made available through an ISA, and offered by HSBC in the United Kingdom to raise funds from personal investors and pay them a competitive return for their funds and so to protect children in LDC from life-threatening diseases.[92] The global pool of resources under various initiatives for drug and vaccine research, production, and marketing to the world's poor, whether by donation or price discounting

[85] Examples include GlaxoSmithKline Biologicals; Novartis Vaccine; Merck & Co Inc etc.

[86] Developing Country Vaccine Manufacturers Network (DCVMN) represents a voluntary, public health-driven alliance of enterprises—state-owned and private, large and small—from developing and middle-income countries. (Indonesia, India, Brazil, Senegal, and Korea) All DCVMN are pre-qualified by WHO to supply vaccines both to domestic and international markets, including UNICEF and WHO and GAVI.

[87] Eldis HAI Team supra n. 84.

[88] GAVI Alliance, 'Innovative Partnerships', available at http://www.gavialliance.org (accessed 27/04/09).

[89] Ibid.

[90] Micklewright and Wright 2005, p. 148.

[91] GAVI Alliance, 'Innovative Vaccine Investment ISA', available http://www.gavialliance.org (last accessed 27/04/09).

[92] Ibid. IFFIm has raised more than US$1.6 billion to support GAVI immunisation programmes since 2006.

should be applauded. However, some operational concerns still remain which are addressed hereunder.

In their review of IHPs, Conway et al. recommend that there is the need to develop greater policy coherence among collaborating institutions and donor partners in order to realise positive results.[93] The reviewers further recommend that 'organisations must start to operate with a different mindset, where attribution and control become less important driving forces, replaced by the higher aspirations of achieving the MDG through cooperative *mutual accountability*.'[94] Bernstein and Sessions recently examined the operation of three major funds directed at combating HIV/AIDS in Ethiopia and Uganda.[95] These include the GFATM, the PEPFAR, and the World Banks' MAP. They report that in 2005 alone the three funding bodies disbursed three billion US dollars, through governments, local non-governmental organisations (NGOs), international NGOs, consulting agencies, and other bodies for addressing HIV/AIDS at the country-level. They find that the large scale of the increase in funding, and the difference in disbursement procedures between the three funders, made the new funding difficult to manage in Ethiopia and Uganda.[96]

A similar concern emerges from a study of the health systems in Botswana, Sri Lanka, Uganda and Zambia to assess the role of PPPs in improving access to donated or discounted drugs for diseases including malaria, and HIV/AIDS.[97] Caines and Lush reveal that the relevant LDCs are not given appropriate support at the international arena, to assess for themselves which strategies (discounted/donated) or offers of support (funding) could provide the maximum cost benefit.[98] Even more unsettling is their finding that, for the LDC to benefit from donated drugs precludes, the use of generics while the lack of overall price transparency means that governments were not always sure if or when they could negotiate further discounts from companies.[99]

Moreover, the African strategy in respect of TB Control PPPs, operates within concepts like 'strictly private for profit', 'private for profit' and 'private not for profit'.[100] Examples of 'private for profit' LDCs with the Global Fund support for specific TB PPP include Burundi, Malawi, Liberia, Mali, Mozambique, Senegal, and Sierra Leone.[101] It seems paradoxically strange that amidst the billions that are garnered for disease prevention, control, and research through the Global Fund, LDC countries tend to be grouped according to the nomenclature of profitability for access to affordable TB drugs. Also, Tubman has examined how PPP research and

93 Conway et al. 2008, p. 7.

94 Ibid. [emphasis added].

95 Bernstein and Sessions 2007, p. 4.

96 Ibid.

97 Caines and Lush 2004, pp. 4–5.

98 Ibid.

99 Ibid.

100 Nkhoma 2008.

101 Ibid. On the cost effectiveness of PPP programmes see generally: Yukich et al. 2007.

development agreements with access conditions have been developed, negotiated, and implemented, and how they are structured to ensure the widest effective access to the finished product. He concludes that there is a need to develop new hybrid forms of intellectual property management, which allow public players to negotiate access to effective health delivery, while at the same time providing incentive for private players to develop product research and manufacturing resources.[102]

In light of the forgoing examples, it is not implausible to suggest the appearance of either collusion between the international public partners and their private counterparts to defraud LDC; or that an inherent conflict exists between the commercial interest underpinning health PPP and the goals of public health (in the *developmental context*) that is irreconcilable. There is thus an urgent need for LDC governments to re-examine and refocus their public health priorities to investments in building skills in their health sector, health institutions, and manufacturing capacities, over and above the current system of drug cartelisation that is flagged through international health PPP.

9.3 International Development and PPP

Outside the remit of the IHPs of the global fund and other alliances, donors, NGO, and civil society involvement in LDC health development is still substantial. This may not directly connect with the global initiatives but they are not sufficiently distinguished from it. Currently, apart from cases of humanitarian assistance and transitional processes, the health concerns in MDGs tend to supplant broader health policy framework in LDCs. Development PPP (unlike some Global PPPs) are not merely financial instruments, but are operative locally. In this section I discuss development PPP for health (DPH). I attempt closer scrutiny of partnership (including government) agendas and implementation methods. The goal is to ascertain a *developmental context* of health PPP as opposed to the traditional business-led PPP arrangement that is echoes in other sections of this paper.

9.3.1 Financing for Health versus Financing Healthy Business

In the realm of international development, PPP has become an 'essential tool' in the US government's 'development toolbox' to help the Americas and the world meet the challenges of the 21st century including health care in developing

[102] Tubman 2004 (accessed 26/05/2009). For a corporate perspective on Health PPP in Tanzania, see Njau et al. 2009, pp. 235–249. They identify three key themes that are critical for developing countries to emulate in the implementation of PPPs. They conclude from their case study that '… PPPs may begin from very humble and loose beginnings but with perseverance, a vision, and trustworthiness may become powerful advocates for meeting prescribed health agendas in the developing world.'

countries.[103] The US development model PPP is the USAID concept of 'Global Development Alliance (GDA).[104] The GDA is a business model of public–private alliances that institutes private sector partners as full collaborators in the implementation, design, and funding of development projects including health services. It links the US development institutions—civil society and private (profit-making and non-profit)—with those in the developing world, overlapping business and development interests with traditional NGO and host government partners.[105]

The GDA uses Global Framework Agreements (GFA) to create further strategic partnerships with key private sector partners.[106] This helps to reduce the start-up effort required for creating public–private alliances on an individual basis; and they also help to integrate development outcomes into business agendas more broadly.[107] GDA has 'elevated partnerships from the realm of charitable contributions and corporate social responsibility to focus on core business interests of private firms and long-term investment of private philanthropy.'[108]

But international development PPP go beyond business concerns. It includes health and other social policy initiatives which aim to strengthen the interface between public partners and non-state actors in order to make government more responsive to users of health services. In this regard, philanthropy partnership plays a vital role in international health development especially in terms of addressing or attaining a common health and social goal through development charities and private donations. These are partnered by a wide variety of people or organisations giving gifts or subscriptions without necessarily having control of the direction and outcome of the funds. The private charities could then partner with the international public partners or operate within the beneficiary-recipient developing countries to further the national health priorities identified by the public partners or those within their specific mandate.

Autonomous agencies of the UN undertake development activities with respect to advancing various social development goals including the health MDG. For example, UNICEF, WHO, UNDP, UNFPA being public international agencies, could partner with private individuals, entities or foundation donors and in some cases franchising through national charities.[109] UNICEF promotes a system of allowing national charities otherwise designated as 'national committees' to use

---

[103] Green 2008 [emphasis added].

[104] USAID: 'History of the Global development alliance' (USAID GDA) available http://www.usaid.gov/our_work/global_partnerships/gda/frameworks.html. The alliance leverages more than $9 billion in combined public–private sector resources.

[105] Ibid.

[106] For example, USAID/GFA partners with Microsoft Corporation, the Millennium Challenge Corporation and the US President's Emergency Plan for Aids Relief (PEPFAR) combined resources, to advance activities globally in six key areas including health.

[107] USAID GDA supra n. 104

[108] Ibid.

[109] Micklewright and Wright 2005, p. 148.

the name and logo of the agency in order to raise money.[110] This arrangement should not be confused with government contributions to UNICEF or WHO, and must also be distinguished from governments' overall official development assistance channelled through regional or national development agencies which may (or not) be operational at country level. Examples include EC-EDF, DFID, and IRISH AID.

Further forms of international development partnership have been identified by Micklewright and Wright in forms of 'corporate giving' particularly with reference to MNCs. This is taking place in two areas, namely 'cause related marketing' (CRM) and corporate social responsibility (CSR).[111] CRM is derived from corporate recognition that an association with worthy cause can benefit their brands. According to them, it is 'a commercial activity by which businesses and charities or causes form a partnership with each other to market an image, product or service for mutual benefit'[112] CSR is linked with firms building its reputation through investing in social goals from its 'core budget' as opposed to a 'peripheral benevolence fund'.[113] Such act of partnership through a sense of social responsibility is commonly exemplified in MNCs commitments to improving the health of their work force in LDCs by building health clinics.

The analysis has revealed complex mix of partners, with variable structure and models of PPP in international financing relevant to health development. The United States GDA business model of public–private alliances overlaps business and development interests and links the developing world through so called 'global framework agreements'. Then, there is the health and other social policy oriented PPP between international public partners and non-state actors who may not necessarily have control of the direction and outcome of the funds. We also have autonomous public international agencies of the UN partnering with private individuals, entities or foundation donors to undertake health development activities. There is also the developed government overall official development assistance that is channelled through regional or national development agencies. Further partnership derives from forms of 'corporate giving' evidenced through CSM or CSR schemes. The legal aspects of such partnerships in terms of obligations, enforceable rights, duty, and accountability to the LDC is not always visible or certain which leaves the respective arrangements pretty much on the faith of 'to thy own self be true'.

The following section will examine the extent to which the varying categories of DPH identified in the forgoing analysis are representative of donor activities in Sierra Leone's health sector.

---

[110] Ibid.

[111] Ibid.

[112] Ibid.

[113] Ibid.

9.3.2 Government Services, Development Partnerships and Regulatory Paradoxes

Donors make a significant contribution to health sector budget in Sierra Leone. There are 96 registered Health partners operating in the country as Donors (international public institutions and agencies), NGOs (international, national or mission NGOs) with a declared annual cost of operation totalling millions of dollars in 2008.[114] Recently further resources have been mobilised to support a new Reproductive and Child Health (RCH) strategy (2008–2010), aimed at reducing child mortality and improving maternal health- (MDG 4 and 5). Funds have been pledged by the World Bank, DFID, and technical assistance from UN agencies. The range of public and private participants acting on 'common-but differentiated-goals' and responsibilities in a reasonably small health sector as Sierra Leone does have implications for governments' health care policy planning, and financing, implementation, and regulation.

Regulatory tensions and strains are prevalent in health development financing. There is difficulty on how to reconcile vertical approaches, which create and utilise managerial, operational and logistical structures as separate health initiatives on the one hand, with those of government health system initiatives including those that address disease prevention and control.[115] This situation is believed to have created a '*power culture*' as opposed to a *'task culture' in Sierra Leone's health sector.*[116] A new model of health sector financing known as Sector Wide Approaches (SWAps) is currently instituted. According to UNICEF, the rationale is to ensure that the major funding contributions for the health sector support a single plan for sector policy, strategy, and expenditure backed by government leadership.[117] SWAps were created for several purposes, namely:

- to address the limitations of project-based forms of donor assistance;
- to ensure that overall health reform goals are met;
- to reduce the large transaction costs for countries and establish genuine partnerships between donors and countries;

---

[114] MOHS/SL *A Hand Book of Health NGOs, Donor Partners in Sierra Leone*, January Sierra Leone Government, MOHS Youyi Building Freetown (2008). The Main Donors and the amount of funds committed by each public partner for the year 2008 alone is as follows: EU (40 million Euros), DFID (40 million pounds), JICA (5 million and 7 hundred thousand dollars (USD) and Irish Aid (1 million USD). The GFMAT has now pledged up to 50 million (USD), while the World Bank IDA grant is 30 million (SDR). The main international NGOs are: Oxfam UK (7 million pounds); CARE International (4 million USD); Concern World Wide/SL (1 million and 400 hundred thousand Euros). Note that the regulatory requirement is for NGOs to disclose statement of accounts, but the Partners have refused to provide a complete outlay of their spending.

[115] UNICEF 2008 (last accessed 04/03/09).

[116] Siegel et al. 1996 (also in Govt of Sierra Leone, MOHS Staff Appraisal Report No. 13947-SL) Freetown (Dec. 1997).

[117] UNICEF Report (2008) supra n. 115, at p. 106.

- to adopt common approaches to health service delivery across the sector;
- to ensure that government procedures are made to increasingly control the disbursement and accounting of funds.[118]

Concerns still remain over rationalising and reconciling donor and GOSL accounting, procurement, disbursement, and auditing requirements.[119] In terms of project support and implementation, PPP is the main mechanism used in the fight against Malaria, HIV/AIDS, and TB. These three initiatives are prioritised to benefit from huge allocations from the Global Fund. It is therefore not surprising that about 90% of the listed NGOs (including NGO clinics) in the health sector are inscribed as having expertise or operational mandate in these areas, with the highest being for HIV/AIDS.[120] The recently launched RCH programme is reportedly the current attraction and darling of international NGOs partners.

According to the MOHS Donor Liaison Officer, the Ministry finds it difficult to regulate this trend because it filters from the international policy and financing mechanism and instruments through to particular NGO from the funding countries.[121] Such a measure is pursued by JICA, which uses its contribution of 850 million(USD) to the Global Fund to foster the participation of Japanese NGOs in STOP TB Control efforts in Sierra Leone and other efforts conducted by international organisations.[122]

The malaria initiative is a useful example of PPP collaboration on implementation. According to the UNICEF Executive Director, wide spread distribution of insecticide-treated nets is a significant factor in altering the trend of 100 million people dying of malaria a year.[123] So Sierra Leone's main strategy for Roll Back Malaria (RBM) is in using PPP to promote the use of Long Lasting Insecticidal Nets (LLINs) in the fight against malaria.[124] Even the recent World Bank IDA

---

[118] Ibid., at p. 106.

[119] Siegel et al. 1997; see also Canavan et al. 2008. Commissioned by the Health and Fragile States Network in Collaboration with the Royal Tropical Institute, Amsterdam October 2008, 1–80 especially 13–39 at http://www.kit.nl/net/KIT_Publicaties_output/showfile.aspx?e=1484 (09/05/09).

[120] There is limited information on the prevalence of HIV/AIDS in Sierra Leone. However a modelling exercise carried out for the World Bank calculated the annual cost of scaling-up AIDS programmes to meet the current need to be between US$ 9–14 Million USD. This represents per capita cost of around US$ 2-US$3 and approximately 1.8% of GDP (Landell Mills 2007 at p. 55).

[121] Fofana supra n. 35.

[122] Ministry of Foreign Affairs of Japan Public–Private Partnership for International Cooperation towards the Elimination of Tuberculosis 24 July 2008; available at: http://www.stoptb.jp/english/pdf/StopTB%20Japan%20Action%20Plan.pdf (accessed 02/04/09).

[123] UNICEF—Executive Director UNICEF World Malaria Day Announcement by: http://www.gawkk.com/unicef-world-malaria-day-2009-announcement-1/discuss

[124] Creating Sustainable Impact Through Public Private Partnerships In The Fight Against Malaria, Roll Back Malaria, *Scaling up Insecticide-treated Netting Programmes in Africa*, August 2005.

Agreement ensures the use of this product as measurable outcome of the Governments' evaluation and reporting obligations in terms that:

> the number of insecticide-treated bed nets purchased under the project and distributed to the population exceeds 160,000 and the percentage of children under five years of age and pregnant women … who sleep regularly under insecticide-treated bed nets, is at least 40% each.[125]

The government policy of free LLIN distribution is now the problem because it jeopardises the market–based programmes of private partners, social marketing, and other commercial interest in the PPP that is promoted by international public and private partners including the World Bank.[126] The government partners in the Sierra Leone RBM initiative include:

- Ministry of Health & Sanitation—National Malaria Control Programme (MOHS/NMCP) Government of Sierra Leone:—owners of the health program;
- The World Bank (WB)—funding the social marketing and distribution program;
- Universat Logistics Company (ULC)—the local distributor implementing the social marketing program and being supported to build capacity for eventual commercial operation;
- Vestergaard Frandsen S.A.(VF)—Vestergaard Frandsen S.A.(VF)—supplier of PermaNet® LLINs and funding agent for commercial marketing activities;
- Canadian International Development Agency (CIDA)—funding Measles and Malaria Initiative Canadian Red Cross (CRC)—implementing the Measles & Malaria Initiative (MMI);
- Other donors/stakeholders—Participating in campaigns: Médecins Sans Frontières (MSF), CARE International and the Sierra Leone Red Cross (SLRC).

This DHP model aims to collaborate closely for promotion of LLINs' in order to close the gap between free public distributions and time limited subsidised approaches, and sustainable market development.[127] The WHO and the EU ensured that the GOSL waived tariffs and taxes on mosquito nets, insecticides, and anti-malaria drugs, so to address the need of other groups of people not catered for under the Government Policy for Vulnerable Groups.[128] But in this

---

[125] World Bank/SL HSRD Project supra n. 36 [emphasis added].

[126] Roll Back Malaria Partnership 'Creating Sustainable Impact through Public Private Partnerships in The Fight against Malaria', Roll Back Malaria, *Scaling up Insecticide-treated Netting Programmes in Africa*, August 2005 at http://www.gbcimpact.org/files/transfers/Sustainable_Impact_Sierra_Leone_Allan.doc (06/05/09). See more generally—Roll Back Malaria Partnership: Working Group for Scaling-up Insecticide-treated Netting 'A Strategic Framework for Coordinated National Action, Roll Back Malaria, WHO Geneva, Switzerland available at http://www.rollbackmalaria.org/partnership/wg/wg_itn/docs/WINITN_StrategicFramework.pdf (06/05/09).

[127] Ibid.

[128] MOHS/SL 'Mission, Objective, Achievements and Aims of the Malaria Control Programme', 11 August 2006, http://www.health.sl/drwebsite/publish/page_46.shtml (accessed 04/03/09).

dispensation no strict distinction is made between nets under market targeted programmes or social marketing schemes. Also two important factors are not considered in the arrangement: how they afford the nets for the poorest households; and the fact that the effectiveness of the insecticide treated nets declines after 3–4 years.

Similarly, some legal complications could also arise in implementation method that impact on the government's health services regulatory efficiency. For example, there is inherent conflict between the Hospital Boards' Act, 2003 and the Local Government Act, 2004 (LGA). Both legislation effectively confer the same authority to different administrative functionaries and empower both over financial matters, including procurement services, to raise loans and to award contracts.[129] This anomaly is seemingly taken advantage of by the international Donor partners who are keen on instituting un-planned and un-sequenced decentralisation process, and their NGOs who would gladly operate within an unregulated framework. For instance, a DFID award (GB£ 782,043) was made directly payable to CARE International for the implementation of the new RCH initiative on the justification that it would allow NGOs already active in the field to continue to contribute to RCH as the government establishes a functional contracting system.[130] Sierra Leone's official position is that these methods inhibit transparency, accountability, effective regulation, and monitoring of outcomes of such arrangements, the responsibility and risk of which always remains with the government.

This outlook illustrate that the government health sector benefits as much from its DHPs as it is challenged by their predominance in the sector. It puts in sharp focus the need for an effective regulatory mechanism to ameliorate the challenges—especially for regulating health NGOs or charities. One such mechanism could be in finding a criterion to applying incentive systems, as opposed to the prevailing measure which is based on share of expenditure cost, and, huge duty and tax waivers. Sierra Leone could consider adopting the measure adopted by the United Kingdom in its 'Millennium gift aid' scheme between 1998 and 2000 as a useful guide.[131] Under such scheme, in order to qualify for tax deductibility, donations had to be to 'UK charities' running projects in the areas of health, education or poverty-relief in eighty countries eligible for IDA/IBRD funding from the World Bank.

[129] GOSL/MOHS—Report (2005).

[130] CARE International—Project Proposal: Joint Reproductive and Child Health Programme, 'A Collaborative approach to Reducing Maternal and Child Mortality in Sierra Leone', submitted to DFID UK, 20 November 2008.

[131] Micklewright and Wright 2005.

9.4 Conclusions

This chapter sought to identify within the concept of PPP the *developmental context* of government health services in LDCs. It has examined the doctrine of PPP and evaluated its application to LDCs' health delivery systems through various models including the developmental context. The analyses on international trade and economic arrangements reveal that the development context of PPP could be possible within the WTO services and IPR arrangements provided commercially oriented partnerships can be sufficiently distinguished from it. The international and global health partnerships uncovers some contemporary innovative mechanisms for facilitating increased aid flows for funding a 'technical' solution to health problems, albeit with vital operational concerns remaining. The analyses on IDP expose complex mix of partners, with variable structure and models of PPP in international financing for health development. The legal aspects of such partnerships in terms of obligations, enforceable rights, duty, and accountability to the LDC is not certain which leaves development PPP pretty much on the faith of 'to thy own self be true'. The respective distinctions of PPP are implicated in Sierra Leone's health sector. The country benefits as much from its DHPs as it is challenged by their predominant involvement in its health sector. The regulatory tensions and strains that are prevalent in health development financing find easy accommodation in Sierra Leone.

Overall, there seems to be an inherent conflict between the commercial interest underpinning health PPP and the goals of public health (in the *developmental context*) that is irreconcilable. There is also a paradox in having aid funds channelled through 'public–private for profit partnerships' and the fact of legal ambiguities on the rights and obligations of partners is a travesty. The health PPPs tend to predicate on gain and the pursuit of partner self interests. While not entirely adverse to the prospects of gain underlying partnerships generally, in the developmental context this element could undermine LDC governments' genuine effort and national endeavour to provide accessible and affordable health delivery system for their population. It brings into the equation important considerations like: what standard could one use to measure gains?—is it to be measured by the overall wellbeing of a state's population or designated 'vulnerable groups'? Should the gains be measured by selective project gains as 'little-drops' in filling the ocean of health challenges? Should it be measured by good donor relations with consequential implications for other sectors of the economy; or by the politics of how much aid a government can attract? All of these questions represent differing goals, values, and perceptions on how to realise health development goals in LDCs. While these goals and values may still somehow work into partnership agreements for health development, it is imperative that LDC governments are reserved explicit right to use choice of regulatory mechanisms and provide institutional capacity to meet the health challenges they face.

References

Abbott FM (2002) The Doha declaration on the TRIPS agreement and public health: lighting a dark corner at the WTO. JIEL 5(2):469

Abbott FM, Reichman JH (2007) The Doha round's public health legacy: strategic for the production and diffusion of patented medicines under the amended TRIPS provisions. JIEL 10(4):921

Adlung R (2005) Public services and the GATS. WTO ERSD working paper, 3 July 11

Adlung R, Carzaniga A (2001) Health services under the general agreement on trade in services. Bull World Health Organ 79(4):352–364

Adlung R, Carzaniga A (2009) MfN exemptions under the general agreement on trade in-services: grandfathers striving for immortality? JIEL 12(2):1–36

Adlung R, Mattoo A (2008) The GATS. In: Mattoo A et al (eds) A Handbook of International Trade in Services. Oxford University Press, Oxford, pp 52–53

Bernstein M, Sessions M (2007) A trickle or a flood: commitments and disbursement for HIV/AIDS from the global fund, PEPFAR, and the World Bank's multi-country AIDS program (MAP). Centre for Global Development, USA

Caines K, Lush L (2004) Impact of Public-private Partnerships Addressing Access to Pharmaceuticals in Selected Low and Middle Income Countries: A Synthesis Report from Studies in Botswana, Sri Lanka, Uganda and Zambia, Initiative on Public-Private Partnerships for Health. Global Forum for Health Research, Geneva

Canavan A et al (2008) Post-conflict health sectors: the myth and reality of transitional funding gaps. KIT Development Policy & Practice, Amsterdam

Conway S et al (2008) International health partnership: external review. London School of Hygiene and Tropical Medicine, London

Cutler CA (1999) Locating 'Authority' in the global political economy. Int Stud Q 43(1):59–81

David F (2004) Legal Review of the General Agreement on Trade in Services (GATS) from a Health Policy Perspective. WHO: Globalization, Trade and Health Working Papers Series, Geneva

Green E (2008) Public-private partnerships maximize development assistance. http://www.america.gov/st/foraid-english/2008/August/20080818171615xeneerg0.7114527.html#ixzz0DzE1p1Lp&

Handbook on the Least Developed Country Category (2008) http://www.un.org/esa/policy/devplan/cdppublications/2008cdphandbook.pdf

Haochen S (2004) The road to Doha and beyond: some reflection on the TRIPS agreement and public health. EJIL 15(1):123

Harford T et al (2005) Private Finance Are Private Loans and Charitable giving Replacing Aid?' Public Policy for the Private Sector. The World Bank Group, April Note No 290, 1–2

Krajewski M (2003) Public services and trade liberalization: mapping the legal framework. JIEL 6(2):341–367

Landell Mills (2007) Development Consultants: Sierra Leone EPA Impact Study Project 112-Sierra Leone. Final Report vol 2

Lang A (2004) The GATS and regulatory autonomy: the case study of social regulation of the water industry. JIEL 7(4):813

Lang A (2007) Rethinking trade and human rights. Tulane J Int Comp 15(2):336

Marek T et al (2003) Private Health: Policy and Regulatory Options for Private Participation. The World Bank Group, June Note No 2

Matthews D (2005) TRIPS flexibilities and access to medicines in developing countries: the problem with technical assistance and free trade agreements. EIPR 2(11):420

McCreevy C (2005) (European Commissioner for Internal Market and Services) Public-Private Partnerships—Options to Ensure Effective Competition, PPP Global Summit—The 6th Annual Government-Industry Forum on Public Private-Partnership Copenhagen, 17 November

SPEECH/05/698. http://europa.eu/rapid/pressReleasesAction.do?reference=SPEECH/05/698&format=HTML&aged=0&language=EN&guiLanguage=en

Messerlin PA (2005) Trade, drugs, and health-care services. Lancet 365:1198–1200. www.unmillenniumproject.org/documents/TheLancetTrade.pdf

Micklewright J, Wright A (2005) Private donations for international development. In: Atkinson A (ed) New Sources of Development Financing. Oxford University Press, Oxford, p 148

Njau RJA et al (2009) Case studies in public-private-partnership in health with the focus of enhancing the accessibility of health interventions. Tanzan J Health Res 11(4):235–249

Nkhoma W (2008) Regional focal point, WHO/AFRO public-private partnerships form TB control in the African region: progress and future plans. In: Fifth meeting of the Subgroup on Public Private Mix for TB Care and Control, Cairo, Egypt, 3–5 June

Paas K (2009) Compulsory licensing under the trips agreement—a cruel taunt for developing countries? EIPR 31(12):609

Pascal L (2008) (WTO Director General) Access to Medicines has been Improved, The 11th Annual International Generic Pharmaceutical Alliance Conference, Geneva 9 December. WTO News: Speeches. http://www.wto.org/english/news_e/sppl_e/sppl111_e.htm

Siegel B et al (1996) Health Reform in Africa: Lessons from Sierra Leone, World Bank, Discussion Paper Health sector reform series. No 347, Washington DC

Siegel B et al (1997) Health Reform in Africa: Lessons from Sierra Leone', World Bank Discussion Paper (1997)

Smith R et al (2008) Trade in health services and the GATS. In: Mattoo A et al (eds) A Handbook of International Trade in Services. Oxford University Press, Oxford, pp 437–446

Taylor R, Blair S (2002) Public Hospitals: Options for Reform through Public-Private Partnerships, Public Policy for the Private Sector; The World Bank Group, January Note No 241

Trubek DM (2009) The political economy of the rule of law: the challenges of the new developmental state. Hague J Rule Law 1:31

Tubman A (2004) Public-private Management of Intellectual Property for Public Health Outcomes in the Developing World: The Lessons of Access Conditions in Research and Development Agreements, PPPs for Research and Development; Publisher: Initiative on Public-Private Partnerships for Health. http://www.eldis.org/go/topics/resource-guides/health-systems/global-initiatives-and-public-private-partnerships/ppps-for-research-and-development&id=16748&type=Document

Tuosto C (2004) The TRIPS council decision of August 30, 2003 on the import of pharmaceuticals under compulsory licences. EIPR 26(12):542–547

UNICEF (2008) The state of the world's children report (UNICEF Report 2008). http://www.unicef.org/sowc08/docs/sowc08.pdf

Watson AG (2009) International intellectual property rights: do trips' flexibilities permit sufficient access to affordable HIV/AIDS medicines in developing countries? BC Int Comp L Rev 32(1):143

Woodward D (2005) The GATS and trade in health services: implications for health care in developing countries. Rev Int Polit Econ 12(3):511

Yukich J et al (2007) Operations, costs and cost-effectiveness of five insecticide-treated net programs (Eritrea, Malawi, Tanzania, Togo, Senegal) and two indoor residual spraying programs (Kwa-Zulu-Natal, Mozambique). Final Draft 12 July, Swiss Tropical Institute, Basel, Switzerland

Chapter 10
Universal Service Provisions in International Agreements of the EU: From Derogation to Obligation?

Markus Krajewski

Abstract The EU is aware that international trade agreements such as the WTO and the GATS may affect the internal EU response to trade in public services and the Commission has publicly stated that international trade agreements should not impede the EU capability to pursue its policies on public services. *Markus Krajewski* adopts a different approach and asks the question: to what extent can the international agreements signed by the EC/EU reflect, or even advance, a *positive* understanding of public services? This is an important perspective now that the Treaty of Lisbon 2009 places external relations policy in a larger value, and principle, driven framework. *Krajewski* also examines the role of the WTO and in particular the GATS. The telecom sector is the focus of attention because telecom provides an important model for liberalisation and the development of universal service obligations which are mirrored in other sectors opened up to competition. Two case studies follow, first the EC–Chile bilateral association agreement and second, the EU–CARIFORUM Economic Partnership Agreement which is of particular interest in that it contains positive universal service obligations. *Krajewski* also examines a number of agreements which are currently under discussion to determine if there is an emerging trend to include and define PSO and USO in the external agreements of the EU. Underlying this approach is a quest to determine whether in its external role the EU is continuing internal trends of seeing public services not only as exemptions and derogations from EU law, but also as a positive requirement.

M. Krajewski (✉)
Fachbereich Rechtswissenschaft, Universität Erlangen-Nürnberg, Schillerstraße 1, 91054 Erlangen, Germany
e-mail: Markus.Krajewski@jura.uni-erlangen.de

E. Szyszczak et al. (eds.), *Developments in Services of General Interest*, Legal Issues of Services of General Interest, DOI: 10.1007/978-90-6704-734-0_10,

Contents

As we pursue social justice and cohesion at home, we should also seek to promote our values, including social and environmental standards and cultural diversity, around the world (European Commission 2006, p. 5).

10.1 Introduction

The debate about services of general interest in European law has focussed so far on internal law, that is, fundamental freedoms, internal market, competition, state aid and procurement law. The impact and the role of external EU law, as laid down in the international agreements to which the EU is a party, has not been at the centre of attention. If external aspects have been addressed, the discussions mostly concerned the potential limitation and restrictions of the provisions of the General Agreement on Trade in Services (GATS) on the provision and organisation of public services.[1] This issue also informed the debate about services of general interest in the EU as reflected in the *White Paper of the European Commission on Services of General*

[1] Adlung 2006, p. 455; Krajewski 2008a, pp. 173–213.

Interest. Under the heading 'Reflecting our internal policies in our international trade policy' the Commission argued that 'international trade agreements should not go beyond the positions agreed within the European Union'.[2]

The present contribution takes a different approach. Instead of asking whether and how much international law impedes on the EU's capability to pursue its ideas of public services, this contribution discusses to which extent the international agreements signed by the EC/EU reflect or even advance a positive understanding of public services. The background of this approach can be found in the current trade policy of the EU and at a more general level in the provisions on the external relations in the Treaty of Lisbon 2009 which seek to place the external relations of the EU in a larger value and principle-driven framework. As indicated by the quote at the beginning of this contribution, which is taken from the agenda-setting trade policy document 'Gobal Europe' of 2006, the EU seeks to promote similar, if not the same, values in its external relations which it seeks internally. This internal value-driven approach is also reflected in the common normative framework for the Union's external relations established by the Treaty of Lisbon. All EU external policies, including the common commercial policy are subject to the overall goals and objectives of the Union's external relations as laid down in Article 21 TEU.[3] According to Paragraph 2 of that provision the Union shall define and pursue its external policies and actions, inter alia, to 'safeguard its values, fundamental interests, security, independence and integrity'.

As stated in Article 14 TFEU and the Protocol on Services of General Interest, the functioning of services of general interest ranks highly among the values of the Union and its Member States.[4] The present contribution attempts to link the value-driven EU's external policies with the values underlying the organisation and supply of services of general interest by asking whether the EU's external policies aim at protecting and promoting the values of services of general interest. The analysis will be focused on public/universal service obligations as a prominent manifestation of these values. Hence, the contribution will analyse whether and to which extent the EU incorporated such obligations in its international agreements.

The analysis of the paper will proceed in four broad steps: Section 10.2 will briefly outline the notion and function of public/universal service obligations and explain why they can be seen as an exemplification of the values underlying services of general interest. Section 10.3 addresses the WTO's General Agreement on Trade in Services (GATS), in particular its regime on telecommunications. Specifically, the section analyses two important provisions addressing public/universal service obligations in the GATS telecommunications regime, because they served as a template for subsequent agreements. The section will also mention

---

[2] European Commission, *White Paper on Services of General Interest,* COM (2004) 374 final, 20.

[3] Dimopoulos 2010, p. 164 et seq.

[4] Treaty of Lisbon amending the Treaty on European Union and the Treaty establishing the European Community, signed at Lisbon, 13 December 2007, *OJ* 2007 C 306/1. For a consolidated version see *OJ* 2010 C 83/1. The protocol on Services of General Interest can be found in 308.

the 2005 proposal on postal services of the EC which contains a reference to universal service obligations built on the telecommunications model. Section 10.4 analyses reference to universal service obligations in the 2002 bilateral association agreement between the EC and the Chile, the first major bilateral trade agreement of the EU. Section 10.5 discusses the EU–CARIFORUM Economic Partnership Agreement which is of special interest since it is the first agreement which contains positive universal service obligations. Section 10.6 will look at drafts of agreements and proposals for provisions of agreements currently under negotiation to determine whether there is an emerging trend regarding public services obligations in these agreements. The concluding section of the chapter will ask whether the different agreements reflect a development which moves from including justification and derogation clauses for public service obligations to positive requirements of such obligations. Such a move from derogation to obligation could be seen as a parallel movement to the development of the internal EU law on services of general interest.[5]

10.2 Notion and Function of Public Service Obligations

A commonly accepted and widely used definition of public service obligations refers to specific requirements that are imposed by public authorities on the provider of the service in order to ensure that certain public interest objectives are met.[6] This definition is also used in the literature.[7] Public service obligations can take different forms, they may have different scopes and they may apply at different government levels (that is, local, regional, national and supranational). Public service obligations normally aim at securing a certain quality of the service, general (if not universal) access and affordable prices. Often they are based on notions of solidarity or territorial cohesion. Public service obligations can be seen as a central element of the values of the EU and its Member States concerning services of general interest.[8] This proposition is also supported by the Protocol on services of general interest of the Lisbon Treaty. Article 1 of that Protocol contains a clear reference to public service obligations. It mentions ‘a high level of quality, safety and affordability, equal treatment and the promotion of universal access and of user rights’ as a crucial element of the values of the EU and its Members according to Article 14 TFEU.

---

[5] Ross 2000, pp. 22–37.

[6] *White Paper on Services of General Interest*, COM (2004) 374 final, 23.

[7] Neergaard 2009, p. 17; Houben 2008, p. 7(10). See also Chap. 7 of this book.

[8] Neergaard 2009, p. 17.

The terms public service obligations and universal service obligations are sometimes used interchangeably.[9] However, it seems more convincing to view universal service obligations as a subgroup of public service obligations, which specifically apply in electronic communications (telecommunications) and postal services. In this respect, Article 3(1) of Universal Service Directive of 2002 defines universal service as a certain set of services at a defined quality 'which is available to all users regardless of their geographical location and, in the light of specific national conditions, at an affordable price'.[10] Similarly, Article 3(1) of the Postal Internal Market Directive holds: 'Member States shall ensure that users enjoy the right to a universal service involving the permanent provision of a postal service of specified quality at all points in their territory at affordable prices for all users'.[11]

In the context of energy services, EU legislation uses the term 'public service obligation' in a broader sense. Article 3(2) of the 2009 Directive on the internal market in electricity holds that.

> Member States may impose on undertakings operating in the electricity sector, in the general economic interest, public service obligations which may relate to security, including security of supply, regularity, quality and price of supplies, and environmental protection, including energy efficiency, energy from renewable sources and climate protection.[12]

An identical provision can be found in the 2009 internal market in natural gas directive.[13] Furthermore, EU Regulation 1370/2007 defines public service obligation with regard to public passenger transportation as 'a requirement defined or determined by a competent authority in order to ensure public passenger transport services in the general interest that an operator, if it were considering its own commercial interests, would not assume or would not assume to the same extent or under the same conditions without reward'.[14]

This short overview of the use of the term public service obligation or universal service obligation in EU secondary legislation shows that public service obligations typically aim at non-market objectives, that is, they seek to ensure an outcome which could not be provided by the market alone. As a consequence, they restrict the full application of free market principles and competition law in order to ensure societal values which would otherwise not be protected. Based on this conceptualisation of the notion of public service obligations it is now possible to analyse if and how the term has been used in international agreements concluded by the EU.

---

[9] Houben 2008, p. 7(10). See also the other chapters of this book.

[10] Directive 2002/22/EC of 7 March 2002 (Universal Service Directive) [2002] *OJ* L 108, 51.

[11] Directive 97/67/EC of 15 December 1997 (Internal market of Community postal services) [1998] *OJ* L 15, 14.

[12] Directive 2009/72/EC of 13 July 2009 (Internal market in electricity) [2009] *OJ* L 211, 55.

[13] Ibid., 94.

[14] Regulation (EC) No. 1370/2007 of 23 October 2007 (Public passenger transport services) [2007] *OJ* L 315, 1.

10.3 Public Service as Derogation: The General Agreement on Trade in Services (GATS)

The WTO's General Agreement on Trade in Services (GATS) is the only multilateral framework for the liberalisation and regulation of trade in services. It went into force together with all other WTO agreements on 1 January 1995. The core of the GATS framework consists of rules which apply to all services sectors; it does not contain any sector-specific obligations. None of these general provisions, neither the obligations nor the exceptions, refer to public service obligations. However, the GATS also contains a special regime for telecommunication services which contains two references to public service obligations.[15]

10.3.1 Safeguarding Public Service Requirements on the Basis of the Annex on Telecommunications

The Annex on Telecommunications is an integral part of the GATS and aims to ensure that specific market access and national treatment commitments of WTO Members are not frustrated through the lack of access to and use of telecommunication services.[16] The main obligations of the Annex can be found in Paragraph 5. It requires WTO Members to ensure that 'access to and use of public telecommunications transport networks and services on reasonable and non-discriminatory terms and conditions'.

However, Members may impose conditions on the access and use of public telecommunication transport networks and services which are necessary for the maintenance of public service obligations. In this regard, Article 5(e) of the Annex states:

> Each Member shall ensure that no condition is imposed on access to and use of public telecommunications transport networks and services other than as necessary: (i) to safeguard the public service responsibilities of suppliers of public telecommunications transport networks and services, in particular their ability to make their networks or services available to the public generally; to safeguard the public service responsibilities of suppliers of public telecommunications transport networks and services, in particular their ability to make their networks or services available to the public generally (...).

Based on Article 5(e)(i) of the Annex, public service responsibilities can be used as a justification for deviations from the requirements of the Annex. In the telecommunications sector such responsibilities typically consist of universal service obligations which is why Article 5(e) of the Annex is understood to be a

[15] For a detailed analysis of the GATS telecommunications regime see Bronckers and Larouche 2008, pp. 319–379.

[16] Roseman 2003.

justification for restrictions imposed on service providers to ensure universal service.[17] For example, if a Member imposes discriminatory access rates or rates which are not deemed reasonable, because they are very high, it may be possible to justify such charges on the basis that they are necessary to safeguard universal service obligations.

To benefit from Article 5(e)(i) of the Annex, public service obligation conditions must adhere to that necessary to meet the Members policy goals. The notion of 'necessary' has been interpreted in a number of key decisions of the WTO dispute settlement organs and has been subject to controversial debates in the literature. Generally, a measure is considered necessary under WTO law if there is 'no alternative measure less restrictive of trade which may be reasonably available to a member to achieve the same policy goals'.[18] It is also generally agreed that the term 'necessary' can have different meanings in different contexts. In the 2004 *Mexico—Telecommunication Services* (*Telmex*) case the Panel held:

> The term "necessary" in Sect. 5(e) describes the relationship between a "condition" of access to and use of a public telecommunications transport networks and services, and one of the three listed policy goals. What may be "necessary" with respect to one policy goal may not be with respect to another.[19]

However, the Panel did not clearly decide on which standard to use in the context of Article 5(e) of the Annex. While the Panel rejected a narrow approach which would only regard measures which are indispensable to reach the policy objectives of Article 5(e)(i) of the Annex, it left open the question of which other standard should be applied. The Panel seemed to favour an approach which would assume measures as necessary as long as they make a contribution to the objectives of Article 5(e)(i) of the Annex.[20]

In the meantime, the *Mexico—Telecommunications* Report was issued in 2004 and the case law of the WTO Appellate Body has evolved further. In particular, in *Korea—Beef*, the Appellate Body held that 'necessary' involves 'in every case a process of weighing and balancing a series of factors which prominently include… the importance of the common interests or values protected by that law or regulation, and the accompanying impact of the law or regulation on imports or exports'.[21] Taken literally this could mean that a WTO panel or the Appellate Body would put itself in a position to assess the importance of the public service obligation of a particular WTO Member. This would raise difficult questions of competence and legitimacy of the WTO dispute settlement system regarding such

---

[17] Batura forthcoming, p. 258.

[18] *Thailand—Restrictions on Importation of and Internal Taxes on Cigarettes*, Report of the Panel, adopted on 7 November 1990, BISD 37S/200, para 74.

[19] *Mexico—Measures Affecting Telecommunication Services*, Report of the Panel, WT/DS204/R, 2 April 2004, para 7.338.

[20] *Mexico—Measures Affecting Telecommunication Services*, para. 7.342.

[21] *Korea—Measures Affecting Imports of Fresh, Chilled and Frozen Beef, WT/DS161/AB/R, WT/DS169/AB/R, Report of the Appellate Body*, paras 164–166.

issues which are a key aspect of country's regulatory autonomy.[22] It should be noted, however, that despite its emphasis on weighing and balancing, the Appellate Body has never actually engaged in such an exercise.[23] Instead, it has usually accepted the policy choices and level of protection of the respective Member.

In this context, it is worth noting that Article 5(e)(i) of the Annex can be seen as functionally equivalent to Article 106(2) TFEU [ex Article 86(2) EC] which can also serve as an exception from competition law principles for public service obligations.[24] It is beyond the scope of the present contribution to conduct of full comparative study of the ECJ's jurisprudence on Article 106(2) TFEU [ex Article 86(2) EC] with regard to public service obligations and the WTO's dispute settlement practice regarding the elements of Article 5(e)(i),[25] but it is suggested that any future panel or the Appellate Body could reflect the ECJ's case law and the idea of judicial self-restraint when they evaluate fundamental policy choices of the WTO Members with regard to public service obligations.

10.3.2 Universal Service Obligations in the Reference Paper on Telecommunications

The second element of the GATS telecommunications regime which addresses public service obligations can be found in the so-called Reference Paper on Telecommunications.[26] The Reference Paper contains additional pro-competitive regulatory requirements of WTO Members in telecommunication services. It was agreed by the Negotiating Group on Basic Telecommunications and published in April 1996. The additional requirements of the Reference Paper do not apply to all WTO Members but do become binding if a WTO member explicitly includes the Reference Paper or parts thereof in its schedule of commitments: 69 of the 154 Members of the WTO have done so. The purpose of the Reference Paper is to ensure that a so-called major supplier dominating the market does not use its market power to the detriment of new market entrants and where, often, the major supplier in a national market is the former public monopoly operator. Paragraph 1 of the Reference Paper obliges WTO Members to prevent major suppliers from engaging in or continuing anti-competitive practices. In particular, the Reference Paper prohibits anti-competitive cross-subsidisation, the use of information

---

[22] Krajewski 2008, pp. 397–404.

[23] Regan 2007, pp. 347–369.

[24] See Chap. 4 by Bekkedal.

[25] So far, the *Mexico—Telecommunications* case is the only decision which discusses Art. 5(e)(i). However, being an exception clause, the WTO's decisions on other exception clauses, in particular Art. XX GATT and Art. XIV GATS, could serve as guidance.

[26] Reference Paper on regulatory principles of 24 April 1996, available at: http://www.wto.org/english/tratop_e/serv_e/telecom_e/tel23_e.htm (last accessed 31 May 2010).

obtained from competitors with anti-competitive results and withholding technical and commercial information from other service suppliers. The Reference Paper can, therefore, be seen as a nucleus or very basic framework of a specific telecommunication competition regime. It is, therefore, fitting that the Reference Paper also addresses universal service obligations.

Paragraph 3 of the Reference Paper States:

> Any Member has the right to define the kind of universal service obligation it wishes to maintain. Such obligations will not be regarded as anti-competitive per se, provided they are administered in a transparent, non-discriminatory and competitively neutral manner and are not more burdensome than necessary for the kind of universal service defined by the Member.

This provision has three aspects. First, it accepts the right of each WTO Member to define a particular universal service obligation. As a consequence, the relative importance of the elements and objectives of a universal service obligation which could be questioned under Article 5(e)(i) of the Annex on Telecommunications[27] are not subject to review by WTO dispute settlement institutions. Second, the Reference Paper clarifies that universal service obligations will not 'be regarded as anti-competitive per se', suggesting that universal service obligations can never be challenged as such on the basis of WTO law. A challenge will always have to be based on the argument that a particular universal service obligation does not meet the requirements of Paragraph 3. Thirdly, universal service obligations have to be administered in a transparent, non-discriminatory and competitively neutral manner and should not be more burdensome than necessary for the kind of universal service defined by the Member. Hence, the administration of a universal service obligation must be transparent, non-discriminatory, competitively neutral and no more burdensome than necessary if it should conform to the Reference Paper.

This raises a number of questions.[28] The first concerns cross-subsidisation. The Reference Paper prohibits cross-subsidisation which is not competitively neutral [Paragraph 1(2)(a) Reference Paper]. Universal services obligations using cross-subsidization are, therefore, only compatible with the Reference Paper if they are applied in a manner which does not negatively affect competitive relationships. Whether this is the case seems to depend on the direction of cross-subsidisation: if the operator under a universal service obligation uses profits gained in a competitive sector to fund losses in the sector with the universal service obligation, this could be competitively neutral, because presumably there would be no competition in the loss-making sector of the market. For example, combining the licences to provide mobile telephone services (presumably profit-making) with the requirement to invest in land-line telecommunications infrastructure in remote rural areas (presumably loss-making and part of a public monopoly) seems competitive-neutral, because funds flow from the competitive sector to the loss-making

---

[27] See Sect. 10.3.1 supra.

[28] For a more detailed discussion of the following see Krajewski (ed) 2003.

monopoly segment of the market. In fact, this is the logic behind creating public monopolies for public services.

On the other hand, using monopoly rents to subsidise activities in a competitive sector may adversely affect competition. For example, if an incumbent telecommunications operator retaining a monopoly in land-line telephony and required to extend this service on a universal service obligation would use profits from the monopoly to cut costs in mobile telephony to offer lower prices than a competitor, this could be seen as anti-competitive. Because of the dynamics of telecommunications sector, it is possible that an unprofitable market segment may become a profitable and vice versa. Consequently, a universal service obligation, which was designed in a competitively neutral way, could become anti-competitive.

A second aspect of the requirements of the Reference Paper concerns the selection of the provider of the universal service and the imposition of this obligation. For example, imposing a universal service obligation on just one operator could be anti-competitive, because it adversely affects the competitive situation of the universal service operator. On one hand, the obligation could also be seen as more burdensome than necessary, because alternative measures could be used.[29] On the other hand, the universal service obligation may provide benefits, because it applies to a large segment of the market which gives the supplier of the universal service a dominant position. Furthermore, in situations of a natural monopoly, e.g., satellite telecommunications service for an archipelago country, the selection of one provider might be competitively neutral. Another problem in this context concerns the selection process which must be transparent and non-discriminatory. This may require the government to submit the universal service obligation to an open tender.

Another area of potential conflict between universal service obligations and the Reference Paper concerns interconnection charges. Such charges can be used to generate additional revenue to fund infrastructure investments, especially if the tax base of the government is not sufficient for this objective. While such extra charges may already be questionable on the basis of the Annex on Telecommunications, the Reference Paper seems also to reject them on the basis that it requires interconnection charges to be 'cost-oriented'. It has been suggested that the inclusion of a charge for funding universal service obligation would make it impossible to achieve cost-oriented interconnection charges.[30]

It is not entirely clear, whether Sect. 3 of the Reference Paper would exempt interconnection charges aimed to fund universal service obligations from the obligation to be cost-oriented, because it could be argued that an interconnection charge above a cost-oriented level is more burdensome than necessary. In the *Mexico—Telecommunications* case the Panel decided that the requirement of cost-oriented interconnection in Sect.2.2(b) of the Reference Paper excluded the possibility to incorporate costs other than those directly related to the

[29] Peha 1999, pp. 369–373.

[30] OECD 2001, p. 21.

interconnection.[31] Mexico did not rely on Sect. 3 of the Reference Paper because it did not include universal service costs in its rates. Hence, the Panel did not decide on the possibility of justifying a deviation from the cost-orientation standard based on Sect. 3 of the Reference Paper. However, it should be noted that WTO case law suggests that a measure can be seen as less burdensome (or trade restrictive) than necessary even if it implies higher costs for the government.[32] If this approach were to be applied to the Reference Paper, interconnection charges aimed at financing universal service obligations could be seen as more burdensome than necessary, because alternative government funding is less burdensome. This argument is not restricted to interconnection charges. Indeed, any cost-sharing system could be seen as more burdensome than necessary if compared with direct government funding.

Following this line of argument, even the system of sharing the costs of universal service obligations authorised in the 2002 EC Universal Service Directive may be questionable. Article 13(b) and (c) of Directive 2002/22/EC allows cost-sharing arrangements between the providers of communication networks and services to finance universal service obligations. These arrangements can involve special charges imposed on service providers, but they must be transparent, non-discriminatory, proportionate and least-market distortable. The crucial question is whether cost-sharing arrangements are less burdensome than necessary. Even if these arrangements would comply with the Reference Paper, applying a cost-sharing arrangement in a transparent, non-discriminatory and proportionate way remains a difficult task in practical terms. The EC's Universal Services Directive sets firm guidelines on how to calculate and how to share the costs. These guidelines show that the administration of transparent, non-discriminatory and proportionate cost-sharing arrangements requires precise and complete data on costs of services, which could be difficult to collect.[33]

10.3.3 The EU's Proposal for a Reference Paper on Postal and Courier Services

Despite the many open questions concerning the exact content of Paragraph 3 of the Reference Paper on telecommunications, the EU seems to consider it as a

---

[31] *Mexico—Measures Affecting Telecommunication Services*, para 7.170–7.174.

[32] *Korea—Measures Affecting Imports of Fresh, Chilled and Frozen Beef*, WT/DS161 and WT/DS169, Report of the Appellate Body adopted on 10 January 2001, para 181; *Dominican Republic—Measures Affecting the Importation and Internal Sale of Cigarettes,* Report of the Appellate Body adopted on 19 May 2005, WT/DS302/AB/R, para 72.

[33] In 2001, the ECJ declared France in breach of its obligations under the Universal Services Directive. France's defence was partly based on difficulties associated with collecting and assessing the required data, but the Court held that these difficulties could not justify the breach of those obligations, ECJ, Case C-146/00 *Commission* v. *France* [2001] *ECR* I-0767.

template for further regulatory regimes in the GATS context. In the course of the ongoing WTO services negotiations, the EU (then the EC) proposed a Reference Paper on postal and courier services in 2005.[34] According to the EU such a Reference Paper could be used by WTO Members willing to take specific commitments in the postal and courier services sector. Like the Telecommunications Reference Paper, the proposed Reference Paper on postal and courier services would be aimed at preventing suppliers who have 'the ability to affect materially the terms of participation (with regard to price and supply) in the relevant market for postal and courier services as a result of use of their position in the market, from engaging in or continuing anti-competitive practices' (Paragraph 1 of the Proposal).

The proposal also contains a paragraph on universal service obligations which mirrors precisely Paragraph 3 of the Reference Paper on telecommunications. In explaining this proposal the EC claimed that universal service is a key component of the postal sector for most Members. Hence, the principle of universal service should be expressly mentioned in additional commitment rules. The EU state that its proposal would confirm 'the possibility to impose universal services obligations provided that they respect certain basic rules, such as transparency, non-discrimination and a neutral administration'.

The EU's proposal on universal service obligations in postal and courier services is clearly inspired by the EU's own policy regarding the internal market for postal services. The proposal is to be welcomed because it strengthens the position of universal service obligations vis-à-vis the liberalisation requirements of the multilateral trading system. However, it is regrettable that the EU forgave an opportunity to make proposals for clarifying the scope and the contents of a universal service obligation in the GATS regime. It is hoped that in subsequent services negotiations the EU improves its proposal by addressing some of the problems discussed in the context of Paragraph 3 of the Reference Paper on telecommunications.

10.3.4 Conclusion

The references to public or universal service obligations in the GATS telecommunications system and in the proposed Reference Paper on postal and courier services analysed above reveal a common structure and objective. They are drafted as exception clauses aiming at protecting the rights of WTO Members to maintain such obligations within certain limits and under certain

[34] Council for Trade in Services Special Session, Communication from the European Communities and their Member States, Postal/Courier: Proposal for a Reference Paper, TN/S/W/26, 17 January 2005.

conditions. In particular, public or universal service obligations must not be applied on a discriminatory basis and they must not be more burdensome or trade-restrictive than necessary. These provisions, therefore, are structurally comparable to the general exception clauses such as Article XX GATT and Article XIV GATS. Furthermore, they also seem to serve a similar function as Article 106(2) TFEU [ex Article 86(2) ECT] which also provided for a derogation from the obligations of the EC Treaty for the application of public service obligations. The references of the GATS to public service obligations do not contain any positive obligations to maintain or introduce public or universal services. A WTO Member is, therefore, free to fully liberalise a particular service sector without maintain any public service obligations.

It is also important to note that the GATS references to public, or universal service, obligations are not part of the main agreement. Instead they are codified in an Annex (which is, however, an integral part of the agreement) and in voluntary commitments of WTO Members such as the Reference Paper on telecommunications. This suggests that even the value of a derogation clause for public or universal service obligations is not generally shared by all WTO Members. As will be shown in the next sections, the bilateral and regional trade agreements signed by the EC/EU after the foundation of the WTO in 1995 give provisions on universal service obligations a more prominent place.

10.4 Consolidating the GATS Approach: The EC–Chile Bilateral Association Agreement

In 2002, the EC and its Member States and Chile concluded a comprehensive association agreement[35] comprises a large range of trade and trade-related issues which go beyond WTO standards ('WTO plus' agreement). Title III of the EC–Chile Agreement on trade in services and establishment follows a different structure than the GATS but serves similar functions. Apart from general rules on services and establishment the EC–Chile Agreement also contains a section on telecommunication services which incorporates the principles and objectives of the Reference Paper on telecommunications into the main part of the agreement. Hence, there is also a specific provision on universal service obligations, Article 115, which holds:

[35] Agreement establishing an association between the European Community and its Member States, of one part, and the Republic of Chile, of the other part of 18 November 2002, *OJ* 2002, L 352/3.

> 1. Each Party has the right to define the kind of universal service obligation it wishes to maintain. 2. The provisions governing universal service shall be transparent, objective and non-discriminatory. They shall also be neutral with respect to competition and be no more burdensome than necessary.

This provision has the same contents and pursues the same function as Paragraph 3 of the Reference paper. The different wording of the two provisions does not indicate a difference in meaning. In fact, the wording of Article 115 of the EC–Chile Association Agreement seems clearer than Paragraph 3 of the Reference Paper. Paragraph 1 of Article 115 which has the same wording as the first sentence of Paragraph 3 of the Reference Paper unmistakably states that the parties have the 'right' to define the kind of universal service it wishes to maintain. This right is not restricted or linked to the condition that the universal service obligation meets a particular standards. Paragraph 2 then contains requirements for the provisions governing universal service and their application, which is a slight deviation from the wording of the Reference Paper. The actual requirements are the same as the ones of the Reference Paper with the exception of the requirement of objectivity which cannot be found in the Reference Paper. However, this omission does not lead to any substantial difference, because the notion of 'objective' does not seem to a have a meaning which deviates from the combined effect of the notions of transparent, non-discriminatory, competition-neutral and no more burdensome than necessary.

There is no comparable provision on public service obligations in postal and courier services. Instead, the EC only included the following sentence in its commitments on postal and courier services: 'the right to a postal universal service is ensured'. The legal value of this commitment is not entirely clear because it does not contain restrictions or limitations such as the provisions on universal service obligations discussed so far. Instead it seems like a general carve-out for any measure which can be somehow related to a universal service obligation. Yet, a contextual interpretation of this additional commitment would conclude that the criteria to be found in the Reference Paper also, in general, apply to the specific commitment of the EC regarding postal universal services. In other words, it is not conceivable that the EC's commitment would be interpreted so as to also cover discriminatory, non-transparent or competition-distorting requirements.

In sum, it can be said that the EC–Chile Agreement does not go beyond the scope of the GATS with regard to universal service obligations in telecommunication services. It also provides a derogation clause for these obligations with similar restrictions and limitations on the use of such obligations. However, the EC–Chile Agreement incorporates the respective standards into the core of the agreement and makes them mandatory. This distinguishes it from the GATS approach which is built on voluntary acceptance. The EC–Chile Agreement, therefore, consolidates the GATS approach and extends it to bilateral trade arrangements of the EC.

10.5 Beyond Derogation: Universal Service Obligations in the Cariforum Economic Partnership Agreement

The Economic Partnership Agreement (EPA) between the EC and the CARIFORUM States[36] contains the most explicit and elaborate reference to public service obligations. The EC negotiated with all countries of the ACP (African, Caribbean and Pacific) group of countries such economic partnership agreements based on the Cotonou Agreement between the EC and the ACP countries.[37] These agreements became necessary because the EC had to bring its special regime with those countries in accordance with WTO requirements. So far, however, the only comprehensive and final agreement is the one concluded with the CARIFORUM states.[38] It has been applied provisionally since December 2008.

The CARIFORUM–EPA contains specific regulatory provisions on postal and courier services and telecommunications. Both sections contain articles on universal service obligations, Article 91 EPA for postal services and Article 100 EPA for telecommunications. These provisions partly reflect the standards of the GATS and partly go beyond them.

10.5.1 Incorporating the GATS Approach

Like the EC–Chile Association Agreement the CARIFORUM–EPA incorporates elements on universal service obligations which also exist in the GATS. In particular, the first two paragraphs of Article 100 EPA resemble the existing provisions on universal services in the WTO's Reference Paper.[39] Article 100(1) EPA recalls that the EC and the CARIFORUM states have the right to define the kind of universal service obligations they wish to maintain. Article 100(2) EPA states that universal service obligations 'will not be regarded as anti-competitive per se, provided they are administered in a transparent, objective and non-discriminatory way'. Furthermore, the administration of such obligations shall 'be neutral with respect to competition and not more burdensome than necessary for the kind of universal service defined by the EC Party and by the Signatory CARIFORUM

[36] The CARIFORUM States comprise Antigua and Barbuda, the Bahamas, Barbados, Belize, Dominica, Grenada, Guyana, Haiti, Jamaica, Saint Lucia, Saint Vincent and the Grenadines, Saint Kitts and Nevis, Suriname, Trinidad and Tobago and the Dominican Republic.

[37] Partnership agreement between the members of the African, Caribbean and Pacific Group of States of the one part, and the European Community and its Member States, of the other, signed in Cotonou on 23 June 2000, *OJ* L 317/3. On the general policy changes see Desta 2006, p. 1346 et seq.

[38] Economic Partnership Agreement between the CARIFORUM States, of the one part, and the European Community and its Member States, of the other, [2008] *OJ* L 289, 3.

[39] Sauvé and Ward 2009, p. 39.

States'. Article 91 EPA contains a provision on universal service obligations in postal services which uses the same language as the Reference Paper on telecommunications of the WTO.[40] It is, therefore, also identical with the paragraph on universal services in the proposal for a reference paper on postal services submitted by the EU in the context of the GATS negotiations.[41]

Article 100(1) and (2) EPA does not add anything substantially new to the approach established in the WTO context. However, like the EC–Chile agreement these paragraphs incorporate the standard of the Reference Paper into the main text of the agreement, and therefore, make them binding on all parties. As not all CARIFORUM states have adopted the Reference Paper in the WTO context, this approach of the EPA is a 'WTO plus' obligation from their perspective.[42] This is even more so for Article 91 EPA on a postal universal service. Since the GATS does not contain a universal service provision in postal services, this article of the EPA is in fact 'WTO plus' for all EPA parties.

10.5.2 Establishing a Basic Regulatory Framework for Universal Service Obligations

The EPA does not only incorporate the standards of the GATS telecommunications reference paper with regard to universal service obligations, but also contains provisions which are more elaborate than the Reference Paper.[43] A first important innovation of the EPA is that it defines the notion of universal services both regarding postal services and telecommunications. According to Article 89(2)(b) EPA universal service in the context of postal and courier services 'means the permanent provision of a postal service of specified quality at all points in the territory of the EC Party and of the Signatory CARIFORUM States at affordable prices for all users'. Article 94(1)(f) EPA defines universal service in telecommunications as:

> the set of services of specified quality that must be made available to all users in the territory of the EC Party and of the Signatory CARIFORUM States regardless of their geographical location and at an affordable price; its scope and implementation are decided by the EC Party and by the Signatory CARIFORUM States.

Both definitions strongly resonate the definition of public or universal service obligation under EU internal law.[44] They refer to the key elements of affordability, availability, quality and security or continuity of service ('permanent provision'), and therefore, clearly incorporate a model of universal service into the EPA which is similar to, if not identical with, the European model of universal service.

---

[40] Schloemann and Pitschas 2009, p. 101(114).

[41] See Sect. 10.3.3 supra.

[42] Schloemann and Pitschas 2009, p. 101(117).

[43] Sauvé and Ward 2009, p. 40.

[44] See Sect. 10.2 supra.

Article 100(3) EPA already adds an element to the universal service provision which goes beyond the standard of the WTO's approach. This paragraph reads:

> All suppliers should be eligible to ensure universal service. The designation shall be made through an efficient, transparent and non-discriminatory mechanism. Where necessary, the EC Party and the Signatory CARIFORUM States shall assess whether the provision of universal service represents an unfair burden on organisations(s) designated to provide universal service. Where justified on the basis of such calculation, and taking into account the market benefit, if any, which accrues to an organisation that offers universal service, national regulatory authorities shall determine whether a mechanism is required to compensate the supplier(s) concerned or to share the net cost of universal service obligations.

At the outset, it should be noted that this paragraph reads like a brief summary of the internal EU law concerning universal service obligations in telecommunications.[45] In fact, the wording of Article 100(3) EPA provision follows closely the relevant provisions of the EU Universal Service Directive, that is, Articles 8(2) on the designation of undertakings, Article 12(1) on the calculation of costs and Article 13 on the methods of financing the universal service obligations. It can, therefore, be argued that the EU 'exports' its own regulatory model regarding universal service in telecommunications to its trading partners in the Caribbean.

Unlike the GATS Reference Paper, Article 100(3) EPA does not leave the content and structure of the universal service obligation completely to the autonomy of the parties of the agreement. Instead it holds that all service suppliers should be eligible to participate in the universal service. This seems to prohibit models which impose the universal service obligation a priori only to one service supplier. It is not entirely clear, however, whether the provision would also exclude models utilising tendering the universal service if the tendering procedures are open to all service suppliers. It could be argued that the second sentence of Article 100(3) EPA would allow the designation of a single universal service supplier as long as this designation process did not exclude any service supplier. Article 100(3) EPA, therefore, contains a specific clarification of the principle of non-discrimination regarding the application of universal service obligations. Furthermore, the designation process has to be efficient, transparent and non-discriminatory.

The background of Article 100(3) EPA seems to be the fear that the market share of new market entrants could be restricted through the definition of the universal service and the exclusion of foreign service suppliers from that segment of the market. Article 100(3) EPA, therefore, serves two functions: on one hand, it restricts the potential scope for countries to deviate from the obligations of the agreement by relying on universal service provisions. This ensures the economic value of the commitments in telecommunication services, and therefore, supports a liberalisation model. On the other hand, Article 100(3) EPA can also be seen as a positive obligation to establish or maintain a universal service model which is based on the principles of non-discrimination, transparency and efficiency.

---

[45] I would like to thank Olga Batura for this observation.

In particular, the requirement of an efficient designation method indicates that the universal service model should also be effective even though the requirement formally only applies to the designation of the universal service supplier and not to the supply of the universal service in general.

The remaining part of Article 100(3) EPA reflects the fact that the imposition of a universal service does not have to be a burden. In fact, in some cases, the universal service obligation can been seen as an economic asset.[46] That is why the EPA requires the parties to assess whether the provision of universal service represents an unfair burden on the organisation which have to provide it. If this is not the case, in particular because the organisation which offers universal service may be accrued a market benefit, there may not be a need to compensate the supplier concerned or to share the net cost of universal service obligations. The last reference to methods of financing the universal service is also noteworthy. It does not prescribe for a particular method, but it indicates that the compensation method and the cost-sharing method are acceptable. Both methods are also part of the internal EU telecommunication law. It can, therefore, be argued that the parties of the CARIFORUM–EPA are of the opinion that the cost-sharing method is not more burdensome than necessary. This perception could be considered by a panel or the Appellate Body in the interpretation of the GATS telecommunications Reference Paper which does not contain such a specification of the necessity standard.[47]

Another innovation of the EPA with regard to universal service obligations can be found in Article 100(4) EPA. It states:

> The EC Party and the Signatory CARIFORUM States shall ensure that: (a) directories of all subscribers are available to users in a form approved by the national regulatory authority, whether printed or electronic, or both, and are updated on a regular basis, and at least once a year and (b) organisations that provide the services referred to in subparagraph (a) apply the principle of non-discrimination to the treatment of information that has been provided to them by other organisations.

This provision is nothing less than a positive commitment towards ensuring a minimum standard of a universal service. It requires the parties to establish or maintain directories of all telephone subscribes and to update them at least annually. This requirement can be seen as an element of a universal service. In this context, it is important to note that Article 5 of the EC's Universal Service Directive 2002/22/EC contains a similar obligation regarding directory services. Even though this is a small and possibly uncontroversial element of a universal service, it is a positive obligation and not just a derogation.

---

[46] Schloemann and Pitschas 2009, p. 101(122). See also the decision of the British Postal Regulator, the Postal Services Commission (POSTCOMM), which concluded in 2001 that the universal service did not represent a significant burden in the market at that time, see POSTCOMM, Cost and benefit of the universal service, available at http://www.psc.gov.uk/universal-service/cost-of-the-universal-service.html (last accessed 31 May 2010).

[47] On this problem see Sect. 10.3.2 supra.

The background of including this provision could be practical commercial interests, because directories allow telephone service providers to market their services more efficiently. However, from a conceptual perspective the positive obligation of at least one—albeit minor—element of a universal service obligation should not be underestimated. Article 100(4) EPA establishes a positive obligation of the EPA parties to establish or maintain an element of universal service. The provision, therefore, clearly departs from the GATS model which is designed purely as a derogation clause. Article 100(4) EPA indicates a small, but noticeable step towards a positive obligation of a universal service.

10.6 Towards a 'Next Generation' of Public Service Provisions?

The EU is currently negotiating bilateral free trade agreements (FTA) with some of its trading partners. The state of the negotiations differs and in some cases agreements have already been reached while in others the negotiations are still ongoing. This section will briefly look at the proposed or likely provisions on public services in the agreements with Korea, Colombia and Peru and Canada. Korea and the EC and its Member States have been negotiating a bilateral FTA since 2007. The Draft EU–Korea FTA has been initialled in Brussels in October 2009, but has not yet been formally signed. Negotiations between the EU and Peru and Colombia were concluded in March 2010, but the agreement has not yet been finalised. However, since there are no major disagreements any longer the agreement could enter into force as soon as 2011. Finally, the EU is negotiating a FTA with Canada. These negotiations have not yet been concluded. The analysis, therefore, relates to proposed texts which have not yet been agreed upon.

The Draft EU–Korea FTA builds on language of the existing trade agreements.[48] It defines 'universal service' in the same way as the CARIFORUM–EPA. According to Article 7.27(h) of the Draft EU–Korea FTA universal service means 'the set of services that must be made available to all users in the territory of a Party regardless of their geographical location and at an affordable price'. A footnote clarifies that scope and implementation of universal services shall be decided by each Party. Article 7.34 of the Draft EU–Korea FTA contains a clause on universal service obligations in telecommunications which follows the model of the EC–Chile Agreement. However, the Draft EU–Korea FTA does not go as far as the positive universal service obligations of the CARIFORUM–EPA. The Draft EU–Korea FTA also mentions universal service obligations in postal services, but does not regulate them. However, the parties have instructed their joint Trade Committee to set out the

---

[48] The draft text is available from webpage of the European Commission's Directorate General on External Trade, http://trade.ec.europa.eu/doclib/press/index.cfm?id=443 (last visited 31 May 2010).

principles of the regulatory framework applicable to postal and courier services which should also address universal service no later than three years after the entry into force of the agreement (Article 7.26 Draft EU-Korea FTA).

Apart from incorporating the GATS standard, the draft FTA between the EU and Peru and Colombia of 2010[49] also contains a provision on universal service obligations in a section on telecommunications which is similar to Article 100(3) CARIFORUM–EPA requiring that '[a]ll suppliers should be eligible to ensure universal service and no supplier shall be a priori excluded. The designation shall be made through an efficient, transparent and non-discriminatory mechanism, in accordance with the Party's domestic legislation'. A separate provision requires the publication of telephone directories. Furthermore, the Draft EU–Peru/Colombia agreement contains a provision on universal services in postal and courier services. If these draft provisions would be agreed upon the EU–Peru/Colombia agreement would contain similar provisions as the CARIFORUM–EPA.

Finally, in the negotiations with Canada, the EU proposed a provision on telecommunication services the same language as in Article 100 of the CARIFORUM.[50] Canada has proposed a different text which would not go as far as the proposed EU text. The EU has also proposed a provision universal service in postal services which would be similar to the respective EPA provision. It remains to be seen which view will inform the final text. If the EU convinces Canada the EU–Canada agreement would further strengthen the perception that basic elements of a law on universal services in telecommunications could be emerging at the global level. Much will depend on the outcome of the EU–Canadian negotiations and on the potential impact of these new developments on the negotiations in the WTO.

Despite the evolving trend in the most recent EU trade agreements, it seems too early to say whether the incorporation of some elements of positive universal service obligations in EU bilateral trade agreements can be seen as an attempt of the EU to promote its own values regarding universal service obligations in its external relations or whether the incorporation of these elements are predominantly directed by commercial interests.

10.7 Conclusion

The preceding analysis of provisions on public service obligations in the EU's international agreements shows that universal service obligations are generally considered as a possible ground for the justification of deviations from the obligations of these agreements. However, the administration of these universal

[49] The draft text is available from the webpage www.bilaterals.org, http://www.bilaterals.org/spip.php?article17138&lang=en (accessed 31 May 2010).

[50] The Draft is available from the website of the Canadian Trade Justice Network: http://www.tradejustice.ca/tiki-download_wiki_attachment.php?attId=14 (31 May 2010).

Table 10.1 Scope and function of Universal Service Obligations (USO) in EU Trade Agreements

	Telecommunications			Postal services
	USO as derogation: not mandatory	USO as derogation: mandatory	USO as positive obligation	USO as derogation
GATS	X			
EC–Chile agreement		X		X
CARIFORUM–EPA		X	X	X
Draft EU–Korea FTA		X		
Draft EU–Peru/Colombia FTA		X	X	X
EU proposals for EU–Canada FT		X	X	X

service obligations must be non-discriminatory, transparent and no more burdensome than necessary to achieve their objectives. This approach was first incorporated into the GATS framework on telecommunications and has also been used in bilateral trade agreements. In some of the bilateral trade agreements the 'derogation model' of universal service obligations has also been applied to postal services. Even though the provisions on public or universal service obligations have not yet been fully applied in a dispute, it can be assumed that the standards developed in the WTO jurisprudence on the general exception clauses (Article XX GATT and Article XIV GATS) could also be applied to the universal service obligations.

More recent (draft) trade agreements of the EU have moved beyond the derogation standard. In particular the EC–CARIFORUM–EPA but also proposals for bilateral FTAs include positive obligations which require the parties of the agreement to maintain or establish universal directory services. This can be seen as the nucleus of a positive obligation of universal services. The scope and function of the different universal service obligation models is summarised in Table 10.1.

Whether the approach of the CARIFORUM–EPA and the proposal for the EU–Canada FTA indicate a new trend remains to be seen. It may, therefore, be still too early to give a definite answer to the question whether international trade law provisions on public service obligations will move from derogation to obligation in a way which could—at least on a very fundamental level—be compared with the redefinition of Article 106(2) TFEU (ex Article 86(2) ECT) regarding services of general economic interest. However, the new developments show the need to embed the liberalisation of public services, such as telecommunications and postal services, through international agreements in a regulatory framework. The EU will have to contribute to the development of such a framework if it aims to pursue the same values it is promoting internally in its external relations.

Acknowledgement I would like to thank Olga Batura for helpful comments on an earlier version of this contribution.

References

Adlung R (2006) Public Services and the GATS, 9 JIEL, 455

Batura O (forthcoming) Embedded transnational markets in telecommunications. In: Joerges C, Falke J (eds) Karl Polanyi, globalisation and the potential of law in transnational markets. Hart Publishing, p 245

Bronckers M, Larouche P (2008) A review of the WTO regime for telecommunications services. In: Alexander K, Andenas M (eds) The World Trade Organization and trade in services. Nijhoff, Leiden, pp 319–379

Desta M (2006) EC-ACP economic partnership agreements and WTO compatibility, CML Rev 43:1343

Dimopoulos A (2010) The effects of the Lisbon Treaty on the Principles and Objectives of the Common Commercial Policy. Eur Foreign Affairs Rev 15:150

European Commission (2006) Global Europe—competing in the world, a contribution to the EU's growth and jobs strategy, p 5

Houben I (2008) Public service obligations: Moral counterbalance of technical liberalization legislation? Eur Rev Private Law 16:7

Krajewski M (2008a) Comment: Quis custodiet necessitatem? Adjudicating necessity in multilevel systems and the importance of judicial dialogue. In: Panizzon M, Pohl N, Sauve P (eds) GATS and the regulation of international trade in services, CUP, Cambridge, pp 397–404

Krajewski M (2008b) Protecting a shared value of the union in a globalized world: services of general economic interest and external trade. In: Van de Gronden JW (ed) The EU and WTO law on services. Kluwer Law International, Alphen aan den Rijn, pp 173–213

Krajewski M (2003) National Regulation and Trade Liberalization in Services—the legal impact of the General Agreement on Trade in Services (GATS) on National Regulatory Autonomy. Kluwer Law International, London

Neergaard U (2009) Services of general economic interest: the nature of the beast. In: Krajewski M, Neergaard U, Van de Gronden J (eds) The changing legal framework of services of general interest in Europe. TMC Asser Press, The Hague, pp 17–50

OECD (2001) Working party on telecommunication and information services policies: interconnection and local competition, 7 February, DSTI/ICCP/TISP(2000)3/FINAL

Peha J (1999) Tradable universal service obligations. Telecommun Policy 23:369–373

Regan D (2007) The meaning of 'necessary' in GATT Article XX and GATS Article XIV: the myth of cost–benefit balancing. World Trade Rev 6:347–369

Roseman D (2003) Domestic regulation and trade in telecommunications services: experience and prospects under the GATS. In: Mattoo A, Sauvé P (eds) Domestic regulation and service trade liberalization. Oxford University Press, Washington, DC

Ross M (2000) Article 16 E.C. and services of general interest: from derogation to obligation? EL Rev 25:22–37

Sauvé P, Ward N (2009) The EC-CARIFORUM economic partnership agreement: assessing the outcome on services and investment. European Centre for International Political Economy (ECIPE)', Brussels, January http://www.ecipe.org, 39

Schloemann H, Pitschas C (2009) Cutting the regulatory edge? In: Zusammenarbeit (ed) How to ensure development friendly economic partnership agreements, Gesellschaft für technische p 101

Chapter 11
Conclusion

Jim Davies

Contents

This book is divided into three distinct parts: the first part addresses general issues in the development and application of the legal base for Services of General Interest (SGIs), applied in this Conclusion as a generic label, in the Single Market; the second provides a more specific analysis of the development of the regulatory and policy environment for SGI in the Single Market; and the third develops the policy context of the book, to place the debate on SGIs within an international development setting. That said, there are important connections between the general, specific, and international aspects to SGIs that emerge in the essays. The book is concerned with the modernisation processes of services delivery and the conceptual development of the category of services of general interest that has emerged in parallel with the development of global markets, technological advancement and an emergent new model of citizenship.

The thematic approach of this book has been to address the development of SGIs through the parallel strands of their organic and functional conceptions: to balance our research of the problematic comprehension of the 'public service' or 'utility' labels that we attach to SGIs and their organisational and governance

J. Davies (✉)
Department of Law, The University of Northampton, School of Social Sciences,
Park Campus, Boughton Green Road, Northampton, NN2 7AL, UK
e-mail: jim.davies@northampton.ac.uk

E. Szyszczak et al. (eds.), *Developments in Services of General Interest*,
Legal Issues of Services of General Interest, DOI: 10.1007/978-90-6704-734-0_11,

models with the development of consumer orientated operational and convergent output models. This concluding chapter aims to highlight both the trends associated with the developments in SGIs and the issues and questions that arise from the analysis provided by the contributors: it draws from the contributions, an emerging set of core values that define, in generic terms, the shape of a more solidaristic public service delivery model that places the citizen at its centre.

11.1 Issues and Debates: Problems of Definition

In his chapter, *Bauby* suggests that for the founders of European Union, 'the economy was only a way of integration serving a political objective, of federal nature', and that the invention of the expression 'services of general economic interest' was, in excluding the word 'public', a device to avoid any misunderstanding. But it was also a device that has come to define, since the mid-1980s a functional 'general interest' model applicable to general economic services, non-economic services, and to social services. His forensic analysis of the primary law of the EU is supplemented with recognition of the effectiveness of soft law instruments in developing a set of guiding principles for generic operational public service models. The nine guiding principles extracted from the Commission's 2004 White Paper[1] discussed in *Bauby's* chapter resonate with the model of the generic operating provisions of public service obligations identified in the secondary sectoral law instruments, analysed in the chapter by *Davies and Szyszczak.*[2]

It is ultimately the capacity of the secondary legislation to set the economic and financial principles and conditions for SGEI's to fulfil their missions that *Bauby* questions: together with a call for a legislative clarification of the rules necessary for defining the categories and operating norms of social services of general interest and non-economic services of general interest.

Whilst *Bauby* identifies the provisions of the Treaty of Lisbon 2009 as 'quite a step forward' in the opportunities, it presents to clarify the EU rules for defining services of general economic interest and their organisational and operational parameters: he also questions the efficacy of the existing secondary legislation to provide for the delivery of public service missions. Should, he ask, further legislative initiatives be introduced at the EU level to clarify the conditions under which Member States can define SGEIs? And, more generally, should a centralised EU level legislative framework, based on regulation and the setting of EU norms on which international trade negotiations could be based, be the way forward? These are not questions based upon curiosity but are central concerns in the light of the Commission's statement that it will not pursue the new legislative opportunities offered by the Treaty of Lisbon 2009.

---

1 European Commission, White Paper on Services of General Interest, COM(2004) 374 final.

2 See Chap. 2 by Bauby and Chap. 7 by Davies and Szyszczak.

Neergaard's contribution elaborates the debate over the role of soft law instruments in developing a European public service model. Her exposition of the various communications from the Commission that, since 1996, have stimulated the discussion, draw attention to the problems associated with attempting to draft a general instrument, perhaps a framework Directive, setting out a model definition for services of general economic interest. The question of what value would such an instrument add to sector or issue specific measures, must surely be complicated by the risks associated with the lack of any defining boundary between services of general economic interest and the broader category of services of general interest, including social services of general interest.

Whilst failing to result in a legislative outcome, the soft law instruments, and the debate they stimulated, have been influential. As *Neergaard* explains, they have contributed to a more uniform thinking: the communications have been taken seriously and have drawn references from the Advocates-General and the Court of First Instance (now the General Court). Whether recognised as soft law or not, the various communications, and the responses they have elicited, evidence a debate in which the pros and cons for a framework instrument have been elaborated and clarified. The debate is incomplete, but without a defining model of the boundaries between the services' categories we are reliant on the functional analysis developed by the Court of Justice to influence our argument in any sector specific deliberation. *Bekkedal's* analysis of the case law of Article 106 TFEU helps to chart this development in the case law. He suggests that the Court initially adopted a competition law approach to Member States invoking the exception in Article 106(2) TFEU, and a position whereby the measure should not be allowed to serve as a justification for barriers to free movement, but that it has more recently adopted something of this functional approach: an approach, *Bekkedal* argues, that has emerged from the Court's classical assessment of the mandatory requirements doctrine and the application of its traditional proportionality test.

On the issue of the distribution of competencies with regard to services of general economic interest, the debate has proved to be more constructive. The various responses have matured into an acknowledgement that responsibility for SGEI's is a shared responsibility. Protocol 26, Article 1, to the TEU and the TFEU explicitly recognises,

> the essential role and the wide discretion of national, regional and local authorities in providing, commissioning and organising services of general economic interest as closely as possible to the need of users.

The Treaty also identifies that the shared values of the Union include 'a high level of quality, safety and affordability, equal treatment, and the promotion of universal access and of user rights' that place operational process obligations on the service providers. At the EU level, responsibility is focused on economic and social cohesion, balanced with a respect for the principle of subsidiarity and recognition of the national competence to define, organise, finance and monitor *all* services of general interest. A recognition reinforced in Article 2 of Protocol 26 that provides for 'the competence of Member States to provide, commission, and organise non-economic services of general interest.' This distribution of competencies is maturing into more than a mere multi-level welfare system, it is producing a common business ethos for delivering citizen focussed and consumer involved services, within competitive and marketised sectors, irrespective of a functionally assessed 'economic' categorisation or not.

11.2 Cohesion and Rights: Towards an Essential Public Services Doctrine?

Maintaining the focus on Article 106 TFEU *Skovgaard Ølykke* examines the exception in the context of public procurement, which she introduces through reference to a doctrinal approach by the Court that it has developed for the in-house provision of services. A doctrinal approach that rests on an assessment of the functional and organisational relationship through which control over the service provider is exercised by public authority and in which the essential part of the service output is provided to the public authority. In the same vein, she suggests that recent public procurement case law rests on Article 106(2) TFEU and that the approach by the Court can be conceived of as making its assessments on a case-by-case basis in which it is the public service obligation, or a special or exclusive right to provide a service, that provides for the exemption of a SGEI from the public procurement rules, where that obligation or right is found to operate efficiently in general interest.

Taking a broader perspective, it has been argued elsewhere that the dominant trend in Article 106 TFEU case law compels the Luxembourg Court and the national courts to balance the requirement to comply with competition rules with the need for an undertaking to carry out particular tasks mandated by a public authority (the State or devolved authority).[3] This is no straightforward task for at least two reasons. Firstly, such 'balancing' decisions will be applicable wherever services, identified as essential by a public authority at the national level, are provided by way of an obligation or exclusive right that can only be delivered with an exemption from the competition, public procurement and/or state aid rules. Secondly, the uncertain reliance on the available framework of definitions for services of general economic interest, services of general interest, social services of general interest, etc., is a distraction that diverts attention away from considering a single strategic European Social Model for essential services. *Van de Gronden's* chapter highlights the shortcomings of this framework. His contribution brings to this volume, an analysis of part of the category of services that falls under the ambit of social services of general interest: a construction of the soft law instruments of policy processes that can be further divided into economic and non-economic sub-categories where those sub-categories classified as economic fall

[3] Nicol 2010, p. 109.

subject to market forces. However, *Van de Gronden's* conclusions reinforce that there is no clear distinction between non-economic and economic activities, and that consequential tensions, that may arise between the free movement and competition rules, could be reconciled by a greater reliance on the Article 106(2) TFEU exemption and the modelling of social services constituting economic activities as services of general economic interest.

Van de Gronden's analysis shows that re-thinking the concept of social services of general interest is of eminent importance, and that elements of competition will increasingly apply to services that encompass a social dimension. But is it necessary to pursue or maintain the confusion of terminology and the opaque distinctions between 'general' and 'social', and between 'economic' and 'non-economic' essential services? Should we not develop a broader conception for SGI's (here, applied again as a generic label): one that could still rely on the legal base of Article 14 TFEU and the exception provided by Article 106(2) TFEU, one that can build on the reinforcement of the principles of subsidiarity and diversity enshrined in Protocol 26 of the TEU and TFEU and the solidaristic intentions of Article 36 of the Charter of Fundamental Rights of the European Union? *Davies and Szyszczak* argue that the increasing use of the concept of (and phrase) 'universal service obligations' marks a movement, at the EU level, away from the 1957 purpose and use of the phrase 'services of general economic interest'. Universal service obligations can now be seen as specific extensions of a new generation of public service obligations that have a universal aspect to their geographic or social reach: whilst the new generation of public service obligations have been accepted by the Luxembourg Courts as corresponding to the concept of SGEI's.

If we put aside the nuanced categorisations of SGEI's, SGI's, SSGI's, and any sub-categories, what emerges from the new generation of public service obligations is a governance model for essential public services that places the consumer citizen in an increasingly influential role for a renewed social agenda. Delivery of such essential services lies within a cohesive European model that accommodates marketisation and competition, whilst providing for an exception from *full* marketisation and competition, in order to meet potentially non-economic but socially desirable outcomes. It is a model that embraces the fundamental rights of free movement, and in which responsibility for the effectiveness and efficiency of the service is shared between the EU institutions, the Member States and their independent regulatory bodies, the service provider and, increasingly, the consumer citizen. This is a shared responsibility engendered by a developing set of transparency and rights provisions that introduces a focus on the *form* of economic organisation as a potential adjunct to the functional pro-market ideology of Article 106 TFEU jurisprudence.[4]

[4] Cf., Ross 2007 at p. 1079.

11.3 European Principles and International Dimensions

The final chapters from *Schwartz* and from *Krajewski* help us to move away from an introspective European focus: the debate on how to provide essential public services and on where the balance should be drawn between pro-market ideology and a social paradigm established on the principles of solidarity has an international dimension. *Schwartz* argues that in less developed countries, their governments need the freedom to reach their own conclusions but also highlights the familiar difficulties of defining the organisational function and form appropriate for justifying exemptions from standard regulatory mechanisms in the delivery of essential public services and the need for transparent measurable standards. With a broader international focus, *Krajewski* positions the principles of transparency and non-discrimination, that in this volume have been argued to comprise common elements of an administrative model for the delivery of essential services, within a GATS framework. His contribution emphasises that the functioning of services of general interest rank highly among the values of the Union and its Member States and that these values are relevant to the Union's external policies.

The public and universal service obligations that provide for the delivery of service outcomes, that the market by itself would fail to deliver, are central to the liberalisation and regulation of trade within the GATS framework. *Krajewski* draws attention to the role of the provisions for public and universal service obligations in the EU secondary legislation that restrict the full application of free market principles and competition law, but identifies that they do so 'in order to ensure societal values which would otherwise not be protected.' Such values are reflected in the transparency and non-discriminatory provisions that have found their way into Article 115 of the bi-lateral EC-Chile Agreement and the EC-CARIFORUM Economic Partnership Agreement.[5] As obligatory, rather than derogative, provisions of international law *Krajewski* suggests that at least at a very fundamental level they can be compared with the redefinition of Article 106(2) TFEU.

11.4 Final Comments

The evolutionary development of the principles associated with public and universal service obligations, and the move away from derogation provisions to positive obligations, may be beginning to influence agreements made in international trade law. Yet, in an EU context these principles have already become embedded in a consumer-oriented model for service delivery. It is an emerging model that embraces the principles of transparency, accountability, objectivity, and non-discrimination in an essential services paradigm where Article 106 TFEU

[5] Discussed in Chap. 10 by Krajewski.

plays a central role and the nuanced categorisations of SGI, SGEI, SSGI, together with the associated difficulty of assessing the economic/non-economic boundary, may be becoming less important. This volume shows that it is possible to discern some unifying themes across the range of SGIs. Transparency as a unifying concept is found in the form of organisational structure, the unbundling of delivery services from content services, the unbundling of financial accounts and through the market monitoring of consumer behaviour and complaints. Accountability is seen in the form of consumer consultation provisions, regulatory, and competition provisions, provisions for consumer complaint processes, switching provisions and in the processing of personal data. Objectivity is now a core obligation and consumer-citizenship empowering approach seen in the form of published quality of service targets, supply and repair time targets, published and comparable tariffs. Non-discrimination, a fundamental EU law principle, is used in the form of access and affordability provisions and through geographic and social universality obligations.

It will be for future policy-makers and commentators to assess the degree to which new legislative developments, soft law instruments and communications, and case law support the proposition that has been contended in this volume: that is, of the emergence of an organisational model for an essential services paradigm in which there is a shared responsibility that rests on the principles of transparency, accountability, objectivity and non-discrimination.

References

Nicol D (2010) The constitutional protection of capitalism. Hart, Oxford, p 109

Ross M (2007) Promoting solidarity: from public services to a European model of competition? CMLRev 44(4):1057

Table of Cases

Cases before the European Court of Justice

Cases before the General Court

Index

The manufacturer's authorised representative in the EU is Springer Nature Customer Service Centre GmbH, Europaplatz 3, 69115 Heidelberg, Germany. If you have any concerns regarding our products, please contact ProductSafety@springernature.com

Printed and bound by CPI Group (UK) Ltd, Croydon, CR0 4YY
28/09/2026
02224076-0008